D. H. Lawrence on Screen

Literature and the Visual Arts
New Foundations

Ernest B. Gilman
General Editor

Vol. 12

PETER LANG
New York • Washington, D.C./Baltimore • Boston
Bern • Frankfurt am Main • Berlin • Vienna • Paris

Jane Jaffe Young

D. H. Lawrence on Screen

Re-Visioning Prose Style
in the Films of "The Rocking-Horse
Winner," *Sons and Lovers,*
and *Women in Love*

PETER LANG
New York • Washington, D.C./Baltimore • Boston
Bern • Frankfurt am Main • Berlin • Vienna • Paris

Library of Congress Cataloging-in-Publication Data

Young, Jane Jaffe.
D. H. Lawrence on screen: re-visioning prose style in the films
of "The rocking-horse winner," Sons and lovers,
and Women in love / Jane Jaffe Young.
p. cm. — (Literature and the visual arts; vol. 12)
Includes bibliographical references and index.
1. Lawrence, D. H. (David Herbert), 1885–1930—Film and video adaptations.
2. Lawrence, D. H. (David Herbert), 1885–1930—Style. 3. English fiction—
Film and video adaptations. 4. English language—Style. I. Title. II. Series.
PR6023.A93Z967   791.43'6—dc21   98-16432
ISBN 0-8204-4047-7
ISSN 0888-3890

Die Deutsche Bibliothek-CIP-Einheitsaufnahme

Young, Jane Jaffe:
D. H. Lawrence on screen: re-visioning prose style in the films
of "The rocking-horse winner," Sons and lovers,
and Women in love / Jane Jaffe Young.
−New York; Washington, D.C./Baltimore; Boston; Bern;
Frankfurt am Main; Berlin; Vienna; Paris: Lang.
(Literature and the visual arts; Vol. 12)
ISBN 0-8204-4047-7

The paper in this book meets the guidelines for permanence and durability
of the Committee on Production Guidelines for Book Longevity
of the Council of Library Resources.

© 1999 Peter Lang Publishing, Inc., New York

All rights reserved.
Reprint or reproduction, even partially, in all forms such as microfilm,
xerography, microfiche, microcard, and offset strictly prohibited.

Printed in the United States of America

for Phil
and in memory of my parents

Contents

Acknowledgments. ix

List of Illustrations. xi

Chapter 1: Introduction: Literature on Film. 1

Chapter 2: "The Rocking-Horse Winner". 13

Chapter 3: *Sons and Lovers*. 75

Chapter 4: *Women in Love*. 151

Chapter 5: Conclusion. 275

Notes. 287

Filmography. 317

Bibliography. 319

Index. 343

Acknowledgments

I owe a profound debt of gratitude to Joy Gould Boyum, professor of culture and communication at New York University School of Education, film critic and author of *Double Exposure: Fiction Into Film*, one of the few definitive works on the theory and practice of film adaptation. Dr. Boyum's stimulating courses on film and on adaptations of literature to the screen inspired me to undertake this challenging study. Her incisive suggestions on revision and her warm friendship made this project truly a labor of love.

Special thanks must go to Howard Prince, former Associate Dean at Borough of Manhattan Community College, who initiated the CUNY Dissertation Completion Program, of which I was a member from 1987 to 1989, and to David Sternberg, of John Jay College of Criminal Justice, who authored *How to Complete and Survive a Doctoral Dissertation*, coordinated the program, and was responsible for narrowing the scope of this project.

Early mentors who nurtured my love and appreciation of literature include my late father Joseph George Jaffe, an avid reader and book collector, whose censored copy of *Lady Chatterly's Lover* led to my lifelong fascination with D. H. Lawrence; my sister, Paula Kopelman, who introduced me to the magic of poetry and fiction; and John Rosenberg, a distinguished scholar of Victorian literature and member of the graduate faculty at Columbia University, who supervised my honors thesis on Gerard Manley Hopkins at the City College of New York.

Much is owed to the members of my extended family who supported me through the research and writing of this book: my late mother, Sybil Simon Jaffe; my late aunt Dorothy Fisher; my former mother-in-law Virginia Brady Young; Margaret Eggers; and my former sister-in-law Mary Elizabeth Young. I am also grateful for the affectionate support of my late mother-in-law Mary Tippett Young; my gifted sister/cousin Marijo Hennagin Mazur; my superbly accomplished daughter, Victoria, whose love, loyalty and sense of humor have long sustained me; and my two wondrously talented stepchildren, David and Wendy, who have brought much joy into my life.

Many friends and colleagues offered excellent advice, encouragement, and enthusiastic support during the process of researching and writing this book. In particular I must thank Harriet Jillings Bachrach, Frank and Maxine Brady, Judith Bush, Kathy Chamberlain, Ellen Conley, Marilyn Faludi, Rivkah Feldman, Deborah Harkins, Bobbie Harrison, Doris Hart, Joyce Harte, Kathy Hopkins, Judy Lemberger, Harry Lutrin, Nan Maglin, Nancy McClure, Ruth Misheloff, Sandra Poster, Rosalie Roffman, Marilyn Rosen, and Naomi Woronov.

Claude Blenman provided invaluable help in the preparation of the original manuscript. Jonas Salganik contributed expert technical assistance and editing advice on the photographs. Deborah Harkins, former Executive Editor of *New York* magazine, graciously and expertly proofread the final text. Susanna Shopsin, Roslyn Freundlich, and Marcia Brenner offered their wise and insightful counsel during the lengthy writing process. The New York Society Library in Manhattan provided the peaceful rooms where I composed much of this book.

The staff of the Motion Picture Section at the Library of Congress in Washington, D.C., allowed me to view the three films on flat-bed viewers and photograph the images on the screen so I would have a permanent, shot-by-shot record, and Mary Corliss, curator of the Museum of Modern Art Film Stills Archive, assisted me in securing illustrations. Every effort was made to obtain permissions for the artwork. If there are any questions about any of the photographs in this book, please contact the author.

I am most grateful to Ernest Gilman, New York University Director of Graduate Studies for the Arts and Sciences and editor of Peter Lang's series on Literature and the Visual Arts, for expertly assisting me in revising, editing, and producing this manuscript.

My greatest debt of all is owed to my brilliant and steadfast secret sharer, Philip Eggers, who fills my heart with love, graces my life, and makes all things possible. His contributions to this project, both tangible and intangible, are immeasurable.

ILLUSTRATIONS

Figure   *The Rocking Horse Winner*

1. The film opens with an aerial zoom shot of the Grahame's mansion, which resembles a doll's house.

2. Hester Grahame (Valerie Hobson) visits newly hired handyman-gardener Bassett in his tack room quarters.

3. Hester (Valerie Hobson) dutifully hears the prayers of her two daughters on Christmas Eve.

4. After putting her children to bed, Hester (Valerie Hobson) mistakenly assures Nannie (Susan Richards) that Paul and his sisters are fast asleep upstairs.

5. On the moonlit night before Christmas, the Grahame children glimpse prophetic horses in the clouds.

6. Paul (John Howard Davies) says his prayers on Christmas Eve; a shadow in the shape of a cross appears on the wall behind him.

7. On Christmas Eve, Paul (John Howard Davies) steals downstairs to preview his Christmas presents.

8. Paul (John Howard Davies) is mystified by one of his gifts.

9. In a match cut (see Figure 8), Paul (John Howard Davies) excitedly strips the wrapping off his new rocking-horse.

10. A backwards zoom reveals the opulence of the Grahame drawing room on Christmas day.

11. Would-be jockey Bassett (John Mills) enthusiastically gives Paul (John Howard Davies) a riding lesson, urging him to ride faster or he'll " be late for his own funeral."

List of Illustrations

12. In a lengthy deep focus shot, Uncle Oscar (Ronald Squire) takes Hester (Valerie Hobson) and Richard (Hugh Sinclair) to task about her profligacy and his gambling debts.

13. As the whispering house takes up Hester's edict, "There must be more money," the camera pans up the stairs until it reaches Paul's ears; stairs are a recurring visual motif in the film.

14. Hearing the house whispering, Paul (John Howard Davies) gazes quizzically at his rocking-horse.

15. Process server hands extravagant Hester (Valerie Hobson) a writ for an unpaid £40 bill.

16. As mother and son discuss luck and money, Paul (John Howard Davies) holds the symbolic figure of a horse in an antique shop where Hester (Valerie Hobson) buys items she can't afford.

17. When Paul (John Howard Davies) picks the horse Safety Pin as a winner, Bassett (John Mills) agrees to place a bet for him "just this once"; the horse loses. (Museum of Modern Art/Film Stills Archive)

18. Accompanied by lightning and thunder, Paul (John Howard Davies), in pursuit of a winning horse's name, furiously rides his rocking horse until he "gets there!"

19. In quick succession, long and close shots of dismayed onlookers Uncle Oscar (Ronald Squires) and Hester (Valerie Hobson) convey the violent to-and-fro of Paul's frantic rocking-horse ride.

20. On a day's outing, Uncle Oscar (Ronald Squire) invites delighted Paul (John Howard Davies) to visit a race track.

21. Crosscut with shots of Uncle Oscar and Paul at the racetrack are shots of Hester (Valerie Hobson) bargaining with Mr. Tsaldouris (Charles Goldner) to sell her clothes so she can pay her £40 debt.

List of Illustrations xiii

22. Bassett (John Mills) shows Uncle Oscar (Ronald Squire) £1200 Paul has won by betting when he's "sure" of the winners: "It's just like he had it from heaven!" (Museum of Modern Art/Film Stills Archive)

23. Bailiff (Cyril Smith) informs outraged Hester that she must pay an additional 7 pence for his unwelcome services.

24. In a rapid montage of superimposed images, Paul (John Howard Davies) rides his rocking-horse as Hester (Valerie Hobson) spends her son's ill-gotten money on jewelry, gowns, and redecorating.

25. Hester (Valerie Hobson) shows off her new gown to her husband (Richard Sinclair) on the night of the charity ball she has organized.

26. Bassett (John Mills) discusses possible Derby winners with other drivers while ball guests dance in a Belgravia mansion.

27. At the ball, Hester (Valerie Hobson) greets guests on the stairs just before her overwhelming anxieties about Paul prompt her to leave.

28. Paul (John Howard Davies) pleads with his rocking-horse for the name of the Derby winner.

29. The shadow of the rocking-horse looms as Hester (Valerie Hobson) bursts in on her son, who falls unconscious after his last, desperate ride to learn the name of the Derby winner, Malabar.

30. After Paul collapses, an extreme closeup of the demonic rocking horse's head fills the screen.

31. After learning that Malabar has won the Derby and that he is £70,000 richer, Paul (John Howard Davies) assures his mother (Valerie Hobson) that he *is* lucky, and dies peacefully. (Museum of Modern Art/Film Stills Archive)

32. At Hester's insistence, Bassett (John Mills) sets fire to the rocking-horse but refuses her order to burn Paul's winnings with it.

Sons and Lovers

33. In the film's opening shot, birds burst into flight as the squeaky mine headstocks start to turn; in sharp contrast, the camera slowly pans right to sheep grazing in a field.

34. "You've ruined it!" cries Gertrude Morel (Wendy Hiller) when husband Walter (Trevor Howard) drips grease on son Paul's charcoal portrait of his mother; Arthur Morel (Sean Barrett), Paul's brother, looks on. (Museum of Modern Art/Film Stills Archive)

35. Visiting Miriam Leivers (Heather Sears) at Willey Farm, Paul Morel (Dean Stockwell) confesses his desire to live in London, "painting life" in his own studio.

36. Removing Miriam's (Heather Sears) beret, Paul (Dean Stockwell) lets her hair flow free. "Looking at you now, there's more religion in you than your mother could ever learn from the saints."

37. Glimpsed through the spokes of a mine headstock, miners' families race to the scene of an underground explosion.

38. After the mine disaster, Paul (Dean Stockwell) and his mother (Wendy Hiller) join miners' relatives as they wait for the bodies of the dead and wounded to be lifted up. (Museum of Modern Art/Film Stills Archive)

39. Walter Morel (Trevor Howard) covers his dead son Arthur's (Sean Barrett) face; in the novel, oldest son William dies instead.

40. After Arthur's funeral, Paul (Dean Stockwell) and Gertrude Morel (Wendy Hiller) grimly return home in the rain.

41. Walter Morel (Trevor Howard) angrily bangs his fist on the table as Mrs. Morel (Wendy Hiller) urges Paul not to be "dragged down" into the mines like his ill-fated brother Arthur.

List of Illustrations xv

42. Gertrude Morel (Wendy Hiller) and Paul (Dean Stockwell) bid goodbye to Paul's older brother William (William Lucas) after learning he is engaged to be married to frivolous Louisa Weston.

43. At a Nottingham art exhibition, Paul (Dean Stockwell), his mother (Wendy Hiller), and Miriam Leivers (Heather Sears) observe patrons' reactions to Paul's portrait of his father.

44. Paul's down-to-earth painting of his father elicits mixed responses from gallery-goers.

45. Wealthy patron Henry Hadlock (Ernest Thesiger) eyes Paul's work critically but appreciatively.

46. Paul (Dean Stockwell) receives a magnanimous offer from Henry Hadlock (Ernest Thesiger) to study art in London. (Museum of Modern Art/Film Stills Archive)

47. Told that Henry Hadlock (Ernest Thesiger) has paid £20 for Paul's portrait of him, Walter Morel (Trevor Howard) angrily challenges him to feel "the real thing— 20 pounds of real sweat!"

48. "Why must you act like that?" Paul (Dean Stockwell) demands when his father (Trevor Howard) is rude to his would-be patron; Morel retorts, "I'm not loved here 'cause I'm low, so I *act* low!"

49. Mrs. Leivers (Rosalie Crutchley) sternly warns daughter Miriam (Heather Sears) to shun "the sins of the flesh."

50. Elated by his artistic success and his future prospects in London, Paul (Dean Stockwell) kisses frightened Miriam (Heather Sears).

51. Tearfully embracing the trunk of a tree, Miriam (Heather Sears) prays not to love Paul, "but if I may love him, let me love him splendidly!" (Museum of Modern Art/Film Stills Archive)

52. In a drunken rage, Walter Morel (Trevor Howard) throws son Paul's food on the floor and locks Mrs. Morel (Wendy Hiller) out of the house. (Museum of Modern Art/Film Stills Archive)

xvi   *List of Illustrations*

53. Unwilling to leave his mother alone with his abusive father, Paul (Dean Stockwell) tells her he has decided not to go to London but to take a job at Thomas Jordan & Sons Surgical Appliances.

54. On his first day as a clerk at Jordan's, Paul (Dean Stockwell) becomes a figure of fun holding a woman's corset frame.

55. After teasing Paul by singing a risqué song, the flirtatious Spiral girls are formally introduced to the new employee. (Museum of Modern Art/Film Stills Archive)

56. When Paul (Dean Stockwell) and Miriam (Heather Sears) make love, Paul grimly observes that they have only been driven further apart. (Museum of Modern Art/Film Stills Archive)

57. On Christmas day, as Paul looks on, Gertrude Morel (Wendy Hiller) helps her husband (Trevor Howard) take a hot bath in the parlor. (Museum of Modern Art/Film Stills Archive)

58. Eldest son William Morel (William Lucas), home from London, introduces his flighty fiancée Louisa (Rosalie Ashley) to his mother (Wendy Hiller). (Museum of Modern Art/Film Stills Archive)

59. Tipsy from holiday champagne, Walter Morel (Trevor Howard) belts out a music hall ditty.

60. At a suffragette rally, Jordan's overseer Clara Dawes (Mary Ure), (right), daringly claims the four freedoms, "speech, thought, opportunity, love." (Museum of Modern Art/Film Stills Archive)

61. When Paul shows Clara the sketch he has made of her (above) at the suffragette rally, she exclaims, "You've made me *too* beautiful!"

62. On the arm of another woman, Clara's estranged husband Baxter Dawes (Conrad Phillips) glares at Paul and Clara as he passes by.

63. On an evening out in Nottingham, Paul (Dean Stockwell) and Clara (Mary Ure) enjoy ribald dancing and singing at a music hall.

List of Illustrations xvii

64. Missing the last train, Paul (Dean Stockwell) is invited to stay overnight with Clara Dawes (Mary Ure) and her widowed mother. (Museum of Modern Art/Film Stills Archive)

65. Sexual tensions mount as Paul (Dean Stockwell) and Clara (Mary Ure) play an erotically charged game of whist while Clara's mother bustles back and forth, then orders Paul to bed.

66. In Clara's bedroom, Paul (Dean Stockwell) gazes at her photograph, then softly caresses her powder puff.

67. As Paul's mother sleeps, Paul (Dean Stockwell) descends the stairs to the parlor where Clara is warming herself.

68. In an over-the-shoulder shot, Paul gazes longingly at partially disrobed Clara (Mary Ure).

69. Paul (Dean Stockwell) and Clara (Mary Ure) passionately embrace.

70. Baxter Dawes (Conrad Phillips) warns Paul Morel (Dean Stockwell) to keep away from his wife.

71. At Jordan's Clara (Mary Ure) and Paul (Dean Stockwell) plan a winter seaside getaway. (Museum of Modern Art/Film Stills Archive)

72. Paul (Dean Stockwell) expresses concern for his mother's failing health as Gertrude Morel (Wendy Hiller), troubled by her son's relationship with Clara, winces in pain. (Museum of Modern Art/Film Stills Archive)

73. During their seaside tryst, amid "iron trees," Clara (Mary Ure) and Paul (Dean Stockwell) reflect on their relationship with each other and with Baxter and Miriam.

74. In a controversial scene omitted from British version of the film, Clara (Mary Ure) complains that Paul seems incapable of giving himself completely in the act of love.

75. Returning from his rendezvous with Clara, Paul (Dean Stockwell) is assaulted and beaten by Clara's husband Baxter (Conrad Phillips).

76. Heartbroken Paul (Dean Stockwell) weeps after his mother (Wendy Hiller) dies quickly and peacefully of heart failure; in the novel, cancer-ridden Gertrude Morel dies a slow, painful death.

77. After his wife's death, Paul's father (Trevor Howard) urges Paul (Dean Stockwell) not to let Mrs. Morel down, as he did, and encourages him to go to London to study art.

78. Kissing Miriam (Heather Sears) goodbye before he parts for London, Paul (Dean Stockwell) rejects her plea that they marry, telling her he wants to be "free."

Women in Love

79. Sculptress Gudrun Brangwen (Glenda Jackson) and sister Ursula (Jennie Linden), right, a schoolteacher in the English Midlands mining town of Beldover, leave their parents' home to attend the wedding of Laura Crich and Tibby Lupton.

80. On their way to the Crich wedding, fashionably dressed Brangwen sisters, Ursula (Jennie Linden), left, and Gudrun (Glenda Jackson), stroll through the working class district of Beldover. (Museum of Modern Art/Film Stills Archive)

81. Discussing the "experience of marriage," Ursula and Gudrun eye a couple wheeling a baby carriage (above): "More likely the *end* of experience," quips Ursula.

82. At the Crich wedding, wealthy arts patron Hermione Roddice (Eleanor Bron) adjusts cravat of lover Rupert Birkin (Alan Bates).

83. As guests at the Crich wedding pose for a group photograph, one of the glass "films" ominously breaks.

List of Illustrations xix

84. "Nothing materializes; everything withers in the bud," muses Gudrun Crich (Glenda Jackson) as sister Ursula watches the Crich wedding from the graveyard opposite the church.

85. In Ursula's classroom, school inspector Rupert Birkin (Alan Bates) examines catkins as unwelcome guest Hermione (Eleanor Bron) exclaims, "Little red flames—aren't they beautiful!" (Museum of Modern Art/Film Stills Archive)

86. Hermione Roddice's "country cottage" Breadalby, where Ursula and Gudrun are invited for the weekend.

87. Hermione's weekend guests assemble for outdoor luncheon.

88. Lecturing embarrassed guests on the "proper way to eat a fig in society," Birkin (Alan Bates) transforms the fruit Hermione (Eleanor Bron) is eating into a woman's sexual organ: " . . . a glittering, rosy, moist, honeyed, heavy-petaled, four-petaled flower."

89. Hermione (Eleanor Bron), Ursula (Jennie Linden), and Gudrun (Glenda Jackson) perform a dance in "the style of the Russian ballet," with Hermione as the widow, Orpah; Ursula as Naomi; and Gudrun as Ruth. (Museum of Modern Art/Film Stills Archive)

90. Herimone (Eleanor Bron) strikes a provocative pose.

91. After a time-consuming costume change, Hermione (Eleanor Bron) throws herself into a seductive solo that annoys Birkin.

92. Birkin (Alan Bates) and Ursula (Jennie Linden) unceremoniously interrupt Hermione's Isadora-Duncanesque "ballet" by leading guests in a spontaneous ragtime dance.

93. Rupert Birkin (Alan Bates) denounces Hermione's (Eleanor Bron) lust for power and her lack of real sensuality and spontaneity; the female nude behind them is ironic decor.

List of Illustrations

94. In a rage, Hermione (Eleanor Bron) bashes Rupert Birkin (Alan Bates) on the head with a paperweight. (Museum of Modern Art/Film Stills Archive)

95. Fleeing Hermione's wrath, bloodied Birkin (Alan Bates) sheds his clothes as he runs through lush green forest, leaning momentarily on the trunk of a birch tree. (Museum of Modern Art/Film Stills Archive)

96. At a funeral for a World War I soldier, a minister extols the virtues of love while Rupert Birkin rants to Ursula about hate, death, and violent destruction.

97. Gerald Crich (Oliver Reed) races his horse beside a speeding train.

98. In a rapid montage, Gerald Crich (Oliver Reed) whips his rearing horse to make it stand still.

99. Forcibly restraining his mount, Gerald Crich (Oliver Reed) draws blood with his spurs.

100. Ursula (Jennie Linden) and Gudrun (Glenda Jackson) react to Gerald's brutal treatment of his horse with shock and anger.

101. In the coal mine, Gerald (Oliver Reed) confronts an aging worker whom he later fires. (Museum of Modern Art/Film Stills Archive)

102. Gerald (Oliver Reed) and his father, colliery owner Thomas Crich (Alan Webb), drive home in luxury amidst the departing miners.

103. "How are your thighs?" Gudrun (Glenda Jackson) teases a miner who accosts her in the working class district of Beldover. "I want to drown in flesh—hot, physical, naked flesh!"

104. Rupert Birkin (Alan Bates) and Gerald Crich (Oliver Reed) greet Ursula Brangwen's parents (Michael Gough, Norma Shebeare) at the Criches' yearly picnic.

List of Illustrations xxi

105. Half-mad Georgiana Crich (Catherine Wilmer), Gerald's mother, remains indoors behind a barred window during the festivities.

106. In an idyllic interlude with Gudrun (Glenda Jackson) at the Criches' picnic, Ursula sings "I'm Forever Blowing Bubbles," a song popular in England in 1920. (Museum of Modern Art/Film Stills Archive)

107. Seductive Gudrun (Glenda Jackson) dances fearlessly before the horned bulls. (Museum of Modern Art/Film Stills Archive)

108. Rescuing Gudrun (Glenda Jackson) from her bizarre dance before the bulls, Gerald (Oliver Reed) tells her he is in love with her; she responds enigmatically, "Well, that's one way of putting it." (Museum of Modern Art/Film Stills Archive)

109. On the Criches' lake at night, Birkin (Alan Bates) tells Ursula (Jennie Linden), "There is a golden light in you which I wish you would give me."

110. Drowned newlyweds Laura (Sharon Gurney) and Tibby Lupton (Christopher Gable) are found in a fatal embrace.

111. Match cut of Ursula (Jennie Linden) and Birkin (Alan Bates) in an embrace nearly identical to Laura and Tibby's (See Figure 110).

112. Rupert Birkin (Alan Bates) and Gerald Crich (Oliver Reed) in their controversial and memorable Japanese-style wrestling match, notable for its sensuality, frontal nudity, and stunning cinematography. (Museum of Modern Art/Film Stills Archive)

113. Birkin (Alan Bates) and Gerald Crich (Oliver Reed) in a strenuous clinch during their free-form encounter.

114. As the two men rest after their wrestling match, Birkin (Alan Bates) proposes to Gerald (Oliver Reed) that they swear blood brotherhood and eternal love.

115. Gerald (Oliver Reed) responds evasively to Birkin's offer of blood brotherhood. (Museum of Modern Art/Film Stills Archive)

116. Birkin (Alan Bates) and Gerald (Oliver Reed) end their wrestling match with a symbolic chalice between them.

117. To her husband's dismay, Georgiana Crich (Catherine Wilmer) lets their dogs loose on petitioning miners.

118. Stroking Winifred Crich's pet rabbit, Gerald Crich (Oliver Reed) asks Gudrun to visit his younger sister again.

119. After agreeing to marry, Ursula (Jennie Linden) and Rupert (Alan Bates) drift sideways in slow-motion, choreographed lovemaking. (Museum of Modern Art/Film Stills Archive)

120. To son Gerald's (Oliver Reed) dismay, Georgiana Crich (Catherine Wilmer) drops a trowel on her husband's coffin lid and laughs hysterically at his graveside.

121. After his father's funeral, Gerald (Oliver Reed) stumbles through the graveyard where Thomas Crich has just been interred.

122. On the night of his father's burial, muddy-booted Gerald (Oliver Reed) sneaks into Gudrun's (Glenda Jackson's) bedroom. (Museum of Modern Art/Film Stills Archive)

123. Under a symbolic modern painting of a woman, Gudrun (Glenda Jackson) awaits Gerald's embrace.

124. Literally pinned down, Gudrun (Glenda Jackson) urges Gerald (Oliver Reed) to leave before daylight when her parents awaken. (Museum of Modern Art/Film Stills Archive)

125. Multiple images reflected in mirrors, Birkin (Alan Bates) and Gerald (Oliver Reed) discuss marriage and "the additional perfect relationship between man and man."

List of Illustrations xxiii

126. Newly married Rupert Birkin (Alan Bates) tells amused Ursula (Jennie Linden), hanging out the wash, that all women are either wives or mistresses. (Museum of Modern Art/Film Stills Archive)

127. The four lovers enjoy winter sports in the Swiss Alps. (Museum of Modern Art/Film Stills Archive)

128. Gerald Crich (Oliver Reed) in a tense moment with Gudrun (Glenda Jackson) during their tryst in the Swiss Alps. (Museum of Modern Art/Film Stills Archive)

129. Birkin (Alan Bates) confesses to Ursula (Jennie Linden) that without her, he couldn't bear the snow in "this cold eternal place." (Museum of Modern Art/Film Stills Archive)

130. Her interest piqued, Gudrun, symbolically "behind bars," learns that Loerke (Vladek Sheybal) is a sculptor who has had a hard life.

131. In the bedroom they share, Loerke (Vladek Sheybal), with his "friend" (Richard Heffer), defends his sculpture of a young girl on a horse from Ursula Brangwen's attack.

132. Renouncing the "ghastly glamour" of the snow, Ursula (Jennie Linden) enthusiastically agrees to Birkin's (Alan Bates) proposal that they travel to Italy "to find Romeo and Juliet."

133. Gudrun (Glenda Jackson) provocatively reveals to Loerke (Vladek Sheybal) that she and Gerald (Oliver Reed) are not married. (Museum of Modern Art/Film Stills Archive)

134. Gudrun (Glenda Jackson) plays Cleopatra in a perverse dress-up game with Loerke (Vladek Sheybal).

135. Loerke (Vladek Sheybal), "behind bars" like Gudrun (see Figure 130), pretends to be homosexual Tchaikovsky on his honeymoon.

136. As Gudrun (Glenda Jackson) cavorts in the snow, Loerke proposes that she live and work with him in Dresden, Germany.

137. In a poignant series of lap dissolves, rejected Gerald (Oliver Reed) climbs to his icy death in the snow.

138. Home in Beldover after Gerald's suicide, Birkin (Alan Bates) tells Ursula that in addition to the love of a woman, he needs "a man friend as eternal as you and I are eternal."

139. Before film's final freeze frame (above), Ursula (Jennie Linden) insists Birkin can't have two kinds of love "because it's impossible."

140. D. H. Lawrence (rear) and bearded look-alike Alan Bates, who plays Lawrence's alter ego Rupert Birkin in the film of *Women in Love*. (Museum of Modern Art/ Film Stills Archive)

Chapter 1

Introduction: Literature on Film

Cinematic adaptations of literary works have often been dismissed as inferior hybrids, damaging both to their sources and to the film medium itself. Yet up to half of all British and American films, and a surprisingly large number of European films, have been translations of short stories, novellas, novels, and plays, many of them significant literary works. Indeed, a list of films nominated for Oscars over the past 60 years reads like a syllabus for a course on works of modern fiction. Few "classic" nineteenth- or twentieth- century novels in English have not been filmed, and quite a few, including F. Scott Fitzgerald's *The Great Gatsby*, Charlotte Bronte's *Jane Eyre*, Emily Bronte's *Wuthering Heights*, Louisa May Alcott's *Little Women,* and Jane Austen's *Pride and Prejudice,* have been remade many times. Generally popular with the film industry and movie audiences alike, cinematic adaptations have overwhelmingly topped "original" films as all-time box office successes[1] and garnered most of Hollywood's top honors. By one estimate, approximately 85 percent of all Academy Award-winning Best Pictures are adaptations, as well as 70 percent of all Emmy award-winning TV movies.[2]

In the past two decades, critically acclaimed serialized adaptations of numerous literary classics have also appeared on television's *Masterpiece Theater*, including John Galsworthy's *The Forsyte Saga*, William Thackeray's *Vanity Fair*, Charles Dickens's *Bleak House* and *Martin Chuzzlewit*, Leo Tolstoi's *Anna Karenina*, Henry James's *The Golden Bowl* and *The Spoils of Poynton*, Robert Graves's *I, Claudius*, Evelyn Waugh's *Brideshead Revisited*, George Eliot's *Middlemarch*, and almost all of Jane Austen's novels, including two versions of *Pride and Prejudice*. Besides "serious" literary works, commercial bestsellers, including *Gone With the Wind, Rebecca, Gentleman's Agreement, From Here to Eternity, Ship of Fools, Love Story, The Godfather,* and *The Exorcist*—all transformed into Academy-Award-nominated films—have long been a staple of the Hollywood film industry. So as well have obscure potboilers and little-known shorter works whose adaptations have earned sizable profits at the box office.

Given the prevailing critical bias against adaptation, why have so many filmmakers of successful movies been drawn to novels and stories as potential sources? Most of the reasons are practical. In Hollywood, the demand for narrative raw material outstrips the supply, and literature provides substantial, well-developed story lines and rounded characters for screenplays. Since film versions of bestsellers are presold, they are often financially profitable and offer choice roles to top stars, while film rights to eighteenth- and nineteenth- century classics cost producers little or nothing. Adapting literary sources of substance gives moviemakers or those backing such artistic projects recognition, respectability, status, and prestige, and adapting a literary work of stylistic difficulty or distinction is an exciting challenge that stimulates filmmakers' creativity and ingenuity even as it advances the art and technique of movie making.

On a more personal level, individual filmmakers may be attracted to classic novels because of a nostalgia for the historical past or because of the story's relevance to or parallels to current events and political trends. Filmmakers may also be drawn to literary works because they deliver important messages or explore issues or themes important to the filmmakers, or because these works can be reinterpreted according to a particular ideological slant, such as feminism. Certain novels appeal because of their explicit sexual content or other controversial material that might shock or offend a mainstream audience. Finally, some filmmakers may have a strong affinity with the sensibility of a particular writer, or a special fascination with a work they read earlier in their lives.

Whatever motive a filmmaker or producer may have for adapting a story or novel, however, there is a considerable difference between transposing to the screen a major literary work and a best-seller written for a mass audience. While a popular novel certainly invites comparison between the filmed version and the original, a moviegoing audience acquainted with a bestseller is likely to object to changes chiefly when the film departs from the plot of the source (especially its ending) or alters the characters, setting, or time period. Changes in the "style" of the original are not likely to register or to raise hackles because the general public is not attuned to matters of style, and also because the narrative or prose style of most popular fiction is, for the most part, not particularly noteworthy.

In the case of stylistically distinctive literary works of current serious fiction, however, moviegoers and critics familiar with the source are likely to be satisfied with film adaptations only if the substance of the plot and the characters have been left intact and, equally importantly, if the aesthetic and emotional effects generated by the text are somehow rendered in the film and

Introduction 3

the essence or spirit of the original is preserved. Even if the film stands up on its own merits as a work of art, comparisons between the novel and its cinematic *doppelgänger* are inevitable. A failure to take into account all of the elements of the work—its plot and characters as well as its unique stylistic characteristics—is likely to open the film to the sort of indignant charges of betrayal leveled against the salacious 1996 version of Nathaniel Hawthorne's *The Scarlet Letter*, sensationalized by Demi Moore's nudity and some improbably steamy sex scenes. Indeed, in quite a few instances, the mere act of adaptation itself, regardless of the excellence of the film, has been viewed as a form of sacrilege.

Apart from the reproduction of style, the achievement of even partial fidelity to the text of a novel poses major problems. Because of the approximately one-and-a-half- to two-hour maximum usually allotted to feature films, the scope of a lengthy work must be reduced, often resulting in the surgical removal of up to two-thirds of the work. Entire sections of the plot, and some or all of the subplots, are often rearranged or entirely omitted, and passages of sociopolitical or philosophical commentary and psychological analysis are usually eliminated, severely compressed, or inappropriately put into the mouths of other characters. The point of view from which the story is narrated is frequently altered. Usually deleted or externalized are characters' observations, thoughts, interior monologues, dreams, reveries, and memories. Certain characters are either excised or combined with others, and others are added; scenes are omitted, altered, or rearranged; and even if dialogue from the original is included, new dialogue must also be written for added or modified scenes. As a result of budgetary or time limitations, unfavorable shooting conditions, commercial pressures, prevailing cultural and social norms, and in some instances, censorship, key incidents and themes may be modified or omitted, time period or settings may be altered, and, most dramatically, endings may be changed. On the other hand, if the fiction adapted is a short story or novella, characters, episodes, and dialogue must usually be added, new themes may also be introduced, locations and time periods may be changed, and the ending, as in a novel, may be significantly altered.

In addition to grappling with major alterations in the scope, structure, characters, and plot of any novelistic source, a filmmaker adapting a stylistically unusual or demanding text is faced with problems the adapter of pulp fiction is spared, for the prose style of certain literary works is not only difficult to characterize and describe but even harder to replicate in another medium. Challenging though it may be for a filmmaker to devise (or stumble upon) cinematic equivalents for aspects of prose style as varied as diction, syntax, rhythm, figurative language, and tone, however, many screenwriters and directors have (particularly recently) demonstrated that such transposition of style, while difficult, is by no means impossible or have shown a remarkable, even heroic, willingness to try. For as Joy Boyum argues in her passionate defense of adaptation, *Double Exposure: Fiction Into Film*, what is the point of transposing a great work to film "if not because of its greatness and the chance it offers to replicate in another work of art some of the qualities that accounted for its greatness"?[3]

In a landmark essay on John Osborne's stylistically mimetic adaptation of Henry Fielding's lengthy eighteenth-century novel *Tom Jones*, which won the Academy Award for Best Picture in 1963, Martin Battestin, acknowledging the obvious differences between the fiction and film, proposed a useful and often-cited criterion for assessing the effectiveness of a cinematic adaptation of a literary work:

> Analogy is the key. To judge whether or not a film is a successful adaptation of a novel is to evaluate the skill of its makers in striking analogous attitudes and in finding analogous rhetorical techniques.[4]

It was to explore the use of such analogous techniques for reproducing the elements of prose style in film that I undertook an in-depth study of *The Rocking Horse Winner* (1949), *Sons and Lovers* (1960), and *Women in Love* (1970), three highly regarded screen adaptations of fictions by D. H. Lawrence, all the works of different producers and directos in three different decades. My intention was to determine whether the films conveyed aspects of the prose style of Lawrence's texts, and if so, how the transposition of such elements as diction, syntax, rhythm, figurative language, and tone was actually carried out. I also hoped to discover whether the transposition of Lawrence's prose style affected the quality of the film adaptation both as a facsimile of the original and as a work of art in its own right.

D. H. Lawrence on Screen

I first encountered D. H. Lawrence at the age of eleven, when I surreptitiously read my father's intriguingly titled expurgated edition of D. H. Lawrence's *Lady Chatterly's Lover*, hoping for thrills. Stripped of its suggestive passages, lovemaking scenes, and four-letter words, however, the novel was tame, preachy, and dull, and I wondered what all the fuss was about. I finally found out in my twenties, when I eagerly devoured the uncensored *Lady Chatterly*, with its startling blend of tenderness and profanity. In the years to come I read and reread with growing appreciation many other Lawrentian stories and novels, captivated by their sensuality and emotional intensity, both baffled and intimidated by their passionate (and often wrongheaded) notions about love, politics, philosophy, religion, and sex. By the time I embraced feminism in the seventies and realized that despite his unusual sensitivity to the feelings of women and his many strong-willed female characters, the novelist was in certain respects a thoroughgoing misogynist, I had already become a Lawrence devotee. Enthralled by the passion and poetry of his fiction, I have remained somewhat apologetically so.

Along with distinctive prose stylists such as Jane Austen, William Faulkner, Henry James, and Ernest Hemingway, D. H. Lawrence was the author of a remarkable number of works that have been transformed into movies. Besides the three adaptations examined in this book, at least 16 feature films based on his stories, novellas, novels, and plays have been released in Great Britain and the United States in the past five decades,[5] including three more versions of "The Rocking-Horse Winner" (1977, 1982, 1998), three versions of *Lady Chatterly's Lover* (1954/55, 1976/77, 1981), two versions of *Kangaroo* (1952, 1985/86), and adaptations of eight other stories, novellas, and novels, including *The Fox* (1967/68), *The Virgin and the Gypsy* (1971), *The Trespasser* (1981), *The Captain's Doll* (1982), *Samson and Delilah* (1984), *The Horse-Dealer's Daughter* (1984), *The Boy in the Bush* (1984), *Kangaroo* (1985/86), and *The Rainbow* (1989). In addition, many serialized television adaptations were produced in Great Britain in the 1980s, including at least two versions of *Sons and Lovers* and a fine production of *The Rainbow*. Despite feminist attacks on D.H. Lawrence in the 1970s (spurred by Kate Millett's *Sexual Politics*, 1969), two well-received biopics of Lawrence—*The Priest of Love* (1981), starring Ian McKellan as the novelist and Janet Suzman as his wife Frieda, and *Coming Through* (1990), starring Kenneth Branagh as Lawrence and Helen Mirren as Frieda—sparked the interest of both scholars and the general public in Lawrence's iconoclastic views, tempestuous marriage, and gypsy life.

Given Lawrence's antagonism towards the melodramatic silent films of his day[6]—an antagonism shared by almost every British and American modernist writer with the exception of F. Scott Fitzgerald and James Joyce[7]—it is certainly ironic that so many of his stories, novellas, and novels have been (and continue to be) adapted to the screen. Lawrence was highly critical of most of the films he saw; his biographer Harry T. Moore, in *The Priest of Love*, noted that the silent version of *Ben-Hur* made Lawrence physically nauseated.[8] In his novel *The Lost Girl* and in essays such as "Sex Versus Loveliness" (1928), "Pornography and Obscenity" (1929), and "A Propos of *Lady Chatterly's Lover*" (1930), Lawrence argued that, unlike live performances, movies appealed to audiences' "mental consciousness" and "counterfeit emotions" rather than to their hearts and spirits; purveyed stereotyped images of love, beauty, and reality; and degraded life-affirming sexuality into obscenity and furtive ugliness. Lawrence claimed that frustrated housewives' deranged desire for Valentino and other male silent film stars exemplified what he termed "sex in the head."[9] In his satirical poem "When I Went to the Film," Lawrence wrote contemptuously of how he saw at the movies "all the black-and-white feelings that nobody felt," though the audience sighed and sobbed "with all the emotions that none of them felt,"[10] and in another poem, he railed against film as a symptom of the mass industrialization of society: "Not monkeys minding machines. . . /the radio or film or gramophone/ Monkeys with a bland grin on our faces."[11]

Despite Lawrence's largely negative attitude toward the mechanicalness of film—or, more fundamentally, what he perceived to be the movie industry's misuse of technology—he did not entirely reject film as a medium or fail to recognize its influence on other arts. Reviewing John Dos Passos' 1927 novel *Manhattan Transfer*, he praised the experimental novel's affinities with cinema, describing the work as being "like a movie picture with an intimacy of different stories and no closeups and no writing in between."[12] Nor was Lawrence insensible to the appeal of film icons such as Charlie Chaplin, noting that there was "a greater essential beauty" in the comedian's "odd face than there ever was in Valentino's."[13]

Although Lawrence reputedly did not strongly object to the filming of *Women in Love*[14] during the heyday of silent films, it is highly probable that, had he lived well past 1930, he would have balked at selling the motion picture rights to his works. Not only would he have had to give up any input into the screenplay or final cut, but the films of many of his fictions would undoubtedly have been (and in fact were) subjected to the kind of censorship and outright banning that his works repeatedly suffered in print. In any case, Lawrence's general distaste for films was evidently not shared by his widow, Frieda, who took up permanent residence in New Mexico soon after his death and—through Aldous Huxley, then a screenwriter for MGM—met and mingled with the film world in the early 1930s.[15]

Frieda's energetic efforts to bring Lawrence's fictions to the screen, however, met with little success.[16] The difficulties of convincing Hollywood agents and film producers of the 1930s, 1940s, and 1950s to adapt Lawrence's fictions are not hard to imagine. *Lady Chatterly's Lover*, his final and most scandalous novel, had been banned in Great Britain, though pirated copies of the notorious book evidently circulated in Hollywood, no doubt creating the impression that most of Lawrence's works would be too hot to handle. In addition, shortly after Lawrence's death in 1930—memorialized in England with many hostile or at least ambivalent obituaries[17]—his reputation suffered when a few of his erstwhile friends, in particular John Middleton Murry (*Son of Woman: The Story of D. H. Lawrence*, 1931) and Mabel Dodge Luhan (*Lorenzo in Taos*, 1931), published extremely unflattering memoirs about Lawrence's life and work, as well as their relationships to him and Frieda.

As a result, Lawrence's worldwide reputation as a writer was dealt a blow from which it did not recover until 1954, when, more than twenty years later, in *D.H. Lawrence: Novelist*, F. R. Leavis championed him as one of the great British novelists of both the nineteenth and twentieth centuries. From that point on, scholarly, media, and popular interest in Lawrence's fictions in both Great Britain and the United States intensified, culminating in Frieda Lawrence's sale of the movie rights to *Sons and Lovers* to Jerry Wald in 1954, two years before she died. The production of *Sons and Lovers,* delayed until 1960, coincided with the loosening of censorship both in Hollywood and British films, and the lifting of the ban on the publication of the unexpurgated *Lady Chatterly's Lover* in New York in 1959 and in Great Britain in 1960. The ban was lifted as a result of a landmark U.S. obscenity trial (Regina v. Penguin Books Limited) that turned largely on the justification of the use in the novel of until-then-taboo sexual terms.

Both the publication of the full text of *Lady Chatterly's Lover* and the production of *Sons and Lovers* occurred around the time of the release of such films as *Room at the Top* (1959), *Look Back in Anger* (1959), and *Sapphire* (1959), which introduced a greater degree of candor into British narrative films than had previously been tolerated. However, it was not until the late sixties that sexually explicit film adaptations of such erotically charged Lawrence fictions as *The Fox* (1967), *Women in Love* (1970), and *The Virgin and the Gypsy* (1970) could be shown without cuts of possibly offensive scenes, and it is no accident that none of these were British productions. Film historian Robert Murphy notes that these groundbreaking adaptations, along with the *Lady Chatterly's Lover* obscenity trial, made D. H. Lawrence "a potent cultural influence in the sixties."[18]

Paradoxically, the threat of censorship that restricted the publication of several of Lawrence's major works and prevented both American and British filmmakers from adapting many of his novels in the decades following his death[19] is undoubtedly the main reason why, during the increasingly permissive post-1960s decades, a number of adaptations of Lawrence's more controversial works were undertaken. Indeed, had it not been for Lawrence's reputation as a sexual outlaw and the eroticism that pervades his writing, his fictions, many of them idiosyncratic in terms of characters, relationships, plot, setting, ideas and themes, would probably never have been transformed into commercial feature-length films.

Permeated with myth, metaphor, ritual and repetition, Lawrence's stories and novels—especially his later ones—are peopled by overtly symbolic, psychologically peculiar characters spouting strange ideas and desires. Many of them behave in bizarre and often inexplicable ways, experience rapid and extreme shifts of emotion and metaphysical states of being (often ineffable), think inexplicable thoughts, and are involved in tortured, often sado-masochistic relationships. Although sections of Lawrence's fictions are often powerful and interesting, many of them simply do not hang together to create a cohesive narrative. The eccentric, loosely plotted story lines in a number of Lawrence's lesser novels, including *The White Peacock* (1911), *The Lost Girl* (1920), *Aaron's Rod* (1922), and *The Plumed Serpent* (1926)— meandering, episodic, disjointed, implausible, repetitive, and ambiguously resolved—are for the most part unsuitable for adaptation to classical Hollywood narrative films. Several of his novels are far too long to be condensed neatly into two-hour movies; like Emily Bronte's *Wuthering Heights*, *Sons and Lovers* and *The Rainbow* are epic narratives spanning three generations. Conversely, most of Lawrence's short stories, masterpieces of economy, do not lend themselves to the sort of expansion of plot and characters required in a feature-length film.

In addition to the odd characters and loose, disjointed, or improbable plots in his novels, Lawrence's prose style itself—characterized by biblical rhythms; repetition of word, phrase and sound; distinctive vocabulary; richly figurative language; pervasive symbolism; cosmic mysticism; and urgently serious or strident tone—was undoubtedly a barrier to film adaptation. On Frieda Lawrence's behalf, Harry T. Moore tried to persuade several Hollywood agents and studios to produce Lawrence's novels; he had particularly high hopes for *The Boy in the Bush* (1924), co-written with Australian Mollie Skinner. When an agent who was considering one of her upcoming male stars for the lead role of Jack Grant read the first line of the book, "He stepped ashore like a lamb," she demanded to know how her young star "could play that," refused even to read the rest of the paragraph, and sent Moore on his way.[20]

If Lawrence's verbal excesses and peculiarities put off some members of the film industry, others were attracted to Lawrence's work precisely because

Introduction   9

of the challenges of finding cinematic equivalents for his distinctive style. Few filmmakers, of course, are sophisticated or motivated enough to analyze his prose as a stylistician would. Accounts by producers, screenwriters, and directors who adapted Lawrence's fictions, however, reveal that they were not only intuitively aware of most of the significant aspects of his style but, realizing that for many filmgoers the movie *is* the book, they felt responsible for incorporating elements of Lawrence's prose style into their films and actively sought to find equivalents. Alone and collaboratively, they read and reread the novels, underlined significant passages, noted the effects the language created, and considered various ways to convey such elements as symbolism and tone. In interviews and essays about the process they went through in adapting Lawrence's fictions, all of them claimed that they had tried to reproduce the properties of the original. As Christopher Miles, director of two film adaptations of Lawrence's works as well as a film version of Harry T. Moore's *The Priest of Love* (1974), commented about the process of adapting a fiction by a major literary figure, "Anybody that felt in tune with the author's original work, as I have in the case of *The Virgin and the Gypsy*, should stick to it."[21]

But what does it mean for a film adapter to "stick to the style" of a Lawrentian work—or any other? Although much has been written about the transposition of narrative strategies from fiction to film, and a few critics—notably George Bluestone in *Novels Into Film* (1957) and Joy Gould Boyum in *Double Exposure: Fiction Into Film* (1985)—have explored the film/literature nexus in both theoretical and practical terms, little critical attention has been paid exclusively to the transposition of verbal style. Comparing the prose style of a literary work with the cinematic style of a film is quite different from comparing narrative style in the two media. Narrative style encompasses plot and structure, modes of characterization, the vantage point (or points) from which a story is told, rendition of mental states, descriptions of settings, and authorial commentary. Prose style, on the other hand, refers to elements of language such as diction, sentence length and syntax, figurative language (including simile, metaphor, symbol, irony, paradox), and tone. It is far easier to make an explicit comparison between the structure of a prose narrative and the narrative structure of a film than to make a detailed comparison between the diction and syntax of an author's prose and the "diction" (individual shots and images) and "syntax" (type, sequence, and length of shots) of a filmmaker who attempts, in any sense, to translate the writer's style. Comparisons of this sort are necessarily approximate.

Method in My Madness

In researching and writing this book, I wanted to do what no other scholar of film had done in similar depth and scope: to analyze in precise and rigorous detail the prose style of certain literary texts I admire and to determine, through an equally rigorous examination of the film adaptations based on each of them, whether the movies contained identifiable equivalents of the various components of the author's style. Commentary on the stylistic aspects of film adaptations in newspapers or magazines—almost invariably offhand and impressionistic—rarely pinpoints the specifics of transposition. A reviewer complains that "something is missing" from the film; it fails to capture the spirit or essence of the novel; it lacks subtlety, intensity, complexity, irony, passion, wit. But where do these qualities reside if not in the language of the text? And how can these qualities be reproduced except through countless cinematic components, including pictorial decor and composition, camera movement and editing, transitional devices and light, score and sound effects, which can be individually identified and, taken together, appreciated for re-creating at least some of the aesthetic, emotional, and intellectual effects which the text has upon its readers?

Stylistic studies of prose and film can be approached from several angles. Some linguists use transformational-generative grammar to describe and analyze a writer's style, while semiotics is a popular method for analyzing film style, as are auteurist, genre, structuralist, post-structuralist, Marxist, feminist, and Lacanian Freudian approaches. In my close readings of the texts I relied on a traditional approach to analyze grammar and syntax. I also applied the quantitative stylistic method to determine the prevalence of certain grammatical and syntactic features as well as sentence length and paragraph "shape." Similarly, I used a quantitative method[22] to analyze the pace and rhythm of the films.

When I discuss the elements of prose style in this book, I refer to diction; sound; parts of speech; sentence type; syntax of sentences; sentence length; paragraph length, shape, rhythm, and organization; figurative language; and tone. To analyze Lawrence's prose and identify its key features, I made a qualitative and quantitative word-by-word, sentence-by-sentence, and paragraph-by-paragraph analysis of "The Rocking-Horse Winner" in its entirety, and a similarly detailed analysis of the first four narrative or descriptive paragraphs of each chapter in *Sons and Lovers* and *Women in Love*, as well as selected passages of narrative description and dialogue. I noted the prevalence of certain parts of speech and vocabulary, the exact length and syntax of sentences, and the pattern of sentence length in paragraphs. In *Women in Love*, I exhaustively identified and catalogued metaphors and similes.

To identify and describe the cinematic style in all of the films, I analyzed each shot in terms of composition, lighting, distance of the camera from subject, point of view, camera angle, optical distortion or special effects, type of shot, length of shot, transition between shots, and the construction of shots into scenes and sequences. Other stylistic elements of film I noted included the use of color vs. black-and-white film, sound (nonmusical and musical), editing, rhythm and pace, scenery, costumes, make-up, and acting cast and acting styles. Finally, I examined the use of "literary" elements, including metaphor, metonymy, synecdoche, symbol, personification, hyperbole, understatement, irony, allusion, and paradox—all achieved through cinematography, sound, and editing.

My study of the stylistic aspects of the films took me first to the Audio Brandon film distribution warehouse in Mount Vernon, New York, where I viewed Anthony Pelissier's *The Rocking Horse Winner*, and then to the Library of Congress in Washington, D. C., where I screened *Sons and Lovers* and *Women in Love* on a flatbed viewer, taking detailed notes and also extensive 35-mm black-and-white photographs of the images on the screen. In addition, I made audiotapes of all three films which I transcribed into an annotated script. Later, I was able to tape showings of *The Rocking Horse Winner* and *Sons and Lovers* in 1992 and 1993, respectively, and to secure a videotape of *Women in Love*, so I was able to clock the approximate length (in seconds) of each shot in the three films, and so determine the average shot length (ASL) and the editing rhythms in each of them.

For critical reactions to each film, I read contemporary reviews and extended critiques of *The Rocking Horse Winner*, *Sons and Lovers*, and *Women in Love* which appeared in newspapers, magazines, journals, and collections of essays. To understand the historical context for each film, I also consulted articles and books on American, British, and European films of the decades in which each of the adaptations was made, as well as articles or books on or by the individual filmmakers.

To determine which, if any, stylistic equivalencies exist between the fiction and film versions of Lawrence's works, I compared features of the prose style with features of style in the film. I considered a cinematic stylistic feature analogous to its counterpart in fiction if it conveyed or evoked aesthetic, psychological, or conceptual effects similar to a corresponding feature in the text. I compared the diction of each work of fiction to shots and images in the films in terms of such qualities as simplicity, abstractness, orateness, and idiosyncrasy. I also noted the structure, pace, and editing of shots, scenes, and sequences in the films to see whether aspects of prose syntax such as simple or complex sentences, parallelism, antithesis, parataxis and mimetic effects—as well as the pace and rhythmic effects of the prose—were cinematically replicated. I observed whether the editing of scenes and sequences paralleled the "shape" of paragraphs, indicated by relative length of sentences. I checked to see if recurring figures of speech in the text, including metaphor, metonymy, and irony, were replicated in the films, and if so, how. I also compared symbolism in the fictions with the symbolic imagery and sound in the films. In addition, I noted whether the various tones in the fictions were reproduced in each of the films, and how alterations in tone changed my response to the characters and events. Finally, I took into special account cinematic equivalents of stylistic characteristics unique to each of the works, such as irony, paradox, realism, and fantasy in "The Rocking-Horse Winner" and metaphors in *Women in Love*.

Although my methodological approach is mainly formalist, focusing on structure and style rather than the historical conditions in which each work was produced, on other works in the same genre, or on ideological issues, few analyses of fiction or film are *purely* formalist, and neither is this one. Consequently I included material on the production history and critical reception of each work and film, as well as changes made in the plot of the film and an overview of each film's style in the context of the style of other films made in the same period or by the same filmmaker.

In undertaking this study, I wanted above all to find out whether the transposition (or lack of it) of the key elements of Lawrence's prose style would make a significant difference in the quality of each film, both as an adaptation that captures some of the unique qualities that make Lawrence's fictions "Lawrentian" and as a work of film art in its own right. What I discovered was that the filmmakers who paid serious attention to Lawrence's distinctive prose style and tried to find equivalents for it made movies that are not only cinematically outstanding but also bring filmgoers closer to the experience of the texts than skeptics would like to acknowledge. It seems to me that my findings have implications not only for future adaptations of D. H. Lawrence but for adaptations of any stylistically distinctive literary work.

Chapter 2

"The Rocking-Horse Winner"

D. H. Lawrence wrote his much-praised and often anthologized tale "The Rocking-Horse Winner" four years before his death in 1930 at the age of 44.[1] The story of Paul, a doomed boy gifted with an uncanny ability to predict horse race winners, apparently had its origin in the troubled relationship between Lawrence's long-time friend Lady Cynthia Asquith and her autistic son John, whose bizarre and sometimes violent behavior destroyed his mother's ability to love or even tolerate him. In Lawrence's view, the boy's tragic affliction was caused by his parents' skepticism and cynicism, by the materialism of an upper-class lifestyle which they could hardly afford, and, despite Lady Cynthia's kind and gentle demeanor, by her "hard and stoical" spirit.[2]

First published in 1926 in *The Ghost Book: Sixteen New Stories of the Uncanny* (collected, ironically, by Lady Cynthia Asquith herself), the story is a parable of an unloved son who destroys himself in the effort to satisfy his hardhearted mother's boundless appetite for luxury—one of several Lawrentian fictions on the theme of the "devouring mother." It has been interpreted chiefly as an attack on bourgeois materialism, a reading not far off the mark, judging by the author's sentiments about the "curse of riches."[4] Lawrence's leading biographer, who called the narrative "a tale of the supernatural...in the truest sense, a horror story," characterized it as "a study not only of the gambling neurosis—even the winners are destroyed—but also of the entire money neurosis that destroys so many modern families, often crushing the children."[5] By extension, the story has been viewed as an attack on industrialism and the artificiality of modern society in which human beings are cut off from others and their authentic selves:

> The symbolic meaning of Paul's rocking horse depends precisely on the fact that it is not a 'big living presence' but an artificial object.... Modern man, Lawrence implies, has lost the real living universe which is still present to the unreflective child and the savage.[6]

Attesting to the story's richness and ambiguity, and to its power to generate and justify many analytical approaches, a few critics have constructed multi-leveled interpretations of "The Rocking-Horse Winner," taking into consideration the psychosexual aspects of the tale, the sociological implications, its use of the "uncanny" and supernatural, its religious, mythical and anthropological meanings, and its fairy-tale elements.[7]

The Film of "The Rocking-Horse Winner"

Even if he had gone to the trouble of reading the detailed, passionately argued interpretations of "The Rocking-Horse Winner" written from the fifties onward, none of them was available to British screenwriter Anthony Pelissier, who wrote and directed a feature-length adaptation of the story that was released in 1949. The first of many film versions of Lawrence's fictions, it was also one of a number of distinguished films based on literary classics produced during the decade or so after World War II, a period characterized as "an age of adaptation."[8] The chief adapters of the period—Asquith, Reed, and Lean—portrayed a society in which class differences play a significant part. However, postwar socialist Britain, under Clement Atlee's labor government, exhibited a more egalitarian spirit, a new sympathy for proletarian experiences and values, and an evident distaste for capitalistic greed and materialism. Thus, Pelissier's choice of "The Rocking-Horse Winner" for adaptation was in harmony with the times.

When the film was released in England in 1949 and in the United States in 1950, the public reacted with indifference, and critical responses were mixed. Several reviewers praised it for its authenticity and adherence to the style, theme and mood of the text, as well as for its direction, cinematography, and acting.[9] However, despite the critics' appreciation of Pelissier's earnest efforts to capture the essence of Lawrence's grimly ironic tale and their almost unanimous approval of the actors' performances—in particular, Valerie Hobson's as Hester, the mother and ten-year-old John Howard Davies's as Paul, her tormented son—some reviewers had misgivings, in particular about the slow pace of the film,[10] its monumental orchestral score, and the relentlessly tragic mood.[11]

A few complained about the film's softening of Lawrence's bitter message, citing in particular the tacked-on moralistic ending (a bow to antigambling censors). In the film, Paul's tearfully remorseful mother orders the gardener Bassett to burn her ill-gotten gains after Paul's death, along with the rocking-horse, and Bassett insists on giving Paul's £80,000 winnings to the family lawyer to be used for charitable purposes.[12] Such moralistic endings, however, were typical of most British film adaptations of literary works in the 1940s.[13] Whatever their reservations, there was general respect for the film, as reflected in the judgment of often acerbic Pauline Kael, who later lauded the "little known English production" as "a demonstration of how good a movie intelligent people can make when they have better-than-intelligent material to work on."[14] Although few critics focused on style, the film is perhaps most impressive in its grasp of the essentials of Lawrence's style. As in all feature-length adaptations of fiction, however, screenwriter Anthony Pelissier made significant changes—omissions and additions, as well as condensation and transformation of events.

Plot Changes in Pelissier's Film of "The Rocking-Horse Winner"

Pondering the problems of adapting D. H. Lawrence's story to the screen, director-scenarist Pelissier stressed his fidelity to the original.

> Instead of following my first impulse of extending the surface areas of the story material . . . which would have been the easier way to write the screenplay, I decided it would be wiser and safer to dig underneath the surface. In this case, the adapter leaned on Lawrence and rightly or wrongly believed that a sincere regard for the writer's integrity would carry both through to something approaching the desired result.[15]

In keeping with Pelissier's claim that he "leaned on Lawrence," the final screenplay, with few omissions, incorporates and expands on almost all of the incidents and dialogue in the original narrative.[16] Like most feature-length adaptations of short stories, however, the film also contains many scenes not included in the narrative but merely suggested by it.

More symmetrically than the story, Pelissier framed his script by the arrival of Bassett, the kindly gardener, at the beginning of the action and Bassett's dramatic departure at the end. The film's opening scene, in which Paul first sneaks out on Christmas Eve to meet the newly hired gardener-handyman in his harness-room digs is suggested by a brief expository passage one-third of the way through the story:

> The uncle was delighted to find that his small nephew was posted with all the racing news. Bassett, the young gardener, who had been wounded in the left foot in the war and got his present job through Oscar Creswell, whose batman he had been, was a perfect blade of the "turf." He lived in the racing events, and the small boy lived with him. (152)

In the story, Bassett has been living with the family for an indeterminate period of time; at the beginning of the film, we see Paul introduced to him soon after his arrival and witness the rapid formation of a relationship.

Immediately following Paul's introduction to Bassett comes the crucial sequence which introduces the major characters and motifs of the film, and sets the plot in motion. Paul surveys the holiday presents in a darkened drawing room on Christmas Eve, discovers his rocking-horse on Christmas Day, and is taught to ride it by Bassett, while Hester, her husband Richard, and her brother Oscar argue about Richard's gambling debts and the couple's extravagance. The camera finally tracks upstairs, pans the toy-filled nursery, and comes to rest on the rocking-horse while a voice-over whispers, "There must be more money!" All of these scenes originate in one brief paragraph in the story:

> And so the house came to be haunted by the unspoken phrase: There must be more money! There must be more money! The children could hear it all the time, though nobody said it aloud. They heard it at Christmas when the expensive and splendid toys filled the nursery. Behind the shining modern rocking-horse, behind the smart doll's house, a voice would start whispering: "There *must* be more money! There *must* be more money!" (148-149)

Some scenes and sequences, however, are pure Pelissier. Richard's dispensing coins to young carolers on Christmas Eve introduces the story's money theme. A sequence in the film in which Paul bets at his first real horse-race while his mother attempts to sell her evening clothes to a Greek tailor has only partial roots in the text. The racetrack scenes are drawn directly from the story, but the gloomy pawn-shop sequence (Hester arrives by cab, bargains weakly with the tailor, finds herself too short of coins to pay for taxi-fare home, and is finally forced to walk) was entirely Pelissier's invention, as was the scramble of the children for coins the cabdriver contemptuously throws on the pavement, paralleling Richard's handout of coins on Christmas Eve. To further highlight the class distinctions between rich and poor which pervade the film, Pelissier also added shots of Bassett chatting with other chauffeurs about the upcoming Derby outside the Belgravia mansion where Hester and her husband attend a society party on the fateful night of their son's "fall."

Evidently taking his cue from the scene in Lawrence's narrative in which Hester makes negative comments to Paul about his unlucky father, in

Lawrence's narrative, Pelissier interspersed a number of scenes throughout the film showing Hester and Richard arguing with one another and with Oscar over Richard's debts, Hester's extravagance, and Oscar's loans. A scene *not* in the story is a confrontation in front of the house, after the newly fired Richard arrives home early. The trio's argument is witnessed from a distance by Paul, who immediately runs to Bassett and asks to bet on a horse. The scene in which a bailiff duns Hester for £40 to pay for an art object is not in the story, either, but is implied by Paul's anxious comment to his Uncle Oscar, "You know people send mother writs, don't you?"

Scenes with the children were undoubtedly also added to illustrate Hester's superficial attentiveness (she oversees their bedtime prayers) and her lack of awareness of their real feelings and behavior. For example, a scene in which Paul attempts to give his mother money to pay a creditor and is angrily rebuffed indicates her lack of sensitivity. Similarly, a brief scene in which Hester, admiring herself before her vanity mirror, praises her skill in calming the children down before bed is undercut by a parallel scene showing the children wildly romping in the nursery. Unique to the film is the previously noted sequence after Paul's death, in which a remorseful Hester orders Bassett to burn the rocking-horse and Paul's winnings as well. Bassett burns the horse but convinces Hester to allow the "blood money" to be used to help others. In a distinct departure from Lawrence's story, Bassett (not Uncle Oscar) has the last word, moralizing, "You'll never see the end of it, Ma'am, and nor'll I. As long as ever we'll live we'll remember and we'll know each in our own way, just what it is was done."

Apart from expanding Lawrence's text sufficiently to create a 90-minute feature-length film with both indoor and outdoor locales, Pelissier's additions made Bassett more important and appealing,[17] Paul more poignant and sympathetic, Uncle Oscar more sarcastic and amusing. Pelissier also invented scenes that highlight Hester's lust for material possessions and social status, as well as her financial irresponsibility, which results in several humiliating incidents not included in the story. Indeed, as both scenarist and director, Pelissier portrayed Hester throughout the film as selfish, narcissistic, imperious, dismissive, and intemperate, conspicuously lacking in genuine wifely and maternal warmth. In the sequence in which she impulsively leaves her party, rushes home to check on her ailing son, reacts with horror as he falls unconscious from his rocking-horse, and holds a tearful vigil at his bedside, she is shown to undergo a sincere change of heart. This sequence prepares us for the sentimental finale in which Hester appears to be overcome with remorse and guilt for Paul's death[18] and cured of her materialism and lust for money. However, Hester's reformation is not in keeping with Lawrence's portrayal of her as essentially greedy, hardhearted, and unloving to the end.

Style in the Story and the Film

If Pelissier managed to reproduce much of the narrative content of Lawrence's story as well as to elaborate on subtle hints contained in it, finding equivalents for elements of prose style in "The Rocking-Horse Winner" posed more of a challenge. Although "The Rocking-Horse Winner" differs in important aspects from most other short fictions by Lawrence, its distinctive prose style connects it with all of his writings. Links both in content and in style with fairy tales and biblical parables are forged by the tale's subject matter, use of expletives, simple diction, and the relatively short sentences and paragraphs that alternate with longer sentences and paragraphs to create a rhythmic "rocking" effect. "Rocking" is also evoked by frequent use of antithesis, created by contrasting conjunctions (*but* and *yet*) as well as negative conjunctive adverbs (*nevertheless*).

As in almost all of Lawrence's writings, repetition in general (and incremental repetition in particular) is pervasive with respect to scenes, dialogue, units of language (words, phrases, clauses, sentences), rhythm, and sound. Figurative language in the story consists mainly of personification and symbolism, in terms of objects and actions. Paradox is also fundamental to the story and is evidenced, among other things, by Lawrence's frequent use of antithesis and chiasmus (a reversal in the order of words in two other otherwise parallel phrases). Finally, all sorts of ironies—situational, dramatic, and verbal—abound.

Although director-scenarist Anthony Pelissier was basically faithful to the narrative content of Lawrence's story and claimed to have kept the "essence of the story intact,"[19] Julian Smith found Pelissier's *The Rocking Horse Winner* "not particularly Lawrentian," observing that "the style of the film owes less to Lawrence than to the way Dickens' classics were filmed in England in the 30's and 40's: the lush attention to production values and the full range of characterizations."[20] In Smith's view, John Mills's portrayal of "humble Bassett is reminiscent of Bernard Miles's Joe Gargery in David Lean's adaptation of *Great Expectations*, in which Mills had played Pip and Valerie Hobson the grown-up Estella" and John Howard Davies's portrayal of Paul recalls "the watchful innocence" of his characterization of Oliver Twist in David Lean's 1948 version of Dickens's classic.[21] Smith also found striking similarities between the opening and closing shots of *The Rocking*

Horse Winner and the cinematography in Orson Welles's classic *Citizen Kane*:

> Not only do both project the same classic quality, but Pelissier's film has several small visual links to Orson Welles' 1941 masterpiece, chiefly in the opening shot traveling in on a model of the subject's home, the first view of the protagonist as a child playing in snow, the use of oppressively distorting lenses and camera angles, and the burning of the "toy" at the end—Rosebud on the one hand, the rocking-horse on the other.[22]

Since any film adaptation of a literary work mirrors the cinematic techniques as well as the political, social, and cultural climate of the times, Smith's linkage of *The Rocking Horse Winner* with the cinematography in Orson Welles's classic *Citizen Kane* is not surprising. Many of Welles's techniques were derived from those of German expressionism and the works of German filmmakers of the 1920s and 1930s, including F. W. Murnau, Fritz Lang, Max Ophuls, and Otto Preminger. When these filmmakers came to the U. S., they helped post-World War II filmmakers of the forties and fifties to create the film style known as *film noir*, an offshoot of German expressionism with which the style of *The Rocking Horse Winner* has marked affinities.[23]

Film noir was a multifaceted visual technique characteristic of several hundred darkly pessimistic, cynical Hollywood crime dramas of the 1940s and early 1950s directed by such German and Austrian expatriates as William Wilder, Otto Preminger, and Fritz Lang and by Alfred Hitchcock and Michael Curtiz.[24] These films, including *The Asphalt Jungle*, a movie which a critic in *The Saturday Review* compared to and contrasted with *The Rocking Horse Winner*,[25] are distinguished by what one film scholar described as "the unvarnished depiction of greed, lust and cruelty."[26] Their basic theme is "the depth of human depravity and the utterly unheroic nature of human beings."[27] David Cook ably summarized the visual style of *film noir*:

> Moral ambiguity is translated into visual style by these technicians through what has been called "anti-traditional cinematography." The pervasive use of wide-angle lenses permits greater depth of field but causes expressive distortions in close-ups; low-key lighting and night-for-night shooting (that is, actually shooting night scenes at night rather than in bright daylight with dark filters) both create harsh contrasts between the light and dark areas of the frame, in which the dark predominates, paralleling the moral chaos of the world they represent.[28]

Additional hallmarks of *film noir* relevant to *The Rocking Horse Winner* include claustrophobic framing devices, the foregrounding of objects which assume more power than people, extreme high- and low-angle shots, a relative absence of outdoor locations, and sparing but effective use of camera movement.

Whatever Pelissier owed to David Lean's adaptations of Dickens's novels, to Welles, and to *film noir*, the cinematic style of *The Rocking Horse Winner* is, in most respects, distinctly Lawrentian because he managed to find equivalents for almost all of the features of Lawrence's style through the use of a variety of visual and aural techniques. These include, but are not limited to, confined, theatrical interior sets; musical leitmotifs; claustrophobic framing devices; close-ups of objects and faces; tracking and panning shots and deep focus photography; superimposition; subjective shots; low- and high-angle shots; low-key lighting with deep shadows; parallel editing and dissolves; ironic juxtaposition of shots and scenes; impressionistic aural and visual montage; and symbolic images.

Fantasy Elements in the Story and the Film

One of the most distinctive aspects of "The Rocking-Horse Winner," created partly by its prose style, is a fairy-tale quality blended with realistic elements. The opening sentence, which starts with an expletive ("there was") repeated in the first three paragraphs and intoned by an omniscient narrator, suggests a classic fairytale.[29] The narrator's use of the jarringly modern word "advantages" and the flat, harsh-sounding, sardonic word "luck," however, quickly cancel out the initial benign effect, creating ominous opposition, as does the clause "and the love turned to dust" in the second sentence ("She married for love, and the love turned to dust"); it is hard to miss the funereal overtones of the word "dust." Thus, the first two sentences establish a brooding, troubled atmosphere that intensifies as the story progresses, suggesting an ironic, *mock* fairy tale, like Shirley Jackson's gothic story "The Lottery," with normal expectations reversed.[30]

As in a folk or fairy tale, no last name is given for the fractured family; the mother is not named until nearly the end of the story (she is called "Paul's mother" throughout); the father also remains nameless, as does one of Paul's two younger sisters. So does the rocking-horse, which Paul never gives a fixed name, since it takes on the identities of the winning race-horses he rides it to discover. Nor, in keeping with fairy-tale vagueness, is any specific time period mentioned, though mention of cars, whiskeys-and-soda, prams, and telephones implies modernity. Most of the specific names that Lawrence used in the story have an exotic or romantically fanciful cast, as in the case of the racehorses (Mirza, Singhalese, Lancelot, Sansovino, Malabar, Daffodil, Lively Spark, Blush of Dawn). They also have allegorical/symbolic overtones and literary or mythical associations.

Another fairy-tale aspect of the story is the frequent use of personification and its reverse, which might be termed "depersonification," in which the animate is rendered lifeless. In the opening paragraph, for instance, "love" turns into "dust"; when her children are present, the mother feels "the center of her heart go hard." When Paul's mother reads the lawyer's letter informing her that she is to £1,000 a year on her birthday, "her face hardened and became expressionless." On his deathbed, Paul's eyes "were like blue stones," although his mother felt "her heart had gone, actually turned into stone."

Conversely, the inanimate house echoes the parents' (especially the mother's) unspoken urgency over the need for funds. "The Children could hear it all the time. . . . 'There *must* be more money! There *must* be more money!'" The edict came "whispering from the springs of the still-swaying rocking-horse;" even the toys hear the house whispering. The rocking-horse itself takes on human characteristics. After one "mad little journey" Paul stares into its "lowered face," its mouth "slightly open" and its big eye "wide and glassy bright."

As might be expected in a mock fairytale, references to the supernatural abound. A number of critics have identified the supernatural elements in "The Rocking-Horse Winner" as *the uncanny*—having or seeming to have a supernatural basis, mysterious, frightening, preternatural, according to the Unabridged Random House dictionary.[31] Lawrence's "amateur essays" in psychoanalytic theory, *Psychoanalysis and the Unconscious* and *Fantasia of the Unconscious* (1925), which acknowledge Freud's contribution to an understanding of the unconscious, are cited by W. S. Marks III as evidence of the novelist's familiarity with the concept of the uncanny, defined by Freud as "a product of narcissistic regression to a primitive belief in animism."[32]

Evidence of mysterious, inexplicable, secret forces at work beyond the characters' control or volition is introduced in the opening paragraph. Apart from its fairly obvious sexual overtones, "she had bonny children, yet she felt they had been *thrust upon her*" suggests a violent external power compelling Hester to produce offspring she does not want. When her children are present, she always feels "the centre of her heart go hard," suggesting a process over which she has no control. The mother and children share the unspoken yet pervasive anxiety about money that mysteriously agitates their home. "And so the house *came to be haunted* by the unspoken phrase: There must be more money." A voice, an impersonal "it," comes "whispering from the springs of the still-swaying rocking-horse" as the impersonal "it" later becomes "luck" itself. "He wanted *luck*, he wanted it, he wanted it"—"luck" implying the intervention of supernatural forces.

Paul's ability to divine the names of winning horses is "uncanny"— both marvelous and strangely frightening. The boy's weird powers blaze in his "uncanny blue eyes," to which Lawrence refers a number of times in the story. When his mother begs him to go to the seaside before the fateful Derby, he lifts his "uncanny blue eyes" in protest; as the Derby nears, his "eyes were really uncanny." Paul's mother is disturbed by his uncanniness; before the Derby, she "had sudden strange seizures of uneasiness about him." At a big party, "one of her rushes of anxiety about her boy, her first-born, gripped her heart till she could hardly speak."

References to the supernatural in the story also include conventional religious allusions. Early in the story, Paul confides in his mother that he is a lucky person. When she asks "Why?" he replies, "God told me." Confiding in Oscar about Paul's talent for choosing winning horses, Bassett, who is described variously "as if he were speaking of religious matters" and as being "serious as a church," explains to Oscar that the two are all right when they're "sure": "'It's Master Paul, sir,' said Bassett, in a secret religious voice. 'It's as if he had it from heaven."

Like the story, the film has many elements of fantasy. Since all films of the 1930's and 1940s in both the U.S. and Britain were shot on studio lots and sound stages with very few, if any, location shots, the sets as well as the lighting were inevitably artificial,[33] and such artifice was admirably suited to adapting "The Rocking-Horse Winner." From the opening shot of the film, the fairy tale and fantasy elements of D. H. Lawrence's story are replicated primarily through the use of theatrical interior sets or stagy outdoor environments as well as through the use of unrealistic, artificial *film noir* lighting. Pelissier also endows inanimate, mechanical objects and natural phenomena with demonic qualities and incorporates a variety of expressionistic techniques—deep-focus and zoom photography; montage; tracking shots; close-ups; extreme low- or high-angle shots; melodramatic, often janglingly ominous music accompanied by a "surrealistic" soundtrack—to convey the supernatural, occasionally surrealistic aspects of Lawrence's tale.

Fairy-tale artificiality is suggested from the opening of the film by the previously noted aerial establishing shot of the Grahame house[34] at night, a shot that resembles a still photo of an architectural or toy model. Other long shots in the film have a similarly stagy, still-photograph look about them: an establishing shot of Goodwood racetrack, for example, was actually taken on location (according to the shooting script),[35] but because the shot is static and the viewer quite conscious of the edges of the frame, it looks like a picture-postcard.

A medium long shot of the rundown slum street where the tailor/pawnbroker has his shop appears similarly theatrical. Because we see only a small section of the block, a realistic context is missing. Indeed, Joan Mellen laments the unreality of the two main outdoor scenes in *The Rocking-Horse Winner*, complaining that "the street somehow does not seem a real street" and that "the racetrack scene, done partly within a studio and partly on location, also suffers from an air of unreality, a sense of the contrived and artificial."[36]

Like the outdoor locations, the sets of the Grahame house are almost all theatrical in their elegance and in their limitedness and self-enclosure. In the Belgravia mansion where Hester's society affair is held, only the stairs going up, the library off the main entrance hall, and the front door itself are visible; it is as though the rest of the house does not exist.

Not only the artificial outdoor settings but also the indoor settings come under fire from Joan Mellen. Evaluating the film from a purely cinematic point of view, she concludes that Pelissier failed to exploit the medium:

> Too much confinement and too many theatrically designed set-ups make for a sense of "filmed theatre." Too frequently does the viewer feel that he is watching an enactment. The film suffers from this element of finiteness; its portrayal of a closed world, suitable to the theme of the tragic fate waiting the boy who must exhaust himself daily in the pursuit of "luck" is fatal to the film. For, as a medium, film best realizes its potential when it can convey a feeling of endlessness, create a world so replete with sensibility and perception that it seems as if it will maintain its rhythm long after the final fade.[37]

The film's "elements of finiteness" and its "portrayal of a closed world," however, powerfully render the intensely suffocating, anxious feelings generated by the story. It is as though the narrow constrictions and tunnel vision of the characters have affected their perception of the world (and consequently, ours).

Indeed, in many scenes, the disquietingly large figures, especially of Hester and Paul, loom in the foreground, filling up the entire screen, with no preceding long shot to establish a sense of space and distance or a visual context. Since the characters themselves cannot see beyond their own single-minded obsessions and are destroyed by a lack of vision, Pelissier did not permit filmgoers to "see" beyond the confines of his own often restricted and static compositions.

More to the point: intentionally or unintentionally, the theatrical aspects of the film accurately convey the fable and fairy-tale elements of Lawrence's tale. In seeking fidelity to the essence of Lawrence's story, Pelissier would have been off the mark in creating a totally realistic, naturalistic, "open" film style, for artificiality and artifice pervade Lawrence's "The Rocking-Horse Winner."

The nonrealistic, fantastical aspects of the film are also manifested in the artificiality of the lighting, in particular the indoor lighting. From the first nighttime sequence in which Paul spies on Bassett through the transom of the gardener's tack-house lodgings, the lighting is exaggerated and extreme; the characters' faces appear either in dark shadows or untempered, harsh pools of light. The planes and surfaces of the faces are simplified, almost abstracted, with no visible imperfections or subtleties.

In a two-shot, if one character's face is in the light, the other's is usually in shadow. Most often the major oval or circular pool of light falls in the center of the composition like a theatrical spotlight, leaving the rest of the frame in darkness. Shadows that fall on the figures' faces and upper bodies are pronounced and unmodulated; no fill lights mold the features of the principals. In outdoor scenes, such as the seaside, the racetrack, the river, and outside the Grahame house, the illumination is relatively even, but there is still unnaturally sharp contrast between dark and light tones and a strong suggestion of artificial illumination.

The eerie soundtrack of the film also underscores the supernatural and fairy-tale aspects of the narrative. Even before the appearance of titles, a nerve-shattering blast, first of cymbals, then of high-pitched strings, announces the four-note trumpet theme associated with Paul's rocking-horse rides. The monumental fanfare, which sounds like a royal alarum in an Elizabethan drama or the opening of a medieval pageant full of jousting, heraldry, and "derring-do," summons up the fairy-tale world of Camelot; one is reminded of Laurence Olivier's film of *Henry V*. In its second incarnation more discordant and "modern," the fanfare takes on an ominous, disturbing quality with thumps in the bass. The frenzied, accelerating third section anticipates Paul's demented rides, while the final section of the "overture" is elegiac, almost funereal, echoing the rather operatic endings of several melancholy sequences in the film, including Paul's death.

Ever-critical Joan Mellen disapproved of the film's musical score: "Pelissier frequently uses an entire orchestra for his musical accompaniment. The film suffers from having too monumental a soundtrack for the minimal quality of its visuals."[38] Gordon Hendricks, however, praised William Alwyn's use of music in the style of Mozart, Rossini, Verdi, Wagner, and Puccini:

> I was struck right away by the excellence of the background music for the titles, which forecast in a very satisfying manner the various "motifs" of the story. This was particularly true of the rocking horse music and the house music . . . . An extremely skillful and unpatronizing setting was composed for the first appearance of the rocking horse and contained the fundamental musical materials for which the film was noteworthy. Augmented, extended brass chords promoted the very feeling of "wild and horrid glee" for which the director strove.[39]

Complementing the melodramatic music score in creating a ghostly, supernatural effect is the intermingled sound of the whispering house—Hester's voice transformed. It is first heard at the end of the sequence in which the Grahames and Oscar are arguing about Richard's gambling debts. Closing the door to the drawing room, Hester announces, "There must be more money, Oscar." The phrase, at first echoing quite loudly, is reiterated as it fades away towards the upper part of the house. The camera tracks and pans up the stairs as the hoarsely whispered phrase is repeated over and over; the fading echo ends up as a diminishing whisper in the nursery, where Paul, standing by his rocking-horse, hears it issuing from the horse's mouth: "More money, money." The second and final time the whispering house is heard is when Paul is about to take his last ride; as he surveys the newly opulent sitting room, he hears, "There must be more money!" mixed with anarchic music and horses' hooves.

Another aural effect contributing to the "fantastic" aspect of the film is the sound of thunder, heard when Paul rides his horse. In the sequence in which Paul's nanny alerts Hester and Oscar, chatting in the garden on a sunny summer day, that the boy is behaving bizarrely in the nursery upstairs, thunder and lightning unaccountably accompany Paul's frenzied ride.

Realism in the Story and the Film

Fantastic and supernatural elements in Lawrence's "The Rocking-Horse Winner" are offset by realistic or quasi-realistic details that generate a willing suspension of disbelief that seductively draws the reader into Paul's nightmare. The realistic references are sometimes vague: Paul's father goes to town "to some office" while his mother "draws the figures of ladies in fur and ladies in silk and sequins for newspaper advertisements." When Paul's mother gets a £5,000 gift from him, "there were certain new furnishings" and "a blossoming of the luxury Paul's mother has been used to."

However, many of the details about horseracing are concrete and believably specific: for a British reader, at least, the names of the races are recognizable (the Lincoln, the Leger, the Grand National, the Derby) and for any reader, the exact amounts bet on each race and the specific sums realized sound authentic. Mention of the family lawyer, the writs that are sent to Paul's mother, Paul's tutor, the governess, cars, taxis and prams, his mother's "white fur cloak" which she slips off while her husband is downstairs "mixing a whiskey and soda," the "shining modern rocking-horse" itself—all suggest a realistic, relatively contemporary context for this tale of the supernatural. Finally, the colloquial, stychomythic dialogues between Paul and his mother, and among Paul, Bassett, and Uncle Oscar, seem quite true to life.

Despite the theatricality and artificiality typical of the film, Pelissier managed to achieve a degree of realism through the black-and-white photography, the crisp architectural and decorative details of the indoor sets, the modernity of the costumes, and in, particular, through telling nuances of characterization and the naturalness of the dialogue. Valerie Hobson acts, at times, the role of the solicitous, loving mother but reveals the true nature of Hester's character in her brittle, loud voice, rapid speech, and arrogant, dismissive manner; John Mills, in his performance as the down-to-earth gardener Bassett, contributes even more strongly to the film's illusion of reality. Natural and unaffected, the earnest, good-natured Mills softens the otherwise harsh effect created by the other adults and is a foil for sardonic, witty Uncle Oscar. John Howard Davies's earnest portrayal of Paul is a credible rendition of a sensitive, nanny-reared English schoolboy. Charles Goldner as Mr. Tsaldouris, the hard-nosed Greek tailor to whom Hester sells her clothes, has a convincingly seedy appearance, a harsh demeanor, and a foreign accent, contrasting sharply with Hester's upper-middle class hauteur.

In scenes drawn directly from the text, Pelissier relied heavily on Lawrence's dialogue. In added episodes, the lines have a gritty sharpness and realism—for example, the scene in which Hester sells her clothes or the two scenes in which she upbraids both her husband and brother about their reaction to the couple's financial crisis. The specificity Lawrence accords money in the story is mirrored in the film's multiple images of money and checks. Some of the outdoor settings look realistic enough—the seaside, the racetrack, a slum street, an antique shop, a tailor shop, the facade of a Belgravia mansion. However, as Joan Mellen points out, the limited contexts of these settings do attenuate their realism: static, self-contained, and selective, they do not convey the degree of verisimilitude—or at least the illusion of it—normally expected in film.

Aside from balancing fairy-tale elements with certain aspects of everyday reality, Pelissier also managed to create equivalents for the distinctive aspects of Lawrence's prose style—notably diction, syntax, paragraph structure and rhythm, as well as repetition, symbolism, paradox, and irony—which, in the view of many critics, would be nearly impossible to reproduce cinematically.

Diction in the Story; Shot and Image in the Film

Maryanne Felter's stylistic study of ten fictions by D. H. Lawrence (excluding "The Rocking-Horse Winner") documents overall similarities of diction and syntax, as well as paragraph shape and structure.[40] Felter cites 26 words that form the core of a Lawrentian vocabulary—almost all one-syllable nouns and adjectives, such as *blood, mind, fire, strange, wild, heavy, curious,* and *warm.* Not surprisingly, a number of words on Felter's core list, including *strange* and *wild, heavy,* and *curious,* can be found in "The Rocking-Horse Winner."

The relatively simple diction in the story, which suggests an almost childlike point of view, is often monosyllabic or bisyllabic and includes many common nouns, chiefly of Anglo-Saxon and Middle English derivation (*house, money, luck, horse, car, children, love, eyes, whisper, winner*) with a sprinkling of Latin and Old French (*secret*). Many of the nouns are either abstract (*love, luck, prospects, attention, stealth, frenzy*) or, if concrete, of a very general nature (instead of *mansion, house*; instead of *daughters* and *sons, children*).

The verbs are remarkably unvaried and ordinary: verbs of being and the verb *to have* predominate (*is, was, were, must be, had, had been*), along with such basic emotive, cognitive, and physical verbs as *love, feel, know, live, go, come, do, love, try, whisper, listen, hear, speak, ask, mean,* and *say.*

Comparatively heightened active verbs—there are relatively few—include *whisper, trick, scream, frighten, gaze, grip, fight, steal, cry,* and *toss.*

Certain repeated key words in "The Rocking-Horse Winner" signify the crass materialism that Lawrence portrays and attacks throughout the story. The word *money* and offshoots of it (coins, pounds, specific sums) as well as the related words *luck, lucky,* and *unlucky,* are found on almost every page of the text, along with words denoting the luxuries symptomatic of Hester's greed (the children's toys, including the rocking-horse, "flowers in the winter," "piles of iridescent cushions" and "a dress of pale green and crystal"). As previously indicated, words referring to the supernatural—*uncanny, God, religious, heaven,* and *heavenly*—are also interjected throughout the story, both in dialogue and commentary, and the phrase "Honour bright" is repeated numerous times. The atmosphere of weirdness and hysteria that intensifies as the plot unfolds is conveyed in distinctively Lawrentian nouns, such as *rushes, seizures, uneasiness, anxiety, fear, amazement, anguish, ecstasy,* and *madness*; adjectives, such as *secret, mad, strange, furious, wild-eyed, powerful, glittering, startled, rushing, tossing, tormented*; and adverbs, such as *anxiously, madly, suddenly,* and *fiercely.*

The scaled-down simplicity of the diction in "The Rocking-Horse Winner," and in particular the blandness and nonspecificity of the nouns and many of the verbs, has its equivalent in the film version in the restrictiveness of settings as well as of shooting techniques. Much of the action takes place indoors in confined spaces, with only occasional outdoor shots that look rather artificial. Scenes are mainly shot at eye-level with two or three characters viewed at medium or medium close-up range. Many of the two- and three-shots are relatively static; in most shots, even in those filmed outdoors, if there is motion, only one character moves within a narrow range followed by the camera. More often than not, distance or angle of shots within scenes remains fixed; if the characters are shot in medium close-up, there is rarely a shift to close-up of one of the character's face to show a reaction shot. Indeed, close-ups are rare, used only for maximum emotional or dramatic effect.

As a counterpart to Lawrence's repeated use of the word *money* and words associated with it, Pelissier also makes numerous verbal and visual references to money. Words suggesting Hester's materialism are reflected in the film's elegantly appointed sets and fashionable clothes; indeed, the rapid montage of evening gowns, fur coats, jewelry, furnishings, and cash over which is superimposed an image of Paul frantically rocking on his horse is a distillation of the conspicuous consumption described in the story. The sense of escalating weirdness and disturbance in the story, conveyed by

Lawrence's characteristically intense nouns, adjectives, and adverbs, is mirrored in the offbeat cinematography, editing, and soundtrack in many shots, scenes, and sequences throughout the film. In particular, the mounting anxiety and agitation of both Paul and his mother, captured in a few heightened action verbs as well as increasingly ominous adjectives and adverbs, are evoked in the long takes of Paul climbing the stairs towards his rocking-horse, in the rapid montage depicting Hester's material acquisitions, and in the sequence portraying Paul's final desperate ride.

Syntax and Paragraph Rhythm in the Story; "Rocking" Rhythms in the Film

Consistent with a story that has a youthful protagonist, the average length of most sentences in "The Rocking-Horse Winner" is 14 words—very short (under 10 words) or of medium length (10–20 words) in the slower, repetitive passages, offset by increasingly longer sentences in the five, climactic, speeded-up passages. In the frequent passages of dialogue, the average sentence length is about six words. Syntactically, sentences are primarily simple (62 percent) with a much smaller number of complex sentences (22 percent) expanded by many relative clauses that begin with *who* or *that* and a sprinkling of compound sentences (12 percent) and compound-complex sentence (3 percent).

A key feature of syntax in "The Rocking-Horse Winner" is parallelism, a device by which phrases, clauses, or sentences of similar construction and meaning are juxtaposed. Examples are numerous:

> The mother had a small income, and the father had a small income, but not nearly enough for the social position which they had to keep up. (148)

> . . . The horse, bending his wooden, champing head, heard it. The big doll, sitting so pink and smirking in her new pram, could hear it quite plainly. . . . (149)

> He lived in the racing events, and the small boy lived with him. (152)

Antithesis is as prevalent as parallelism. In both simple and compound sentences, coordinating conjunctions such as *and*, *but*, and *yet* are legion (polysyndeton); indeed, many simple sentences begin with *and*, *but*, or *yet*. This feature is especially noticeable in the first paragraph in the story:

> There was a woman *who* was beautiful, *who* started with all the advantages, *yet* she had no luck. She married for love *and* the love turned to dust. She had bonny children, *yet* she felt they had been thrust upon her, *and* she could not love them. They looked at her coldly, as if they were finding fault with her. *And* hurriedly she felt (that) she must cover up some fault in herself. *Yet* what it was she must cover up she never knew. (147)

The predominance of contrasting and contradictory coordinating conjunctions (even *and* is used as a contrasting conjunction) and conjunctive adverbs (*nevertheless*) is a primary feature of "The Rocking-Horse Winner," signaling constant tension and opposition. The frequent *but*s, *yet*s, and *and*s that carry the force of *but* suggest that Paul's quest for luck and his perpetually dissatisfied mother's quest for money are doomed. Moreover, the frequent use of balanced yet antithetical statements creates a sort of rocking effect, noted earlier—a syntactical metaphor for the action of the rocking-horse and analogous to the "pulsing, frictional to-and-fro which works up to culmination" identified by Lawrence, in his famous foreword to *Women in Love*, as the sine qua non of his distinctive style.[41]

In *English Prose Style*, Herbert Read points out that although the sentence is the unit of rhythm, the sentence is not the whole of it.[42] Rhythm "is an affair of the paragraph"[43] which is "the first complete and independent unit of prose rhythm"[44] and which "exactly reproduces what we should call the contour of our thought."[45] Further, Read contends, "true rhythm is dictated by emotional tension" and is a question of immediacy, which, as "direct expression, creative thought," is "always poetical even when it has the appearance of prose."[46]

Like the individual sentences, narrative paragraphs in "The Rocking-Horse Winner" are quite brief, averaging three sentences, including 54 percent which are two sentences long or less. Of those over two sentences long, the average paragraph length is about six to seven sentences. In the frequent passages of dialogue, the average sentence length is about six words. The length of the compact sentences in sections of commentary and description varies, depending on the emotional subtext. Generally, a few longer sentences are followed by one or two shorter ones, creating a swelling effect, a constantly rising and falling rhythm like the contraction and expansion of a bellows (or the heaving movements of a mechanical horse), and analogous to the balanced antithesis within many sentences.

In many paragraphs, sentences follow a pattern of length consisting of medium (11–15 words), short (under 10 words), longish (16–20 words), short (under 10 words), medium (10–15 words), longish (16–20 words):

> Although they lived in style, they felt always an anxiety in the house. (M) (*13 words*) There was never enough money. (S) (*5 words*) The mother had a small income, and the father had a small income, but not nearly enough for the social position which they had to keep up. (L) (*27 words*) The father went into town to some office. (S) (*8 words*) But though he had good prospects, these prospects never materialized. (M) (*10 words*) There was always the grinding sense of the shortage of money, though the style was always kept up. (L) (*18 words*) (148)

After three such rising and falling paragraphs, containing successions of medium to long sentences punctuated by short ones, Lawrence followed with a sustained, climactic paragraph in which each of three sentences is relatively longer than the next:

> It came whispering from the springs of the still-swaying rocking-horse, and even the horse bending her wooden, champing head, heard it. (*23 words*) The big doll, sitting so pink and smirking in her new pram, could hear it quite plainly, and seemed to be smirking all the more self-consciously because of it. (*30 words*) The foolish puppy, too, that took the place of the teddy-bear, he was looking so extraordinarily foolish for no other reason but that he heard the secret whisper all over the house, "There *must* be more money!" (*38 words*) (149)

This climactic paragraph is similar to four other such passages in the story, two occurring near the beginning when the money-whispers are first mentioned, one describing Paul's mad rides on his horse in quest of luck, one when the house clamors for even more money after Paul's mother gets her anonymous gift, and the final one when Paul's mother discovers him on his last, fateful ride. All of these paragraphs are characterized by a speeded-up effect which embodies Paul's compulsive and ever-escalating frenzy to satisfy his mother's insatiable greed and parodies her desire for money and material possessions.

Longish passages of dialogue, which constitute the bulk of the narrative, consist of relatively short, staccato sentences and questions, averaging six words and no more than a line or two. Like the internal rhythm of the paragraphs, the story's dialogue sections, numbering 14, also have a rising and falling rhythm, both internally (a longer quote balanced by a shorter one) and in terms of their relative length as the story progresses.

At the outset, Paul and his mother have a fairly lengthy discussion of luck and its connection with "lucre," followed by a much shorter talk while Paul is riding his rocking horse. Following is a very short talk between Uncle Oscar and Bassett, and then a long three-part discussion between Uncle Oscar and Paul about the boy's betting. The pattern of long/short/long conversations continues throughout the story, the last long dialogue taking place between Paul and his mother when she urges him to go to the seaside, and he begs to stay at home for the Derby.

Although the average sentence length in the story is fairly short (under 14 words), the average shot length in the film is relatively long, about 12 seconds, and in many scenes and sequences, very lengthy indeed— approximately one to two minutes, leading a few critics to criticize the film for its sluggish pace and tedious sections. The rhythm of the shots, scenes, and sequences in the film, however, mirrors the "rocking" effect within sentences. The film also simulates the rising and falling pattern and climactic conclusions within the paragraphs and climactic paragraphs in and of themselves. In fact, the "rocking" effect pervades the film, most obviously in the parallel cut sequences.

The climactic paragraph typical of Lawrence's story is mimicked in the film by a number of slowish sequences culminating in a climactic shot. The brief opening shots in the first two scenes of the film, for example, yield to a relatively slow, lengthy-seeming Christmas Eve sequence (the average shot length is 25 seconds) in which Paul descends to the ground-floor drawing room to inspect his unopened presents, among them the mysteriously wrapped rocking-horse. Only at the end of this relatively sluggish segment does the camera move in for medium shots of Paul touching the Christmas tree and other presents, and finally to a climactic 27-second-long medium close-up of Paul, moving from left to right, encountering the rocking-horse's head wrapped in brown paper. The sequence terminates abruptly with a clever match-cut transition in which Paul, in a paper crown and holiday clothes, stands in the exact same position the next day, eagerly tearing open the mysterious gift.

The pattern of short scenes intercut with longer ones is repeated in the next sequence, in which Bassett carries the rocking-horse to the stairway landing and tutors Paul on the finer points of racing his new rocking-horse, while in the drawing room below, Uncle Oscar needles the embattled couple about their excesses. In each locale the action and dialogue reach a climactic pitch. As Paul tentatively rocks back and forth on his new horse in a three-shot scene with two shots lasting one minute each, Bassett urges him on in a lengthy pep talk, in which he ironically warns the boy, "You'll have to go a great deal faster than that or you won't be in time for your own funeral."[47] Bassett's exhortation is followed by a short scene of one 24-second shot in which Oscar tells Richard he's covered his nephew's debt because he doesn't want to get thrown out of his own club. Next there is a quick cut to a long 36-second take of Bassett urging Paul on to a prolonged gallop, after which the boy slows sheepishly to a halt and slides off the rocking-horse. This climactic scene is paralleled by an increasingly loud and angry argument between Richard and Hester, filmed in one long take of nearly two minutes, during which she slams the drawing room door, sending the phrase "There must be more money!" up the stairs and out into the hallway.

A third sequence analogous to the rhythmic pattern of intercut short scenes followed by a relative long, climactic scene shot with special camera effects occurs when Hester and Oscar, lounging in the summer garden, are alerted to Paul's frenzied ride in the nursery, a shot lasting 38 seconds. A quick intercut shot of seven seconds reveals the boy, like a real jockey, "careening madly as if chased by devils."[48] Back in the garden, in a shot lasting 21 seconds, Nanny tells Oscar and Hester that Paul is upstairs having a fit. In the nursery again, thunder and lightning in the background, Paul orders the rocking-horse to "take me to where there's luck."[49] In the scene that follows, made up of shots only a few seconds long, we see Paul frenziedly riding his horse, interspersed with glimpses of Nanny entering and closing the window, and Hester and Oscar gazing at him from the doorway.

When his mother and uncle open the door, Paul is rocking furiously; from his vantage point, the walls of the room swing, loom, and recede "like the horizon of sea at full gale."[50] In the midst of the mounting, climactic frenzy, which ends with Paul claiming, "I got there!" the zoom-like shots rapidly cut back and forth between Paul's bobbing, twisted face filling up the screen, Paul's sisters huddling in the corner, and Oscar and Hester standing near the doorway—alternately large and small, perceived from Paul's distorted point of view. The scene ends with a 20-second shot of Oscar discussing betting with the boy. In the single long take of 42 seconds that follows, Hester and Oscar walk downstairs and then upstairs.

Repetition in the Story and the Film

Along with recurring "rocking" rhythms, perhaps the most noticeable stylistic feature of Lawrence's "The Rocking-Horse Winner" (and of his writing in general) is repetition, not only in regard to recurrent episodes, passages, and rhythm, but of words, phrases, clauses, sentences (parallelism), and sounds. Lawrence alluded to this quirk in a rare defense of his own writing method:

> In point of style, fault is often found with the continual, slightly modified repetition. The only answer is that it is natural to the author and that every natural crisis in emotion or passion or understanding comes from this pulsing, frictional to-and-fro which works up to culmination.[51]

Analyzing another story by Lawrence, "The Horse-Dealer's Daughter," Thomas M. McCabe generalized, "The rhythmic form of Lawrence's stories rests . . . on the conventional devices of repeated scenes, phrases and characters . . . ."[52] Daniel J. Schneider's comments on Lawrence's pervasive use of repetition seem especially relevant to "The Rocking-Horse Winner":

> The dangers of his repetitive style are obvious: the repetitions may become mechanical or may even be unnecessary. Yet they are generally required by Lawrence's effort to present the actualities of psychic process. . . . The frictional to-and-fro exhibits Lawrence's conception of the dualism of the psyche. . . . Beyond this, repetition serves the purpose of presenting the pressures of psychic necessity. . . . The repetition of key words or phrases fixes attention on the single undeniable need. The repetitions build the intensity until a culmination is reached.[53]

Sometimes the verbal repetition in the story is exact; more often it is incremental (or, as Lawrence described it, "slightly modified"), with elements of the original retained and new elements added. Frantic, insistent repetition is also metaphorical in "The Rocking Horse Winner," embodying the obsessive drive for money and material possessions which leads to tragedy.

Repetition of individual words is pervasive throughout the story. In the first paragraph, for example, the words *love* and *children* occur five times each, *felt* and *knew* three times each; *fault, hard, cover up*, and *heart*, twice. In the second paragraph, the words *smirking, foolish, heard*, and *whisper* are each repeated twice. In one relatively short passage in which Paul and his mother are discussing the meaning of "luck," the words *lucky* and *unlucky* appear 15 times, and in yet another passage, in which Paul discusses horse-racing with Uncle Oscar, the words *honour bright* recur six times. Often repeated are adjectives that convey both the story's meanings and its tense, ominous atmosphere, including *expensive, secret, dark, strange, furious, sudden, powerful, uncanny, cold,* and *heavy*. Recurring adverbs, such as *madly, terribly, suddenly, uneasily,* and *stonily* suggest the increasingly frenzied pace of the narrative and the unhealthy intensity generated by it.

Parallel phrases, too, recur constantly, often with minor variations. In the first paragraph, for instance, "she always felt the centre of her heart go hard" is echoed and amplified two sentences later in "at the centre of her heart was a hard little place that could not feel love, no, not for anybody." Similarly, the clause "only she herself knew" is repeated, with slight variation, two sentences further on as "Only she herself, and her children themselves knew it was not so." In the second paragraph, the second sentence, "There was never enough money" is embedded in the more elaborate last sentence, "There was always the grinding sense of the shortage of money, though the style was always kept up" and is repeated throughout the story as the "unspoken phrase" which haunts the house: "There must be more money!"

Examples of this sort of incremental repetition abound in "The Rocking-Horse Winner," as do instances of anaphora, the repetition of a word or a group of words in successive clauses: "There was a woman *who* was beautiful, *who* started off with all the advantages . . ." and "*Behind* the shining rocking-horse, *behind* the smart doll's house. . . ." A driving intensity is conveyed by the three repeated short clauses, "He *wanted* luck, he *wanted* it, he *wanted* it," and by Paul's repeated commands to his rocking-horse, "Now take me to where there is luck! Now take me!" And the degree of Paul's hysterical anxiety and obsessiveness is reflected in his repeated pleas to his mother not to worry about his fixation on "horse-racing and *events*"— or, beyond that, about some unnamed possible catastrophe. Indeed, Paul repeats "You needn't worry," or a variation of it, four times during a single brief exchange with Hester.

Quite a few critics, most notable among them F. R. Leavis, called Lawrence a "prose poet."[54] More than many of his stories, "The Rocking-Horse Winner" is self-consciously and flamboyantly poetic, both in its cadenced rhythms and in its pervasive use of repetitive sound effects. Recurring sounds play a major symbolic role in "The Rocking-Horse Winner"—the increasingly loud and demanding whispers of the house urging Paul on in his quest for "luck" and the rushing, powerful "soundless noise" which Paul's mother hears outside the door of his bedroom on the night of his final, fatal ride.[55]

Stylistically, repetitive sound devices include rhyme and near-rhyme, alliteration, assonance, and onomatopoeia. A polyphony of repeated sounds knits many of the paragraphs in "The Rocking-Horse Winner" together, creating a hypnotic, incantatory effect and the sense of a multi-leveled, intensely self-enclosed world. Typical is the first paragraph of the story, with its many repeated words, initial and internal consonants, and vowels:

> There was a woman who was beautiful, who started with all the advantages, yet she had no luck. She married for *love* and the *love* turned to dust. She had bonny *children*, yet she *felt* they had been thrust upon her, and could not *love* them. They looked at her coldly as if they were finding *fault* with her. And hurriedly, she *felt* she must *cover up* some *fault* in herself. Yet what it was she must *cover up* she never *knew*. Nevertheless, when her *children* were present, she always *felt* the *centre* of her heart go hard. This troubled her, and in her manner she was all the more gentle and anxious for her *children* as if she *loved* them very much. Only she herself *knew* that at the *centre* of her *heart* was a *hard* little place that could not feel *love*, no, not for anybody. Everybody else said of her: "She is such a good mother. She adores her *children*." Only she herself, and her *children* themselves, *knew* it was not so. They read it in each other's eyes. (147)

Just as Lawrence repeated himself compulsively in "The Rocking-Horse Winner" (and elsewhere), Pelissier used formal repetition of scenes and visual motifs as an organizing principle in scripting and directing his screen adaptation. The most obvious instance of this is that the film opens and closes symmetrically with a scene involving Bassett, the gardener-handyman, and Hester. In both of the above-mentioned scenes, horses figure prominently. During Bassett's initial conversation with Paul at the beginning of the film, we see a close-up of a photo of young Bassett on a race horse, and at the end of the film, Bassett, at Hester's command, burns the infamous rocking-horse. Aside from the rocking-horse itself, the emblematic horse motif appears repeatedly, sometimes subliminally, throughout the rest of the film, suggesting the work of both overt and hidden "occult" forces. In the antique/furniture shop scene, for example, Paul picks up a small statue of a horse and, unnoticed by his mother, examines it as she speaks to him. Before Paul takes his last rocking-horse ride, he gazes out of the large nursery window at exaggeratedly white clouds moving rapidly across the night sky; briefly glimpsed is the clearly superimposed image of three white horses, manes flying. Real horses, naturally enough, appear in the outdoor scene at Goodwood racetrack. The flesh-and-blood animals become ironically superfluous, however, compared with the mechanical horse and its various representations, which come to seem more intensely real than the genuine article.

Scenes involving stairs are repeated over and over. In the opening scene of the film, Paul climbs on cartons (improvised stairs) to spy on Bassett and falls off them. Soon after, Hester and Richard ascend the stairs in the house as she questions her husband pointedly about his possible new job. Paul descends the stairs on Christmas Eve to look at the presents in the drawing room, and climbs them with Bassett on Christmas Day to receive his riding lesson. On the same day, after Hester ends her heated argument with Oscar and Richard about the need for more money, the camera tracks upstairs.

After the impressionistic montage showing Hester's extravagance, a second tracking shot up the stairs ends with a shot of Paul astride his rocking horse. A triple-stair sequence in the final parallel-edited series of shots shows Hester mounting, then descending, the ornate stairs at her charity ball, alternating with Paul ascending the stairs at home for his last ride. The series ends with Hester climbing the stairs after she rushes home to discover Paul shouting out the name of the Derby winner. The last stair scene occurs when Bassett carries the rocking-horse down to the yard to burn it.

Also featured in the movie are doors. Most of them are being closed—the front door of the Grahame mansion shut by Richard at the beginning, when Hester complains of a draft, and several times later, when Hester closes the door, or attempts to close it on Paul to keep him from the adult world and its secrets. Several times we see long shots of children framed in an open doorway—Paul's sisters saying their prayers with Hester, Hester putting Paul to bed, and Paul kneeling in prayer at night with a prophetic shadow in the shape of a cross over his head.

Windows, though emphasized less frequently, are significant elements too. In the opening sequence, Paul spies on Bassett through a transom. Soon afterward, Bassett closes his window of his tack room after Hester and Paul leave. In other scenes, windows in the nursery let in or shut out thunder and lightning and the eerie light of the moon. In the dark basement tailor's shop, the pawnbroker pulls down the window-shade to shut out the prying eyes of outsiders. After an argument with her brother, Hester glares moodily out of the French door in the drawing room, as if dreaming of escape.

Stripes and bars of light or shadow appear in many scenes. Stripes turn up in the drawing room and automobile upholstery (Hester sits on a striped sofa and chair), on Paul's pajamas, on Oscar's striped valise, on the wallpaper and lampshade in Paul's room, and on the awning at the Belgravia mansion where Hester's charity ball is held. Bars of various kinds are also featured in many scenes: bars on the nursery window, spindles on the banisters in several scenes going up or down the stairs or on landings, spindles and vertical bar-shadows on the wall when Bassett demonstrates rocking-horse technique, and the wide wooden slats of the fence seen when

Paul and Oscar are on the beach near the racetrack.

Money—paper and coins—is another recurrent visual motif through the film. Finally, parallel-cut sequences abound.

Repeated aural motifs are drawn from the Wagnerian-style overture. The trumpet motif that heralds a horse race and Paul's rocking-horse rides is heard over and over, in brief snatches, reminding us of the boy's obsession. Almost the same soundtrack plays when Paul ascends for his last ride and when his mother mounts the stairs to find him. A second ominous musical motif accompanies Paul's rocking-horse rides; this motif is in a lower register, and consists of four notes in a speeded-up consecutive downward progression. A third motif is a melancholy dirge played by a bassoon.

In addition to its three repeated musical themes, the soundtrack at various points blends nonmusical sounds, including the "whispering house," thunder, horse's hooves, hawkers, announcers, and shouting crowds at the racetrack. As in the story, the sound of the house clamoring for more money is repeated in key sequences during the film, becoming a ritualistic refrain and underscoring the frantic climax of Paul's last ride.

Symbolism in the Story and the Film

Clearly connected with Lawrence's repetitiveness in "The Rocking-Horse Winner" is his use of symbolism. David Lodge describes Lawrence's writing as "a mode . . . that is continually turning its realistic particulars into symbols"[56] and Mark Schorer observes that "in many of his short stories and novels, Lawrence managed to maintain a realistic framework within which rich symbolic modulations that far transcend realism can be beautifully contained."[57] Because "The Rocking-Horse Winner" is a complex blend of fairy-tale and realistic elements, the symbolic aspects of the story and the film adaptation are especially numerous and pronounced, calling for detailed explication.

In film, symbolism is created by repetition of aural and visual effects, by a character's placing value and importance on an object, by charged associations with other objects or adjacent shots, or by special visual, aural, or musical emphasis—lingering close-ups, unusual camera angles, freeze frames, or lighting effects.[58] To be discussed in the following sections are the symbols in Lawrence's story and Pelissier's equivalents for them, as well as symbolic elements added by the director that are either based on or suggested by material in the original text.

In "The Rocking-Horse Winner," inanimate objects and forces acquire symbolic meaning through frequent repetition, the nameless rocking-horse, of course, foremost among them. Several explicators of the story have waxed eloquent on the symbolism of horses in general. W. S. Marks III sees horses in Jungian terms, as "common symbols for the libido in a state of repression,"[59] and points out that "the equestrian, used as an emblem of modern man's tragic attempt at conscious domination of the libido,"[60] is a recurrent figure in Lawrence's fiction, appearing in *Women in Love*, "The Prussian Officer," *St. Mawr*, and most of the New Mexico stories. Kingsley Widmer reminds us that for Lawrence "horses symbolize the passions."[61]

The rocking-horse, though powerful in its own way, is inanimate, mechanical, a counterfeit of the real horses that run in the races, and the race-horses themselves are facsimiles of the steeds of knights and warriors of the past. "The symbolic meaning of Paul's rocking-horse depends precisely on the fact that it is not a 'big living presence' but an artificial object," argues Marks. In his view, Lawrence implies that modern man "has lost the real living universe that is still present to the unreflective child and the savage."[62] According to Caroline Gordon and Allen Tate, the rocking-horse is "a link between the visible and invisible worlds,"[63] while Michael Goldberg sees it as "an extension of the unlived, unfulfilled quality of the parents' life."[64]

W. D. Snodgrass contends that although the rocking-horse reaches symbolically "into the occult, into the modern intellectual spirit, into the financial and imperial manipulations of the modern state," its sexual symbolism is basic to the story, and Paul's frenzied rides are masturbatory: "Just as the riding of a horse is an obvious symbol for the sex act and 'riding' was once the common sexual verb, so the rocking-horse stands for the child's imitation of the sex act, for the riding which goes nowhere."[65] Finally, Michael Goldberg sees Lawrence's rocking-horse symbolism as more Dickensian than Freudian, and attacks Snodgrass's widely accepted psychoanalytic interpretation as weakening the force of Lawrence's central symbol by narrowing its range of effectiveness:

> The point is not that the horse may symbolize a masturbating activity, but that masturbation is itself a symbol, representing a kind of futility which describes the parents' life as well as the boy's and the general activity of society itself.[66]

To Goldberg, the tale is not primarily an account of sexual aberration but of the larger dislocation implied by social malfunctioning.

The whispering mansion, a symbol more restrictive than that of the rocking-horse, represents the money-madness that afflicts the household and is embedded in capitalist society itself. Constantly heard, the whispering—a sort of schizophrenic or drug-induced aural hallucination—permeates the children's consciousness and their subconscious as well. The house is inanimate yet alive, impersonal yet intimate. Like the rocking-horse, it has a demonic life of its own. It is a force that is unleashed by human beings yet exists independent of them and profoundly affects their relationships and actions. The notion of the *house* urging Paul on is, of course, symbolic of the dissociation of parts of the self. Paul is deeply affected by his parents' acrimony and greed, but in a household of secrets and lies, he cannot bear (and is not permitted) to acknowledge the true source of his anxiety. His solution is to deny his awareness and ascribe the clamor for money to the house, a poignant projection that lets his guilty parents off the hook but condemns the acquisitive society that spawns and sustains them.

In "The Rocking-Horse Winner," ever-escalating sums of money are symbolic of luck (if you are lucky, you have or acquire money) and are also used as a replacement for the father figure and for love. In Freudian theory, money is associated with feces—hence, the appropriateness of Oscar's calling it "filthy lucre," which Paul ironically confuses with "luck." W. D. Snodgrass argues that "the money in the story must be taken literally, but it is also a symbolic substitute for love and affection (since it has that meaning to the characters themselves) and ultimately for sperm."[67] Snodgrass insists that the money has no intrinsic value to Paul; it is only a way to win his mother's affection and attention. Nor, he argues, has it any real use for Hester; when she receives her anonymous gift of £5,000, she becomes even more insatiable.

Pervasive throughout "The Rocking-Horse Winner" are two symbolic organs of the body—the heart and above all, the eyes, both of which are mentioned in the first paragraph. Although the heart is not referred to as frequently as the eyes, the story is studded with mentions of it. "Hard-hearted" may be a trite metaphor, but Lawrence uses it imaginatively to show the anomie that afflicts Paul's mother. When her children are present, Hester feels "the centre of her heart go hard"; as her son lies dying, she is "heart-frozen," feeling her heart "had gone, turned actually into stone"(165).

The eyes of the children, the adults, even of the demonic rocking-horse itself ("Its big eye . . . wide and glassy-bright") are ubiquitous in "The Rocking-Horse Winner"—almost literally, windows of the soul. Everyone else believes Hester to be a good mother; only she herself, and the children, know it is not so: "They read it in each other's eyes." During a crucial discussion about luck, Paul anxiously watches his mother "with unsure eyes" and when she backtracks on her comment that she is unlucky, Paul "looked at her to see if she meant it," perceiving that she is trying to hide something from him.

Throughout the story, Paul's eyes project his preternatural awareness and power. As he rides his rocking-horse in a frenzy, "his eyes had a strange glare in them." When Paul's nurse warns him that he will "break his horse" and his sister urges him to stop riding, "he only glared down on them in silence." The "blue glare from his big, rather close-set eyes" silences his mother and Uncle Oscar when they seek to curb his riding.

Normally, the color blue denotes coldness, but Lawrence paradoxically and oxymoronically describes Paul's eyes as fiery (at the core of any flame, of course, is a blue fire). "The boy gazed at his uncle from those big, hot, blue eyes, set rather close together." At the racetrack, when Daffodil wins and Paul receives his £20 earnings, the boy is flushed and his eyes are "blazing." When he is explaining to his Uncle Oscar that he started betting on horses for his mother's sake and to stop the house from whispering, he watches his uncle "with big blue eyes, that have an uncanny *cold fire* in them."

In many of his other works, Lawrence often associated blueness with "northernness," intellectuality, a desire to know and dominate the natural world (Gerald in *Women in Love* or Lord Chatterly in *Lady Chatterly's Lover*) or with suppressed passion, as in the case of the tormented, sadistic homosexual captain in "The Prussian Officer" with eyes "bluey like fire," murdered by the young orderly to whom he is sexually drawn but cannot admit he desires. Paul is also an individual with a Faustian desire to "know" and to be loved; he attempts to fulfill both desires, with disastrous consequences. The "blazing blueness" of eyes is a peculiarly Lawrentian paradox, perhaps symbolic of Lawrence's own oxymoronic nature but more probably literally reflective of his own physiognomy. Like Paul's, Lawrence's eyes were intensely blue and electric, a facet of his otherwise unremarkable appearance often noted in the memoirs of his friends and relatives.[68]

As the story unfolds, Lawrence describes Paul's eyes in increasingly fevered and surrealistic terms. Repeatedly failing to come up with the names of winning horses, Paul becomes "wild-eyed and strange . . . his big blue eyes blazing with a sort of madness." When his mother urges him to go to the seaside, he lifts "his uncanny blue eyes" and begs to be allowed to remain in the house until after the Derby. As the Derby draws near, the boy grows more and more tense "and his eyes were really uncanny." In the climactic rocking-horse scene, before Paul falls unconscious at his mother's feet, "his eyes blazed at her for one strange and senseless second." As he lies in a coma, his eyes are "like blue stone": something organic turns hard and lifeless, just like the heart of Paul's mother, which is already stone.

In Pelissier's film of "The Rocking-Horse Winner," some of the symbols in the narrative have been altered in the process of adaptation, whereas visual and aural symbols *not* included in the original have been added to reinforce mood and theme. As in the story, much of the symbolism in the screen version is created through repetition, which is one of the chief cinematic techniques for investing an image with symbolic significance. Indeed, many of the recurring visual motifs already discussed in the section on repetition are in fact symbolic.

The primary symbol in the film, as in the story, is of course the rocking-horse, subliminal variants of which, as noted, appear as a small statue of a horse in an antique shop and in the briefly glimpsed image of three horses racing through clouds viewed through Paul's nursery window. The rocking-horse is first seen in its entirety on Christmas Day when Bassett shows Paul how to ride it. Following this scene, most of the shots show Paul with only the horse's head and shoulders, suggesting that the toy has now become, to Paul at least, a flesh-and-blood animal.

Through the rest of the film, the reification of the rocking-horse intensifies. On Christmas Eve, when Paul's mother announces "There must be more money," the camera focuses on the boy standing beside the rocking-horse in the nursery, listening to its whisper. Closeups of Paul, his head turning this way and that, are followed by a high-contrast, low-angle, three-quarter closeup of the malevolent horse's head, in deep shadows, its mouth cut off and only one demonic eye visible. In the following shot, the sounds of the whisper seem to come from the horse's mouth, which Paul stares at from the left. In this scene, and in a later one, Pelissier's grotesque closeup of the horse's head is drawn directly from Lawrence's text: "Its red mouth was open, its big eye was wide and glassy bright."

In the nursery riding sequence, photographed in subjective zoom-like shots and from various angles, Paul rides like a jockey on a real horse. We next see Paul frantically riding his rocking-horse in a shot metaphorically superimposed over an impressionistic montage of Hester's buying spree, directly linking the boy's rides with the frenzied materialism of his mother. In the last sequence in which the boy rides his rocking-horse, a shadow profile of the boy is projected from a low angle onto the wall opposite the moonlit window in the nursery as his horrified mother, in closeup, gazes at him from the doorway. In the extreme foreground, Paul falls unconscious at the feet of the horse. A low-angle, eerily lit closeup of the horse's head, triumphant and diabolical, ends this sequence.

The Rocking-Horse Winner

The progression in the film is from the rocking-horse as inanimate object to flesh-and-blood animal (from Paul's perspective) to ghostly chimera, as Paul's equestrian shadow fills the screen, and he and the horse become one. The shadow also partially covers Hester, standing in the doorway, in her ironically white dress, visually and psychically wedding mother and son in an unholy union. At the end of the film, when Bassett burns the terrifyingly magical rocking-horse (once again, as at the beginning, we see the toy in its entirety), the flaming object fills the entire screen, emblematic of a ritualistic sacrifice to "strange gods"[69] and paralleling Paul's sacrifice of himself. In this respect, perhaps, Pelissier's ending, reluctantly added by the director/scenarist as a concession to the anti-gambling bias of the post-World War II British censors,[70] is more in keeping with the fairy-tale quality of Lawrence's story than Lawrence's deliberately ambiguous and ironic conclusion.

How much of the symbolism Lawrence's critics ascribed to the rocking-horse and to Paul's frantic rides on it was reproduced in Pelissier's adaptation? As portrayed in the film, the rocking-horse is clearly associated with unbridled acquisitiveness. A seductive, dominating, diabolical presence, inhuman yet all-too-human, it symbolizes the deadly destructiveness of boundless wants and needs that can never be satisfied. The mechanical qualities of the nameless horse stressed by a number of interpreters of Lawrence's story are, however, downplayed in the screen adaptation, and the sexual aspects of the boy's riding episodes, despite his unbuttoned shirt, tossing hair and feverish look, are not overtly suggested; Paul is far from the psychotic adolescent in Peter Shaffer's *Equus*. Conditioned as we are to a Freudian subtext, it will undoubtedly occur to us that Paul's rocking-horse rides are onanistic, but the urgently melodramatic music that accompanies them and the ritualistic way they are photographed signals that the rides are far more meaningful than mere preadolescent masturbatory paroxysms. The close-up head shots focus our attention on Paul's mental and emotional state rather than on his sexuality.

In fact, Pelissier's Paul is somewhat desexualized in the film, and that desexualization detracts from the film's Lawrentian aura. Though it is clear that the boy wants attention from his mother and longs to satisfy her demands, there is little to suggest that he has openly Oedipal desires, which Pelissier could have shown in any number of ways, as Laurence Olivier did in his screen version of *Hamlet*. If, as W. D. Snodgrass argues, misdirected sexuality is fundamental to the story and Hester's frustrated libido is the goad to her materialism, then Pelissier, perhaps self-censoring, prudently side-stepped the erotic implications of Paul's "secret" and, in keeping with the postwar focus on traditional and egalitarian values in Great Britain, opted for a far more straitlaced sociopolitical or economic interpretation—Dickensian or possibly Marxist rather than Freudian.

The whispering house in Lawrence's story is symbolic of the acquisitive society as a whole; the whispers are built into the system, and no one (including the audience) is really immune from them. They are directly linked, in both text and film, with the mother's insatiability. However, the sound in Lawrence's narrative is heard by all of the children; in Pelissier's adaptation, only Paul seems to become aware of its urgent demands.[71] Nor, in the film, is it the house itself that actually whispers; as pointed out previously, the loud echo of Hester's Christmas Day pronouncement, "There must be more money!" travels up the stairs to the nursery, where it seems to come out of the mouth of the rocking-horse, identifying the message with Paul's mother and the rocking-horse as her agent.

Certain aspects of the Grahame mansion take on special significance. Closed doors, for instance, signify the damaging separation between the adults' and children's lives and the futile attempt to hide secrets that ultimately cannot be hidden. Windows and lenses, too, are symbolic: staring wistfully out of or through them, both children and adults seem trapped, longing to escape (the nursery windows have bars on them) or looking for supernatural intervention. The shade is drawn on the window in the pawnbroker's basement shop where Hester tries to sell her clothes, suggesting both illicitness and imprisonment. Paul prays alone in his little bedroom under a shadow on his window in the shape of a cross. At the racetrack, he mistakenly reverses the lenses on his uncle's binoculars, parodying the ironic inversion of values which causes his untimely death.

The often repeated motif of stripes and bars also symbolizes imprisonment, as well as victimization and mortality. Stairs, too, are one of the central symbols in the film. Upward climbs, already described, represent the endless quest for elevated status and wealth (upward mobility) which results in Paul's madness and death.[72] Downward movements—for example, Hester's descent into the pawnbroker's basement, her abrupt descent at the charity ball when she grows anxious about Paul, and Bassett's carrying the rocking-horse downstairs at the end of the film—symbolize the consequences of unbridled greed and desire for status.

To suggest the uncanny in the film, Pelissier uses moonlight, which he connects with Paul. The moon, a peculiarly Lawrentian symbol often associated in non-Lawrentian contexts with witchcraft and ghosts, elicits Paul's occult powers. (Bassett tells Paul that his rocking-horse will take him "halfway to the moon and back" if he rides it right, and the figurative is translated into the literal.) In the last riding sequence, we see Paul staring at the moonlit clouds in which horses with flying manes are embedded, further linking his powers of divination with the supernatural.

If money—the word itself and specific sums—is a recurring motif in the story, paper money is also an important visual symbol in the film—for example, in the scene in which Bassett shows an amazed Uncle Oscar Paul's substantial winnings in a money box (a close-up shot), or at the end of the film, when Bassett shows Hester the £70,000 the dead boy won on Malabar (another close-up). In the first instance, the money (£1,200) is seen in a positive light; in the second, it is clearly supposed to be "blood money," sinister and evil. "Burn it, burn it!" cries ever-extravagant Hester, who seems to be its sole owner. "How can anyone ever touch money like that?" Presumably, only Bassett can hold it without being contaminated.

Though Lawrence makes no overt moral judgment about the huge sum of money Paul wins in the Derby and does not indicate what he will do with it, the "narrator" in the film leaves us in no doubt as to how evil Paul's winnings are, and how Hester, chastened and transformed by tragedy, has come to regard them. The audience, however, could certainly have been expected to feel ambivalent at so large a sum going up in smoke, and despite the censors, Pelissier could not bring himself to have Bassett burn it, preferring to "launder" it instead by having it used for charity.

At certain points in the film, Pelissier added scenes in which money in small sums symbolizes the hypocrisy and stinginess of the affluent classes: Richard's coins given to the young Christmas carollers; Hester's sixpence over which the street urchins fight when the disgusted taxi driver throws his "tip" into the gutter; the 7s which Hester borrows from her servant and angrily gives to the bailiff; and the meager £40 which the bailiff demands ("You'll have every filthy penny!" cries Hester) and which Hester manages to extract from the pawnbroker for her expensive finery.

In other scenes, offers of money are used to symbolize its uselessness as a substitute for authentic feeling. Paul pathetically attempts to give his mother small sums, which she rejects. When Hester takes Paul to the antique shop, he offers her the 22s sevenpence he has saved because she "needs it," to which she replies, ironically, "I don't need money so badly I'd take it away from you." After he returns from the racetrack with Uncle Oscar, Paul also offers his mother money to pay the bailiff, but she takes Nanny's sweepstakes pocket money rather than any part of Paul's considerable winnings, and rebuffs him harshly. In these scenes, we see Paul's failed attempts to win his mother's love, attention and appreciation, as well as his attempts to ease her anxiety, through the use of money—symbolic actions that are replicated in his frantic rocking-horse rides, money-seeking ventures with much higher stakes.

Symbolism in a film can be perceived to arise out of repeated placement of certain characters or objects in the same location in any composition that includes them. For example, in his speculative ideological interpretation of the film and of director Pelissier's intentions, Henry Becker III has identified Paul's position to the left of center, whenever he is shown with his rocking-horse, as indicative of the wrongness of the values he has absorbed from his mother, who is also shown at left of center. According to Becker, in the antique-shop scene, in which Hester eyes some pictures she cannot afford, she stands to the left of center. In a later scene at home, Hester and Paul regard the expensive pictures she has bought from the left, while the bailiff "correctly" views them from the right "as expensive, unnecessary items that are certainly not worth £40, especially when one cannot afford them."[73] In the last scene of the film, in which Bassett stands to the left of the rocking-horse, Hester stands to the right, leaning against the fence. "Symbolically and visually, she has found the right way to view the money. She is convinced that she is responsible for her son's death."[74]

Becker's interpretation of the ideological significance of the actors' "left" and "right" positions within the frame may be quixotic and arbitrary. However, the frequent physical separation between Paul and the other characters in the film—we often see him alone, turning away or at a distance from the other actors—certainly symbolizes the spiritual and emotional distance between Paul and his parents that Lawrence conveys in the story. The boy attempts to bridge this distance, both in the story and the film, through the medium of money. Aggressive and dominating, Hester looms large in almost every scene she appears in, almost always positioned in the foreground and tracked by the camera. For example, in the Christmas Day scene in the drawing room, while Richard and Oscar stay in place in the background, Hester moves from left to right and back again; our eyes are focused almost exclusively on her. In a bedroom scene, Hester sits at left in the foreground at her vanity while speaking to Nanny in the doorway. Like Paul, she is occasionally pictured alone, his counterpart in isolation, though in medium close-ups instead of head-and-shoulder shots.

Pelissier did not attempt to find equivalents for all of the symbols in Lawrence's narrative. For example, there is no counterpart for the symbolism of the heart and the eyes, which pervade the story. In the case of the heart, it's not hard to see why such an obvious metaphor for human feeling—or lack of it—cannot be reproduced except, all too obviously, through the actual sound of a heartbeat. The director conveys the sense of Hester's stony heart, however, through her self-centered, arrogant, dismissive behavior and in several scenes, when her reserve breaks down, by having her actually lift her hand to her heart.

Pelissier also chose not to emphasize the eyes through which Paul and his mother reveal their iciness or crazed intensity, though he could have done so, like Jack Cardiff in *Sons and Lovers*, by using frequent extreme close-ups. (In fact, the viewer rarely gets close enough to the faces of the characters in *The Rocking-Horse Winner* to penetrate their souls, perhaps a shortcoming in Pelissier's approach to filming the story.) Lawrence refers to Paul's uncanny blue eyes to suggest the grotesque and the supernatural. To evoke the uncanny in the film, Pelissier used external phenomena—lightning and thunder, moonlit clouds in the shape of horses, weird lighting, and specialty lenses, along with melodramatically distorted camera angles, music and sound effects—and kept Paul as realistic a figure as possible.

Paradox and Irony in the Story and the Film

Two of the most striking aspects of style in Lawrence's "The Rocking-Horse Winner"—typical of a number of his later stories—are paradox and irony. According to one definition, a paradox is "an apparently self-contradictory (even absurd) normative statement which, on closer inspection, is found to contain a truth reconciling the conflicting oppositions,"[75] although paradox, by extension, can also be said to inhere not only in verbal constructs but also in situations and personalities.

Analogous to paradox are four types of irony—tonal, situational, dramatic, and verbal—all pervasive in "The Rocking-Horse Winner." Wayne Booth defines tone as "the implicit evaluation which the author manages to convey behind the explicit presentation,"[76] although Fred B. Millett describes tone as "the general feeling which suffuses and surrounds the work" and which "arises ultimately out of the writer's attitude towards his subject."[77] An ironic tone implies a discrepancy between what is stated, either by the narrator or one of the characters, and what the author actually feels or believes. Situational (or circumstantial) irony exists when "there is a discrepancy between what might reasonably be expected and what actually occurs—between the appearance of a situation and its reality."[78] With regard to dramatic irony, a character "may utter words that have a hidden meaning intelligible to the audience of which he himself is unaware," and verbal irony occurs "when the speaker means the opposite of what he says."[79]

Commenting on Lawrence's prose style as an embodiment of the writer's psychology, Daniel J. Schneider notes that Lawrence "needs to make us aware of a continual paradox or irony."[80] In "The Rocking-Horse Winner," paradox is conveyed mainly through sentence structure, specifically by the use of antithesis—the juxtaposition of sharply contrasting ideas in balanced or parallel words, phrases, and grammatical structures.

Examples of paradox generated by antithesis are numerous, not only within and between sentences, produced by the words *but*, *and*, and *yet*,[81] but between entire paragraphs that are contradictory, expressing opposing thoughts that are equally "true."

Chiasmus is another form of verbal antithesis in "The Rocking-Horse Winner," as in "She married for love and the love turned to dust," and "He was unconscious and unconscious he remained." Several oxymorons can also be found in the story—for example, "cold fire" and "soundless noise."

If paradox in "The Rocking-Horse Winner" is created by juxtaposition of opposites, it is frequently replicated or generated in the film version by contradictory visual and/or aural effects within shots and by contrasting parallel cut shots and sequences. For example, throughout the film we are constantly made aware of the disparity between the material affluence which surrounds the members of the family and their emotional and financial "poverty." This conflict is underlined in many scenes in which the subject of conversation is debts, gambling losses, and lack of funds—in the drawing room on Christmas Day or in the antique shop just after Hester has been served with a writ by a bailiff and she is shown hunting for new things to buy, at the same time lamenting her lack of luck and money to her son.

Paradox is also suggested in the parallel cut sequence in which elegant Hester is selling her evening clothes and Richard's gift of a traveling case in a pawnbroker's basement for a meager £40, while Oscar and Paul are at the racetrack winning a far greater sum. There is paradox also in the montage sequence in which Hester buys and buys while a superimposed Paul rides and rides. A subtle visual paradox is created in the Christmas Day scene in which we see a medium close-up of Paul, wearing a gold paper crown—suggestive both of his God-given powers and also of Christ's crown of thorns—examining his newly unwrapped rocking horse. As the camera dollies backward, revealing the magnificent room and its well-turned-out family, Paul recedes into the background, no longer remotely regal, a small "figure in the carpet." In yet another paradoxical scene, Bassett enthusiastically teaches a reluctant Paul to ride his rocking-horse against a backdrop of barlike banisters and wall shadows forecasting the spiritual imprisonment and death that will be the boy's fate.

Paradoxes involving Hester's superficial motherliness and her real feelings toward her children are also frequently suggested throughout the film. For example, in the opening scene, she pretends to be solicitous toward her son, yet her treatment of him—cutting him off, hustling him away, talking of his being a possible "nuisance"—strongly conveys the opposite. A paradoxical parallel cut sequence shows Hester praising her own skill in getting the children settled down on Christmas Eve ("They're quiet as mice!") while the children cavort in the nursery.

Irony in the Story: Situational, Dramatic, Verbal, and Tonal

A perverse sense of ironic doubleness permeates "The Rocking-Horse Winner"; illusion continually conflicts with reality. Hester is thought to be a good mother who adores her children; in truth, she does not love them at all and feels they have been "thrust upon her." Husband and wife perceive themselves as "superior to everyone in the neighborhood," yet they are continually at the point of bankruptcy. After Hester receives her anonymous gift of £5,000, instead of softening and finding relief, she becomes even harder and colder than before. At the end of the story, when Paul is dying, he asks his mother if he has ever told her he is lucky. She replies ironically (and forgetfully), "No, you never did." The statement immediately following, "But the boy died in the night," implies that Paul's luck, which his mother claims not to have known he possessed, is a curse instead.

In Lawrence's story, grimly ironical misunderstandings and quirky twists abound. Paul's nurse worries that he "will break his horse" from riding it so vigorously; it is not, of course, the mechanical toy she needs to worry about but the boy himself. When Paul begs not to be sent away to the seaside before the Derby, his mother uncomprehendingly remonstrates with him about the ill effects of gambling on their family and the possible harm it will do him in the adulthood he is fated not to have. Later, when Paul begs her not to be made to leave the whispering house, his mother wonders what suddenly makes him "care" about the house. "I never knew you loved it," she says, with stunning obtuseness.

Since secrecy and illicitness are basic motifs in the story, dramatic irony (the reader or a character is aware of something another character is not aware of) is also pervasive in "The Rocking-Horse Winner." Although the reader is told that Paul's mother does not love her children, and the children themselves realize it, no one else in the story seems to know. Neither Hester nor her husband realize from whom she is receiving her windfall, but the reader does, along with Paul and his uncle. No one, including the reader, knows exactly how Paul is able to learn the names of the winning horses until near the end of the story, when the narrator tells us outright (the reader will probably have guessed early on). Hester and her husband have no idea of the meaning of "Malabar!" but Oscar and Bassett, aware of its significance yet not communicating with one another, separately place successful bets.

The sense of doubleness characteristic of the story is also reflected in Lawrence's use of paronomasia (punning), for example, on the words *luck* and *lucre*, which Paul confuses:

> "Is luck money, mother?" he asked rather timidly.
> "No, Paul. Not quite. It's what causes you to have money."
> "Oh," said Paul vaguely. "I thought when Uncle Oscar said *filthy lucker*, it meant money."
> "*Filthy lucre* does mean money," said the mother. "But it's *lucre*, not luck."
> "Oh!" said the boy. "Then what *is* luck, mother?"
> "It's what causes you to have money. If you're lucky you have money. That's why it's better to be born lucky than rich. If you're rich, you may lose your money, but if you're lucky, you will always get more money." (149-150)

Luck and *lucre* are further confused with Paul's fatal quest for *luck*—in reality, a desperate campaign to win his mother's love. The names of several of the characters are puns, in particular Oscar Creswell ("increase well") and Bassett, an elaborate pun involving the word *base*, which has various meanings,[82] and the word *asset*, another obvious pun.

Yet another ironic play on words is the expression *honour bright,* which occurs repeatedly in the story and is extremely ironic. Paul first uses it when his uncle asks him for a tip on the Lincoln. After Oscar affirms his "honour," Paul responds by telling him the name of the sure winner, Daffodil. Paul reiterates "honour bright" when he reveals his partnership with Bassett and swears his uncle to secrecy. The "bright honour" to which he refers, of course, is violated by the unholy alliance between the two adults, who urge the tormented boy on to his destruction. At the end of the story, Oscar entirely breaks the gentleman's code of "honour" by gambling on Paul's pick while the boy lies dying.

The overall tone of Lawrence's "The Rocking-Horse Winner" is coolly, at times bitterly, ironic: the omniscient narrator distances himself from almost all of the characters. The thoughts and feelings of mother and son are tersely reported by an omniscient narrator with a blunt, unsentimental directness that only covertly conveys negative judgment. For the most part, the speaker feigns ignorance of the tragic significance of the events and conversations he records in the story. In a few narrative passages, however, Lawrence betrays an openly mocking, sardonic stance. After Paul's mother receives her son's anonymous gift, for example, the narrator tells us that something very "curious" happened: "the voices in the house suddenly went mad like a chorus of frogs on a spring evening" and "simply trilled and screamed in a sort of ecstasy." "Curious" and "simply" are ironic understatements, although hyperbolic references to going mad like choruses of frogs and screaming in ecstasy suggest, by way of contrast, orgiastic sexuality—the narrator's view of Hester's sublimated extravagance. Hinting at Paul's betting to Oscar, benighted Bassett is described as if "speaking of religious matters" and "as serious as a church," as if the narrator were actually open to the idea that gambling is a spiritually uplifting activity, when clearly, judging by the outcome of the tale, quite the opposite is true.

Although Lawrence basically retains his distance and control throughout the story, the tone becomes emotional, almost impassioned, toward the end, conveying the mother's and son's agitated feelings and actions. Yet even in passages like the following there is a negative subtext:

> His mother had sudden strange seizures of uneasiness about him, sometimes for half-an-hour. Sometimes for half-an-hour, she would feel a sudden anxiety about him that was almost anguish. She wanted to rush to him at once, and know he was safe. (163)

> His eyes blazed at her for one strange and senseless second, as he ceased urging his wooden horse. Then he fell with a crash to the ground, and she, all her tormented motherhood flooding upon her, rushed to gather him up. (164)

In the first instance, the phrase "half-an-hour" undercuts the mother's apparent concern, while in the second, the phrase "all her tormented motherhood flooding upon her" does not sound as if feelings of love and compassion for her son were welling up inside her but rather as if she were being overcome by feelings of shame and guilt. Lawrence never allows us to forget that Paul's mother, whose heart is "gripped" by "rushes of anxiety" over her firstborn, is an essentially loveless, compulsive woman whose dominating passion is self-reflexive angst.

Irony in the Film: Ironic Counterpoint, Ironic Foreshadowing, Dramatic Irony, Verbal Irony, and Ironic Tone

Even as antithesis is one of Lawrence's favorite syntactical modes, its film equivalent, parallel cutting (also known as cross-cutting), can create exquisite circumstantial and dramatic ironies. Pelissier used cross-cutting as the film's chief editing device: in scene after scene, sequence after sequence, the juxtaposition of two contrasting yet often simultaneous events allows each happening to become an ironic commentary on the other, exposing the underlying delusions of the characters or revealing the terrible consequences of their attitudes and actions. These ironical paired events, most of them invented by Pelissier, are certainly suggested by the story.

A profoundly ironic parallel-cut sequence is the one in which Hester, Richard, and Oscar argue on Christmas Day about finances, while Bassett shows Paul how to ride his rocking-horse to make him a winner. The connection between the dangerous "game" Bassett is teaching Paul and the destructive gamesmanship going on in the drawing room (and in the lives of Hester and Richard) could not be clearer. The scene in which the bailiff presents Paul's mother with a writ is ironically juxtaposed with the browsing scene in the antique shop; just when Hester is being dunned for one item, she can't resist contemplating the purchase of another.

Another parallel-cut sequence is bitterly ironical. While Hester and Oscar are enjoying their bourgeois leisure, relaxing in the garden, Paul is upstairs in the nursery madly rocking to enable his mother to go on lying idly about in the summer sun. In yet another parallel-cut sequence, we are transported back and forth between Oscar and Paul winning at the racetrack and Hester attempting to get the seedy pawnbroker to give her enough cash to pay a bill. Both activities, in fact, are degrading, though Paul and Oscar, arriving home in the uncle's classy car, are delighted at day's end, while Hester, forced to walk home from the pawnbroker and dunned for the bailiff's fee, is angry, humiliated, and frustrated. Oscar's wonderment at Paul's £1,200 winnings (in partnership with Bassett) and Hester's subsequent dismay at the bailiff's demand for *more* money are ironically contrasted.

The episode in which Richard comes home after being fired and confronts Hester and Oscar in front of the house is poignantly ironic. Oscar has just given a small whip to Paul, and he excitedly runs off with it, only momentarily glancing backward to where we can see but not hear the three adults angrily gesturing at one another. Ironically, Paul "hears" only too well. Seeking out Bassett, who is looking at a racing form, Paul tells him, "I know I'm lucky," but picks a losing horse, ironically named Safety Pin. This scene is followed immediately by a heated exchange between Oscar and Hester: "Writs, Hester, writs. How are you going to pay them?" he badgers her. Pelissier then cuts back to Paul, down at the mouth because Safety Pin has lost. In these counterpointed scenes, both parents and child are "losers" heading for further losses.

The last major parallel-cut sequence in the film is bitterly ironic too. On the eve of Hester's greatest social triumph as organizer of a successful charity ball, her son also has his greatest triumph—divining the name of the Derby winner. Both must "ascend" to succeed—Hester the elegant stairway of a Belgravia mansion and Paul the stairs of the whispering house. Both must also descend, Hester anxiously turning back down the stairs and calling home, Paul falling off his rocking-horse as he ironically fell off the piled-up cartons while spying on Bassett in the first scene of the film.

However, there are aural and visual ironic cinematic contrasts too. As immaculately well-coifed, gowned, and befurred as Hester is, her son is tousled and deranged-looking, his pajama top open and hair flying. The charity ball, brightly and artificially lit, contrasts sharply with the dark, foreboding, moonlit shadows in which Paul finds his way from the drawing room to his upstairs bedroom. Cheerful noises and music at the party are offset by the loud cacophony of sounds and music that accompany Paul's final climb and ride. The culminating shot, showing a close-up of Hester, aghast in the doorway, drenched in a pool of harsh light, and beside her, Paul's black equestrian shadow in profile plunging to and fro, ironically juxtaposes the two preceding motifs—darkness and light.

Ironic foreshadowing, not evident in the story, is a device Pelissier uses frequently in the film. One of the most calculated instances of such forecasting occurs during the scene in which Bassett criticizes Paul's slow-paced, sluggish riding: "No, Master Paul, that won't do at all. You'll have to go a great deal faster than that or you won't be in time for your own funeral. . . ." Another instance of ironic foreshadowing occurs during the Christmas day scene in which Hester dismisses Oscar's warnings about bankruptcy and insists on their need for "more money": "It's immaterial where it comes from—we need it, Oscar. We've got to have it and somehow, sooner or later, we shall get it." Ironically, Hester is telling the truth; she doesn't care where "it" comes from (even though "it" turns out to be "blood money"), and cash does materialize in the form of an anonymous gift. After Hester has spent all of her gift on extravagant purchases, Paul has a losing streak and becomes profoundly anxious. Though Bassett and Oscar attempt to reassure him, he bursts out:

> But you don't understand. I've got to know. I've got to be *sure*. Something terrible'll happen if I'm not, I know it will. . . . Don't worry, Uncle. Everything'll be all right. I'm bound to know in time for the Derby. I am, really. And everything'll be all right then, you see.

The irony is heavy: something terrible *does* happen precisely because he *is* sure, and nothing will ever be "all right" again.

Although Pelissier omitted the scene in which Hester receives but fails to acknowledge Paul's secret gift of £5,000—a key example of dramatic irony in the story—there are many other instances of dramatic irony throughout the film. After Hester puts her children to bed on Christmas Eve, she pronounces them "no trouble" and wonders why their nanny has such a hard time getting them to bed. As we watch the children romp in the nursery in the parallel cut scenes that follow, we recognize how foolishly self-deluding Hester actually is, as does their nanny when she returns to find the children at play.

In the scene in which the grimly detached bailiff waits to serve a summons on Hester, he is graciously hosted by Paul, who unlike the film audience, has not idea of the grim reason for his visit. "I expect mother will be awfully pleased to get it, won't she?" the boy asks innocently. When Hester tries to sell her evening clothes to pay her debt, we are aware that the bailiff is waiting for her at home, although she does not admit her real reason for needing immediate cash to the Greek pawnbroker. In the confrontation between Hester and Paul before the Derby, the boy begs to stay at home instead of going to the seaside. We know, as Hester does not, precisely why Paul wants to stay.

Far more than in Lawrence's story, verbal irony abounds in Pelissier's adaptation. In scene after scene, words are spoken which make us wince because of the disparity between what we sense or know to be true and what the characters would have others or themselves believe. Other dialogue ironically foreshadows later events, creates dramatic irony, or underplays a character's true attitudes.

If Hester Grahame's manner is consistently cold and dismissive, she also makes solicitous verbal gestures towards servants and children: "I shall be worrying about you all the time," she tells Bassett in his outdoor harness room. We immediately sense that she couldn't care less about Bassett—or Paul, for that matter, whom she lightly refers to as both "darling" and a "nuisance." After Paul loses his first 5s, Bassett ironically sermonizes, "Let it be a lesson to you, Master Paul. Keep away from the horses and you've every chance of growing to be a happy man." Paul's mother responds to her son's offer of money with a laughably ironic disclaimer: "I don't need money so badly I'd take it away from you. I'd never do that, however badly I needed it." Near the end of the story, Hester ironically moralizes about gambling: "You'll never know until you grow up how much damage it's done," she says prophetically.

Understatement is another form of verbal irony which, in Pelissier's adaptation, is assigned mainly to urbane Oscar, who constantly displays an Oscar Wildean sarcasm. "A deplorable vice, gambling," he tells Richard. "Personally, I adore it." Explaining why he has paid off Richard's debt, he ascribes his generous act to selfishness: "I am fond of my club; sometimes I even find myself liking the members. I should find it extremely tiresome having to give it up on your account." When Paul wins £10,000 on Lively Spark, he asks his uncle, "Is that a lot?" "It's enough," replies Oscar. Ironically, of course, it isn't; for Hester, no amount of money can ever be.

Sarcasm is yet another type of verbal irony which Pelissier injects into his script. Paul asks the bailiff if the paper he means to present to his mother is "special." "I'll say it is," he replies. "Very extra super special is what I call it." Hester's diatribe against her brother for lecturing them on their perilous financial situation is fiercely sarcastic:

> Thank you, Oscar. There's so much to thank you for, isn't there? . . . How *does* one thank an older brother for being brotherly? or a trustee for being a trustee? . . . I'll tell you one thing we *can* thank you for; your unbearable superiority. Believe me, darling, that made the necessity of begging from you infinitely easier. . . . You see, Oscar, there's so *much* to thank you for.

The taxi-driver who receives a mere sixpence as a tip from Hester throws it to the pavement. "Here, Lady," he shouts after her derisively. "You forgot something. You was too generous. I couldn't take all that money from you, really I couldn't!"

In an attempt to create cinematic excitement, Pelissier chose not to reproduce the detached, ironic tone of the narrator in Lawrence's story; his "narrator" is not a dry-eyed, sardonic chronicler apparently withholding judgment of his misguided characters but rather a latter-day Edgar Allan Poe beguiling us with witchcraft, portents, heavy handed paradoxes, and melodramatic emotionality. Unlike the narrator in the story, Pelissier foreshadows and editorializes throughout the film, in part by the use of striking musical leitmotifs that tell us the way we are supposed to feel or what we are going to experience and that continually remind us of the film's somber subtext. For example, there is a montage sequence that consists of a rapid series of lap dissolves of Hester trying on gowns, furs, and jewelry, intercut with shots of checks, invitations, and workmen redecorating the house; images of Paul fiercely riding his rocking-horse are superimposed over all the shots. We hear lilting waltz music which quickly becomes weird and distorted, merging into "There must be money" on the soundtrack and increasingly frenzied riding music. The benign waltz music takes over again for a while, but once more dissolves into the disturbing riding music. We know, from the background score, that Hester's glittering purchases are cursed.

Visually, a brooding, ominous, surrealistic atmosphere and tone is created through the use of deep shadows, hard-edged pools of light, offbeat tracking shots, low-angle shots, zoom-like shots and occasional isolated closeups (especially of Paul riding his horse and the horse's demonic head). There is no matter-of-factness in this extremely theatrical film: almost every shot and scene bristles with tension and with significance that is hard to miss, not merely because of the script, visuals, and soundtrack but because of the rather exaggerated way the characters play their roles. Valerie Hobson as Hester, for example, is blatantly obnoxious, cold, self-centered—ignoring or barely listening to others, interrupting, denouncing, imperiously demanding, perfunctory in her affections, scathing in her mockery and self-serving anger. In no uncertain terms, Pelissier makes us see and hear the hardness of her heart as well as the recklessness and ineffectuality of her husband, the bemused arrogance of her brother Oscar, and the pathetic anxiety and neediness of her rejected son. The melodramatic tone is especially noticeable at the end of the film: melancholy, dirge-like bassoon music accompanies the death of Paul and also the burning of the rocking-horse while a remorseful Hester weeps against the garden fence. By comparison, at the end of Lawrence's story, Hester's feelings about her son's death, which would be ambivalent at best, remain unrevealed; it is her brother Oscar who has the last word: "My God, Hester, you're eighty-odd thousand to the good, and a poor devil of a son to the bad; But, poor devil, poor devil, he's best gone out of a life where he rides his rocking-horse to find a winner."

Although screenwriter-director Pelissier chose to reproduce neither the dry-eyed, ironic detachment of the narrator in Lawrence's disturbing story nor its rapid pace and a few of its unvisualizable symbols, he was quite successful in devising imaginative visual and aural equivalents for most of the stylistic components of the work. Incorporating both the fairy-tale and realistic aspects of the original, Pelissier managed to replicate not only the story's dialogue but analogously—through screenplay, settings, cinematography, and editing—the simplicity of the diction, the pervasive antithesis between sentences and paragraphs, the shapes of paragraphs, and the constant repetition and incremental repetition of episodes as well as of words, phrases, clauses, sentences, and sounds. He also found equivalents for most of the symbols and almost all of the various types of disturbing paradoxes and ironies present in the story—situational, dramatic, and verbal.

Commercial rather than artistic considerations were undoubtedly responsible for the melodramatic tone of Pelissier's adaptation and its sentimental, moralistic ending, but the negative response of the reviewers to the film's morbidly gloomy atmosphere and darkly satirical subject matter as well as its lagging tempos doomed the genteel horror film to a quick, unprofitable run. Despite its lack of popular success, however, Pelissier's version of Lawrence's much-anthologized short story has come to be ranked high in the canons of certain influential film critics and historians and has earned a well-deserved reputation both as a British movie classic and as a haunting screen adaptation of considerable subtlety, complexity, integrity, and power.

1. The film opens with an aerial zoom shot of the Grahame's mansion, which resembles a doll's house.

2. Hester Grahame (Valerie Hobson) visits newly hired handyman-gardener Bassett in his tack room quarters.

The Rocking-Horse Winner

3. Hester (Valerie Hobson) dutifully hears the prayers of her two daughters on Christmas Eve.

4. After putting her children to bed, Hester (Valerie Hobson) mistakenly assures Nannie (Susan Richards) that Paul and his sisters are fast asleep upstairs.

5. On the moonlit night before Christmas, the Grahame children glimpse prophetic horses in the clouds.

6. Paul (John Howard Davies) says his prayers on Christmas Eve, a shadow in the shape of a cross on the wall behind him.

The Rocking-Horse Winner 61

7. On Christmas Eve, Paul (John Howard Davies) steals downstairs to preview his Christmas presents.

8. Paul (John Howard Davies) is mystified by one of his gifts.

9. In a match cut (see Figure 8), Paul (John Howard Davies) excitedly strips the wrapping off his new rocking-horse.

10. A backwards zoom reveals the opulence of the Grahame drawing room on Christmas day.

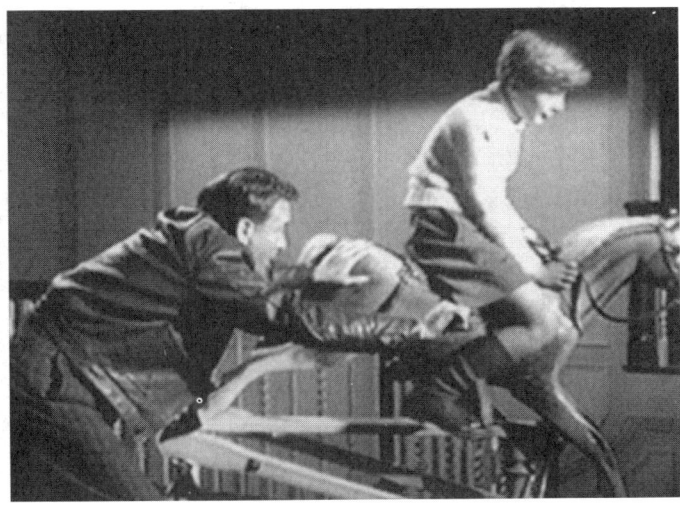

11. Would-be jockey Bassett (John Mills) enthusiastically gives Paul (John Howard Davies) a riding lesson, urging him to ride faster or he'll " be late for his own funeral."

12. In a lengthy deep focus shot, Uncle Oscar (Ronald Squire) takes Hester (Valerie Hobson) and Richard (Hugh Sinclair) to task about her profligacy and his gambling debts.

13. As the whispering house takes up Hester's edict "There must be more money!" the camera pans up the stairs until it reaches Paul's ears; stairs are a recurring visual motif in the film.

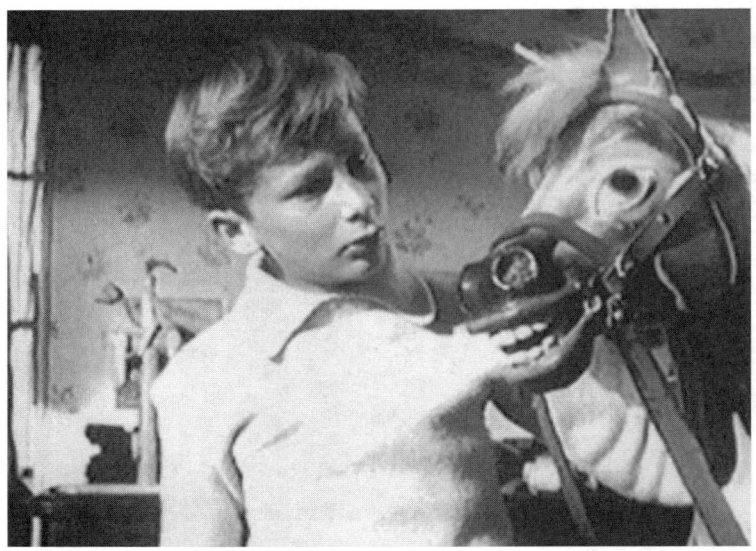

14. Hearing the house whispering, Paul (John Howard Davies) gazes quizzically at his rocking-horse.

15. Process server hands Hester (Valerie Hobson) a writ for an unpaid £40 bill.

16. As mother and son discuss luck and money, Paul (John Howard Davies) holds the symbolic figure of a horse in an antique shop where Hester (Valerie Hobson) buys items she can't afford.

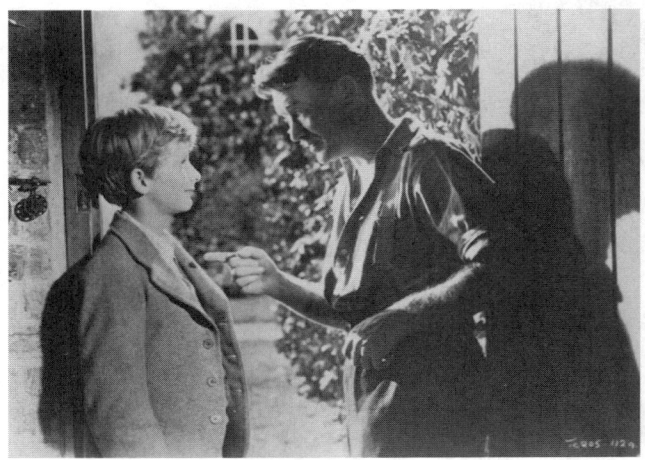

17. When Paul (John Howard Davies) picks the horse Safety Pin as a winner, Bassett (John Mills) agrees to place a bet for him "just this once"; the horse loses. (Museum of Modern Art/Film Stills Archive)

18. Accompanied by lightning and thunder, Paul (John Howard Davies), in pursuit of a winning horse's name, furiously rides his rocking horse until he "gets there!"

The Rocking-Horse Winner 67

19. In quick succession, long and close shots of Uncle Oscar (Ronald Squires) and Hester (Valerie Hobson) convey the violent to-and-fro of Paul's frantic rocking-horse ride.

20. On a day's outing, Uncle Oscar (Ronald Squire) invites delighted Paul (John Howard Davies) to visit a race track.

21. Crosscut with shots of Uncle Oscar and Paul at the racetrack are shots of Hester (Valerie Hobson) bargaining with Mr. Tsaldouris (Charles Goldner) to sell her clothes so she can pay her £40 debt.

22. Bassett (John Mills) shows Uncle Oscar (Ronald Squire) £1200 Paul has won by betting when he's "sure" of the winners: "It's just like he had it from heaven!" (Museum of Modern Art/Film Stills Archive)

The Rocking-Horse Winner 69

23. Bailiff (Cyril Smith) informs outraged Hester that she must pay an additional 7 pence for his unwelcome services.

24. In a rapid montage of superimposed images, Paul (John Howard Davies) rides his rocking-horse as Hester spends her son's ill-gotten money on jewelry, gowns, and decorating.

25. Hester (Valerie Hobson) shows off her new gown to her husband (Richard Sinclair) on the night of the charity ball she has organized.

26. Bassett (John Mills) discusses possible Derby winners with other drivers while ball guests dance in a Belgravia mansion.

The Rocking-Horse Winner 71

27. At the ball, Hester (Valerie Hobson) greets guests on the stairs just before her overwhelming anxieties about Paul prompt her to leave.

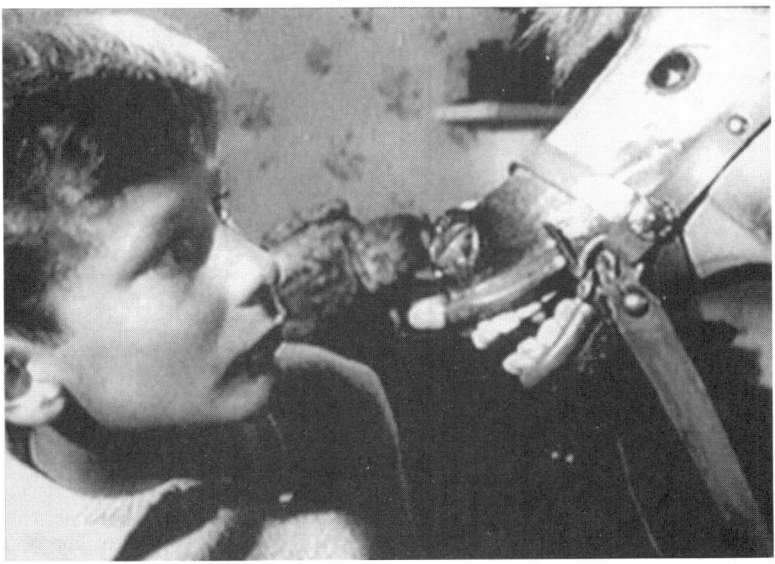

28. Paul (John Howard Davies) pleads with his rocking-horse for the name of the Derby winner.

29. The shadow of the rocking-horse looms as Hester (Valerie Hobson) bursts in on her son, who falls unconscious after his last, desperate ride to learn the name of the Derby winner, Malabar.

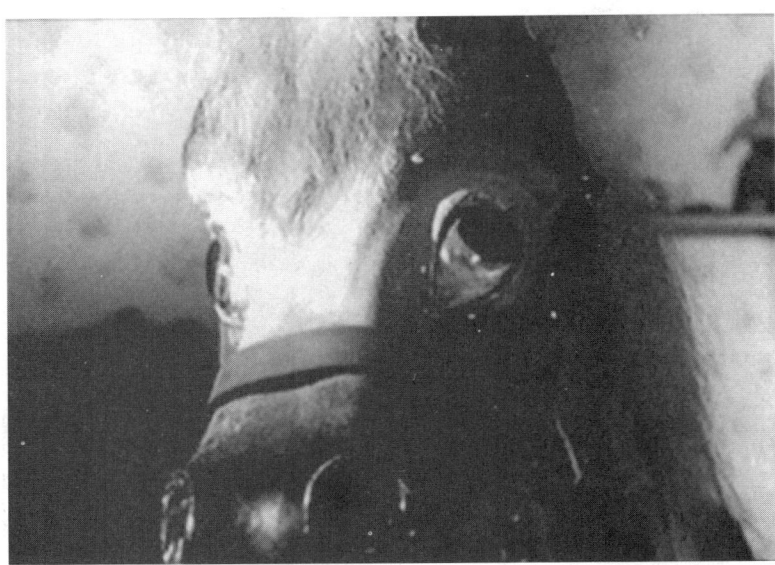

30. After Paul collapses, an extreme closeup of the demonic rocking horse's head fills the screen.

The Rocking-Horse Winner

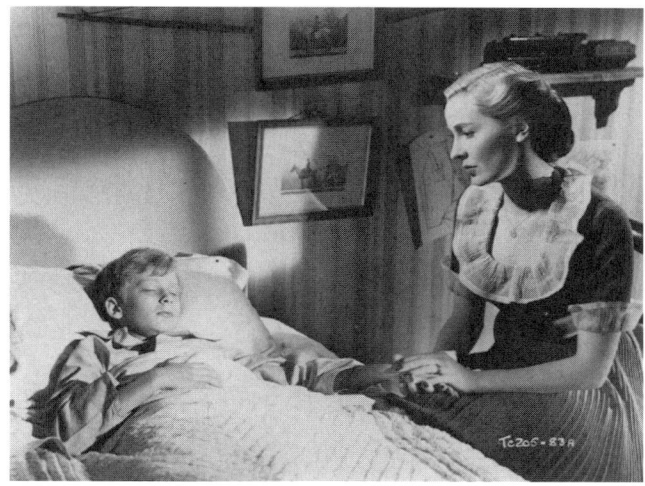

31. After learning that Malabar has won the Derby and that he is £70,000 richer, Paul (John Howard Davies) assures his mother (Valerie Hobson) that he *is* lucky, and dies peacefully. (Museum of Modern Art/Film Stills Archive)

32. At Hester's insistence, Bassett (John Mills) sets fire to the rocking-horse but refuses her order to burn Paul's winnings with it.

Chapter 3

Sons and Lovers

After receiving his first copy of *Sons and Lovers* in May, 1913, D. H. Lawrence wrote to his editor, Edward Garnett, who had pruned and shaped the overly long, loosely constructed last draft of the famous autobiographical novel into its final form, "I am fearfully proud of it. I reckon it is quite a great book."[1] Indeed, although a few libraries and booksellers refused to stock the novel because of its candid treatment of sexuality,[2] initial response to *Sons and Lovers* in the British press was extremely favorable and established Lawrence as a significant figure on the literary scene. Several reviewers acclaimed Lawrence as a major writer, and nearly all lauded "the sincerity, authenticity, vividness and vitality of the novel."[3] If some complained of a lack of plot or form,[4] others acknowledged that rules had been broken but discerned coherence in the novel anyway, ascribing to it a poetic quality they could not quite explain.[5]

Over the past seven decades, critics have tended to agree with the writer's self-congratulatory assessment of his third novel,[6] ranking it with *The Rainbow* (1915) and *Women in Love* (1920) as one of his finest works. Although praising the first part of the novel chronicling the Morels' disastrous marriage and the young lives of their children (chapters 1 to 6), many critics, however, have echoed the reservations of earlier reviewers by pointing out serious literary flaws in the lengthy, somewhat repetitive second part (chapters 7 to 15) devoted to Paul Morel's ambivalent love affairs with Miriam Leivers and Clara Dawes. Earlier critics, in particular Mark Schorer, noted inconsistency and stridency of tone and suggested a failure of technique with regard to point of view. In Schorer's view, "Lawrence could not separate the investigating analyst, who must be objective, from Lawrence, the subject of the book; and the sickness was not healed, the emotion not mastered, the novel not perfected."[7]

Later critics, however, viewed the novel's confusion in point of view as a truthful expression of the writer's ambivalence,[8] and affirmed the conceptual unity and complex, multi-layered structure of the novel, as well as its vivid descriptiveness and richness of character and incident. Dorothy Van Ghent argued that the book is organized not only "on a chronological plan" but with a structure rigorously controlled by "an idea of an organic disturbance in the relationships of men and women—a disturbance of sexual polarities that is first seen in the disaffection of mother and father, then in the mother's attempt to substitute her sons for her husband, finally in the sons' unsuccessful struggle to establish natural manhood."[9] According to Mark Schorer, the novel has two themes—"the crippling effects of a mother's love on the emotional development of her son; and the 'split' between different kinds of love, physical and spiritual, which the son develops, the kinds represented by two young women, Clara and Miriam."[10] Julian Moynahan, who described *Sons and Lovers* as "Lawrence's most popular book," sees a tripartite underlying structure in the novel:

> The first matrix is autobiographical narrative; the second a scheme taken over from psychoanalytic theory; the third is difficult to name because Lawrence was the first novelist to use it as a context, as opposed to a quality, of human experience, but it might be called the matrix of "life."[1]

Judith Farr identifies the most inclusive theme of *Sons and Lovers* as "the familiar Romantic one of bondage"—the imprisoning effects of industrialism and rigid sex roles. "Much of the radiant energy of *Sons and Lovers*," she contends, "rises in its consistent revelation of human quest for fulfillment despite limitation."[12] Mark Spilka interprets the novel as "mainly an exploration of destructive or counterfeit loves—with a garbled Freudian 'split' imposed upon it."[13]

The Film of *Sons and Lovers*

In a lengthy correspondence with noted producer/adapter Jerry Wald,[14] who bought the rights to *Sons and Lovers* from Frieda Lawrence in 1954, the writer's widow generally praised the first film adaptation of one of her late husband's fictions, but worried about its projected sequel:

> Of course, I am just as anxious as you are to have a good Lawrence movie. Did you see *The Rocking-Horse Winner*? It was good except for the last few minutes, when they altered it to give the false moral touch. That will be the difficulty, to get Lawrence's special quality over, and most movies are according to a pattern. . . . It won't be easy, but a new, fresh approach would do it, I believe. (March 30, 1954)[15]

The considerable difficulty of translating Lawrence's "special quality" to the screen was a constant refrain in Mrs. Lawrence's letters to Wald—as it turned out, a legitimate concern.[16]

Shot partly on location in the English midlands—in Eastwood, Lawrence's birthplace, and in nearby Nottingham—the one-hour-and-43-minute[17] black-and-white CinemaScope production, budgeted at a mere $535,000,[18] was directed by distinguished cameraman Jack Cardiff.[19] Although the official cinematographer was another illustrious lensman, Freddie Francis, who also shot *Room at the Top* (1959) and *Saturday Night and Sunday Morning* (1960), and most recently won at Academy award for his cinematography in *Glory* (1990), most critics credited Cardiff with the excellence of the camerawork in *Sons and Lovers*. An almost entirely British cast was headed by Hollywood child actor Dean Stockwell in the lead role of Paul Morel—a rather unpopular choice in Great Britain, though well-tolerated by most newspaper critics in the United States.[20] The otherwise much-praised cast also included veteran actors Trevor Howard as Walter Morel and Wendy Hiller as Gertrude Morel, as well as younger rising stars Mary Ure as Clara and Heather Sears as Miriam.[21]

Released in 1960, one year after the groundbreaking, X-certificated adaptations *Look Back in Anger* and *Room at the Top*,[22] *Sons and Lovers* was one of a number of controversial but commercially successful films produced in England between 1956 and 1963. These films were distinguished by an unprecedented focus on the industrial working class, frankness about race relations and sexuality, and by the filmmakers' "determination to tackle real social issues and experiences in a manner which matched a style which was 'honest' and 'realistic' as well."[23]

Although most British reviewers were lukewarm toward *Sons and Lovers*, and a few were totally negative,[24] almost all U.S. critics responded enthusiastically to the film,[25] as did the American public, whose curiosity had been piqued by pre-release media hooplah about the uncut film's sexual explicitness.[26] Wrote *Newsweek*'s critic, "The Anglo-American collaborators who have dramatized D. H. Lawrence's *Sons and Lovers* have done a fine job of bringing a genuine classic to the screen; it is treated with affection and respect in a performance that is first-rate."[27]

At the time *Sons and Lovers* was released, American critics' glowing response to the cinematography and acting in Wald's adaptation tended to obscure the fact—noted by at least a few British reviewers[28]—that the screenwriters took considerable liberties in condensing and modifying the plot of the original.

Plot Changes in Wald's Film of *Sons and Lovers*

The episodic, chronological narrative structure of *Sons and Lovers* is hardly complicated, yet it is impossible not to be struck by the wealth of realistic, vividly described incident that crowds its densely textured 400+ pages, especially in Part One (chapters 1 to 6). This section recounts the courtship and stormy married life of former schoolteacher Gertrude Coppard and "mining contractor" Walter Morel, as well as the intense experiences of their children, William, Annie, Paul, and Arthur; the section ends with the death of the eldest son, William, at 23. There are memorable scenes of domestic conflict and tragedy: Mrs. Morel, pregnant with Paul, locked out by her drunken husband and communing mystically with madonna lilies in the moonlight; Mr. Morel hurling a cutlery drawer at Mrs. Morel's head and drawing blood that drips, symbolically, onto baby Paul's glistening hair; neighbors unsteadily carrying brother William's huge coffin into the Morels' parlor.

Juxtaposed are minutely detailed vignettes of the youthful protagonist's everyday life: Paul picking up his father's wages, burning his sister's broken doll as a sacrifice, playing outdoor games with siblings and neighborhood children, and interviewing for a job at a surgical appliance company when he is 14. Tenderer scenes include Mr. Morel telling the children stories about the "pit," hammering glowing iron on his "goose," making fuses, mending his pit-bottle or the kettle; Mrs. Morel window-shopping, buying a piece of china, ironing, going on outdoor excursions with the children, sharing delight over garden or wild flowers.

Part Two of *Sons and Lovers* (chapters 7 to 18) focuses on Paul's ambivalent relationship with Miriam Leivers, which begins when she is 14 and Paul nearly 16, and ends, after four breakups initiated by Paul, when Miriam is 23 and Paul almost 25. Less attention is given to Paul's comparatively brief affair with Clara Dawes, which overlaps his ongoing relationship with Miriam, and to his peculiar friendship with Clara's estranged husband Baxter Dawes, to whom Clara returns at the end of the novel. The narrative culminates in Mrs. Morel's slow, agonizing death, Paul and Miriam's final separation, and Paul's hard-won decision not to follow his mother to the grave but rather to embrace life.

Interspersed throughout the narrative and permeating all else are glimpses of Paul's intense, Oedipal love affair with his mother which led Lawrence's sarcastic wife, Frieda, to subtitle the novel *His Mother's Darling*.[29] Also pervasive are scenes in which Paul interacts with significant women in his life in outdoor settings that reflect, evoke, and sometimes define their emotions, behavior, and the nature of their relationship—walking along the beach under a setting sun with Clara or making love to her by a river bank, shaking cherries down on Miriam at dusk, picking field flowers or jumping over haystacks with Miriam and Clara, or delightedly sharing with his mother the discovery of a previously hidden flower in her garden.

Unlike the novel, which begins with the courtship and marriage of Gertrude and Walter Morel, the film version of *Sons and Lovers* opens around 1910, when their son Paul is in his early twenties, and focuses entirely on one year in his life. Compared with the novel, the screenplay of the film version, written by Gavin Lambert and T. E. B. Clarke, is considerably shortened and streamlined.[30] The film entirely omits Part One of the book—making no allusions at all to Paul's early life and giving only one mention of the father's going down into the mines when he was a boy and only two passing references to the parents' originally passionate relationship and its painful breakdown. Many incidents from Part Two, recounting Paul's relationships with Miriam, Clara, and Baxter Dawes are also omitted, and changes in the substance and sequence of remaining episodes are numerous.[31]

The film version of *Sons and Lovers* greatly simplifies and condenses the part of the novel it actually covers.[32] In the book, for example, Miriam and Clara are friends, and it is Miriam who precipitates a love affair between Paul and Clara by introducing them. Before becoming Paul's lover, Clara persuades him to initiate a sexual relationship with Miriam—hardly the film's one-night stand. Paul's prolonged ambivalence toward Miriam during their nine-year relationship, and his gradual estrangement from Clara during their passionate love affair are barely indicated. Also omitted entirely in the film is Paul's rivalrous yet homoerotic relationship with Clara's husband, Baxter Dawes. which spans several chapters near the end of the novel. The subtle, cumulative tensions that arise out of these interrelationships create a dense psychological subtext in the novel that is entirely absent from the film. Paul's relationship with his mother is similarly simplified in the film adaptation. Numerous scenes in the novel showing Paul on holidays and excursions with her or sharing intimate domestic moments are omitted. The eroticism of their love is minimized. Also missing from the film are the many scenes in the novel in which Paul, Miriam, Clara, and Mrs. Morel, separately or together, experience the beauty and power of nature.

Another type of simplification in the film involves the complex, often ambivalent feelings and motivations of the characters. For example, the film portrays William's infatuation with his fiancée, Louisa, as wholehearted, portrays William's infatuation with his fiancée, Louisa, as wholehearted, whereas in the novel, he feels obligated to marry her but is increasingly disgusted by her extravagance and empty-headedness. In the film, Paul's break-up with Miriam on Christmas Day is prompted by his doubt about the future of Louisa and William's relationship and his mother's warning not to take his affair with Miriam lightly; in the novel, Paul's repeated rejections of Miriam stem from far more complicated emotions. Similarly, Paul's decision in the film not to take the scholarship in London so he can protect his mother from his father's outbursts greatly simplifies the motives of Lawrence's Paul, who remains by Mrs. Morel's side for far less conscious reasons.

The screenwriters took considerable liberties with the chronology of *Sons and Lovers*. Although Paul Morel's boyhood and adolescence are omitted from the film, a few altered incidents from Part One of the novel are inserted. For example, the episode in which Mrs. Morel is locked out of the house by her drunken husband occurs in the novel when she is pregnant with Paul; the event portrayed in the film has a completely different significance from the event portrayed in the film. In Lawrence's version, Mrs. Morel has a mystical experience among the madonna lilies. In the film, Mrs. Morel has no mystical experience in the garden (or anywhere else); the episode merely provides an occasion for Paul to come to her rescue and a convenient excuse for him to remain with her instead of going off to London to study art. In the novel, Paul is hired as a clerk at Jordan's at age 14, and works there for 13 years; in the film he begins work at Jordan's in his early twenties. In the book, Clara is an employee at Jordan's who leaves before Paul arrives and returns as overseer after Paul has been there many years; when Paul starts work at Jordan's in the film, Clara is already overseer.

The most controversial modification in the film concerns Mrs. Morel's death. In the novel, Lawrence spares us none of the harsh, graphic details. Mysteriously ailing for almost two years, Paul's mother reveals the presence of a huge abdominal tumor. Brought home to die, she lingers for months in drugged agony. Paul and his sister Annie, anguished by her suffering, take turns nursing her and finally poison her milk with a huge overdose of morphine; her breathing labored and face distorted, she finally expires. In the film, Mrs. Morel takes to her bed one night and dies quickly and serenely the next morning. Screenwriter Gavin Lambert contended that Lawrence's description of Mrs. Morel's death had to "be reconceived to make its effect in another medium":

> The long, despairing passage. . . is a *tour de force* of "static" writing—writing that creates a deliberate suspension of time: the surface is

uneventful, almost a blank, but there is fierce turbulence and struggle beneath it. Visually, this crucial episode contains little more than a single image of a woman wasting away on a sick-bed; dramatically, little more than her son asking her how she feels, and telling other people that he can't bear to watch her suffer much longer.[33]

Not surprisingly, Lambert's argument struck Frank Baldanza as somewhat specious:

One wonders where the 'reconception' is felt, since Mrs. Morel *is* seen in bed and her son *is* concerned at her suffering. No one has suggested that the motive for the change might be commercial, that euthanasia was considered too controversial—but the possibility exists, since the visual and dramatic execution of her death scenes are precisely what Mr. Lambert described as impossible.[34]

In several instances, the screenwriters achieved simplification by condensing successive scenes in the text. In the novel, for example, Paul makes two separate visits to Clara's home; in the film, Paul makes only one, during which he first makes love to Clara by the fireside. Later in their affair, Paul and Clara repeatedly go to the seaside, occasionally taking Clara's mother with them; in the film, they have only one seaside tryst. Paul breaks off with Miriam four times; in the film, there are two scenes in which Paul rejects Miriam. The screenwriters also combined dialogue from different scenes in the novel in individual scenes in the film. For example, the final conversation between Paul and Miriam is a composite of a dialogue Paul has with himself and a conversation he has with her at another point.

Besides cutting and splicing scenes from the text, the screenwriters also added major scenes and sequences, bits of comic relief, and even characters. In the film, a mine disaster in the film which kills Arthur and demonstrates the perils of Morel's occupation; this is a complete invention, as is a controversial scene in which Morel castigates his wife for her destructive possessiveness towards Paul. Humor enlivens the exhibition at Nottingham, Paul's first day at Jordan's, the Morels' Christmas gathering, and Clara's suffragette rally. Henry Hadlock, the "wizzened-hearted old stick" who buys Paul's painting of his father and offers to be his patron, does not appear at all in the novel.

Both major and minor characters from the novel are missing or altered in the film. Paul's sister Annie, who conspires with him to end their mother's life, is absent, as is Miriam's brother Edgar, Paul's close friend, and the rest of the Leivers family, with the exception of Miriam's mother and her young brother Hubert. Paul's restless brother Arthur, who marries and settles down as a family man in the novel, makes only a brief, cautionary appearance at the beginning of the film.

However radical, the differences between the narrative structure of the original text of *Sons and Lovers* and that of the film adaptation do not fully account for the un-Lawrentian "feel" of the film, noted even by admiring British and American critics. In fact, only a comparison of the prose style of the novel with the cinematic style of the film can reveal why Jerry Wald's adaptation fails to capture what Frieda Lawrence referred to as the "special quality" of the novel.

Style in the Novel and the Film

Literary critics have unanimously characterized *Sons and Lovers* as a traditional nineteenth-century British novel similar in narrative style and subject matter to works by Lawrence's contemporary Arnold Bennett.[35] However, they have also consistently remarked on the unique stylistic features of *Sons and Lovers* which have prompted many critics, paradoxically, to categorize it as the first twentieth-century novel.[36] Detailed, vividly realistic narrative and descriptive passages that capture the immediacy and particularity of physical objects and experiences,[37] coupled with a pervasive poetic lyricism that suffuses the novel with a highly charged intensity,[38] are the qualities most often cited as the hallmarks of prose style in *Sons and Lovers*. Lawrence described the style he was aiming at in the novel in negative terms: he wanted, above all, to purge it of the excesses of his first two works, *The White Peacock* (1911) and *The Trespasser* (1912): "Paul Morel will be a novel—not a florid prose poem, or a decorated idyll running to seed in realism but a restrained, somewhat impersonal novel" (Letter, Oct.18, 1910).[39] Only half a year after the novel was published in May 1913, however, Lawrence had serious reservations about its narrative and prose technique. "I shan't write in the same manner... again, I think—in that hard, violent style full of sensation and presentation," he wrote his editor, Edward Garnett (Dec. 30, 1913)[40] and a year later, working on *The Rainbow*, "I have no longer the joy of creating vivid scenes, that I had in *Sons and Lovers*, I don't care much more about accumulating objects in the powerful light of emotion, and making a scene of them...." (Letter, Jan. 29, 1914)[41]

Lawrence infused all aspects of the novel's prose with intense lyricism and concrete immediacy, none more so than its diction. The simplified, predominantly Anglo-Saxon diction, often colloquial, alternates with more elevated, rhapsodic, philosophical, literary or biblical language in the narrative and descriptive sections. A much higher proportion of nouns than verbs defines Lawrence's style as nominal; verbs tend to be intransitive rather than transitive. The frequent use of intensifiers throughout the novel creates a highly charged, eroticized subtext.

Sentences tend to be relatively short and direct, consisting mainly of independent clauses with subject-verb-object word order, often expanded with participial modifiers. Longer sentences, though not numerous, are almost always composed of fairly short units—two to four independent clauses joined by commas or semi-colons. Antithesis—a pervasive feature of the novel's narrative and thematic structure as well as of the psychology of the characters—occurs frequently with and between sentences and paragraphs.

Paragraphs, like sentences, tend to be brief, as in "The Rocking-Horse Winner," averaging six to seven sentences, but also varying widely in length. Although the overall effect of the paragraphing is choppy, the typical longer paragraph in *Sons and Lovers* is climactic, starting with sentences of short or medium length, swelling to longer and longer sentences (often interspersed with extremely short ones), and dropping to one or two relatively short sentences in the end. The rhythms of a typical Lawrentian paragraph in *Sons and Lovers* approximate the *vers libre* cadences of Walt Whitman's poetry[42]—circular, flowing, wavelike rhythms created by the modified repetition and parallel structures characteristic of the language of the Old Testament. Lawrence's Congregationalist upbringing, permeated with scripture and hymns, had deeply embedded these rhythms in his consciousness and memory.[43]

Repetition with modification, common to all of Lawrence's prose, is a major element in both the narrative structure and the language of *Sons and Lovers*. Key words and images weave and interconnect throughout the novel like Wagnerian motifs, creating a multi-layered, highly charged subtext. Many critics have noted that there is symbolism in *Sons and Lovers*,[44] at the same time pointing out that the symbolism is not artificially superimposed on the narrative; images in the novel grow naturally out of a realistic context and become symbolic chiefly through repetition.[45] Sounds are cumulatively repeated; alliteration and assonance abound in *Sons and Lovers*, as well as the occasional use of onomatopoeia, prompting a number of critics to call the novel a "dramatic poem"[46] and many others to pay tribute to its poetic suggestiveness and to the connotativeness of the diction. Much of the language is also kinesthetic and mimetic; words and sentences move propulsively forward, often imitating the turbulent physical and emotional experiences being described.

Finally, although the narrator's point of view changes in *Sons and Lovers*, merging with that of one character or another, the tone of the novel remains remarkably consistent. In sharp contrast to the distanced irony that characterizes the narrator's tone in "The Rocking-Horse Winner," the narrator's tone in *Sons and Lovers* is passionately and insistently serious throughout.

Even as the unique prose style of Lawrence's first major novel was widely praised, the striking cinematic style and visual effects of Jerry Wald's *Sons and Lovers* received a positive response from most American and British viewers. *New York Times* movie critic Bosley Crowther wrote appreciatively of the film's "stunning pictorial style,"[47] while Paul Beckley, reviewer for the *New York Herald Tribune*, was enthusiastic not only about the photography but also about the settings and decor.[48] A number of British critics also praised the look of the film. The reviewer in the *London Times* commended the location shots,[49] although C. A. Lejeune, in the *London Observer*, waxed eloquent over the cinematography:

> Jack Cardiff, the director, was once regarded as England's top cameraman, and it is plain to see that "Sons and Lovers" was made by someone with a passion for photography. Time and time again, the camera digs deep into a close-up, trying to lay bare everything behind the face. Time and again the eye is caught and held by some subtle composition on the screen. In all that he does here, Mr. Cardiff has been splendidly served by Freddie Francis, the director of photography. The pair have worked in black and white and every subtle tone between.[50]

Other critics, however, were enthusiastic about neither the cinematography nor almost any other aspect of the film. Even those who found much to commend in the adaptation complained that something absolutely crucial was missing from the film—something not explainable by the glaring omission of characters, episodes, and psychological complexity, by poor casting and hammy acting. Margaret Tarratt panned both the movie's truncated screenplay and its "lack of visual expressiveness."[51] Neil Sinyard turned thumbs down on both the photography and the score: "The weak visual imagination and Mario Nascimbene's lush music dampen the Lawrentian complexities," he wrote.[52] Noting the film's "emotional monotone" and its "restraint," Bosley Crowther was typical in his reservations: "The powerful passions that race and foam through the original tale, which shocked and dismayed a lot of people when it was published in 1913, do not surge up," he charged.[53] Although Pauline Kael acknowledged *Sons and Lovers* to be "one of the best movie adaptations of a major novel," ironically she ascribed what she perceived as an un-Lawrentian lack of passion in the film to the very cinematic style praised by other critics:

> It's a curiously quaint, pastoral sort of film; the rhythm is off—the pictorial style, exquisite as it is, is neither Lawrentian nor a visual equivalent or even approximation of Lawrence's prose. The visual beauties aren't informed by Lawrence's passionate sense of life. The artist's fire simply isn't there—the movie is temperate, earnest, episodic. . . . Pick up the book again at almost any point, and the movie simply disappears. There's a richness and a fullness in the novel.[54]

Part of the reason that both British and American critics faulted *Sons and Lovers* for inadequately conveying the poetic lyricism and emotional fervor and power of the original is that the style of the film is, in fact, an attenuated hybrid. If Anthony Pelissier's *The Rocking-Horse Winner* bears the stylistic imprint of *film noir*, Jerry Wald's Anglo-English production of *Sons and Lovers* rather cautiously blends two distinctive cinematic styles—those of the British "New Wave" films of the late fifties and early sixties and those of the films of Hollywood's classical era, the mid teens to the late sixties. The result is a curiously tepid mix.

The films of the British "New Cinema" or "New Wave" (1959 to 1963) had their genesis in John Osborne's anti-establishment play *Look Back in Anger*, adapted for film in 1959, and the social realism of the working-class novels of David Storey, John Braine, Alan Sillitoe, and Shelagh Delaney, adapted as *This Sporting Life* (1963), *Room at the Top* (1959), *The Loneliness of the Long-Distance Runner* (1962), *Saturday Night and Sunday Morning* (1960), and *A Taste of Honey* (1961). Featuring unknown young actors, set in the industrial midlands, shot on location in black-and-white, and focusing on the lives of vulgar, brawling, beer-drinking working-class youths, the British "New Wave" films are stylistically distinctive, in sharp contrast to the artificial conventions of studio-made films.

It's not hard to see why film scholars generally include Jerry Wald's *Sons and Lovers* among the films of the British "New Wave."[55] Besides the fact that the film was shot in black-and-white and focuses on vernacular-speaking working-class characters, the most obvious link between *Sons and Lovers* and films, such as *Saturday Night and Sunday Morning* and *Room at the*

Top is location shooting in the English midlands (*Sons and Lovers* was filmed, in part, in the town of Eastwood, where Lawrence grew up, and in the city of Nottingham, where he worked and attended both high school and college).[56] Other elements in *Sons and Lovers* reminiscent of both Italian neo-realist films and the films of the British "New Wave" include the gray bleakness of many scenes; the consistent use of deep focus, wide-screen mise-en-scène photography permitted by new CinemaScope lenses; the use of natural lighting made possible by newly introduced fast film; the shooting of most shots from eye-level; the use of relatively inexperienced screen actors, such as Mary Ure and Heather Sears and of 200 local nonprofessionals as extras in the crowd scenes at the mining disaster; the absence of makeup on the male actors and a bare minimum of it on the women; the simple, unadorned, authentic period costumes of almost all of the characters; and the contrast between the freedom and spontaneity evoked by a pastoral setting and the imprisonment symbolized by an urban environment.

Although Wald's *Sons and Lovers* shares certain elements of Italian and British realist films, the adaptation lacks both the psychological and the sensory realism that pervades Lawrence's novel. Although the film captures certain very limited aspects of the mining-town's milieu, it omits many of the locales that appear throughout the novel as well as much of the life of the community beyond the Morels' household and the experiences of the miners underground. Moreover the novel's vivid and frequent vignettes of everyday life are almost entirely missing in the film. The period costumes are too tidy, tailored, and pressed to convey the crumpledness of personal grooming and dress suggested by the novel and by period photographs of actual coalminers and their families. In general, despite occasional hints of domestic squalor, the poverty, harshness and drudgery of the Morels' life are underplayed, and interiors are prettified and glamourized.

The relative lack of realism in the film is a direct result of cinematic technique, for despite its links with British "New Cinema," Wald's *Sons and Lovers* is closer in many respects to "classical cinema," a term used to designate "the style of mainstream fiction films produced in America roughly from the midteens until the late 1960s":

> Classical cinema avoids the extremes of realism and formalism, in favor of a slightly stylized presentation that has at least a surface plausibility. . . . The classical paradigm is a movie strong in *story*, *star*, and *production values*, with a high level of technical achievement, and edited according to conventions of *classical cutting* . . . a style of

editing developed by D. W. Griffith, in which a sequence of shots is determined by a scene's dramatic and emotional emphases rather than by physical action alone. . . . The human materials are paramount in the classical cinema. The characters are generally appealing and slightly romanticized. . . . The visual style is functional and rarely distracts from the characters in action. Movies in this form are structured narratively, with a clearly defined conflict, complications that intensify to a rising climax, and a resolution that emphasizes formal closure.[57]

Point-of-view shots, medium closeups, closeups, and extreme closeups; tightly framed two- and three-shots; use of high-angle and low-angle shots and montage traveling shots; dissolves to link scenes and sequences; even lighting; repeated visual motifs; casting of extremely well-known actors in principal roles (in this case, Trevor Howard and Wendy Hiller); softening and sentimentalizing of characters; a conventionally romantic score—all of these features of *Sons and Lovers* clearly belong to classical cinema.

The hybrid cinematic style of Jerry Wald's *Sons and Lovers* is largely responsible for the tepidness of the film. It was shot in black-and-white CinemaScope with a "fast" film that permitted considerable depth of focus and less lighting than previous black-and-white films had, and with a prism on the camera lens that allowed the shooting of closeups from a distance of only seven to eight inches from a subject instead of the six-foot distance previously required.[58] The film adaptation of *Sons and Lovers* consists, with one notable exception, of a series of fairly brief, self-contained scenes—medium closeups of two or three actors earnestly exchanging Lawrentian dialogue—linked almost entirely by lap dissolves. Interspersed are transitional shots and sequences, either brief picture-postcard establishing shots of landscape or cityscape, or rapid montages or "traveling shots." Within many individual shots filmed indoors, there is little shifting of camera angle or distance; like actors on a stage, the characters generally move within the frame, fairly close to the camera, while the camera itself remains stationary.

In outdoor scenes there is much more variety of camera distance and angle than in indoor shots, but the filmmakers rarely took advantage of the breadth of the CinemaScope screen to capture epic expanses of space. Instead, they paradoxically used the wide screen to create an almost suffocating, larger-than-life intimacy. At peak moments, the camera zeroes in for extreme close-ups of the characters' faces and parts of their faces—notably, their eyes.

A few visual motifs are repeated throughout the film; visual or aural "surprises" are few. The lighting, natural or artificial, is relatively even and uniform throughout; in contrast to *The Rocking Horse Winner*, little use is made of expressionistic lighting. Although there are a number of subjective shots in the film, the point of view is predominantly objective. The numerous depth-of-focus shots lack the complexity and detail associated with a mise-en-scène approach. Low-angle and high-angle shots are used mainly for variety, resulting in some striking frame-by-frame compositions.

The orchestral score, lush and melodic, is executed by a Mantovani-like string ensemble with lots of bass and some bassoon. Intrusive and manipulative, the music has three main themes—heavily romantic, liltingly pastoral, and ominously tragic—to trigger the viewer's emotional responses. The filmmakers also make nonmusical sounds—a clock ticking, a mine whistle or foghorn blowing—function like music.

With the exception of several imaginative lap dissolves between shots, scenes, and sequences, a few "traveling" shots to show movement, and some artful frame composition, there are almost no "special effects" to create visual interest, excitement, or depth in Wald's adaptation of *Sons and Lovers*—no parallel editing, prolonged tracking or panning shots, expressionistic montages, slow or fast motion, jump cuts, freeze frames, rack focus, superimposition, exaggerated or offbeat lighting, distorting lenses, soft-focus photography; almost no unusual camera angles, syncopated rhythms, or heightened contrasts. Nor is there distorted sound to suggest subjective or dream states, sound to bridge shots and sequences, ironic juxtaposition of sound and image. On the contrary, the cinematic techniques used in *Sons and Lovers* are relatively simple and straightforward, even for a classical Hollywood film. As director Jack Cardiff described the challenge before him, "It's a gimmickless picture; there's no chariot race or anything like that to pull us through."[59]

The "gimmickless" simplicity of the cinematic style in *Sons and Lovers*, however, is not necessarily analogous to the far more complex prose style of Lawrence's novel, as I discovered when I compared stylistic elements in Lawrence's *Sons and Lovers*—diction, grammar and syntax, antithesis, paragraph shape and rhythm, imagery and symbolism, and tone—with their equivalents in Wald's screen adaptation.

Diction in the Novel; Shot and Image in the Film

As in "The Rocking-Horse Winner," diction in Part One of *Sons and Lovers* is relatively simple and concrete, mono- or bisyllabic and predominantly of Anglo-Saxon, German, or French origin (Lawrence rather self-consciously sprinkled the novel with French words, phrases, and snatches of poetry). In the narrative and descriptive passages of Part Two, however, simple, concrete diction is intermixed with a Latinate vocabulary consisting of polysyllabic abstract nouns, adjectives, and adverbs. In all of his narratives, Lawrence exhibits a nominal style, typically favoring nouns over verbs; *Sons and Lovers* is no exception.[60] John Russell has noted Lawrence's preference for abstract nouns ending in *ity* and *ness*, of which there are many in Part Two, along with nouns ending in *ion*.[61]

Throughout the novel, the vocabulary is often colloquial and regional, reflecting the Midlands dialect of Lawrence's youth. Narrative and descriptive passages, as well as dialogue, contain down-to-earth bits of local slang, such as *bobby-dazzler* (finery), *gaby* (fool), *mardarse* (spoiled child), and *wessel-brained* (giddy, thoughtless). Words such as *barkled* (encrusted), *twitchel* (a narrow passage), *crozzly* (crisp, well-done) and *mucky* (dirty) alternate in narrative passages with exalted and religious words such as *soul, ecstasy, communion, reverence, sanctity, peace,* and *firmament*. Lawrence's detailed knowledge and love of botany accounts for his constant references to specific flowers, plants, trees, and birds. The frequent use of colloquial contractions, especially in dialogue, is another feature of Lawrence's diction in *Sons and Lovers*. Abbreviations, such as *shonna* (should not), *didna* (did not), *sh'lt* (shall) and *nobbut* (no one but) turn up often in conversation among Paul Morel's friends and siblings, as well as between Mr. Morel and members of his family or his mining comrades.

The majority of verbs, by a proportion of two to one, are intransitive, most often verbs of being that link a noun with predicate adjectives. The prevalence of intransitive verbs, especially linking verbs, is indicative of Lawrence's focus on inner, self-referring mental and emotional states rather than on external events involving two or more persons as the source and locus of significant—sometimes violent—activity; indeed, in *Sons and Lovers*, "action" is as often emotionally as physically violent. Intensifiers—highly charged verbs, adjectives, and adverbs that are the language of intoxication—create a Dionysian subtext throughout the novel. The italicized words in the following passage from Part One are illustrative of Lawrence's unique method:

> The moon was *high* and *magnificent* in the August night. Mrs. Morel, *seared* with passion, *shivered* to find herself out there in a *great white light*, that fell cold on her, and gave a shock to her *inflamed* soul. She stood for a few moments helplessly staring at the *glistening great* rhubarb

leaves near the door. Then she got the air into her *breast*. She walked down the garden path, *trembling* in every limb, while the child *boiled* within her. For a while she went over the last scene, then over it again, certain phrases, certain moments coming each time like a brand *red-hot* down on her soul; and each time she enacted again the past hour, each time the brand came down at the same same points, till the mark was *burnt in*, and the pain *burnt out*, and at last she came to herself. She must have been half an hour in this *delirious* condition. Then the presence of the night came again to her. She glanced round in fear. She had wandered to the side garden, where she was walking up and down the path beside the currant bushes along the long wall. The garden was a narrow strip, bounded from the road, that cut transversely between the blocks by a *thick* thorn hedge.

She hurried out of the side garden to the front, where she could stand as if in an *immense* gulf of white light, the moon *streaming high* in face of her, the moonlight *standing up* from the hills in front, and filling the valley where the Bottoms *crouched* almost *blindingly*. There, *panting* and half *weeping* in reaction from the stress, she murmured to herself over and over again: "The nuisance! The nuisance!"

She became aware of something about her. With an effort she *roused* herself to see what it was that *penetrated* her consciousness. The tall white lilies were *reeling* in the moonlight, and the air was *charged* with their perfume, as with a presence. Mrs. Morel *gasped* slightly in *fear*. She *touched* the *big*, pallid flowers on their petals, then *shivered*. They seemed to be *stretching* in the moonlight. She put her hand into one white bin: the gold scarcely showed on her fingers by moonlight. She bent down to look at the binful of yellow pollen; but it only appeared *dusky*. Then she *drank* a deep draught of the scent. It almost made her *dizzy*.

Mrs. Morel *leaned* on the garden gate, looking out, and she *lost* herself awhile. She did not know what she thought. Except for a slight feeling of sickness, and her consciousness in the child, herself *melted out* like scent into the shiny, pale air. After a time, the child, too, *melted* with her in the mixing-pot of moonlight, and she *rested* with the hills and lilies and houses, all *swum together* in a kind of *swoon*. (23-24)

An underlying verbal progression in these four paragraphs is generated by words relating to light, heat, and fire (*seared, white light, inflamed, glistening, red-hot, burnt, burnt out*) overlapping with words that suggest feverishness and illness (*trembling, delirious, weeping*) and later, words— almost entirely verbs—associated with sexual arousal and gratification, and with intoxication (*streaming, standing up, panting, roused, reeling, charged, gasped, touched, stretching, penetrated, drank, leaned, lost, melted out, rested, swum together, swooned*). The erotic connotations of these words, along with the hyperbole of adjectives, such as *great, high, magnificent, immense, deep, big,* and *thick*, combine with typically Lawrentian rhythmic cadences and repetition of vocabulary and sound to create a powerfully affecting, multi-layered polyphonic prose poem. These paragraphs are characteristic of a number of significant, quasi-mystical passages in the novel which, like previously cited passages in "The Rocking-Horse Winner," convey and embody Lawrence's eroticization of both human and non-human experience, and indeed, of the entire cosmos.

Another passage in *Sons and Lovers* that exemplifies Lawrence's eroticized diction is the one in which, after flying through the air with abandon, Paul aggressively pushes Miriam on a swing in her barn:

> "It's so ripping!" he said, setting her in motion. "Keep your *heels up*, or they'll *bang* the manger wall."
> She felt the accuracy with which he *caught her,* exactly at the right moment, and the exactly proportionate *strength of his thrust,* and was afraid. *Down to her bowels* went the *hot wave of fear.* She was *in his hands.* Again, *firm* and inevitable, came *the thrust* at the right moment. She *gripped* the rope, almost *swooning*.
> "Ha!" she laughed in *fear*. "No higher!"
> "But you're not a bit high," he remonstrated.
> "But no higher."
> He heard the *fear* in her voice, and desisted. Her heart *melted in hot pain* when the moment came for him to *thrust* her forward again. But he left her alone. She began to breathe. (151)

The sexual connotations of *heels up, bang, caught her, strength of his thrust* (repeated three times), *hot wave of fear* (also repeated three times), *afraid, fear, down to her bowels, firm, in his hands, gripped, swooning, melted in hot pain*, generate the highly charged lexical subtext present in many passages throughout the novel, and suggest the constant tension between the powerful libidinous impulses of the principal characters and their attempts (sometimes too successful) to repress them.

Finally, as in "The Rocking-Horse Winner," there is much lexical repetition in *Sons and Lovers*, especially of vocabulary, peculiar to Lawrence's fictions, that carries the weight of accumulated meanings—words such as *blood, dark, fire, wild, intensity, wonder,* and *intimacy,* as well as key nouns describing emotional states that reverberate significantly throughout the novel—in particular, *bitterness, terror, horror, cruelty, misery, suffering, anguish, restlessness, communion, love*, and *hate*. Above all, the words *bondage, battle,* and *sacrifice* appear in various contexts.[62]

Bondage, associated with words such as *prisoner* and *imprisoned*, is used frequently. Of Mrs. Morel, Lawrence wrote, "The prospect of her life made her feel as if she were buried alive," and indeed, all of the characters in *Sons and Lovers*, in one way or another, feel thwarted in their attempts to satisfy their deepest needs and to feel spiritually and physically free. The related word *battle* (or *struggle*) appears more often than *bondage* or *sacrifice*, suggesting the principal characters' fierce attempt to escape their restrictive lives as well as the unresolved internal and external conflicts that ultimately destroy them.

Like the diction in Part One of the novel, the filmic images in *Sons and Lovers* are mostly simple, concrete, and, like Lawrence's shortish words, abbreviated and foreshortened. Key actors are filmed mainly in medium closeups—classical Hollywood two- or three-shots or group tableaus permitted by the wide CinemaScope screen—shot either at eye-level or at a slight low angle. The characters are depicted mostly as "talking heads," earnestly speaking to one another while moving within a confined space, or physically interacting during lovemaking or an emotional conflict. In keeping with Lawrence's preference for nouns over verbs, and for intransitive verbs over transitive verbs, a majority of scenes are relatively static, confined to small interiors; even outdoors, the movements of the characters tend to be restricted, occupying little physical space. Similarly, as in *The Rocking Horse Winner*, the establishing shots of landscapes, villages, and cities are static and oversimplified, like picture postcards.

At the same time, analogous to the arresting vocabulary in Part Two of *Sons and Lovers*, cinematographer/director Cardiff devised a number of picturesque compositions that create momentarily stunning visual effects that call attention to themselves and also convey hidden layers of meaning. One example is the panning shot at the very beginning of the film that moves from sheep grazing in a lush field to a distant view of the outbuildings of a local mine. The next shot is a closeup of the silhouetted headstock of the mine, which dominates the left side of the large screen. When the wheel at the top suddenly turns with a piercing shriek of gears, an eye-filling explosion of birds fills the sky. The striking headstock motif recurs in the mine-disaster sequence, at the end of which an extreme high-angle bird's-eye view of the villagers swarming toward the mine is shot through the spokes of the headstock wheel.

Another example of strikingly artful composition is the tracking shot of Paul and Clara cavorting along the deserted beach at a wintry seaside resort; the shot ends inside a diagonal construction of iron girders (an extension of a jetty) to which Paul euphemistically refers as "trees." Other tastefully composed, semi-decorative compositions in the same sequence include a high-angle shot, from Paul's point of view, of Clara in her white underclothing warming herself by the fire in her parlor; another high-angle shot of Clara sitting on the wintry beach, looking up at Paul; and a prolonged shot of Clara's partly clothed body and tousled head seen through the ornate curves of a wrought-iron bedstead.

Snippets of dialogue from *Sons and Lovers* are repeatedly reproduced in the film, often out of their original context. The Midlands regionalisms and dialect that pervade the novel are also reproduced in the conversations of both Paul and his father, creating some semblance of authenticity and documentary realism. "I brought thee a coconut, lass," says Morel to his wife, whom he calls a "mucky little lassie" who has "taken the curl out of" him. As in the novel, Paul uses regional words, referring to his mother's "nubbly old bonnet" and, using a word that appears several times in the novel, Mrs. Morel calls the fancy hat her son has sketched for her a "bobby-dazzler."

The film version of *Sons and Lovers* is quite uneven in its reproduction of the eroticized subtext embedded in the novel's distinctive prose. The passage I cited in which Paul pushes Miriam on her swing, for example, is filled with suggestive words and phrases. One might reasonably expect all of Lawrence's cinematic adapters to devise a variety of visual and/or aural equivalents for the reverberating, highly charged intensity of his diction. But the sanitized swing scene in the movie version barely hints at the eroticism of words and phrases like *in his hands, thrust, bowels, firm, grip, swooning,* and *hot wave of fear*. Instead, we are shown an elated Paul surprising Miriam as she swings (we only glimpse her from the rear and cannot see her face). As she rather weakly protests, he pushes her a few times from the front (we still don't see her face or a closeup of his) and excitedly takes over the swing himself, standing and facing the camera as he lunges forward and disappears into the hayloft. Instead of focusing on the subtleties of the scene—Miriam's ambivalent reactions to Paul's pushing her, and Paul's face and body as he aggressively thrusts her into the air—the filmmakers chose to bypass the erotic byplay between them and focus instead on Paul's botched attempt at lovemaking a few moments later. The scene offers no visual equivalent for Lawrence's highly charged verbal pyrotechnics—nor do most of the other scenes and sequences in the film, with one notable exception.

Regrettably, only one segment of the film truly does justice to Lawrence's eroticized prose. With its skillful choreographing of movement, rhythmic cutting, and counterpoint of dialogue, physical movement, subtle gesture, and facial expression, the complex, finely detailed sequence depicting Paul and Clara's developing love affair exquisitely captures the multi-leveled connotativeness of Lawrence's diction as no other segment of the film does. When Paul approaches Clara after a suffragette rally in Nottingham at which she asserts her belief in the "four freedoms for women—speech, thought, opportunity, and love," she tells the young man that she has left her husband because of his infidelity (which has been underscored by an earlier cutaway shot of a glowering Baxter Dawes with a woman on his arm). Despite Clara's protest, Paul picks some snowdrops and gives them to her. An extreme closeup of his hand intertwined with hers as she takes the flowers speaks volumes: "When you hold the snow in your hand a little, it melts," says Paul provocatively. After his first encounter with Clara, Paul tells his mother he is "serious" about her, preparing us for the seduction that will follow.

A quick cut to clashing cymbals that look like breasts with prominent nipples shifts rapidly to an extreme long shot of can-can dancers, photographed on a low-angle diagonal revealing frilly petticoats and a sexually ambiguous lead dancer. The prancing high-kickers alternate with quick off-center medium closeups of laughing Clara and Paul, animated and aroused. The growing tension between Paul and Clara is evident as the last train pulls out of the nearby station and Clara tells Paul that he will have to stay overnight in her mother's house. As in the novel, the sequence that follows builds to a high pitch of intensity: visuals convey the growing illicit passion between the lovers, while the restrained, often double-leveled dialogue heightens the sexual tension between them.

The widow Radford—Clara's feisty, vigilant mother—needles Paul about his breaking off with Miriam Leivers, and makes not-so-subtle cracks about liking to have a man in the house and Baxter Dawes having slept without the bottoms of the pajamas she lends Paul. Afterward, Paul and Clara—photographed in two shots, shot/reverse shots and, as minutes tick by, larger and larger closeups—stall for time alone by attempting to prolong a bogus card game, while Mrs. Radford, rattling pans in the kitchen and bustling about the parlor, censoriously stalks back and forth behind and in front of the would-be lovers, a foreign body irritatingly entering, exiting, and re-entering the frame.

Exchanging intense glances, slightly moving their half-open mouths, the couple, framed in time-stretching, increasingly closeup shot/reverse shots, reveal their mutual desire; in this highly charged scene, "real" time seems elongated. Shot from Clara's point of view, an extreme closeup of Paul's fingers cutting the deck of cards is highly suggestive. When Mrs. Radford thrusts a lighted candle at Paul—a rather obvious phallic symbol—he scowls angrily and reluctantly goes upstairs.

Clara remains downstairs, ostensibly to warm herself at the fire, while Paul, in her bedroom, caresses her powder puff, stares at an extreme closeup of Clara's photo, blows out the candle, and removes his collar and boots. Standing at the half-open door, he hears Clara asking her mother to undo her dress. After Mrs. Radford closes the door to Clara's room on her way to bed, Paul waits a few moments, then quietly leaves the room, pausing at the top of the stairs. We see him in a frontal medium closeup transfixed by the vision of Clara, captured in a stunning high-angle shot, bare-shouldered in her white undergarments, her hair down, illuminated by firelight and defined by the surrounding darkness. Slowly and noiselessly, Paul descends the stairs and approaches Clara from behind, touching her bare shoulder. Kneeling by her side, he lunges at her with sudden fierceness as they exchange passionate kisses; simultaneously, there is a burst of heavily orchestrated romantic music. A slow lap dissolve ends a sequence crackling with psychological and erotic tension.

The repetitiveness that is characteristic of Lawrence's use of words and verbal motifs in *Sons and Lovers* is broadly echoed in the film in the repetition (with variation) of shots, locales, and visual and aural motifs. As in the novel, elements of cohesion in the film are Paul and Mrs. Morel, one or both of whom appear in almost every shot and scene. Although the detail in most of the interiors is not nearly as dense, various, and loaded with symbolic significance as in Pelissier's adaptation, visual motifs are repeated in three settings: the lamp, fire, table and china in the Morels' kitchen and parlor; the poles of the brass bedstead in their bedroom; the windowed doors and Clara's desk at Jordan's. Outdoor locales are also repeated, in particular the mine, the lake and forest on Miriam's farm, the Bestwood railroad station, and the Bestwood street on which the Morels live. A constantly recurring visual motif is the water wheel on Miriam's property; in some scenes, the wheel fades into the decor, in others it figures prominently. The circularity of the water wheel is mirrored by that of the mine headstocks, the round clock in Nottingham, and the round bobbins at Jordan's.

A few specific shots also recur. At the outset of the film, workers emerge from the mine entrance. A little later, at the same entrance, the wounded and dead are cranked up on a lift. A closeup of the mine headstock early in the film is repeated just before the traveling montage of the townspeople running to the scene of the disaster, and again at the end of this sequence, when all are motionless, staring as the wheel turns the miners up.

Other recurring shots are Clara's head and neck, stared at by Paul from behind as the camera zooms in closer, and Paul and Miriam walking by the lake on her farm in fall and winter. We see the pair in the forest, a poignant scene of leave-taking repeated twice in the film, the last time just before Paul boards the train for London. Particularly noteworthy is the twice-repeated visual motif of separation in which Paul turns his back on Miriam and walks off into the woods while she turns and moves forward toward the camera. There are a number of shots of Paul and Clara embracing and kissing, in sharp contrast to the scenes in which Paul kisses Miriam—awkwardly before a haystack in the barn, solemnly standing by the lake in twilight, patronizingly when he takes his final leave of her. Shots of Paul's painting of his father are repeated twice, as are matched shots of daffodils, painted and real, and throughout the film we are shown extreme closeups of Paul's drawings of his mother and of Clara, and photographs of Louisa and Clara.

Three conventional musical themes—sweepingly romantic, heavily tragic, and liltingly dancelike—recur almost monotonously throughout the film, almost always lushly orchestrated. The musical motifs underscore mood, announce characters, and are occasionally keyed to the physical actions of the principals, starting and stopping at critical moments.[63] Natural sounds, too, are repeated throughout the film—rippling water on Miriam's farm, the mine whistle, a train in transit, the rhythmic chuffing of machinery and whir of bobbins at Jordan's, the miners' heavy boots, the loud ticking of a clock, and the piercing shriek of the headstock wheel as it cranks up the lift in the mine.

The novel's verbal motif of bondage or imprisonment is expressed repeatedly in the film's dialogue,[64] although it is translated only sporadically into cinematic images. The sense of the principal characters being trapped by their environment, class, and gender is repeatedly suggested by the tightly framed shots in small interiors and even out of doors (Paul, for example, is usually photographed hemmed in between two walls). There are occasional prison-like motifs of bars and restraints—the spokes of the mine headstock wheel through which the villagers are seen running to the mine, the four glass-paneled doors before which Paul stands on his first day at Jordan's; the criss-crossed iron girders that engulf and divide Paul and Clara on the beach; Mrs. Morel's brass bedstead; and the ornate iron bedstead behind which "liberated" Clara seems trapped in her tryst with Paul. The theme of freedom is visually conveyed in the traveling montage in which Paul runs to Miriam's, the scene in which Clara and Paul cavort on the beach, and the final extreme long shot in which Paul boards a train for London.

Finally, sacrifice is a repeated motif, exemplified in the film by Paul's renunciation of a London art school scholarship to remain at home with his mother and take a clerical job. A visual emblem of sacrifice is the shot of Miriam fully dressed, lying motionless on a wooden slab after a night of unhappy lovemaking with Paul.

Syntax in the Novel and the Film

Lawrence referred to the prose style of *Sons and Lovers* as "hard and violent,"[65] and there is agreement among critics that the sentences in the novel are more compact, plangent and direct than those in any of his other major fiction or in the novels of his contemporaries—Conrad, Hardy, and Bennett. Lawrence's earliest interpreters especially noted the succinctness of the writing: "Although this is a novel of over 500 closely printed pages, the style is terse—so terse that it produces an effect as of short, sharp hammer strokes," observed the *New York Times* reviewer.[66] Virginia Woolf also noted the speed, spontaneity, and fluidity of Lawrence's prose: "Words, scenes flow as fast and direct as if he merely traced them with a free rapid hand in sheet after sheet. Not a sentence seems thought about twice; not a word added for its effect on the architecture of the phrase."[67]

Using statistical methods, investigators of style from the 1960s on have amply documented the rapidity and intensity of Lawrence's prose, citing his syntax as his "most distinctive stylistic feature."[68] In *Sons and Lovers* Lawrence makes extensive use of simple and complex sentences, a stylistic feature common to much of his fiction. In her study of ten of Lawrence's short stories, Maryanne Felter found that in a sample of 66 paragraphs, 52.6 percent of the sentences were simple and 29.04 percent were complex. Although Lawrence used a variety of sentences in *Sons and Lovers*, the proportion of simple sentences is even larger than Felter found it to be: of 92 sentences (the first four paragraphs of each of 15 chapters), 62 percent were simple, 24 percent complex, and 13 percent compound or compound-complex. Moreover, Lawrence's simple sentences in *Sons and Lovers* are in straightforward subject-verb-object order, conspicuously lacking both the passive voice and circuitous words.[69]

Analyzing prose style in the early novels of D. H. Lawrence, Marion Smith McKeown found that the average length of sentences in *Sons and*

Lovers, including passages of dialogue, was 11.65 words, shorter than the average sentence length of four contemporary novelists—Arnold Bennett, Thomas Hardy, Joseph Conrad, and Virginia Woolf.[70] In comparison, my sample of 60 paragraphs (the first four paragraphs of each of 15 chapters) indicates that average sentence length in *Sons and Lovers* is 13.7 words, excluding dialogue, in which sentences tend to be shorter.

In *Sons and Lovers*, a distinctive aspect of syntax in complex sentences is the frequent use of subordinate clauses (often relative clauses and adverbial clauses expressing time relations) following main clauses. Another is Lawrence's recurring use of appositives.[71] Adverbs such as *almost, always, occasionally, often, quickly,* and *suddenly* often appear at the beginnings of sentences. As in "The Rocking-Horse Winner," so also do coordinating conjunctions *and* and *but*, and less frequently *yet* and *so*.[72]

The use of *and, but, so, yet,* and *then* at the beginnings of sentences, along with the frequent insertion of semicolons between two short, simple sentences, accounts for the paucity of regular compound or compound/complex sentences that tend to create the impression of both expansiveness and looseness. Instead, the effect of Lawrence's simple and complex sentences, and of successive sentences linked by initial coordinating conjunctions, is of rather brief yet connected waves of words that propulsively carry the reader along. Lawrence's use of parataxis—short sentences linked by commas rather than by coordinating conjunctions—also creates the impression of forward movement, vitality, and speed.

Within clauses Lawrence often used adjectival and adverbial phrases—frequently beginning with a past participle, or even more frequently, with a present participle—*after* the noun or verbs they modify. He also employed *ing* words, either as verbs in the progressive present or past tense (*is going, was going*) or as adjectives before nouns (*living* thing). The repeated use of verbs that end in *ing* is emblematic of key elements in Lawrence's metaphysic—the Heraclitean flux, the eternal process of becoming, the constant flow of emotions between polarities. When Miriam responds positively to one of Paul's sketches but cannot say why she likes it so well, he explains the "truth" of it to her:

> It's because—it's because there is scarcely any shadow in it; it's more shimmery, as if I'd painted the shimmering protoplasm in the leaves and everywhere, and not the stiffness of the shape. That seems dead to me. Only this shimmeriness is the real living. The shape is a dead crust. The shimmer is inside really. (152)

Sons and Lovers

It is the "shimmeriness"—what Lawrence would have called the "livingness" and "quickness"—of inanimate and animate objects as well as of life experience that is captured through the novelist's language; his frequent use of *ing* words and phrases is, in grammatical and syntactical terms, but one surface manifestation of this quality.

Another feature of Lawrence's prose style in *Sons and Lovers*—parallelism, or, in general, the repetition of key elements or structures in a sentence—is an aspect of sentence structure, as well as of diction, that is pervasive in Lawrence's prose, as I pointed out in the preceding chapter on "The Rocking-Horse Winner." Certainly, it permeates *Sons and Lovers*: scarcely a paragraph in the novel fails to manifest Lawrence's tendency to repeat words and phrases and sometimes, with or without incremental variation, entire clauses. Frequently, Lawrence constructs sentences in units of two or three, especially three verbs:

> Mr. Pappleworth *picked up* the whitey blue knee-band, *examined* it, and its yellow order paper quickly, and *put* it on one side. Next was a flesh-pink "leg." He *went* through the few things, *wrote* out a couple of orders, and *called* to Paul to accompany him. (106)

Even more blatantly, he repeats verbs and participles, phrases or variations of phrases, and even the structure of entire clauses:

> Frequently he *hated* Miriam. He *hated* her as she *bent forward* and *pored over* his things. He *hated* her way of patiently casting him up, as if he were an endless psychological account. When he was with her, he *hated* her *for having got him*, and yet *not got him*, and he tortured her. (293)

As I noted in my analysis of paradox in "The Rocking-Horse Winner," Lawrence's prose, both within and between sentences and paragraphs, is saturated with antithesis as an expression of the inner and external conflicts that dominate the individual psychology and relationships of his characters, and also as a manifestation of his sense of the duality underlying all experience.[73] As in "The Rocking-Horse Winner," antithesis in *Sons and Lovers* is epitomized by a constant use of the coordinating conjunction *but*, along with a less frequent use of *nevertheless*, *however*, and *and yet*. It is also reflected in opposites like *love* and *hate*, *freedom* and *imprisonment*, *distance* and *closeness*, *life* and *death*. Often, contradictory statements are juxtaposed without the use of conjunctions, or a question or series of statements is followed by a brief negative remark. Conversations are full of antithetical statements. On almost any page of the novel one finds sentences and passages such as the following:

> She sat trembling slightly, *but* her heart brimming with contempt. What would she do if he went to some other pit, obtained work and got in with another woman? *But* she knew him too well —he couldn't. She was dead sure of him. *Nevertheless*, her heart was gnawed inside her. (43)

> "We aren't lovers, we are friends," he said to her. "Let them talk. What does it matter what they say?" Sometimes, as they were walking together, she slipped her arm timidly into his. *But* he always resented it, and she knew it. It caused a violent conflict in him. (173)

> She wanted to do penance. So she kneeled to Dawes, and it gave him a subtle pleasure. *But* the distance between them was still very great—too great. It frightened the man. It almost pleased the woman. (304)

> "She's dead. What was it all for—her struggle?" That was his despair wanting to go after her.
> "You're alive."
> "She's not."
> "She is—in you."
> Suddenly he felt tired with the burden of it. (412)

> Always alone, his soul oscillated, first on the side of death, then on the side of life, doggedly. (412)

The see-saw of emotions suggested by Lawrence's constant use of antithesis in syntax and in dialogue is fundamental to Lawrence's preoccupation with the intense, larger-than-life struggles within and between his characters.

Finally, as in "The Rocking-Horse Winner," and elsewhere, a poetic feature of Lawrence's prose style in *Sons and Lovers* is the author's use of diction, grammar, and syntax to mimic visual, aural and kinesthetic experience. The convoluted tangle of Paul Morel and Baxter Dawes locked in combat is embodied in a complicated, repetitive, muscular, rhythmically jerky sentence, with its string of adjectival participial phrases and catalogues of adjectives:

> He lay pressed hard against his adversary, his body adjusting itself to its one pure purpose of choking the other man, resisting exactly at the right moment, with exactly the right amount of strength, the struggles of the other, silent, intent, unchanging, gradually pressing its knuckles deeper,

feeling the struggles of the other body become wilder and more frenzied. (366)

Some elongated, loose, climactic sentences, distinguished by repetitiveness and strings of coordinating conjunctions, encapsulate the cosmic, "swept-away" feelings of passion for which Lawrence is justly renowned:

> As a rule, when he started love-making, the emotion was strong enough to carry with it everything—reason, soul, blood—in a great sweep, like the Trent carries bodily its backswirls and intertwinings, noiselessly. Gradually the little criticisms, the little sensations were lost, everything borne along in one flood. . . . It was as if he, and the stars, and the dark herbage, and Clara were licked up in an immense tongue of flame, which tore inwards and upwards. (363)

The speed, directness, and flow generated by the syntax of Lawrence's propulsive prose in *Sons and Lovers* is re-created only in parts and aspects of the movie. Certainly, in terms of overall narrative and chronological structure, the film progresses smoothly and linearly from the spring of one year to the spring of the following. Although certain events, through artful editing, seem lengthened and thus heightened in impact and significance, nothing impedes the forward movement of time; there are no flashbacks, no slow or fast motion, nor is there any parallel cutting to indicate that events are taking place simultaneously. The film employs a temporal syntax as straightforward and fluid as the syntax of the simple and complex sentences that dominate the text.

Although the leisurely mise-en-scène style made possible by CinemaScope tended to discourage the rapid cutting associated with narrower screens,[74] for the sake of variety Cardiff employed both the mise-en-scène and classical Hollywood editing approaches in most scenes and sequences.[75] Indeed, analogous to Lawrence's conventional, rather simple sentence patterns is Cardiff's alternation of medium shots, medium closeups, close-ups and again medium close-ups, typical of Hollywood's classical style. Considering the brevity of most of Lawrence's sentences, one might expect the individual, shots in Cardiff's adaptation to be fairly short; in some sequences, cutting *is* relatively rapid. The traveling montages near the beginning of the film are marked by accelerating speed, movement and energy. There are also a number of sequences that employ classical cutting of fairly brief shots combined with more leisurely mise-en-scène photography. Despite segments of alternating brief single shots and some rapid sequences, however, Cardiff's distinct preference in *Sons and Lovers* is for longer shots that follow and reframe the figures as they move toward, past, or away from one another, or that track characters as they walk and then focus on them in uninterrupted takes when they come to rest. The director's reliance on longer takes tends to retard the film's overall pace, paradoxically creating the impression of sluggishness, weight and density even when the dialogue and movement within shots is swift and dynamic.[76] In this connection, the leisurely (one might say overly drawn-out) transitions between scenes and sequences—almost invariably lap dissolves or fadeouts to black—constitute a singularly un-Lawrentian type of cinematic punctuation, considering the author's fondness for short sentences ending in commas (parataxis) or semi-colons, and compound sentences artificially divided by periods before the coordinating conjunction.

Also retarding the pace of the film is Cardiff's habit of ending scenes and sequences with prolonged closeups of faces that merge into extended lap dissolves. Undoubtedly meant to convey intensity of emotion, reflectiveness, and inwardness, these close-ups are a cinematic equivalent for the sort of interrogative soul-searching the characters do in Lawrence's novel. However, passages of verbal introspection in the text have a rapid-fire, kinetic turbulence that meshes with the headlong quality of the narrative and descriptive sections: in the film, Cardiff's static, extreme closeups of penetrating narrowed or glistening eyes capture none of the characters' anguished self-questioning and analysis.

Though not nearly as pronounced in *Sons and Lovers* as in "The Rocking-Horse Winner," parallelism—the repetition of grammatical and syntactical structures—is a pervasive feature of the prose style of the novel and also of the structure and composition of shots, scenes, and sequences in the film as well. However, as a stylistic device it is not nearly as deliberate and noticeable as it is in Pelissier's *The Rocking-Horse Winner*, and as a consequence, in this respect at least, Cardiff's adaptation often seems quite un-Lawrentian.

To be sure, the standard classical Hollywood paradigm, characterized by parallel shot sequences, is used repeatedly. Many scenes in *Sons and Lovers* open with an establishing shot which quickly shifts to a medium shot or medium close-up and, during the scene, occasionally shifts back to the medium shot to reestablish the context. Alternatively, scenes open with a medium closeup of a character which expands to disclose an interior or exterior environment that quickly fills up with one or more additional characters. Throughout the film, there are brief medium or full-body shots, but for the most part, once a scene is established, the medium closeup—head to waist or just above waist—reigns supreme, usually shifting to a closeup of head and shoulders and, on a few occasions at the very end of a scene, to a headshot or an extreme closeup of a part of the face (usually the eyes and the nose). Despite the sort of predictable "parallelism" associated with the classical cinema, however, *Sons and Lovers* entirely lacks the pronounced and deliberate parallel cut sequences of *The Rocking Horse Winner*, so evocative of parallelism and antithesis in Lawrence's story.

As in the novel, paradoxical antithesis pervades the film of *Sons and Lovers*, both between and within shots, scenes, and sequences. Visual contrasts abound, such as in the shot of sheep grazing followed by a shot of the mine wheel, and the lengthy dissolve of Paul embracing Clara by firelight that overlaps spinning bobbins at Jordan's. Other obvious instances of antithesis are the parallel but contrasting sequences of Paul running joyfully toward Miriam's farm and, soon after, racing in a panic toward the just-exploded mine. Antithetical to an extreme closeup of Paul's face turned right as he gazes at Clara just after meeting her at Jordan's is a later companion shot of Miriam's tear-stained face turned left after Paul has dismissed their attempt at love-making. A closeup of sobbing Mrs. Morel clutching her bedpost after a tongue-lashing from her husband about her possessiveness towards her son is followed by a sweeping extra-long shot of the seacoast where Paul and Clara run hand in hand across a wide expanse of sand.

In longer sequences, moods are diametrically opposed. Paul's white-haired patron thrills the young man by offering him an art scholarship in London; immediately afterward, coal-besmeared Morel angrily confronts the fastidious Hadlock. A scene at Jordan's, in which Dawes warns Paul to stay away from his wife, is succeeded by an erotically charged closeup between Paul and Clara as they plan their seaside tryst. Comically juxtaposed are dressed-up Louisa and William, arriving early for the Morels' Christmas party, and towel-wrapped Morel, fresh from his bath.

Consistent with the novel's exploration of intrapsychic and interpersonal conflict, both aural and visual opposition pervade the film's individual shots and sequences. In almost every scene, the characters are verbally or emotionally at odds with one another. The visual effects also suggest conflict, tension, and paradox: birds flying explosively out of the mine headstock; Mrs. Morel or Clara contrasted with Paul's glamourized drawings of them; the raucous mine wheel cranking up casualties, counterpointed with the silent *pietà* of Mr. Morel and his dead son; an elegant automobile parked in front of the Morels' grimy proletarian row house; Paul standing stiffly on a balcony at Jordan's, holding a metal corset form, as the animated factory girls tease him; a group of suffragettes preaching against domestic slavery as a houseboat, festooned with billowing laundry, blows its foghorn and passes slowly by. Other antithetical shots and scenes include Paul and Clara's ersatz game of cribbage, their passion for each other visibly frustrated as Clara's mother intrusively patrols back and forth; the iron scaffolding on the beach, a backdrop for Paul and Clara's romantic tryst; and the real daffodils in the forest, harbingers of hope and rebirth, contrasted with Miriam's sadness during her final parting with Paul. Indeed, Paul and Miriam's last meeting is visually antithetical: Paul walks off into the forest as she turns and heads toward the camera in the foreground.

In many scenes, the focus shifts rhythmically back and forth between individuals and groups. For example, in the aftermath of the mine explosion, shots of onlookers alternate with shots of the bodies being brought up from underground. Repeated alternating shots also dominate other scenes—at Jordan's, during Paul's first meeting with the girls; at the exhibition hall as Paul, Miriam, and Mrs. Morel observe gallerygoers appraising Paul's painting; and at the suffragette rally in Nottingham, as Paul watches a group of onlookers question placard-holding demonstrators.

Even though the filmmakers constantly suggest antithesis through dialogue, cinematography, and editing, the screen adaptation of *Sons and Lovers* lacks the tension, thrust, and turbulence of the original, with its endless paradoxes and intimations of deeply divided psyches. This lack of seething and unresolved conflict is caused, in part, by the shrinkage and oversimplification of the narrative and, despite generally picturesque photography, by the conventionality of the shooting and editing techniques. But it is also the consistently tidy resolution of antithesis that is responsible for the un-Lawrentian slackness and tepidness of the film. A number of critics have noted that Lawrence's writing is pseudo-dialectical, containing thesis and antithesis but no synthesis. The prose in *Sons and Lovers* is certainly illustrative of this attribute; to the bitter end, the *buts*, *howevers*, and *nevertheless*es prevail, despite the affirmation abruptly suggested in the last lines of the novel. In the neater, more sanitized film version, however, loose ends are tied up in a manner uncharacteristic of Lawrence's messier, more ambivalent novel. In *Sons and Lovers*, every moment of communion or resolution simultaneously carries within it a dissolution of change of heart: in the film, the built-in contradictions are rendered in a linear fashion, and therefore lose their essential paradoxical Lawrentian quality of opposites rendered virtually simultaneously—yin synonymous with yang.

Finally, with a few notable exceptions, the pacing and editing of the film does not replicate the experiences depicted. Some scenes are appropriately staged quite slowly and statically, as in the lugubrious "morning after" scene between Paul and Miriam and in the dirgelike sequence after the mine explosion. By way of contrast, in one dynamic sequence—Paul's overnight at Clara's—the complex camera work and taut editing skillfully evoke mood, atmosphere, tension, and suspense. However, unlike Pelissier's *The Rocking-Horse Winner*, which contains many shots, scenes, and sequences in which the cinematic effects are strikingly analogous to the syntax of sentences and paragraphs in the short story on which it is based, in much of *Sons and Lovers* there is a rather noticeable absence of creative cinematic techniques that mirror Lawrence's distinctive syntax. The film is shot and edited quite conservatively and for the most part unimaginatively, with few unsettling compositions, distorted camera angles, or unusual visual or aural effects that reproduce the rapidity, dynamism, and energy generated by Lawrence's muscular, impetuous prose.

Paragraph Shape and Rhythm in the Novel; Rhythm in the Film

Critics of Lawrence's fiction have long recognized the rhythmic, cadenced sentences and paragraphs, rooted in the King James version of the Bible and in the Congregational hymns that permeated the author's boyhood, as the hallmark of his prose. Few critics. however, have attempted to analyze in detail Lawrentian rhythms in specific works.[77] Such analysis, with attention to repetition of metrical patterns and syntactical structures within sentences as well as the relative length and number of sentences within paragraphs, confirms the impression that Lawrence's prose is indeed highly rhythmic, although, as one might expect, in longer works, such as *Sons and Lovers*, the rhythm, distinctive in certain passages, varies from paragraph to paragraph.

As in "The Rocking-Horse Winner," both the length and the shape of Lawrence's paragraphs in *Sons and Lovers* are significant. In general, paragraphs are remarkably short: among the first four paragraphs which open each of the novel's 15 chapters, the average number of sentences is 6.1 and the average length in words is 90 (in the earlier chapters, paragraphs tend to be even briefer—an average of 62 words). In Part Two, upon which the film adaptation is based, the paragraphs are often longer, averaging 98 words.

The swelling shape of paragraphs noted in "The Rocking-Horse Winner" can occasionally be found in *Sons and Lovers*, but more typically, the sentences in each paragraph grow longer and remain so, or—even more often—alternate between short and long, or long and short, in a seesaw pattern that suggests the undulation of waves. The same swelling or wavelike patterns discernible within paragraphs also prevail in the relative length of succeeding paragraphs. In each chapter paragraphs tend to start at a medium length, grow shortish, and then swell to much greater lengths.

Within and between sentences, hypnotic, insistent rhythmic effects are achieved largely through repetition of metrical patterns, as well as by repetition of words, sounds, and syntactical constructions and by the coupling of repeated sounds with words that are emphasized (that is, receive a heavy beat or accent), as in Anglo-Saxon poetry. The driving, rapidfire propulsiveness typical of much of Lawrence's narrative prose in *Sons and Lovers* stems in large part from the continuity and flow between sentences, to which Anaïs Nin referred when she wrote perceptively of the "undercurrent of rhythm" especially typical of Lawrence's later works (e.g., *Women in Love*) but embryonically present in *Sons and Lovers*:

> The words almost cease to have a meaning; they have a cadence and flow, and Lawrence gives in to the cadence. That is why there are so many "ands" and *enchainements*, repetitions like choruses, words that are made to suggest more than their own determinate, formal significance.[78]

Occasionally, Lawrence's prose rhythms in *Sons and Lovers* are choppy and staccato, especially in passages evoking conflict, tension or distress, or in passages of dialogue, most of which consist of sentences ten words or under. Sometimes the impression created is of bullet-like speed, but more typically, Lawrence breaks up a very brief chronological time segment into short sentences of ten words or under that paradoxically create an illusion of suspended and elongated time. In passages of description, the relative paucity of short, tripping multiple syllables and the frequently heavy accents retard the pace of the prose and inspire contemplation.

Although exact equivalents of a literary text's prose rhythms are rarely apparent in a film adaptation, rough approximations are discernible, as we have seen in the "rocking" rhythms and climactic scenes and sequences of Pelissier's *The Rocking Horse Winner*. As also noted, classic Hollywood cinematic techniques of the forties and fifties dictated certain norms of syntax and rhythm that were intrinsic to the structure of narrative films of the period and that would undoubtedly have been imposed on the film adaptation of *Sons and Lovers* regardless of the rhythms in the original text. The question remains to what extent did the director of *Sons and Lovers* and his film editor deliberately or accidentally replicate Lawrence's uniquely rhythmic prose? The answer, in this instance, is equivocal. Not surprisingly, the film version of *Sons and Lovers* has visual and aural rhythms that conform to Hollywood norms; however, except in specific scenes and sequences, and in certain aspects, the rhythms are not particularly Lawrentian.

Unlike much of the text, with its relatively short sentences and paragraphs that create a generally speedy effect, the overall pace of the film, as already noted, is relatively slow; indeed, the average shot length (ASL) is just under 13 seconds, which is a bit longer than the ASL of 11 seconds in other wide-screen Hollywood films of the period, but far slower than the six-second ASL of typical films of the 1930s.[79] To be sure, the pace of *Sons and Lovers*—like the pace of the novel—is by no means uniform; the opening section of the film, ending with the mine explosion, is relatively rapid, with an average shot length of under nine seconds. The next section, focusing on Paul's troubled relationship with Miriam, is considerably slower, with an ASL of 12½ seconds. The section devoted to Paul's passionate love affair with Clara is the speediest of all, although the pace of the final section of the film, depicting the illness and death of Mrs. Morel, with an ASL of 12 seconds, is quite literally funereal. In the two slower segments, shots last as long as 57 seconds, and a number are 30 seconds to 45 seconds in length. In the faster segments, shots may be no more than one or two seconds long. Despite the alternating variations of speed from segment to segment, which corresponds to the wavelike quality of Lawrence's paragraphs, the overall impression created once the film gets underway is measured and unhurried, not only because of the slow pace but also, perhaps, because there is little strenuous or rapid physical action in the film; 65 percent of the scenes consist of indoor conversations (albeit heated at times) between the principals.

The previously noted temperateness generated by the film's average shot length is heightened by the regularity of smooth, stately, and fluid transitions between scenes—almost entirely dissolves, extended lap dissolves, or, in a few instances, fades to black. A cinematic feature connected to these transitions and reminiscent of the shape of Lawrentian paragraphs which swell to longer sentences is the frequent use of lengthy closeups or extreme closeups at the ends of scenes, which, in conjunction with lap dissolves, prolong cinematic and psychological time. An especially striking transition that occurs after Miriam's futile surrender to Paul is an extreme closeup of the upper part of her tear-stained face superimposed over a prolonged shot of a snowy landscape of Bestwood at Christmas. In one sense, these drawn-out, nonjarring transitions mirror—in slow motion—the fluidity and flow of

Lawrence's sentences. Indeed, in many sections of the film, in terms of camera movement, length of shots, and easy transitions, the effect is as smooth and streamlined as if the film were moving on well-oiled ball bearings. Such unbroken smoothness, however, does not suggest the author's self-described "hard, violent style," with its driving rhythms, nor is it in accord with Lawrence's climactic or wavelike paragraphs.

Despite the un-Lawrentian leisureliness of the film's overall pace, *Sons and Lovers* does contain individual scenes that convey the kinesthetic energy of the novel's prose. For example, the opening scene between Paul and Mrs. Morel, one long fluid take that tracks Mrs. Morel's brisk, bustling movements back and forth from one side of the kitchen/dining room to the other while Paul moves towards and away from the camera, is pulsatingly rhythmic. The brief long shots of Paul, Miriam, Mrs. Morel, and the townspeople racing in the mine, beginning quite uniformly at three seconds each and lengthening to five or six seconds when the bodies are brought up from below, also suggest the rhythms of the text. The tiny figures of Clara and Paul running hand-in-hand together, alternately moving and motionless against a broad, sweeping backdrop of sea and sand, create striking temporal and visual rhythms.

In a number of scenes, a rhythm is deliberately created by symmetrically repeating similar shots, often in trios, of objects or persons. For example, at the suffragette rally in Nottingham, there are repeated cuts from the feminist spokeswoman and Clara to each of several onlookers—Paul, a bearded man, a middle-aged couple. At the art exhibition in Nottingham, Paul, his mother and Miriam look on as a disdainful, well-heeled couple, a white-haired patron, and an admiring pair of middle-aged men assess Paul's portrait of his father: director Cardiff steadily alternates between the anxious threesome and the bemused gallerygoers. In the wryly comical scene in which Paul awkwardly embraces a corset form as the Spiral girls at Jordan's tease him by singing an off-color song, Cardiff cuts four times from a medium shot of Paul to medium closeups of the girls. However, the rhythms achieved through regular repetition in all of these scenes, as in others like it, are schematic, steady, and predictable whereas Lawrence's alternately flowing and choppy rhythms, despite their repetitiveness, are full of nuance and variation. Only in the film's sole relatively complex sequence—Paul's overnight at Clara's house—is the repetition of shots effective in heightening the climactic buildup of tension between the would-be lovers: the shot/reverse shots of Paul and Clara from different angles and increasingly close distances accelerate in speed as the camera zeroes in on their yearning, expressive faces.

To some degree, alternating moods and locales also mimic the wavelike rhythms of the text: the otherwise somber film is leavened by bits of comic relief, especially in the first half, and the settings are varied by consistently alternating outdoor with indoor scenes (about one-third are shot outdoors). Despite the recurrence of shots, locales, actions, sounds, and images, and the patterned, deliberate alternation of moods, however, the use of repetition in the film adaptation of *Sons and Lovers*, so marked in the novel, tends to be perfunctory, superficial, and restrained, with few surprises and little syncopation. Lawrence's repetitiousness in *Sons and Lovers* (and elsewhere) is relentlessly hyperbolic, generating a feverish, even hypnotic intensity that throbs and pulsates; sometimes choppy, sometimes connected and flowing, it is meant to heighten and electrify the reader's experience of the objects and phenomena described. The slack, predictable rhythms in the film, for the most part incapable of startling and arousing viewers or sweeping them away, are faint, attenuated echoes of the driving rhythms of the text.

Imagery and Symbolism in the Novel and the Film

The pervasiveness of concrete, realistic images that are also symbolic—"organic units of consciousness with a life of their own"[80]—has been noted by almost all explicators of *Sons and Lovers*, and indeed, of Lawrence's fictions in general. "Perhaps in no other novelist do we find the image so largely replacing episode and discursive analysis, and taking over the expressive function of these, as it does in Lawrence," observed Dorothy Van Ghent:

> Lawrence's gift for the symbolic image was a function of his sensitivity to and passion for the meaning of real things—for the individual expression that real forms have. In other words, his gift for the image arose directly from his vision of life as infinitely creative of individual identities, each whole and separate and to be reverenced as such.[81]

Like the paradoxical characters and actions explored in the novel, the images in *Sons and Lovers*, according to Judith Farr, are antipodal—contrasting "space and closure, darkness and light, nature, and the machine. . ."[82] Daniel Schneider views the images in *Sons and Lovers* as "issuing from the recurrent conflict between life and life constriction."

Life is quick, open, free, flowing, running, loose, alert, natural, easy or spontaneous. When life is thwarted, it is ill, hurt, awkward, unreal, bound, or imprisoned. These antinomies are everywhere.[83]

One of the "antinomies" central to *Sons and Lovers* is the contrast between nature and industry.[84] As Alfred Kazin has observed, Lawrence is "a great novelist of landscape."[85] Indeed, *Sons and Lovers* is saturated with nature imagery; perhaps no other novel in history is so resplendent with fields and gardens full of flowers—roses, phlox, lilies, sunflowers, fuchsia, daffodils, carnations, honeysuckle, and sweet-peas, among many others. A link between the human and the nonhuman, the fragrant, colorful flowers in *Sons and Lovers* generate bonds between people, give keen aesthetic and sensory (visual and olfactory) pleasure, call forth deep emotions, and convey powerful subliminal messages. They also symbolize a wide range of phenomena.[86]

Death, for example, is represented by the chrysanthemums at William's funeral and the cowslips that Paul scatters over Clara's neck when he first becomes aware of his powerful attraction to her. Romantic love and courtship are suggested by the forget-me-nots, blue violets, and daisies that Paul picks for his mother and the dahlias offered to Clara by an elderly woman in a teashop after she and Paul have become lovers. Purity and spiritual exaltation are symbolized by the madonna lilies in Mrs. Morel's garden and by the white wild rose bush to which Miriam leads a reluctant Paul for a much-desired religious communion. Sexual passion, on the other hand, is epitomized by the purple irises with "fleshy throats" (294) whose coarse fragrance prompts Paul to break off with Miriam. Eroticism is also symbolized by the bunch of scarlet carnations Paul gives to Clara just before he makes love to her beside the Rivert Trent. The powerfully scented madonna lilies that intoxicate and "pollinate" pregnant Mrs. Morel as she wanders in her garden at night, after being locked out of the house by her drunken husband, represent a mysterious and compelling life force.

In the novel, the instinctive response of characters to flowers is an index of their psychic health. Miriam's morbidly possessive, anthropomorphic attitude toward flowers sharply contrasts with Clara's refusal to pick them and with Paul and Mrs. Morel's wholesome, unsentimental enjoyment of both growing flowers and "dead" (picked) ones.[87]

Though not nearly so pervasive as flowers, trees also figure significantly as generators and indexes of feeling in *Sons and Lovers*, in particular the ash tree near the Morels' home on Scargill Street.[88] Morel likes the "shrieking tree" that catches the "west wind sweeping from Derbyshire," although the

Morel children fear the noises it makes and associate it with the "anguish of home discord." (59) The ash tree is also connected with William's death. Awaiting his brother's coffin, Paul gazes out at the tree, "monstrous and black in front of the wide darkness." (138) Later in the novel, when Paul begins work at Jordan's, his altered attitude towards the tree, "which seemed a friend now," (113) reflects a more positive phase in his life.[89]

Trees are also associated with Paul's artistic and spiritual development and with his relationship with Miriam. Painting some pine trees at sunset, Paul characterizes them as "God's burning bush," and awkwardly compares Miriam, "always sad," to one of the singular pine trees that "flares up" (152). Courting Miriam "like a lover," he climbs high in a cherry tree at sunset and, in a pagan ritual, shakes the red fruits down on her. Afterward, they walk into "the thick plantation of fir-trees and pines" where it rains and Paul speaks of "the darkness" that he longs to "melt out into" and "sway there, identified with the Great Being"(285–287). In this instance, trees are associated with sexual ecstasy and with Paul's growing mysticism.

Water imagery in *Sons and Lovers* is usually the backdrop of (and sometimes a metaphor for) romantic and erotic encounters. Paul and Clara consummate their love by the flooded River Trent, characterized as a dark, sinuous animal "intertwining itself like some subtle, complex creature" (305). Later in the novel, the powerfully surging emotions and sensations of Paul's lovemaking are again compared to the river, which "carries bodily its black swirls and intertwinings, noiselessly"(363). On the way to Theddlethorpe, Paul walks with Miriam along "the great sweeping shore of sand," (178) and later bathes with Clara along the Lincoln coast. Rain falls in the forest when Paul and Miriam first become lovers; appropriately, it also falls on the mourners at Mrs. Morel's funeral.

Food, a natural image that recurs frequently in the novel, carries all sorts of symbolic overtones. Shunned by his family, Mr. Morel eats with increasing brutishness; his solitary meals become primitive rituals of alienation.[90] For genteel Mrs. Morel, meals are ceremonies of civility. Offers of food in the novel are symbolic of affection: after a violent quarrel, Mr. Morel brings tea—with sugar—to Mrs. Morel in bed. Sharing food is also associated with romantic intimacy: Paul takes tea in Nottingham with Clara after they have made love the first time, and he and Miriam role-play husband and wife as they dine together during their week of sexual intimacy in her grandmother's cottage. Bread burnt in the oven, an image heavy with Freudian overtones, becomes an emblem of sexual transgression when Paul, distracted by the flirtatious Beatrice Wilde and by the presence of Miriam, lets his mother's precious loaves overbake. A symbol of life itself,[91] the food that Paul longs to withhold from his mother during her final weeks both sustains her and becomes the agent of her death, when he and his sister poison Mrs. Morel's milk with an overdose of morphine.

Animals in *Sons and Lovers* are symbolic of unself-conscious spontaneity, healthy sexuality, and, in general, the joys of the instinctual life. Both fowl and birds are associated with Paul's relationship with Miriam and Clara. Fourteen-year-old Miriam is terrified to allow a hen to peck food from her outstretched hand and is similarly repelled by the rutting livestock on the farm. Paul, on the other hand, is attracted to the vitality, sensuality, and naturalness of birds and fowl. Not long after he first meets Miriam, Mrs. Leivers asks Paul to touch a jenny wren's nest: "It's almost as if you were feeling inside the live body of the bird," he says. "It's so warm. . ." (148). Paul also discerns unself-conscious spirituality in a bird's flight. "It's not religious to be religious," he tells Miriam. "I reckon a crow is religious when it sails across the sky. But it only does it because it feels itself carried to where it's going, not because it thinks it is being eternal" (250–251). Birds are also associated with sexual and emotional rapture: when Paul loses himself making passionate love to Clara, the peewits scream in the field.

Like Paul, Clara is attracted to animals, although she is ambivalent about the animality of men. When Clara, Miriam, and Paul encounter a lonely woman living on a cattle farm, the woman's brother is leading a stallion, "a big red beast." "As loving as any man!" says Miss Limb, to which Clara replies, "More loving than most men, I should think" (235). Later, pondering Miss Limb's isolation, Clara blurts out, "I suppose . . . she wants a man" (236). Clearly, Lawrence sees the stallion as symbolic of the male sexual partner missing in both women's lives.

Contrasted with imagery from nature are largely negative images from the realms of commerce and industry—the coal pits and the railroad; the wooden legs, elastic stockings, trusses, sewing and manufacturing machinery at Jordan's Surgical Appliances firm; and the spinning jenny over which Clara and her mother toil at home. For Paul, entering the urban world of work is like going to jail. Despite Paul's reluctance to submit to the monotonous discipline of the business world, his vision of the mines, connected with the masculine vitality of his father and with the mysterious life force itself, is remarkably benign, even mystical:

> "The world is a wonderful place," she said, "and wonderfully beautiful."
> "And so's the pit," he [Paul] said. "Look how it heaps together, like something alive almost—a big creature that you don't know." (123)

References to moonlight, sunlight, and firelight abound in *Sons and Lovers*. Streaming white light, associated with the moon, is often linked with the feminine principle (specifically Mrs. Morel and Miriam) and represents purity, spiritual ecstasy, and ultimately, death. Goldenness, as well as redness, is connected with maternity and new life, as when contrite Mrs. Morel thrusts her unwanted infant Paul up to the "crimson, throbbing sun" (37) in a primitive act of dedication. Goldenness is also associated with the beauty of sunflowers and daffodils and with fire, a symbol of life and sexual passion. Gertrude Morel is powerfully attracted by youthful Walter Morel: "The dusky, golden softness of this man's sensuous flame of life, that flowed off his flesh like the flame from a candle . . . seemed to her something wonderful, beyond her" (10). Paul's affair with Clara is characterized as "a baptism of fire" (318). When Paul's mother lies dying, he sees "the red firelight leaping in her bedroom window." "When she's dead," he says to himself, "that fire will go out" [92] (390). Indeed, the sustaining hearth fire is the center of family life: Morel comforts himself before it as he eats his solo breakfast at dawn; Mrs. Morel sews beside it; baths are taken publicly in front of it, and the teakettle and iron are forever warming on it. Fire is also associated with ritual sacrifice, as when Paul burns his sister Annie's doll.

Although alluded to far less frequently than light, darkness is a recurring image in *Sons and Lovers*. A symbol for Lawrence of the "unknown, from which all life comes," [93] darkness is associated with the mysterious depths of the female psyche and with the upsurging of intense feelings and awarenesses linked with powerful forces in nature. As Dorothy Van Ghent points out:

> Darkness . . . has in Lawrence a special symbolic potency. It is a natural and universal symbol, but it offers itself with special richness to Lawrence because of the character of the governing vision. Darkness is half of the rhythm of the day, the darkness of the unconsciousness is half of the rhythm of the mind, and the darkness of death is half of the rhythm of life.[94]

For many of the characters, darkness has positive associations. Intrepid Mr. Morel, who disappears each day "down pit" and emerges covered with dirt, prefers darkness even at home, where he keeps the blinds down and the candle lit in daylight. Darkness for Paul is associated with places he loves— the church, the forest—as well as with spiritual exaltation and harmony

("The highest of all was to melt out into the darkness and sway there, identified with the Great Being," 287) and with sexual passion (Paul refuses to make love to Clara in the daylight).

Positive as images of darkness tend to be throughout the novel, in the final chapter darkness is associated with the profound depression Paul experiences during and after Mrs. Morel's terminal illness. Tempted to follow his mother to the grave, Paul leaves Miriam for the last time and wanders aimlessly through the "vastness and terror" of the country night, experiencing himself as a "speck of flesh." Despite his "nothingness," however, he resists suicide and turns towards the lights of the city: "He would not take that direction, to the darkness, to follow her. He walked towards the faintly humming, glowing town, quickly" (420).

Contrasting images of space and closure pervade *Sons and Lovers*, reflecting a "recurrent conflict between life and life constriction."[95] Hilltops, valleys, roads, fields, meadows, pastures, woods, orchards, seaside, and "the great scoop of darkness" (76) outside Paul's boyhood home on Scargill Street, are all settings for joyous, unconstrained activity. Images of quickness and spontaneity are often associated with Paul ("She [Clara] loved him for his unexpected movements, like a young animal," 266; "Clara was conscious of his quick, vigorous body as it came and went, seemingly blown quickly by a wind at its work," 322).

Such images, however, are countered by recurring references to bondage and restriction, against which the characters rebel. Institutions, such as home, school, army, hospital, and business are anathema to Miriam Leivers, Paul, Arthur and Walter Morel, Baxter Dawes, and become so even to William Morel, who returns to Bestwood in a coffin—the ultimate image of confinement. In man-made structures, life is often narrowly oppressive. The pit confines the spirit of Walter Morel, as does the "little darkish room" off the parlour where Clara and her mother make lace (259). Also oppressive are Mrs. Morel's parlor, "the beastly cold sunless hole" (98) where no plant grows; the "dungeon" (108) at Jordan's Surgical Appliance firm; and the gloomy bedroom where Mrs. Morel slowly dies of cancer. Clothing is similarly confining. Stiff collars representing bourgeois gentility are often removed as a gesture of spiritual and physical liberation, as when Paul unfastens his collar before making love to Miriam and Clara. The erysipelas that kills William erupts as a fierce red rash under his overly tight collar—a bitter irony.

The descriptions of clothing worn by various characters in *Sons and Lovers* are revelatory of underlying attitudes as well as of more superficial class distinctions. Puritanical yet tasteful Mrs. Morel, who dresses in black silk most of the time, casts a cold eye on finery, associating it with frivolity, youthful irresponsibility, and sensual indulgence. When William rents a Highland suit for a fancy-dress ball, Mrs. Morel, "afraid of her son's going the same way as his father," (54) refuses to unpack it or look at her son in it. To Mrs. Morel's disgust, Walter Morel, once a snappy dresser, spends most of his waking hours in filthy work clothes; his pit garments, drying nightly before the fireplace, are a constant reminder of the sweaty animality of his life underground. Unaware of her rosy beauty, Miriam, who first appears as a "girl in a dirty apron," (124) wears frayed old dresses symbolic of her lowly class and inferior gender. As her love for Paul grows, she fusses over her blouses and dresses in hopes that Paul will take favorable notice of her.

When Paul first sees Clara Dawes, she is wearing a "large, dowdy hat" and a simple dress that makes her "look rather sacklike" (185). As he becomes more attracted to her, descriptions of her clothing focus on her heightened sensuality—the lack of stays under her blouses, the free movement of her breasts, the way her clothes hug her body and emphasize her "beautiful figure" (305). At one point, Clara divests herself of all clothes; when Paul sleeps overnight at her house, he finds her kneeling naked in a pile of white underclothing on the hearth rug (338).

Boots—dirty or clean, intact or broken—are symbolic in *Sons and Lovers*. In his psychoanalytic interpretation of the novel, Daniel Weiss compares the ritual of Paul's cleaning Clara's boots after they make love by the flooded river, symbolic of restoring her respectability, to his cleaning his mother's boots which, in fact, need no cleaning. According to Weiss, clean boots represent chastity and bourgeois fastidiousness; dirty boots, which Paul abhors, are associated with his proletarian father and with illicit sex.[96]

Not surprisingly, as with the diction in the novel, the common link in much of the imagery in *Sons and Lovers* is a covert and sometimes overt eroticism. The sense of the visual world, animate or inanimate, as charged with a palpable sexuality as well as with sexual metaphors and symbols is the distinctive feature of Lawrence's prose and poetry and the aspect of it that was most revolutionary and therefore disturbing to contemporary readers.

To be sure, the British romantic poets had attributed human feelings to objects in nature, and had also celebrated physical and spiritual responses evoked by natural phenomena. With the possible exception of Blake and Keats, however, none had depicted nature as anthropomorphically bristling with a very nearly human sexuality. Flowers with "fleshy throats" and "coarse fragrance," (294) pine trees that "flare up," (153) rivers that "slide in a body," (306) jenny wrens with "warm breasts," (148) golden flesh that flames "like a candle," (10) burnt bread loaves, a huge red stallion "more loving than most men," (235) coal pits daily penetrated by half-clothed miners—all of these images (some of which verge on metaphor) have obvious sexual connotations. Indeed, almost every setting in the novel, whether the mines, Jordan's factory, the midlands countryside, the seaside, the Leivers' farm, is a backdrop and often a catalyst for the characters' emerging erotic awareness. It would seem reasonable, therefore, to expect that a film based on *Sons and Lovers* would visually (and aurally) convey Lawrence's perception of the underlying eroticism of the animate and inanimate world; that perception, enshrined in his rhythmic, cadenced prose, was his unique gift to the English novel.

In the novel *Sons and Lovers*, nature is a pervasive backdrop and dynamic presence in the experiences of the principal characters. In the film, however, the natural landscape is not nearly as prominently featured; instead, it is used, as it was in British romantic poetry, to convey feeling states, often between lovers. Trees, for example, are a gauge of emotional climate. Near the beginning of the film, when Paul and Miriam's relationship is tender and close and the mood is upbeat, the two stroll along an autumnal, tree-shaded pond. At Christmas, some time after their failed effort at lovemaking, Paul breaks off with Miriam beside the same pond, now frozen and surrounded by snow and bare trees that symbolize the termination of their once promising courtship. After Mrs. Morel's death near the end of the film, a long shot of the forest reveals both trees and daffodils, harbingers of spring, just beginning to bloom. Here, Paul and Miriam accidentally meet and part for good, each presumably moving on to a new and better life. However, the somber expression on Miriam's face as she walks toward the camera belies—for her, at least—the symbolism of rebirth suggested by the budding trees and flowers, as do the dying freesias Paul gives to Miriam in the novel after their last meeting in his rented room.

Individual trees and bushes significant throughout the novel (the ash, cherry, and white rose) are not key images in the film. However, after Paul has attempted to kiss Miriam, and her mother has denounced sex as "horrible," Miriam embraces a tree and prays that if she may love Paul, she may love him "splendidly." In this scene, the bifurcated tree trunk, which resembles outstretched thighs, is subliminally and ironically erotic. Clinging to one of the boughs, Miriam piously gazes heavenward, an image symbolic of the conflict between flesh and spirit that pervades the novel.

Flowers, which saturate the novel and are its primary symbol, are barely visible in the film.[97] If Lawrence was quixotically obsessed with the manner in which his characters picked flowers as indicative of their attitudes toward life, death, and love, the filmmakers used the few flowers in evidence in far less subtle and imaginative ways. In the novel, Clara's priggish refusal to pick flowers and Paul's unself-conscious pleasure in doing so becomes the occasion for a serious dialogue that reveals an underlying conflict that dooms their relationship. In the film, picked flowers become an occasion for Clara's hypocritical moral condemnation of Paul. When Paul pursues Clara after the suffragette rally, he bends down to pluck snowdrops growing along a Nottingham canal. "Don't pick them," says Clara, as in the flower-gathering scene in the novel; "They want to be left." When Paul picks them anyway, as in the novel ("I like them and I want them"), Clara compares his plucking of the flowers to his callous treatment of Miriam: "So you take what you want and when you're tired of it you throw it away?" she inquires acerbically. When Paul thrusts the flowers into her hand, Clara notes how icy they are and Paul archly replies that the ice melts when the flowers are held. In this scene, flowers are primarily a cinematic peg on which to hang tired Hollywood clichés.

Similarly, the daffodils Paul paints for his terminally ill mother are a hackneyed symbol for Paul's love of her and of his desire that she remain alive (in the novel, he longs for her death). The painted flowers can also be interpreted as suggesting the falsity and distortion that underlie Paul's incestuous relationship with his mother, a symbolism probably not intended by the unsubtle screenwriters, for whom the painting merely represented Paul's futile effort to offer hope and comfort to a dying woman. In any case, Mrs. Morel's mercifully quick death in the film, in marked contrast to her slow, agonized death in the novel, is trite and unmoving—a far cry from what could (and should) have been one of the most powerful and affecting sequences of the film.

Although the mines are portrayed far more positively in the novel than in the film, the contrast between the natural and the mechanical central to Lawrence's *Sons and Lovers* is established in the opening panning shot, with its pastoral image of sheep grazing in a field of waving grass followed by the squeaky turning of the mine headstocks that propels a flock of roosting birds into the empty sky. The intrusion of the machine into the unspoiled beauty of nature is also suggested in an episode not in the novel when Paul and Miriam, in the midst of a tender encounter beside a tranquil pond, are alerted to the explosion in the mine by ripples on the water's surface and a loud rumble. The powerful high-angle shot of the villagers running toward the mine, seen through the spokes of the headstock wheels, reduces human beings to mere ciphers and suggests the cruel dominion of industrialism over the villagers' limited and often wretched lives.

In the film, as in the novel, the world of machinery and commerce is repeatedly associated with monotony, oppression, and depersonalization. A series of shots of Paul walking through the streets of Nottingham on his first day at Jordan's surgical appliance factory suggests the restrictions of the industrial world: a low-angle shot of a huge clock which chimes three times (the sound of a clock is also heard after Arthur's funeral) indicates that the world of commerce is dedicated to punctuality.[98] The metal corset form that Paul is obliged to hold on his first day at Jordan's sardonically symbolizes the dehumanization and sexism of the world Paul is about to enter, as does the succeeding high-angle long shot of the factory room in which Mr. Pappleworth introduces the "girls" by the name of the surgical garment each produces ("Claudia and Lil, reinforced corsets; Beatrice, elastic hose; Dotty, knee caps").[99]

The mechanical world intrudes on Paul and Clara's love affair in a variety of shots and scenes. During the first meeting between Paul and Clara at Jordan's, the sound of machinery gets louder and louder as Paul gazes at the back of Clara's neck and she finally turns slowly to gaze back. Directly after they make passionate love by firelight, a scene during which the sound of a ticking clock becomes louder and louder, there is a lap dissolve to a full-screen shot of noisy, oversized, rotating bobbins, which symbolize the workaday industrial world with its repressive, impersonal constraints.

Water imagery plays a larger role in the film version of *Sons and Lovers* than it does in the novel. The pond at Miriam's farm, the canal in Nottingham and the seaside are settings for Paul's relationships with Miriam and Clara. Each, however, is intruded upon by discordant elements—the pond by a mine explosion, the "Venetian" canal by a noisy houseboat hung with laundry, and the sea coast by an iron construction. These intrusions suggest that encroaching industrialism destroys the naturalness, spontaneity, and intimacy of love between men and women. As Paul courts and beds Miriam, we hear water rhythmically driven by a water wheel, the quietly soothing sounds suggestive of their lukewarm sexual feelings for one another. Though not associated with Paul's protracted initial breakup with Miriam in the novel, the Leivers' frozen pond is a fitting if embarrassingly clichéd backdrop for his definitive split with her in the film.

Mr. Morel's once passionate connection with Mrs. Morel is evoked in the scene in which he bathes by the fireside in a metal tub of hot water and his wife reminisces about how attractive he was when he was younger. As Mrs. Morel tenderly washes her husband's back, Paul stares at his father, jealousy palpable in his gaze. After the arrival of William and his clinging fiancée, Paul and Mrs. Morel throw the father's bath water out the front door.

The discarded water, associated with a rekindling of feelings between the embattled Morels, suggests the transiency of passion—Paul's for Miriam and Clara, and Mrs. Morel's for her once-desirable husband.

The association of water and death is established in the scene early in the film in which Arthur reports his daredevil dive into the Nottingham canal, foreshadowing his imminent death underground. Also symbolic of sadness and death is the rain that falls after Arthur's funeral,[100] like that which drenches the mourners at Mrs. Morel's gravesite in the novel. Similarly, the demise of Paul and Clara's love affair is forecast by the rainy weather at their rather gloomy seaside tryst.

If the novel's images of food are associated with simple affection and romantic intimacy, with sexual and spiritual transgression, and with life itself, the film's images of food—even more numerous than those in the text—are used to symbolize the bonds, broken and unbroken, between members of the Morel household. Mrs. Morel's emotional dominance over her son and Paul's half-hearted attempt to challenge it is evident in the scene near the beginning of the film in which Paul refuses breakfast in his haste to run off to Miriam. In subsequent scenes, Mrs. Morel repeatedly offers Paul food when he comes home, and is disappointed when he has already eaten with either Miriam or Clara. Even on her deathbed, when Paul flies to her side, she offers to fix him a meal: "You'll be wanting your supper!"

The preparation and presentation of food is Mrs. Morel's means of binding Paul to her, and is paradoxically symbolic of her bondage to all men, including her sons. In the opening scene, Mrs. Morel hears bootsteps: "They're coming down and the kettle not boiling," she mutters anxiously, rushing to accommodate the menfolk. Mrs. Morel's attempts to convey her love to Paul through food are thwarted in the scene in which drunken Morel comes home, accidentally knocks his food from Mrs. Morel's hand, and appropriates Paul's dinner instead. When his wife protests, he throws Paul's dinner at the wall, shouting, "Then we'll *both* have bread and drippings!" Symbolized in the scene is the oedipal battle between father and son.

Even as Mrs. Morel "courts" Paul through food, Mr. Morel attempts to woo his estranged wife with culinary luxuries: a coconut he brings home from the fair (a reminder of one he won for her during their courtship) and a cup of tea he brings her in bed after a violent quarrel—both present in the novel.[101] Similarly, Mr. Morel tries to placate his son by fixing him breakfast, which Paul angrily refuses to eat until his mother orders him to.

In both the novel and the film, dining with the family is symbolic of being considered part of it. Frequently denied this ritual of social inclusion, Mr. Morel retaliates by behaving brutishly. After Arthur's funeral, Paul,

William, and Mrs. Morel sit together by the fireside having tea and talking enthusiastically about Paul's imminent employment as a clerk at Jordan's while Morel listens offscreen. Enraged by the contempt his family shows for his work and income, he bursts defiantly into the conversation (and the frame), announcing that he will drown his sorrows at the local pub.

In the novel, animals—birds and fowl in particular—are symbolic of the instinctual life and of unself-conscious physicality. In the film, images of animals are seldom featured, except in the opening shots and in scenes on Miriam's farm when, on arrival, Paul races through a bunch of pigs and jokes about one with Miriam:

> Paul: I'm sure she's the dark lady of the sonnets.
> Miriam: Oh no. She's the lady of the lake.

In this scene, the pig represents the earthy reality that Miriam longs to rise above. Birds, symbolic of naturalness and freedom, are also visible in the sky over the wintry beach where Paul and Clara run in romantic abandon and are referred to in dialogue as a symbol of spontaneity when Paul criticizes the religious fanaticism of Miriam's mother. "It's not religious just to be religious. I think a crow is religious as it sails across the sky. It's showing the glory of God but it doesn't know it."

In the novel, light of various kinds and degrees of intensity is associated with spiritual purity, the life force itself, sexual desire, attractiveness, and passion. In the film, light acquires a more specific symbolic significance, in contrast to darkness and shadowiness. In almost all indoor scenes including Mrs. Morel, a lit gas or kerosene lamp on a table, hanging from the ceiling, or carried is the first object we see, establishing maternal warmth and security in an otherwise cold environment. Mrs. Radford, Clara's mother, is also pictured fussing with a round lamp in her parlor.

A seeming contrast to the indoor light of the lamp, associated with binding motherhood and suffocating domestic intimacy, is the outdoor light of the midlands countryside and of Nottingham, where Paul courts Miriam and Clara. However, the contrast is superficial and deceptive: outdoor light turns out to be no more liberating than artificial indoor illumination. The pastoral midlands, in fact, is as much a prison as home or factory. "Will you ever be free?" Miriam asks Paul bitterly, when he rejects her the first time in a wintry outdoor setting. The answer is clear: neither of them will be truly free until they achieve financial and emotional independence and leave a repressive provincial world.

Flame and firelight, associated with sensuality, passion, and life itself in the novel, are used symbolically in the film—though in more conventional and clichéd ways than Lawrence's. In scenes at the Morels', the fire is almost always burning in the grate, symbolic of Mrs. Morel's abiding love for Paul as well as of the physical warmth and sustenance provided for the family. Food is cooked and water boiled for tea on the family hearth, and the family, except for Mr. Morel, eats before it. The lighted candle handed to Paul by Mrs. Radford forecasts the fire before which he and Clara soon embrace. In the following scene, in which Paul makes love to Clara, the phallic forks of flame in the parlor grate symbolize sexual desire and intercourse.

In a few of the film's scenes in which lighting is used expressionistically, there is a sharp contrast between light and darkness. After Miriam resists Paul's sexual advances in the barn, she moves away from him into a high-key pool of light which symbolizes purity and virginity,[102] while lustful Paul remains brooding in the deep shadows. When Mr. Morel visits his dying wife for the last time, he sits isolated and abject in the shadows to the right,[103] in contrast to Paul, who occupies the center of the frame, bent close to his mother in a brightly lit intimate tableau. Also, for the sake of variety, well-lighted scenes alternate with darker or grayer ones: the dimly lit views of the mine entrance and men leaving work at the beginning of the film are softened by the warmly lit interior of the Morels' kitchen and dining room. Succeeding shots of Paul running through a forest to Miriam's are an even brighter contrast in mood and lighting to the rather grim opening shots of the film. Scenes at night or in muted light—indoors or outdoors—are generally succeeded by scenes in bright light, indoors or outdoors.

Although darkness in the novel is generally positive and benign, except in the chapter dealing with Mrs. Morel's death, in the film darkness is repeatedly associated with rejection, loss, conflict, depression, and death. After Arthur's funeral, the Morel family and friends, dressed in dark gray or black and carrying black umbrellas, walk home slowly along a gloomy, rain-soaked, darkened street.[104] When Mrs. Morel is forced out of her house for hours at night by her drunken husband, the darkness and cold underscore her helplessness, her isolation from Morel, and her dependency on her son. Paul seduces Miriam at night, but at dawn their love-making's total failure to bring them closer becomes painfully apparent. Paul also fights Baxter Dawes in the dark near the railroad station. Near the end of the film, Paul sits brooding in the shadows by the fireside on the eve of his mother's death.

In the novel, one of the central themes is the contrast between freedom and bondage; the film, too, deploys contrasting images of spaciousness and closure, though images of constricted spaces predominate. The outdoors is a setting for untrammeled, spontaneous activity, as when Paul joyfully races to Miriam's farm, walks with her beside the pond, and runs on the beach with Clara. Even outdoor scenes, however, suggest enclosure. For example, the sequence in which Paul, Miriam, and the villagers run through the streets of Bestwood and its environs suggests the opposite of spaciousness: all roads lead inexorably to the mine, which dominates and destroys. Paul is frequently photographed outdoors at the apex of a V-shaped angle, hemmed in by walls or other surfaces on either side, as when he walks through the commercial district of Nottingham on his first day at Jordan's.

Consistent with the theme of bondage that runs through the novel, images of restriction and constraint are prevalent in the film. More often than not, the characters are "trapped" by indoor settings and furnishings and by tightly framed compositions, often medium closeups or closeups. Paul is almost invariably shot indoors in small, constricted rooms in which he appears restless, moody, and confined. Even in love-making scenes he is shown turning his back on both Miriam and Clara and staring out of the window toward the rear of the set.[105] The iron-barred bedstead in Mrs. Morel's bedroom and the curvy brass headboard in the seaside hotel room where Paul and Clara spend the night are both images of imprisonment: through the "bars" of the bedstead we see Clara naked under a sheet, clutching them like an inmate in jail.[106] Similarly, Paul and Clara's romp on the beach ends in a series of shots amidst a criss-crossed construction of iron girders, suggesting entrapment and helplessness.[107]

Clothing, too, suggests restrictiveness. In their first scene together, Paul pulls off Miriam's hat, allowing her hair to flow free. Paul wears a stiff collar on his first day at work, and removes an equally rigid high collar before he makes love to Clara. In the film, apparel is also an indicator of class distinctions: Mr. Morel's soiled work clothes contrast dramatically with the formality of Paul's aristocratic patron's. Miriam's repressed sexuality, along with her mother's, is reflected in her functional, dowdy clothes, although Clara's seductiveness and ample figure are suggested by her pretty, form-fitting blouses, body-hugging coats, and revealing evening dress and undergarments. Mrs. Morel's costumes are somber and utilitarian, and her attitude towards clothing, as in the novel, is puritanical (she sternly disapproves of Louisa's bare-shouldered photo). However, she is not above appreciating Paul's drawing of her in a fancy hat, revealing her repressed sensuality, her pleasure in her son's amorous attentions, and her desire for upward mobility. In the novel, William and Louisa, much to Mrs. Morel's disgust, are the flashiest dressers. In the film, however, only Louisa is portrayed as frivolous and extravagant, while a prematurely aged William is attired conservatively, like an office clerk. One final note: boots as symbols of sexuality and class respectability are entirely absent from the film.

One of the unique and memorable aspects of Lawrence's *Sons and Lovers* is the novel's numerous symbolic and often ritualistic scenes, described in realistic details suffused with poetic intensity. These powerful, affecting scenes, many of which feature flowers, blood, moon, sun, and fire, convey the mysteriousness embedded in the ordinary and at times manage to suggest an anthropological and even cosmic significance. Some of the scenes include Mrs. Morel's horrified reaction to Mr. Morel's masculinization of their one-year-old son William by shearing off his "myriad of crescent shaped curls" in "the reddening fire-light"15); Mrs. Morel in her garden communing with the "tall white lilies . . . reeling in the moonlight" (24) when, pregnant with Paul, she is shut out of the house by her drunken husband; Mrs. Morel thrusting her infant son up to the "crimson, throbbing sun" (37) setting over the hills of Derbyshire and naming him, as if by divination, Paul; Paul's curiously sadistic ritual sacrifice by fire of his sister's paraffin doll, the head of which he has accidentally smashed (58); Paul's burning of his mother's bread loaf while chatting with Miriam (206–207); Paul shaking handful after handful of cherries down on Miriam (285); Paul's sudden decision to break off with Miriam after inhaling the "raw and coarse perfume" of "the purple iris" and touching "their flesh throats" (294); and Paul making love to Clara on the clay river bank and afterward noting "scarlet carnation petals, like smashed drops of blood" in the wet roots and "streaming down her bosom" (311).

Because the plot is so truncated in the screenplay that Paul Morel's early childhood and adolescence as well as episodes from Paul's courtships of both Miriam and Clara are entirely omitted from it, all of the powerful, richly symbolic scenes described above are almost entirely excluded from the film version or altered beyond recognition. Furthermore, although the 103-minute film preserves to some extent the symbolist texture of the novel, the symbolism in the screen adaptation lacks the multi-layered complexity and subtlety of the symbolism in the original.

The imagery of imprisonment that pervades the novel was well-captured on screen, as was the contrast between the natural and mechanical worlds. Lawrence's symbolism, however, is mostly covert and idiosyncratic, whereas in the film, as we have seen, the imagery and symbolism are more heavy-handedly explicit, obvious, and clichéd, reduced to no more than two meanings per symbol. Fire, for instance, is associated with home and hearth, and in one instance—a Hollywood cliché—with sexual passion; flowers are associated with violated maidenhood and with rebirth in spring, etc.

Similarly, both the sexuality and the mysticism implicit in so much of

Lawrence's imagery are either absent or greatly subdued. Except for the eroticized sequence in which Paul courts and seduces Clara, the filmmakers seized few visual opportunities to convey Lawrence's sense of the sexuality permeating the physical world—phallic flowers and trees, super-masculine horses, penetrated mines, swollen rivers—and of the intense sexuality of all human relationships, including those who are not normally supposed to be sexual at all. Similarly, the sense of real objects as being suffused by the ineffable is quite lost in the film. Wordsworthian daffodils may be pressed into service as a predictable symbol of spring, but they are nothing like the tall white madonna lilies in Mrs. Morel's garden, "reeling in the moonlight," leaving her gasping "slightly in fear." On the whole, the images in the film are quite straightforward, conveying the surface of reality and fairly obvious cinematic symbolism, but leaving the dense and richly evocative symbolic texture of Lawrence's novel quite literally out of the picture.

Tone in the Novel and the Film

In *Sons and Lovers*, Lawrence's basic attitude toward his material and audience is unvaryingly candid, serious, intense, heartfelt, and impassioned. Despite its urgent seriousness, however, the tone of the narrative varies from passage to passage—alternately didactic, authoritative, and judgmental; affectionate, sympathetic and empathetic; strained, anguished and frustrated; melancholy and despairing; and rhapsodic and reverential.

Lawrence's narrative technique in *Sons and Lovers* was to lay bare the psyches of each of his principal characters and to reveal the subterranean life forces and conflicts that pulse in each of them, beneath conversation which, in Lawrence's fiction, almost always masks real feelings; beneath outward demeanor and behavior; beneath individual consciousness itself. Although identifying the real emotions, motives, and attitudes of his characters was Lawrence's apparent aim, many critics, aware of the autobiographical content of the novel, have pointed out his extreme subjectivity and probable unfairness towards Mr. Morel and Miriam. However biased he may have been, Lawrence's quest to uncover and depict the psychological truth about his characters, as he conceived it, was an urgent and important mission, and the tone of the entire novel underscores the earnestness of his undertaking.

The tone of the film adaptation of *Sons and Lovers*, established during the opening credits by the surging, melodramatic music theme that recurs during critical episodes, is predominantly earnest, even grave, like the tone of the novel—though rarely, as in the novel, fervently impassioned. The seriousness of the mood, particularly during the first half of the film, is lightened by humorous scenes and sequences that are not present in the text and are rather superficially and stagily imposed on the screen version. These cheerful or amusing bits include Paul's joyful dash to Miriam's farm, his playful exchange with her about her pig, Mr. Morel's song and William's recitation at the Christmas party, Paul's holding a corset form while the factory girls sing an off-color song, silly exchanges at the Nottingham suffragette rally, a male can-can dancer's mock-split at a local music hall, and Clara's mother's comic turn as a suspicious chaperon.

In certain respects, the film's intermittent lightheartedness undercuts and trivializes the seriousness of the novel's tone and theme and is distinctly un-Lawrentian. It is likely, however, that the lugubrious tone of the novel, faithfully translated to the screen, would have lessened the film's substantial box office success.[108]

Besides including outright comedy, the film alters the novel's tone by introducing cinematic irony, as in the scene on the beach in which Paul and Miriam discuss their doomed relationship against the backdrop of prison-like metal poles. In this and many other scenes, the director and cinematographer create a type of tonal tension, involving irony and paradox, that is not characteristic of Lawrence's prose style in *Sons and Lovers*.

Mirroring the tone and point of view of the novel, the filmmakers create a sense of emotional intimacy by the use of frequent closeups and by putting overall emphasis on shots of people rather than of landscapes or interiors. Compassion and sympathy are generated towards almost all of the characters, with the possible exception of Mrs. Leivers, who is harshly portrayed, and at certain moments Paul himself. Similarly, although the narrator in the novel is openly critical of certain characters, such as Miriam, Mr. Morel, and even Clara, the text paradoxically (and probably unintentionally) creates sympathy for these characters, especially for Mr. Morel. Virtually in spite of himself, Lawrence portrayed his father and, to some extent, Miriam in a positive light.

Embracing Lawrence's unconscious sympathy for his father, the "narrators" in the film—i.e., the screenwriters, director, and cinematographer—are more openly compassionate toward Mr. Morel and, not surprisingly, toward Miriam than towards Paul and his mother, who are both, by modern standards, portrayed in an unflattering light. Paul is moody, detached, self-centered, and cruel, while Mrs. Morel, though appealingly played by Wendy Hiller, is overtly manipulative, controlling, and possessive toward her son, and cuttingly and unfairly critical of her husband. On the other hand, despite his anger, bad manners, drunken outbursts, and violence,

Mr. Morel, whom his wife nostalgically recalls as handsome and appealing throughout the film, is presented as an attractive, vital figure. In part, this is due to the superb performance of Trevor Howard, but it is also because he is the "mouthpiece" for the post-Freudian consciousness of the late 1950s movie audience and of the scriptwriters who allow him, like a Greek chorus, to identify, evaluate and denounce Mrs. Morel's oedipal seduction of her son. In one added scene, which has raised the eyebrows of many critics, Morel spouts modern psychobabble as he castigates his wife:[109]

> Mrs. Morel: You had your way with Arthur.
> Mr. Morel: He died young, but he died a man. And William, he had the good sense to escape.
> Mrs. Morel: From you, from you —
> Mr. Morel: No woman, no. *You're* the one he had to escape from. He had to find a life of his own, where you wouldn't be there to smother him as you've smothered this one. It's *your* fault, woman, he's in this trouble now, it's *your* fault. Don't put the blame on me. Why do you think he's gallivanting around this minute with a Nottingham tart? He's never had the chance to go courting with an ordinary, decent girl. You've put a stop to that! A thing like that—you with your pride and your jealousy. Any lad of spirit can throw off a low-mannered father. That's not gonna hold him back when he grows up. But a mother who clings on to him and won't let him go for her own selfish sake, that's enough to ruin his life, and that's what you've done to our Paul.

Despite the filmmakers' apparent partiality toward Mr. Morel and Miriam, the point of view in the film is essentially third person omniscient, and is not, as in the novel, inextricably intertwined with the young protagonist's emotions, perceptions, and attitudes. The intimacy created by the close proximity of the camera lens to its subjects notwithstanding, the angle of most of the closeup photography is eye-level, creating an objective, realistic point of view that forces the viewer to take all of the characters with a grain of salt. We may feel sympathy, dislike, or contempt, in turn, for each of them, but the filmmakers, through script and shooting techniques, convey an evenhanded compassion for all of the characters as victims of social and economic forces over which they have little or no control.

In the last analysis, although Jerry Wald's film of *Sons and Lovers* has much to recommend it, even independent of its source, the movie's screenwriter, director and cinematographer were not nearly as effective as Anthony Pelissier (or Ken Russell) in translating Lawrence's substance or unique style. No doubt the film is enhanced by its picturesque black-and unique style. No doubt the film is enhanced by its picturesque black-and-white, wide-screen cinematography; gritty realism; the outstanding performances by veteran screen actors Trevor Howard and Wendy Hiller, and the dark, brooding good looks of Dean Stockwell; entertainingly comic scenes; and a catchy, hummable score. But, compared with the novel, Wald's adaptation is also a disappointingly conventional romantic drama, foreshortened, slick, superficial, and lukewarm, nothing like the lyrical *bildungsroman* it could have been had the filmmakers succeeded in infusing the movie with the concrete sensuousness, passionate poetry, rhapsodic religiosity, and mysticism of the text—the "special quality" of D.H. Lawrence's eloquent language that his widow, Frieda Lawrence, importuned Wald to preserve. However engaging, entertaining, and visually striking the movie version of the novel may be on its own terms, it succeeds only intermittently in capturing the bristling intensity and eroticism of Lawrence's prose. The screen adaptation that does the novel justice has yet to be made.

33. In the film's opening shot, birds burst into flight as the squeaky mine headstocks start to turn; the camera slowly pans right to sheep grazing in a field.

34. "You've ruined it!" cries Gertrude Morel (Wendy Hiller) when husband Walter (Trevor Howard) drips grease on son Paul's charcoal portrait of his mother; Arthur Morel (Sean Barrett), Paul's brother, looks on. (Museum of Modern Art/Film Stills Archive)

35. Visiting Miriam Leivers (Heather Sears) at Willey Farm, Paul Morel (Dean Stockwell) confesses his desire to live in London, "painting life" in his own studio.

36. Removing Miriam's (Heather Sears) beret, Paul (Dean Stockwell) lets her hair flow free. "Looking at you now, there's more religion in you than your mother could ever learn from the saints."

37. Glimpsed through the spokes of a mine headstock, miners' families race to the scene of an underground explosion.

38. After the mine disaster, Paul (Dean Stockwell) and his mother (Wendy Hiller) join miners' relatives as they wait for the bodies of the dead and wounded to be lifted up. (Museum of Modern Art/Film Stills Archive)

Sons and Lovers 131

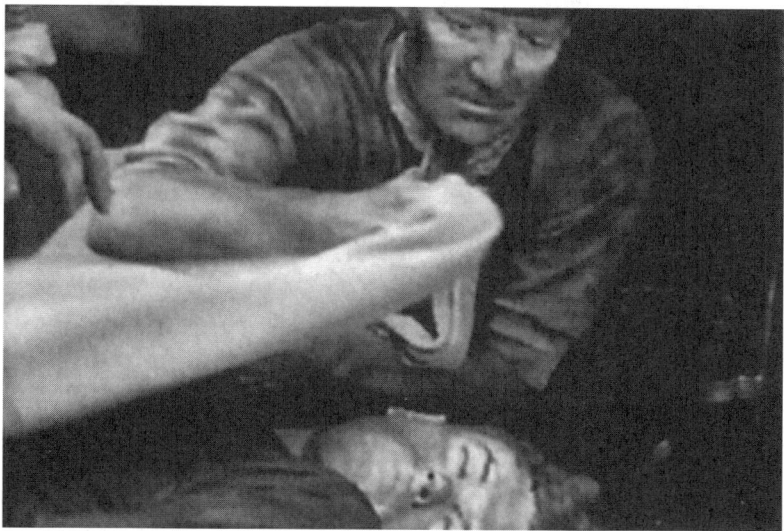

39. Walter Morel (Trevor Howard) covers his dead son Arthur's (Sean Barrett) face; in the novel, oldest son William dies instead.

40. After Arthur's funeral, Paul (Dean Stockwell) and Gertrude Morel (Wendy Hiller) grimly return home in the rain.

41. Walter Morel (Trevor Howard) angrily bangs his fist on the table as Mrs. Morel (Wendy Hiller) urges Paul not to be "dragged down" into the mines like his ill-fated brother Arthur.

42. Gertrude Morel (Wendy Hiller) and Paul (Dean Stockwell) bid goodbye to Paul's older brother William (William Lucas) after learning he is engaged to be married to frivolous Louisa Weston.

Sons and Lovers 133

43. At a Nottingham art exhibition, Paul (Dean Stockwell), his mother (Wendy Hiller), and Miriam Leivers (Heather Sears) observe patrons' reactions to Paul's portrait of his father.

44. Paul's down-to-earth painting of his father elicits mixed responses from gallery-goers.

45. Wealthy patron Henry Hadlock (Ernest Thesiger) eyes Paul's work critically but appreciatively.

46. Paul (Dean Stockwell) receives a magnanimous offer from Henry Hadlock (Ernest Thesiger) to study art in London. (Museum of Modern Art/Film Stills Archive)

Sons and Lovers

47. Told that Henry Hadlock (Ernest Thesiger) has paid £20 for Paul's portrait of him, Walter Morel (Trevor Howard) angrily challenges him to feel "the real thing—20 pounds of real sweat!"

48. "Why must you act like that?" Paul (Dean Stockwell) demands when his father Trevor Howard) is rude to a would-be patron; Morel retorts, "I'm not loved here 'cause I'm low, so I *act* low!"

49. Mrs. Leivers (Rosalie Crutchley) sternly warns daughter Miriam (Heather Sears) to shun "the sins of the flesh."

50. Elated by his artistic success and his future prospects in London, Paul (Dean Stockwell) kisses frightened Miriam (Heather Sears).

51. Tearfully embracing the trunk of a tree, Miriam (Heather Sears) prays not to love Paul, "but if I may love him, let me love him splendidly!" (Museum of Modern Art/Film Stills Archive)

52. In a drunken rage, Walter Morel (Trevor Howard) throws son Paul's food on the floor and locks Mrs. Morel (Wendy Hiller) out of the house. (Museum of Modern Art/Film Stills Archive)

53. Unwilling to leave his mother alone with his abusive father, Paul (Dean Stockwell) tells her he has decided not to go to London but to take a job at Thomas Jordan & Sons Surgical Appliances.

54. On his first day as a clerk at Jordan's, Paul (Dean Stockwell) becomes a figure of fun holding a woman's corset frame.

55. After teasing Paul by singing a risqué song, the flirtatious Spiral girls are formally introduced to the new employee. (Museum of Modern Art/Film Stills Archive)

56. When Paul (Dean Stockwell) and Miriam (Heather Sears) make love, Paul grimly observes that they have only been driven further apart. (Museum of Modern Art/Film Stills Archive)

57. On Christmas day, as Paul looks on, Gertrude Morel (Wendy Hiller) helps her husband (Trevor Howard) take a hot bath in the parlor. (Museum of Modern Art/Film Stills Archive)

58. Eldest son William Morel (William Lucas), home from London, introduces his flighty fianceé Louisa (Rosalie Ashley) to his mother (Wendy Hiller). (Museum of Modern Art/Film Stills Archive)

59. Tipsy from holiday champagne, Walter Morel (Trevor Howard) belts out a music hall ditty.

60. At a suffragette rally, Jordan's overseer Clara Dawes (Mary Ure), (right), daringly claims the four freedoms, "speech, thought, opportunity, love." (Museum of Modern Art/Film Stills Archive)

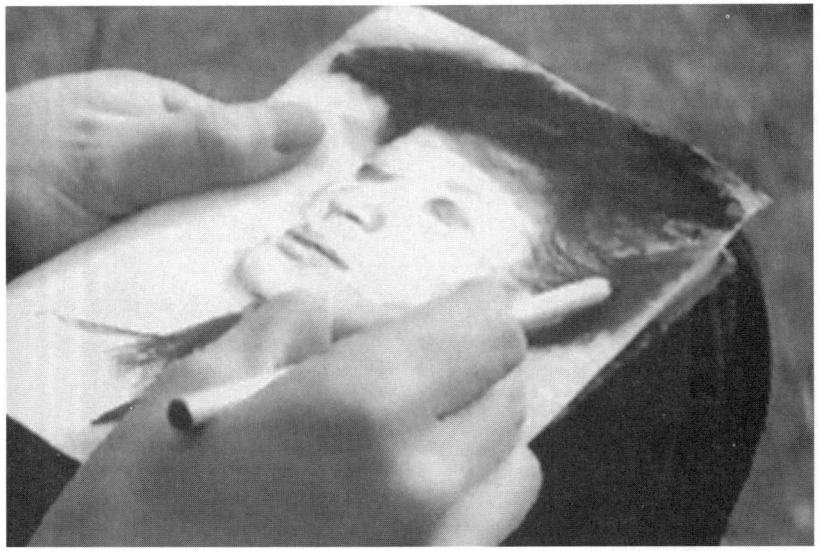

61. When Paul shows Clara the sketch he has made of her (above) at the suffragette rally, she exclaims, "You've made me *too* beautiful!"

62. On the arm of another woman, Clara's estranged husband Baxter Dawes (Conrad Phillips) glares at Paul and Clara as he passes by.

Sons and Lovers 143

63. On an evening out in Nottingham, Paul (Dean Stockwell) and Clara (Mary Ure) enjoy ribald dancing and singing at a music hall.

64. Missing the last train, Paul (Dean Stockwell) is invited to stay overnight with Clara Dawes (Mary Ure) and her widowed mother. (Museum of Modern Art/Film Stills Archive)

65. Sexual tensions mount as Paul (Dean Stockwell) and Clara (Mary Ure) play an erotically charged game of whist while Clara's mother bustles back and forth, then orders Paul to bed.

66. In Clara's bedroom, Paul (Dean Stockwell) gazes at her photograph, then softly caresses her powder puff.

67. As Paul's mother sleeps, Paul (Dean Stockwell) descends the stairs to the parlor where Clara is warming herself.

68. In an over-the-shoulder shot, Paul gazes longingly at partially disrobed Clara (Mary Ure).

69. Paul (Dean Stockwell) and Clara (Mary Ure) passionately embrace.

70. Baxter Dawes (Conrad Phillips) warns Paul Morel (Dean Stockwell) to keep away from his wife.

71. At Jordan's Clara (Mary Ure) and Paul (Dean Stockwell) stealthily plan a winter seaside getaway. (Museum of Modern Art/Film Stills Archive)

72. Paul (Dean Stockwell) expresses concern for his mother's failing health as Gertrude Morel (Wendy Hiller), troubled by her son's relationship with Clara, winces in pain. (Museum of Modern Art/Film Stills Archive)

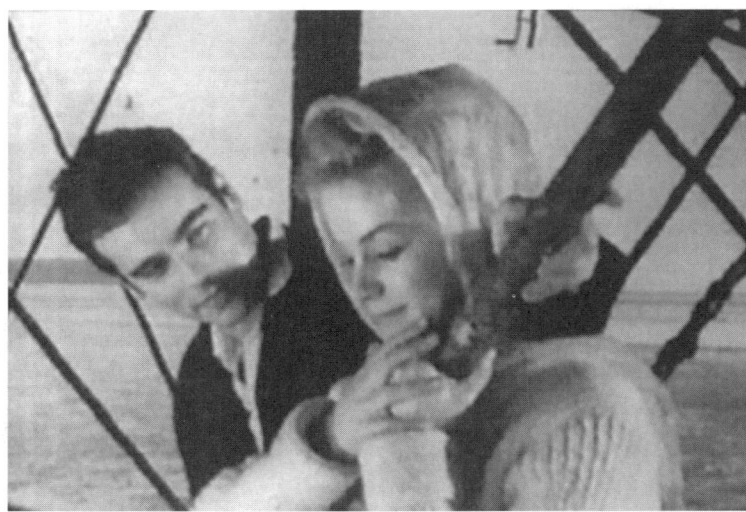

73. During their seaside tryst, amid "iron trees," Clara (Mary Ure) and Paul (Dean Stockwell) reflect on their relationship with each other and with Baxter and Miriam.

74. In a controversial scene omitted from British version of the film, Clara (Mary Ure) complains that Paul seems incapable of giving himself completely in the act of love.

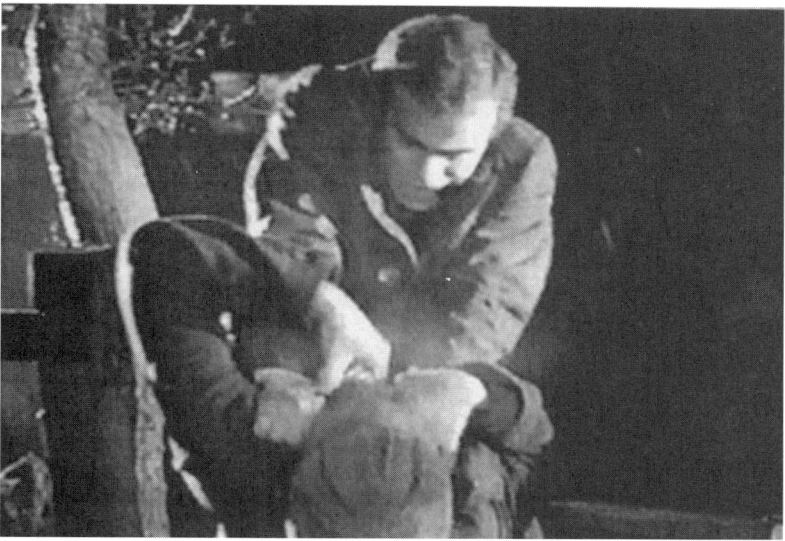

75. Returning from his rendezvous with Clara, Paul (Dean Stockwell) is assaulted and beaten by Clara's husband Baxter (Conrad Phillips).

76. Heartbroken Paul (Dean Stockwell) weeps after his mother (Wendy Hiller) dies quickly and peacefully of heart failure; in the novel, cancer-ridden Gertrude Morel dies a slow, painful death.

77. After his wife's death, Paul's father (Trevor Howard) urges Paul (Dean Stockwell) not to let his mother down, as he did, and encourages him to go to London to study art.

78. Kissing Miriam (Heather Sears) goodbye before he parts for London, Paul (Dean Stockwell) rejects her plea that they marry, telling her he wants to be "free."

Chapter 4

Women in Love

"There is another novel, sequel to *The Rainbow*, called *Women in Love*," wrote D. H. Lawrence to Waldo Frank in July 1917. "This actually does contain the results in one's soul of the war: it is purely destructive, not like *The Rainbow*, destructive-consummating. It is very wonderful and terrifying, even to me who have written it. . . . I suppose, however, it will be a long time without being printed. . . ."[1] Lawrence's gloomy prediction turned out to be accurate. After the banning and burning of *The Rainbow* for obscenity in 1915, no publisher in England would touch his fifth novel. Begun in 1913 under the title *The Sisters*, completed in 1916 at the peak of World War I, revised in 1917 and 1919, the "end-of-the-world" novel[2] that Lawrence variously titled *The Wedding Ring*, *Noah's Ark*, *The Latter Days*, and *Dies Irae (Days of Wrath)*, was printed privately in the United States in 1920 and finally published in England in 1921.

In the years since its publication, *Women in Love* has come to be regarded as Lawrence's most ambitious and difficult work, and a classic of modern literature—"one of the half dozen most important novels of the present century."[3] But with the exception of a few critics, such as Rebecca West, who found the novel "a work of genius,"[4] early critics, and some later ones as well, were almost entirely outraged or dismissive. *The Observer*'s unsigned review condemned the book as "the ravings of some unfortunate being . . ." filled with "nauseating rubbish about the sexes . . . ."[5] E. Shanks in *The London Mercury* fumed, "One would have to sweep the world before getting together such a collection of abnormalities,"[6] and Charles Pilly, in *John Bull*, denounced the novel as "an obscene abomination," calling for its suppression.[7] Even Lawrence's sometime friend and fellow writer, John Middleton Murry, attacked *Women in Love* for its overblown language and undifferentiated characters:

> *Women in Love* is five hundred pages of passionate vehemence, wave after wave of turgid, exasperated writing impelled toward some distant and invisible end; the persistent underground beating of some dark and inaccessible sea in an underworld whose inhabitants are known by this

alone, that they write continually, like the damned, in a frenzy of sexual awareness of one another. . . . We remain utterly indifferent to their destinies, we are weary to death of them.[8]

It was not until the publication of a critique of *Women in Love* by Mark Schorer[9] and of F. R. Leavis's *D. H. Lawrence: Novelist*, linking Lawrence's major novels with the Great Tradition of the nineteenth-century British novel and proclaiming him "the greatest creative writer in English of our time... of anytime"[10] that *Women in Love* received scholarly attention and acclaim. Characterizing *Women in Love* as "a dramatic poem,"[11] Leavis admitted that, like earlier readers, he had at first found the novel difficult, but saw the difficulty as a measure of its "profound originality."[12] Two of the book's worst faults, he acknowledged, were its insistent "jargon"[13] and the inclusion of scenes that do not contribute much to "the needs of thematic definition and development,"[14] yet he demonstrated how the complex, closely organized novel revealed in the "disorder of the individual psyche the large movement of civilization."[15]

Since Leavis' impassioned defense of Lawrence's fiction, legions of critics, especially those familiar with the novelist's intellectual preoccupations,[16] have grappled with the complexities, obscurities, and oddities of *Women in Love* in detailed analyses that are often as jargon-filled, esoteric, and obscure as the novel itself. Frank Kermode called *Women in Love* "so strange" a work "that after half a century of comment there is still no received opinion of it . . . in its fluidity, its unpredictable tonalities, it is surely if disconcertingly close to the essence of the modern."[17]

Despite controversy over the interpretation of many aspects of *Women in Love*, the novel is about a great deal more than the relationships among two pairs of lovers. "In each case the relationship . . . has implications for society as a whole," Pritchard observes. "It seems that the society of values of modern Europe offers only limited possibilities for life-enhancing relationships between men and women—and none for that between men."[18] On a loftier plane, Mark Schorer views the novel as a dramatized struggle between the death impulses of the "Will," associated with the drive to power and with the machinery of industrial society, and "Being," which is "the integration of the self" and of "life forces in total and complete self-responsibility." Thus, Schorer argues, "characters" pretty much disappear:

> Instead we have a large group of minor persons who, colorful as they may be, are caricatures—these are "social beings," the persons who are left with nothing but the external self, the ego-trampling or ego-trampled shell;

and then a small group of the four major persons, still actively seeking out their destiny and presented to us as naked psyches. With this division, Lawrence now specifies his theme: turning away from the many-faceted but superficial impulses of the ego to the primary source of all human action in the psyche, he finds that there all motives reduce themselves to two: the wish to live and the wish to die. The minor characters have already chosen the second way, and dead to their full selves, are frozen in their social roles. Of the four major characters, two, Gerald Crich and Gudrun Brangwen, gradually take that second way, and at the end, one, the woman Gudrun, is like the main characters, frozen in her 'will'; the other, the man Gerald, is literally dead, frozen in the Alpine snows, where she willed him and he willed to go. The other two, Rupert Birkin and Ursula Brangwen . . . take the way of life: removing themselves more and more from social activity, they find—we are told—individual integration rather than self-division, and thereupon, a real and finally fulfilling relationship with one another.[19]

H. M. Daleski points out "the dual motion of the book":

On the other hand . . . there is a continuation of the search . . . for a lasting relationship between the sexes, a search for the 'two in one'. . . . But at the same time . . . both couples are shown to be on board a ship which is rapidly heading for destruction, and their personal relations are not only qualified by their response to the danger but are the measure of a psychic drive towards life or death which such a predicament intensifies. Birkin and Ursula, clinging to the life preserver of their own 'unison in separateness', abandon ship; Gerald and Gudrun, by trying to destroy each other symbolically, prefigure in themselves the desire for death of those who do not attempt to leave the ship—a desire, it is implied, which is to achieve its shattering consummation in the general wreck that lies ahead.[20]

Julian Moynahan views *Women in Love* as "Lawrence's most perfectly integrated study of disintegration":

The heroes and heroines of *Women in Love* live close to the sick heart of a doomed civilization and are implicated in its final illness. The principal statement the novel makes is a deeply pessimistic one. It says that a living man or woman who embraces the social destiny offered by industrial Western society in the early twentieth century embraces his own dying.[21]

Along with Lawrence, in his letters and in the Foreword to the American edition of *Women in Love*, critics have also focused on the novel's revolutionary style. Mark Schorer comments on its "visionary quality":

> He [Lawrence] deliberately attempts, first of all, a kind of incantatory prose through the use of repetition, a kind of drugged choral quality, which is perhaps what E. M. Forster had in mind when he said that Lawrence was the only modern novelist "in whom song predominates, who has the rapt bardic quality." . . .To this development of style we should add the insistent contrast of the diction between the mechanical and the organic, and the attempt of the style to persuade us of the *force* inhering in all life. A third development of style is mentioned in Lawrence's own preface... "modified repetition."[22]

Although Keith Sagar sees the novel's unique style as "a way of forcing the reader to experience that alienation himself . . . to confront it in its most extreme and lurid forms,"[23] Ronald Draper praises the work ". . . for its great scenes of untranslatable symbolic power."[24] The question of whether the extraordinary content and style in Lawrence's novel can be "translated" is answerable only by an effort to convey them in another medium. Ken Russell made such a daring attempt in his 1969 film of *Women in Love*.

The Film of *Women in Love*

When American screenwriter Larry Kramer bought the movie rights to *Women in Love* in the early 1960's, he tried for some time to interest a major Hollywood studio in filming it and worked on a script with Silvio Narrizano, director of *Georgie Girl*.[25] In 1969, United Artists sent Kramer to fledgling British director Ken Russell,[26] who had previously produced three short amateur films (*Peepshow*, 1956; *Amelia and the Angel*, 1957; *Lourdes*, 1958)[27] and two minor feature-length films in the sixties: an obscure comedy, *French Dressing* (1963), and a secret-agent thriller starring Michael Caine, *Billion Dollar Brain* (1967).[28] Between 1959 and 1969, Russell also produced 33 strikingly original television documentaries and biographies ("biopics") of dancers, artists, composers,[29] a body of work that earned him a reputation as "the wild man of the BBC."[30]

After reading *Women in Love*, Russell was dismayed at the liberties Kramer had taken with the original: "It [the novel] made the script look the tawdry piece of sensationalism it was."[31] Although Kramer got final credit for the screenplay and received a 1970 Academy Award nomination for it,[32] the final script was a collaborative effort, and Russell, who was nominated for an Academy Award as best director,[33] was, by his own account, almost entirely responsible for the film's fidelity to the novel. Russell also contributed several Lawrentian touches extracted from the novelist's biography[34] as well as his letters, poems, essays and plays.[35] The filmmaker credited his lead actor Oliver Reed with the authenticity of the famous wrestling scene, with its full frontal male nudity:

> I originally thought of a swimming context for the scene since how else could you explain the two men stripping off for the match? But Oliver Reed said that that setting would be too poetic. He suggested that it should be more of a real physical confrontation between the two men locked in a room sweating and straining, and that is how we did it.[36]

Larry Kramer had recruited Alan Bates years earlier for the role of Birkin. United Artists suggested Oliver Reed, with whom Russell had worked previously and who he acknowledged "wasn't ideal physically for the part,"[37] for the role of Gerald.[38] To play Gudrun, Russell chose Glenda Jackson, a member of the Royal Shakespeare Company who had impressed the filmmaker by her performance as Charlotte Corday in the movie version of Peter Weiss's *Marat/Sade*.[39] After auditioning 300 women for the role of Ursula, Russell selected Jennie Linden, a relatively unknown stage actress who he later admitted was too "perky" for the role.[40]

Near Lawrence's birthplace in Eastwood, Kramer and Russell found suitable locations within a 25-mile radius of Sheffield, Derby, and Newcastle.[41] After approximately three months of shooting in the English midlands[42] and Zermatt, Switzerland, on a tight budget and schedule, and significant condensation of the rough cut by inserting flashbacks during the wedding sequence near the beginning of the film,[43] the uncensored 130-minute edited version was released in London in November 1969 and in New York in March 1970, winning critical acclaim and considerable box office success on both sides of the Atlantic.[44] For her performance as Gudrun, Glenda Jackson won, among other honors, the 1970 Academy Award for best actress.[45]

The film's frank eroticism, made possible by the newfound freedom from censorship of the late sixties,[46] was largely responsible for the film's box office success,[47] but most critics found much to admire in Russell's adaptation, praising its authentic period settings and costumes, lush scenery, sumptuous cinematography and artful editing, superb performances by the entire cast, as well as the screenplay's seeming faithfulness to the text. "Rarely has a great novel been more lovingly, more sensitively or more knowingly brought to the screen," wrote Arthur Knight,[48] and Margaret Tarratt compared *Women in Love* with four other films based on Lawrence fictions and judged it the best of the bunch:

> In many ways, the film comes closer to Lawrence than any of the earlier adaptations. Questions of social realism are never allowed to emerge. Consequently, the film is able to capture some of the strange surreal quality of certain of Lawrence's scenes without appearing virtually ridiculous.[49]

Other critics, including Richard Schickel,[50] Judith Crist,[51] and Kathleen Carroll[52] were enthralled by the film's visual beauty. British critic Penelope Mortimer, who judged *Women in Love* "a triumph of translation . . . that gains in the process," also praised it as "a superbly realised film, a success on the highest possible level."[53]

Despite the enthusiastic response of most movie reviewers to Russell's adaptation, even critics who, like Lawrence's biographer Harry T. Moore, viewed the film as "in many ways a moving-picture masterpiece,"[54] regarded the film as seriously, if not fatally, flawed. For Lawrence's champion F. R. Leavis, "rewriting" *Women in Love* for the screen was an act of sacrilege, "an obscene undertaking," as he charged in a condemnatory letter he wrote to Larry Kramer when he was invited to an advance screening of the film:

> No one who had any inkling of the kind of *thing* the novel is, or how the 'significance' of a great work of literature is conveyed, or what kind of thing significance is, could lend himself to such an outrage. Great writers, even when they are dead, ought to be protected.[55]

John Simon criticized Russell's casting, "cinematic tricks," and obvious, "misleading" symbolism, arguing that the film of *Women in Love*, for all its "superficial fidelity to the novel," was "a profound betrayal of it" and agreed with Leavis that the only safe, wise thing with a novel like *Women in Love* is not to make a film of it all.[56] Almost all aspects of the film came under fire by Pauline Kael, who denounced its "purple style": "The movie is a series of lavish caricatures, bursting with intensity that isn't really grounded in anything. It might seem that Russell confuses being gorgeously lurid with capturing the essence of the novel."[57] For Elliot Sirkin, the film reduces the novel to a series of "breathy fragments...a scrawny bird's-eye view of the book's main events,"[58] and in Neil Sinyard's view, Lawrence's symbolism in *Women in Love* does not travel well to the cinema.[59]

Plot, Character, and Dialogue Changes in Ken Russell's Film of *Women in Love*

The unconventional narrative structure of *Women in Love* has been noted by many critics. Although F. R. Leavis marveled at the novel's "wealth of vivid dramatic creation"[60] and argued that "not a scene, episode, image or touch but forwards the original development of the themes,"[61] some of Lawrence's critics, including Frank Kermode[62] and Eliseo Vivas,[63] view *Women in Love* as loosely organized, with little or no obvious connection between episodes. Observes Graham Holderness, "Chapters are not linked sequentially or in terms of a gradually developing plot; instead the author uses an episodic technique, with chapters tending to adopt their own individual shapes around central controlling metaphors."[64] On the other hand, George Ford echoes Angus Wilson in arguing that, despite outer appearances, *Women in Love* has a form as strict as some court dance:

> Subtle counterpointing, or whatever is its choreographic equivalent, *Women in Love* has in abundance. The intricate linking of scene to scene, the pairings, variations, crossings, repetitions, as the four lovers live their parts, reinforced from time to time by further variations introduced by other characters, by Hermione and Loerke in particular, surely justify the analogy to an artfully designed and patterned dance.[65]

Keith Aldritt highlights the "patterns of contrasts" in the novel:

> Here in *Women in Love* Lawrence has two stories to tell. And the narrative continues to and fro between the Ursula-Birkin relationship and that of Gudrun and Gerald. The result is that successive chapters (for instance, "Excurse" and "Death and Love") constitute a contrast rather than a continuity. The overall effect of the novel is . . . one of a pattern of contrasts that compose a moment of psychological, social, historical and . . . evolutionary tension. . . . *Women in Love* is concerned with antithesis, with counterforces in whose presently uncertain and seemingly untenable balance the continuance of human civilization is seen to depend. These antitheses are presented in the novel largely through the complicated set of relationships which are are at the centre of Lawrence's story.[66]

Transposing to the screen Lawrence's most multi-faceted, complex work crowded with violent encounters, sudden shifts of feelings, impulsive actions, intense discussions, solitary epiphanies, and highly charged ritualistic or symbolic scenes posed many difficulties for a filmmaker, not least of which was the novel's idiosyncratic plot. Unlike Jerry Wald's truncated adaptation of *Sons and Lovers*, Ken Russell's film of *Women in Love* closely follows the episodic plot of the lengthy novel, which begins in the spring and ends in the winter of the same year, and includes most of its characters and much of its dialogue.

Set in a midlands mining town, the novel explores the intense relationships between the two Brangwen sisters—schoolmistress Ursula and unconventional artist Gudrun, and their lovers, irreverent school inspector Rupert Birkin and wealthy industrialist Gerald Crich. It also delineates the principal characters' subsidiary love relationships—Birkin's neurotic affair with affected, aristocratic Hermione Roddice and Gudrun's perverse alliance with the bisexual sculptor Loerke as well as Birkin's thwarted friendship with Gerald. After a somewhat stormy courtship Birkin and Ursula find fulfillment in Lawrentian-style domesticity and marriage, while Gudrun, who takes up with Loerke, torments and coldly rejects Gerald, driving her former lover to commit suicide in the Alpine snowdrifts. "For the story line, I pulled out of the novel's action the bits that would hang together as a narrative," Russell explained.[67] Certain omissions, modifications and additions, however, create a tighter narrative structure with marked parallels and contrasts; simplify and exaggerate the characters and their relationships; heighten the eroticism of the film; and underscore themes in the novel.

Although Russell was aware that he had to cut and condense the lengthy, repetitive novel, he was extremely reluctant to do so. Twenty-five years after he directed the film, Russell compared it with his 1993 four-part adaptation of Lawrence's *Lady Chatterly's Lover*, which ran a total of three hours and twenty minutes, and acknowledging the difficulty of adapting a lengthy work, lamented the deletions he had been obliged to make in *Women in Love*: "It's impossible to film a 600-page novel and be true to the author's vision. . . . Many great scenes had to be sacrificed."[68] Forced by the film's producers to considerably shorten the rough cut, he managed to retain bits of the key classroom scene at the beginning of the novel through the use of brief flashbacks as Ursula watches the Crich wedding.[69] Absent from the film, however, are scenes in London involving Birkin's bohemian friends and the West African statuettes in Halliday's flat, the symbolic significance of which has long been debated and which Russell particularly regretted having to leave out.[70] Also missing are three key symbolic episodes—Birkin's stoning of the moon and a tomcat taming a female cat. As Russell himself noted, he filmed but omitted the scene in which Gerald and Gudrun struggle to subdue a berserk rabbit at Shortlands (a thoroughly tame rabbit was used in the film[71]). Also deleted are various scenes portraying the developing relationships between the principals through revealing conversations.[72] Several incidents involving Hermione are also missing—a swimming party at her estate, her accidental dousing of Gudrun's sketchbook, and her symbolic gift to Birkin of a rug he doesn't want. Birkin's bungled proposal of marriage, his nocturnal lovemaking with Ursula in Sherwood Forest, Ursula's battle with her father over her precipitate marriage plans, and the couple's trip by boat and train to the Austrian Alps are also left out. Finally, many of the interior monologues and debates among the principals concerning philosophical, educational, political, economic, social, and aesthetic issues are omitted.

One important modification is that the film's time period is more definite than in the novel. Although the events in *Women in Love* occur during an unspecified time prior to World War I, Lawrence wrote the bulk of the novel during the later years of the conflict, and indicated in the Foreword that the bitterness generated by the war's carnage pervades the work,[73] so Russell transposed the action to 1920, with appropriate costumes,[74] props, dances, and music. The opening sequence includes a shot of a child beggar carrying the sign "Somme," and later in the film, a public memorial service for a soldier clearly establishes a post-World War I ambiance. A recurring motif in the film, the song "I'm Forever Blowing Bubbles," was the biggest hit of 1920,[75] and the ragtime piano music with which Birkin disrupts Hermione's Russian ballet replaces the Hungarian music in the novel.[76]

To create striking parallels and contrasts as well as narrative continuity from scene to scene, the screenwriters changed certain characters in key episodes and borrowed dialogue from one section of the novel and inserted it into different contexts in the film. Russell and Kramer transformed Hermione's weekend gathering at Breadalby into a celebration in honor of the newlyweds, Laura Crich and Tibby Tupton; in the novel, the couple are not even present. The pair are not only seen making love on the couch during Hermione's "Russian ballet" but also, in a later sequence, swimming nude at the Criches' water party, and finally, locked in a deadly embrace at the bottom of the lake in the same position as Birkin and Ursula in a previous shot. In the novel, on the other hand, the drowning victims are Laura Crich's sister Diana and a young doctor, unconnected to each other. In the film, Birkin and Ursula's stormy courtship is condensed and foreshortened, and the consummation of their relationship, which takes place in the novel at night in Sherwood Forest, occurs in the film in a sun-drenched pastoral setting very similar to the field in which they picnic earlier in the same sequence.

Many passages of dialogue drawn directly from the novel are condensed, transposed, and mixed up. Birkin's denunciation of Hermione's narcissistic sensuality and her lack of true spontaneity, delivered in Ursula's classroom (Chapter II), turns up in an abbreviated version in the film during the confrontation with Hermione at Breadalby, in which, humiliated and rejected, she bashes him on the head with a paperweight. In one instance, Russell and Kramer rather inappropriately put Ursula's thoughts into Hermione's mouth after the drowning of the newlyweds: "Perhaps it is better to die than to live mechanically a life that's repetition, repetition. . . ." Joseph Gomez points out,

> In the novel, this line is part of Ursula's thoughts only a few hours after the unhappy events at Shortlands, and reflects the momentary depths of her despair. In the film, the line is uttered by Hermione during what will be her last appearance. This example seems one of the very few cases where Russell has switched around the dialogue without first considering the effect on characterization.[77]

In the film, Birkin apologizes for destroying the effect of Hermione's dance; her reply ("My ass!") is criticized by John Weightman as inconceivable for "a pre-1914 society lady,"[78] but defended by Joseph Gomez as creating a vivid counterpart to corrupt, vulgar Loerke, and also because Hermione's remark parallels a similar comment Isadora made in an equally "proper" situation.[79]

Several of the modifications, which involve minor additions, make certain characters seem more bizarre and extreme, others merely different from their portrayal in the novel. Satirized but treated with grudging respect by Lawrence, Hermione is savagely caricatured in the film as a vain, laughably pretentious, controlling harpy, especially during her lengthy dance solo. In the novel, Hermione merely presides over the dance of the sisters and the Contessa but does not actually participate. Mrs. Crich, eccentric enough in the text, is depicted as totally crazy in the film. Her daydream of setting dogs on charity-seeking miners is realized in graphic detail on the screen, and her hysterical laughter at her husband's funeral when she drops a trowel onto his coffin is entirely Russell's invention. Though critics attacked Russell for making the sculptor Loerke overtly homosexual as well as excessively crude and brutish, the novel reveals Loerke to be as sexually ambiguous and decadent as Russell represents him.

Although sexuality in the novel is almost always portrayed as vague and mystical, several of Russell's additions in the film make the characters' eroticism more explicit. Along with having Hermione perform a provocative dance, Russell shows her licking spilled champagne from Birkin's chest as they lounge beside her pool. Russell portrays Gerald emerging from a working-class tavern with a prostitute on either arm, and Gudrun, after admiring half-naked miners washing themselves, challenges a drunken wooer with "How are your thighs? Are they strong? Because I want to drown in flesh—hot, physical, naked flesh." Birkin's discourse at Hermione's luncheon on the proper way to eat a fig in society, based on a Lawrence poem,[80] creates an eroticized atmosphere, as does Birkin's and Ursula's frantic attempt to disrobe and make love at the Criches' water party and their subsquent nude lovemaking in a field of wheat.

Finally, some of Russell's additions are visual shorthand for important themes in the novel and also create meaningful parallels. These include a couple with a baby carriage in the opening sequence, Gudrun lying on a tombstone with her arms crossed over her chest, Birkin and Ursula discussing "love versus hate" at a memorial service for a dead war veteran, and Gerald slowly driving his father's white car through a crowd of blackened miners.

Style in the Novel

Recognizing the uniqueness of his prose style in *Women in Love*, Lawrence defended his hypnotic, rhythmic, eroticized prose, with its "continual, slightly modified repetition," in his previously noted foreword to the American edition of *Women in Love* (1920). Besides the repetition characteristic of almost all of Lawrence's prose, the hyperbolic, incantatory and often surrealistic style of *Women in Love* manifests the influence of several modern cultural movements, including Imagism,[81] German expressionism,[82] primitivism,[83] Vorticism,[84] and particular Futurism,[85] in which Lawrence expressed considerable interest. Futurism spurred Lawrence's focus on the nonhuman quality of life and on "the necessity of portraying an essential, unchanging reality which lies beneath the varying moods and personalities of his characters."[86] As Keith Sagar points out, the unique style of *Women in Love*, with its relative inaccessibility and unintelligibile meanings, is a way of forcing the reader directly to experience the alienation he evades in real life, and "to confront it in its most extreme and lurid forms."[87]

Like the writings of the Futurists, characterized by deliberate excessiveness and exaggeration, the prose of *Women in Love* is distinguished by an overblown "special" vocabulary replete with lofty abstractions and emotive adjectives and adverbs, as well as a nominal style in which nouns outweigh verbs by a ratio of almost two to one, and the majority of verbs are intransitive. The diction is also distinguished by the absence of vivid, concrete, mimetic action verbs and by the preponderance of lofty, abstract nouns and indefinite, vague nouns, adjectives, and adverbs; highly emotive adjectives and adverbial intensifiers; and adverbs of degree and manner. Adjectives and adverbs are often used like oxymorons, to contradict words they modify, and words and phrases are constantly repeated, usually in clusters. A unique feature of *Women in Love* is sudden shifts between prosaic language and the specialized, elevated vocabulary that permeates the novel.

In dialogue passages, short sentences predominate; however, in narrative and descriptive sections, sentences are much longer than in "The Rocking-Horse Winner" and *Sons and Lovers*, and the majority are simple and complex. A unique feature of the prose in *Women in Love* is the disjointedness of the syntax. Incremental repetition of syntactic structures, as well as antithesis, paradox, and oxymoron, are pervasive, as are sentences that evoke the experiences they describe.

Narrative paragraphs are generally shorter than in *Sons and Lovers*, and paragraphs of dialogue are more numerous. One quarter of paragraphs alternate, wavelike, between short and longer sentences; one fifth start with long sentences, and a quarter of the paragraphs also end with sentences over 25 words long. In half of the paragraphs the penultimate sentences are shorter than the final one. Only one sixth of the paragraphs evidence the mid-paragraph swelling characteristic of "The Rocking-Horse Winner."

Repetition of metrical patterns is pervasive in *Women in Love*, creating powerful rhythms. Repetition of words and sounds creates a sort of rocking rhythm. Continuity and flow are achieved by repetition of words at the beginning of sentences, by repetition of words and phrases, and by frequent use of parataxis. A slower rhythm and pace are achieved by use of heavily accented syllables and the relative paucity of multiple unaccented syllables.

Women in Love is truly distinctive for its underlying network of interlocking metaphors and similes drawn from a variety of nonhuman sources—natural, inorganic and supernatural. Imagery from the primeval world, and from a medieval cosmos of earth, air, fire, and water, create a mythical, dreamlike and sometimes nightmarish landscape. The metaphors and similes in *Women in Love* refer to plants, animals, and insects; water, snow, and ice; light and fire; shadow and darkness; birth, life, and death; bondage and freedom; and demons, angels, and ghosts.

Symbolism in *Women in Love* is so pervasive and intrinsic to the novel that almost all of the names, persons, animals, objects, natural phenomena, locations, encounters between individuals, and encounters between individuals and the environment are imbued with mythic significance. The basic duality of Lawrence's metaphysic, which is also evident in *Sons and Lovers*, is reflected in opposing images of darkness and light, spontaneity and rigidity, and the natural and the mechanical. Despite Lawrence's animus against modern technology in the novel, literal images of industrialism are scarce in *Women in Love*.

Although the underlying tone of the novel is extremely serious, and quite often urgent, melodramatic and vehement, it ranges from philosophical, resigned, reverent, and exultant to judgmental, mocking, disgusted, and outraged.

Style in the Film

Flamboyant film director Ken Russell was admirably suited to devising visual and aural analogues for key aspects of Lawrence's idiosyncratic "purple" prose. A unique cinematic style that incorporates the techniques of Sergei Eisenstein, Fritz Lang, George Wilhelm Pabst, John Ford, and Orson Welles is the hallmark of almost all of his movies.[88] In general terms, Russell's mature style is characterized by flowing camera movements, "shock" editing, a contrast between simple compositions and an embellished mise-en-scène, the use of closeups to accompany "ebullient acting," the deliberate manipulation of camera angles, and a dependence on elements of nature to function as private symbols.[89]

Most of these stylistic features are present in Russell's adaptation of *Women in Love*, which has been widely praised for its cinematography and editing, as well as for its distinctive settings, costumes, and acting. Conceding that Russell "sometimes gets carried away with his lyric camera," Vincent Canby declared, "The movie does capture a feeling of nature and of physical contact between people, and between people and nature, that is about as sensuous as anything you've probably ever seen in a film. . . ."[90] Thomas R. Atkins commended the director for his "extrardinary use of color,"[91] Penelope Mortimer lauded "the splendid artistry of the sets" and "the brilliance of the photography,"[92] while Judith Crist described *Women in Love* as "a beautiful film, its beauty glowing far beyond the surface . . . a thing of beauty for the eye that the mind too can feast upon."[93]

The cinematic style of *Women in Love*, however, did not impress a number of critics. Characterizing Ken Russell as "one of those directors who one feels might have the necessary daring and deviltry to scale the Lawrentian heights," Neil Sinyard panned *Women in Love* as "one of Russell's most tepid and visually boring movies...."[94] Describing the photography as "affected" and the camera work as "immobile," with "one static shot piled on top of another," Elliot Sirkin complained that "each shot has been obviously scheduled and planned." He also criticized the "synthetic splendor of the scenery" and "the pale quality of the lighting."[95]

Some critics found the style overwrought. Stanley Kauffman adjudged the color photography "overly lush ... in wheat fields and woods," and accused Russell of being "nervous about cinematizing ... he throws in superfluous fancy dissolves, mirror shots, a sideways sequence, and other evidence of insecurity."[96] Wrote Ken Hanke, "[The film] seems overlong, too lyrical, impossibly mannered ... one is disturbed by the freqently pointless artistic camera of Billy Williams, by some of Russell's too clever scene transitions...."[97] Pauline Kael faulted the way the director "pours on the decor and startling camera positions."[98] Russell, however, touted the exuberance and expressiveness of his unique style: "People always say of British pictures that they're muted, that they have great understatement. My films are the opposite. Why a muted masterpiece should be better than a baroque masterpiece, I don't know."[99]

Women in Love may not be Russell's masterpiece, but it is certainly baroque. Compared with the relative simplicity and straightforwardness of Jerry Wald's *Sons and Lovers*, all of the components in Ken Russell's adaptation combine to produce the lushness and artful complexity that impelled Pauline Kael to observe that Russell's "purple style of filmmaking ... might deceive one into imagining that he was providing a film equivalent to Lawrence's prose."[100] But Russell's success in approximating Lawrence's prose style in *Women in Love* is neither deceptive nor illusory. Indeed, I believe that it is precisely because of Russell's ability to create effects strikingly analogous to those in the novel that his adaptation brings us so close to the unique power and expressiveness of the original.

Characterized by semi-static, tightly framed one-and-two-shots juxtaposed with extreme long shots, and tracking and panning shots, the cinematography of *Women in Love* is distinguished by singular compositions, unusual shooting angles, long takes, zooms, slow-motion sequences, and, within scenes, by repeated dissolves. Lavishly decorated interior settings feature fire and fireplaces, mirrors, statuary, paintings, and other symbolic objects, while outdoor scenes are dominated by water, lawns, fields, tropical forests, and snow-covered mountains. In the numerous scenes involving running, swimming, and dancing, the staging, physical movements, camera work, and editing are heavily patterned and choreographed.

So-called "shock editing," a hallmark of Russell's television biopics and of his mature films,[101] is pervasive in *Women in Love*, along with disjointed syntax in several scenes and sequences. Structural and syntactic parallelism permeate the film. Scenes and sequences depicting funerals, dances, and love-making are also repeated. Sharply contrasted shots, scenes, and sequences are prevalent, as are crosscutting, intercut shots, and antithesis within shots, scenes, and sequences. Rapidfire montage is used in scenes of physical conflict, and the photography, sound, and editing in a number of scenes and sequences are mimetic, replicating the experiences depicted.

The rhythms of *Women in Love* alternate dance-like between rapid and slow-paced sequences; Russell consistently contrasts scenes of spontaneous vitality with scenes of deathlike immobility and rigidity. Many scenes build to a physical and psychological climax, then stop abruptly and subside. Syncopated rhythms are created by sudden bursts of violent movement or by "shock editing." The pace of the film is generally rapid but moderated by long takes and several slow-paced scenes. Many patterns of rhythm are repeated, in particular, scenes that accelerate in speed, then get slower and are followed by even slower scenes.

Mimicking the use of metaphor in the novel, the film combines music, words, and images to create pervasive interlocking metaphors. Many of the metaphors in the film are exclusively visual, such as characters' appearance, settings, background elements, and images of objects. Metaphors are also produced by camera movement, by the positioning and motion of figures within the frame, and by the use of light, darkness, and color. "Running metaphors," the repetition of images throughout a sequence of shots and several related sequences, are also featured throughout the film.

Like the novel, the film is permeated with the symbolism of light and darkness, as well as with contrasting images of freedom and spontaneity, or domination and imprisonment. Nudity as well as activities such as running, horseback riding, swimming, and dancing represent vitality and aliveness, while animals represent raw libido and aggression. Nature symbols are pervasive, as are industrial and urban images and many linked images of love and death. Houses, rooms, furniture, art works, and clothing are used to symbolize and comment on the personalities and values of characters.

Lighting ranges from pale and high key in daytime outdoor scenes to low key in nighttime and indoor shots, and golden by fire and candlelight. In many sunlit shots, the hues of the pastoral landscape are intense and brilliant, although indoors, colors tend to be dark and muted. The staging of shots and scenes alternates between static and highly choreographed images of people moving energetically, frantically—swimming, running, dancing, strolling, fighting. Matching the film's editing rhythms, the music is laced with dances and with popular songs and tunes that evoke the 1920s and provide ironic commentary. In some sequences, Russell introduces lugubrious, ominous, or "weird" passages that signal the seriousness or perversity of a scene. Spoken words, as important in Russell's adaptation as music and natural sounds, are drawn almost exclusively from the abundant dialogue in the novel.

The overall tone of the film is markedly different from the novel's.in certain respects. Russell's stance, unlike that of Lawrence's narrator, is cool, detached, at times even critical. Many scenes evoke an amusement inconsistent with Lawrence's intense solemnity, and the background music often creates an ironic counterpoint to the action that has no analogue in the original text. Despite disparities in tone between the novel and the film, however, cinematic equivalents of almost all of the stylistic components of Lawrence's distinctive prose style in *Women in Love* can be found in Russell's adaptation. As Joy Gould Boyum observes, the film achieves its "own kind of fidelity to the Lawrentian spirit . . . by mounting a series of original and daring strategies"[102]—strategies that reward close analysis.

Diction in the Novel

The diction in *Women in Love* has elements in common with that of "The Rocking-Horse Winner" and *Sons and Lovers*. The novel has its share of common-core one- and-two-syllable nouns of Anglo-Saxon and German origin, particularly in descriptive passages—words such as *mother*, *book*, *coat*, *house*, *lake*, *meadow*, and *heart*. As in all of Lawrence's narratives, a nominal style prevails.[103] Nouns outnumber verbs by a ratio of nearly two to one, and in most passages, nouns greatly outnumber adjectives as well.[104] The most common transitive verbs are quite basic—*have, know, see, watch, give, want, hate, love*. Action verbs, unlike the concrete, mimetic verbs in *Sons and Lovers*, tend to be nonspecific—*walk, run, dance, sing, stand*. As in *Sons and Lovers*, however, the majority of verbs are intransitive, with an abundance of verbs of being (*be, see, feel, appear, look*) followed by predicate adjectives or nouns. The constant use of linking verbs, whether introduced by expletives or by nouns and proper nouns, gives the sentences a bounded, self-enclosed quality, presenting an object's or person's feelings or attributes as intrinsic, absolute, and permanent, even if an extremely different feeling or attribute is indicated a few paragraphs or pages later.

Although the nouns and verbs in *Sons and Lovers* are predominantly concrete and precise, *Women in Love* is saturated with distinctive yet indefinite and vague words—abstract nouns, adjectives and adverbs—that, together with syntactic anomalies, give the novel its unique and often peculiar stylistic character. That there was something quite unusual, even revolutionary, about the diction in *Women in Love* D. H. Lawrence acknowledged when he noted in 1913 that *The Sisters*, the earliest version of *Women in Love*, was written in a "new style"[105] and that it was "like a novel in a foreign language I don't know very well . . . ."[106]

Michael Ragussis argues that *Women in Love* "constructs a new vocabulary" that "seems deliberately to defy our educative powers"; each time a word is repeated, it acquires "an additional and sometimes antithetical meaning."[107] Claiming that "this basic confusion in language is at once the novel's texture and text," Ragussis observes that for Lawrence, in *Women in Love* at least, words simply do not have a single consistent meaning; even the book's title, according to Ragussis, is "full of new meanings. . . ."[108] Key conceptual words central to Lawrence's metaphysic are also used in a variety of contexts throughout the novel, acquiring different and sometimes contradictory meanings as the narrative unfolds.[109] Garrett Stewart also notes that in constantly using puns and paradoxical phrases, the novelist is guilty of the same verbal and narrative habits as his protagonist Rupert Birkin.[110]

The "new vocabulary" of *Women in Love* is pervaded by polysyllabic words (often ending, as do most of Lawrence's abstractions, in *ion*, *ity*, and *ness*)[111] that seem more appropriate to treatises on ancient Greek science, philosophy or psychology than to a novel. The idiosyncratic lexicon of *Women in Love* is typified by such polysyllabic nouns as *corruption*, *dissolution*, *disintegration*, *retrogression*, *sensation*, *consciousness*, *conjunction*, *star-polarity*, *star-equilibrium*, *opposition*, and words such as *singleness* and *lapsing out*, as well as by less esoteric but similarly abstract non-Latinic noun such as *love*, *hate*, *death*, *knowledge*, *fate*, *power*, *freedom*, *beauty*, and *silence*. Rupert Birkin, Lawrence's mouthpiece in the novel, regularly uses an ornate, abstract vocabulary in speech and thought, as in a letter to his friend Halliday:

> "And in the great *retrogression*, the reducing back to the created body of life, we get knowledge, and beyond knowledge, 'the *phosphorescent*

ecstasy of acute *sensation*'. Oh, I do think those phrases are too absurdly wonderful." (475)

Abstract Latinate nouns often appear, not singly, as in *Sons and Lovers*, but in pairs, joined by *of*, with indefinite adjectives modifying the first and/or second terms of the phrases:[112]

> the pure duality of polarisation (271)
> a luminousness of supreme repudiation (321)
> a certain pure effluence of maleness (244)
> the grey, awful semi-consciousness of mere pain and dissolution (363)
> the antipathy of visible and audible death (363)
> a full mystic knowledge of his suave loins of darkness (400)
> the pure lambent reality of her forever invisible flesh (403)
> the terrible frictional violence of death (430)
> this small, slow, central whirlpool of disintegration and dissolution (471)
> the voluptuous resonance of darkness (174)
> pure mystic nodality of physical being (402)
> the immemorial magnificence of mystic, palpable, real otherness (403)

Passages that are permeated by strings of such phrases have a hypnotic, incantational, dreamily impressionistic quality that conveys a mysterious sense of the ineffable and unsayable.

Aside from phrases yoking abstract nouns, the language of *Women in Love* is marked by the constant use of vague and inexact modifiers, as in an often ridiculed passage in which Birkin, about to make love to Ursula, is driving a car through Sherwood Forest:

> He felt as if he were seated in *immemorial* potency, like the great carven statues of real Egypt, as real and fulfilled with *subtle* strength as these are, with a *vague, inscrutable* smile on their lips. He knew what it was to have the *strange* and *magical* current of force in his back and loins, and down his legs, force so *perfect* that it stayed immobile, and left his face *subtly, mindlessly* smiling. He knew what it was to be awake and potent in that other basic mind, the deepest physical control, *magical, mystical*, a force in darkness, like electricity. (400-401)

Derek Bickerton cites Lawrence's attempt to transform an ordinary situation...into an experience of supranormal significance" by an accumulation of "highly emotive but almost meaningless adjectives: *immemorial, subtle, vague, inscrutable, strange, perfect. . . mystical.*"[113]

Bickerton also identifies two groups of words accounting for nearly one word in every fifty,[114] which have attracted the notice of many interpreters of *Women in Love* and appear to varying degrees in commentaries on all of Lawrence's fiction: intensifiers (adjectives and adverbs), such as *very, really, complete/completely, utter/utterly, perfect/perfectly, pure/purely, terrible/terribly, horrible/horribly, awful* and *dreadful;* and "structure-words of vagueness," including *as if, almost, rather, some, a certain, a little, sort of, kind of,* and *perhaps.* Words that indicate an indefinable, often uncanny out-of-the-ordinariness—characteristic of almost all of Lawrence's fictions—include *strange/strangely, curious/curiously, queer* and the indeterminate *quite.* Other adjectives of which Lawrence is fond in *Women in Love* include *dark, soft, strong, great, subtle, new,* and more exotic words, such as *abstract, potent,* and *inchoate.*

Both the characters and the narrator in *Women in Love* display a predilection for adverbs of degree (*mostly, slightly*) and manner (*ironically, coolly, angrily*).[115] Four adverbs of time are also used quite frequently: *always* and *again,* which create a feeling of driving relentlessness; *suddenly,* one of Lawrence's characteristic modifiers, which suggests impulsiveness and surprise; and *gradually.* Somewhat like oxymorons, adjectives and adverbs are often used to contradict the words they modify; adverbs and verbs, adverbs and adjectives, and nouns and nouns oppose one another. Indeed, many parts of speech are used to create oxymoronic contradiction, e.g. "purple hedges were *darkly luminous* in the grey air"; "high hedges glowed like *living shadows.* . . ." (6) Contradiction is also suggested in *of* phrases, such as "a foul kind of beauty" and "glamour of blackness."

Incremental repetition, to some degree characteristic of all of Lawrence's fiction, is ubiquitous in *Women in Love*; words and phrases in various forms are constantly repeated, usually in clusters. Language that refers to sensuality and sexual passion also pervades certain narrative passages in *Women in Love*. Words that suggest sexuality include concrete nouns, such as body parts (breasts, buttocks, loins, belly, thighs) as well as abstract nouns, such as *desire, thrill, voluptuousness, passion, ecstasy, intoxication, intimacies, abandonment,* and *consummation.* Adjectives evocative of sexuality include *naked, turgid, soft, palpitating, fleshy, protuberant, licentious, orgiastic, bestial, unrestrained, phallic, obscene, frictional,* and *hot-looking.* Verbs with sexual overtones are less common and are often present participles—*thrusting, surging, pulsing, spreading, shuddering, writhing*—as well as verbs, such as *melt, swoon, penetrate, entwine, touch, vibrate, and violate*

A pervasive characteristic of the diction in *Women in Love* is the sudden shift between prosaic language and Lawrence's specialized, elevated vocabulary. Characters speaking banal words and performing routine acts are portrayed as experiencing unaccountably extreme reactions and feelings. When Hermione realizes that Birkin has not yet arrived at the altar for Laura Crich's wedding, "A terrible storm came over her, as if she were drowning . . . . Never had she known such a pang of utter and final hopelessness. It was beyond death, so utterly null, desert" (65). The first time Gudrun sees Gerald, she has a "keen paroxysm a transport. . . her veins were in a paroxysm of violent sensations" (61). Leo Bersani explains Lawrence's sudden shifts in diction in terms of Lawrence's underlying purpose in the novel:

> In *Women in Love*, Lawrence himself is attempting to destroy the superstructure of personality in order to define human beings in terms of their primary desires to live and to die. The continuous shifts in the novel between familiar social identities and currents of life or death energy train us to recognize the latter in the midst of the former. . . .[116]

Finally, if Lawrence showed off his knowledge of French in *Sons and Lovers*, he added Italian, German, and Latin in *Women in Love*, an index of the characters' worldliness and sophistication. As in "The Rocking-Horse Winner," modern slang enlivens the conversation of Birkin, Gerald, and Ursula, and particularly Gudrun, and transcribed dialect once again typifies the few working-class characters.

Shot and Image in the Film

Ken Russell's *Women in Love* abounds in cinematic equivalents of the types of words and phrases typical of Lawrence's novel. As in the film adaptations of "The Rocking-Horse Winner" and *Sons and Lovers*, most of the shots in *Women in Love*, analogous to the one- and two-syllable words basic to the lexicon of the novel, are tightly framed one- and two-shots. The majority of them are medium closeups and closeups of "talking heads," along with a sprinkling of medium one-, two-, and three-shots of figures.

Although the images in this film are not nearly as static as those in *The Rocking Horse Winner* and *Sons and Lovers*, numerous shots suggest the boundedness of sentences controlled by linking verbs (verbs of being) and, by extension, the rigidity and limitedness of most of the principal characters' lives. In the opening shots of the film, for example, Ursula and Gudrun's stiffly conventional parents are shown in a tight deep-focus interior shot—a long take—with Mr. Brangwen in the foreground systematically tapping at nails in a piece of leather. Symmetrically, the film ends with alternating medium closeups of Birkin and Ursula sitting opposite each other by the fireside in Birkin's cottage, finally freeze-framing Ursula as she expresses skepticism about the two kinds of love Birkin seeks.

Hermione is often photographed in stiff, motionless positions—in Ursula's classroom holding catkins and in her salon describing the characters in her "Russian ballet." During Hermione's solo, closeups of Ursula and Gudrun in comically frozen poses suggest the constraints of Hermione's dominating personality. Often formally dressed, Gerald is monumental, stiff and unmoving, standing over a writhing Gudrun after her dance before the bulls; enthroned in his baronial chair before wrestling with Birkin; or trapped beside his half-crazed mother at his father's funeral. In a disturbingly static sequence shot from a high angle, Gerald makes love to Gudrun and imprisons her beneath him as he sleeps; a series of dissolves reveals his immobility and her discomfort. Mrs. Crich is repeatedly photographed as a prisoner behind grillework, windows, or framed in a doorway, and a defeated Mr. Crich is also shown as nearly immobilized in his mine office, in his wheelchair at Shortlands, and in his death chamber, shrunken and bloody-faced against pillows. Images of boundedness symbolized by prison bars are associated with Gudrun as she banters with Loerke behind the spindles of the stars in the Alpine lodge, and with Loerke as he plays erotic games with Gudrun. Boundedness is also suggested by physical entrapment by other bodies, as in the shot of the colorfully costumed sisters, hemmed in by poker-faced, filthy miners in dark work-clothes on a Beldover streetcar.

The polysyllabic, Latinate nouns, adjectives, and adverbs that distinguish the ornately "purple" vocabulary of *Women in Love* are replicated in the film in a number of ways. For one thing, the principal characters themselves use a polysyllabic Lawrentian vocabulary, including *immortality, megalomania, conductivity, spontaneous, consciousnesss, mechanically, spiritually, mysterious, intimacy, sympathetically, alternative, unpardonable,* and *esoteric.* Lush indoor and outdoor settings—Hermione's castle-like "cottage" with its elegant salon and drawingroom; the baronial chambers of Crich's manor house, Shortlands; a sundrenched field; a semi-tropical forest; the Swiss Alps—convey a luxuriant visual opulence that matches the baroque diction. Decor, too, evokes the ornate "purpleness" of the language—mirrors over mantlepieces, carved and curved furniture, statuary, traditional and modern paintings, patterned Oriental rugs, floral fabric, and diamond-shaped stained glass windows at Shortlands.

The hyperbole created by Lawrence's adjectival and adverbial intensifiers is replicated throughout the film by every conceivable visual and aural means. The vivid colors, striking textures, and elegant designs of the costumes, combined with theatrical eye makeup on Hermione and the Brangwen sisters in several scenes, produce a dramatic effect, as do the rich, deep greens and high-key golds of the outdoor scenes. Textures also create evocatively sensuous effects—the wet pines and semi-tropical fronds that conceal Birkin's naked body, the snowy birch bark that Birkin feels out with his bloody hand, the shaggy reddish coats of the horned cattle, the frothing water that is drained from the lake after the newlyweds' drowning, the thick white fur of a bear rug in the nude wrestling scene, and the beaded room divider in Gudrun's bedroom. Instances of lighting used to intensify the sensuousness and emotional impact of many scenes include the high-key sunlight enveloping Ursula and Birkin in a wheat field; the candlight on the lake at night, in Loerke's room and illuminating Gerald's frozen corpse; and most especially the burnished firelight in both the wrestling scene and the film's final shots, in which Birkin and Ursula sit before a hearth in Beldover.

Camera movements replicate the effects of Lawrence's verbal intensifiers—tracking shots of the newlyweds racing to church, Birkin and Ursula pushing their way through a crowd at a soldier's memorial service, and Birkin fleeing Hermione through a forest, as well as backward zooms of Gudrun and Gerald after lovemaking, of the drowned newlyweds, and of Gerald curled up in the snow. In many shots and scenes, the characters' rapid or explosive movements and gestures also contribute to the overall intensity generated by the film, as, for example, in the running, diving, dance, and wrestling scenes, in the skiing and sledding scenes in the Swiss Alps, and in the sequence in which Gerald brutalizes his horse beside a moving train

Unusual camera angles also function as intensifiers throughout the film. There are many extreme high-angle shots—Gudrun twisting and writhing on the grass, Birkin dashing through the forest, Gerald and his father riding through the crowd of miners, Birkin and Ursula making love during the water party, and Gerald entombed in the snow. Among low-angle shots that generate emotional and visual intensity are those of Hermione bashing Birkin with a paperweight, Gerald restraining his horse, and Gerald viewed from Gudrun's point of view as she writhes on the ground before him.

Striking closeups of the principal characters and medium closeups in one- and two-shots, a pervasive stylistic feature of the film, overwhelm the screen and intensify viewers' reactions. Point-of-view closeups of Gerald, Birkin and Hermione at the Crich wedding capture Gudrun and Ursula's first visions of them from a cemetery across the road. In the "fig" scene, the camera pans slowly around the table, revealing, in medium closeups and medium shots, the embarrassed or bemused reactions of each of the guests. Reaction shots of the sisters reacting in horror and disgust as Gerald disciplines his horse highlight the violence and cruelty of the scene. Throughout the film, closeups of Gudrun, Hermione, Ursula, and Mrs. Crich, as well as many other larger-than-life images, create a powerful visual impact. Finally, in many scenes brooding music underscores the drama of the action and intensifies viewer reaction many scenes—for example, during Hermione's solo dance, Birkin and Gerald's wrestling match, Gudrun's movements before the bulls, Ursula and Birkin's lovemaking, Gerald's seduction of Gudrun, and Gerald's ascent to his death in the snow.

Mimicking Lawrence's use of many abstract nouns, the filmmaker uses several relatively abstract shots and series of shots. These include shots of body parts during Gerald and Birkin's wrestling match and Birkin and Ursula's love-making scenes, as well as shots of parts of a white mare and shaggy horned cattle. Crane shots create compelling semi-abstract compositions—the curved stone stairway at Breadalby which Birkin runs down as he flees Hermione, the horizontal geometry of steps at the outdoor flea market, the backward zooms of the drowned newlyweds' interlocked bodies isolated in a sea of mud, and a rapid high-angle backward zoom of Gerald's body curled up in a fetal position in the snowy expanse of the Alps.

The unusual and distinctive vocabulary in *Women in Love* is replicated in many of the images in the film. Notable is the high-angle shot of Gudrun in a royal blue dress lying with her arms crossed over her chest on a gravestone, as well as shots of her in white posing with uplifted arms against a tree trunk and dancing before bulls. Also notable are frame-filling shots of Hermione posturing in black robes during her solo dance or crooning over catkins. Striking too is the closeup of Birkin's bloody hand pressed against white birch bark as well as high-angle shots of Birkin sprawled naked amid vegetation and the Crichs' immaculate white automobile surrounded by blackened miners. Other memorable images include the high-angle shot of the drowned lovers entwined at the muddy bottom of the drained lake; a medium closeup of Birkin and Ursula, dressed in beige, picnicking in a platinum sunlit wheatfield; and a low-angle shot of Gudrun in royal blue standing before diamond-shaped, broken stained glass windows at Shortlands. Shots of Gerald and Birkin reflected in a mirror from different angles and repeated high-angle shots of Gerald's torso pinning Gudrun to the bed after he has made love to her are also arresting.

If the meanings of many of Lawrence's key words in *Women in Love* are ambiguous (Pauline Kael refers to the novelist's "passionate imprecision"),[117] many of the scenes shot in a field are equally so. Not merely for modesty's sake, the lovemaking scenes are intentionally undefined. In a dreamily impressionistic sequence printed sideways, Birkin and Ursula, hands outsretched and naked in a wheatfield, move in slow motion toward and away from each other. As Birkin and Gerald strive closer and closer during their wrestling match, the identities of their intertwined bodies blur. Birkin and Ursula in light-colored clothing almost blend in with a pale yellow wheat field, as does Birkin's nude body with vegetation on the floor of a forest. In the artfully composed series of shots of Birkin and Gerald photographed from various angles before mirrors, it's almost impossible to tell where they are standing and in what relation to each other. Confusion is also created by juxtaposed shots of Birkin and Ursula and the drowned newlyweds in identical embraces.

Just as Lawrence incrementally repeats words and phrases, Russell uses repetition as a basic visual and aural stylistic device. One example of a visual motif repeated with modification is stripes—on a girl's jacket at the Crich wedding, Gerald's blazer at the picnic and his pajamas in the Swiss Alps, Ursula's headband in the Russian ballet scene, Birkin's striped tie and the striped tent cover at the Crich water party, and, most dramatically, the black- and-white striped fur coat that both Gudrun and Loerke wear. Colors of costumes are also echoed: Ursula and Gerald are generally dressed in yellows, beiges, oranges, and whites, and Gudrun wears a unique royal blue, while Gerald and Birkin frequently appear in black formal wear. Makeup too is duplicated; Hermione's, Ursula's, and Gudrun's theatrical eye makeup in the Russian ballet scene, for example, is similar to Gudrun's in her pantomime with Loerke. Decor includes repeated motifs—"bars" in the form of stair spindles behind which Gudrun peers at Loerke, slats of a headboard behind which Loerke teases Gudrun in his bedroom, and the spokes of a fence at the Crich estate.

Many striking shots and images are echoed, often consecutively. or instance, Mrs. Crich's laughing face at her husband's funeral is intercut several times during the scene in which Gerald makes love to Gudrun in her bedroom. Gudrun's laughing face backlit by the sun flashes intermittently on the screen as Gerald climbs to this snowy death near the end of the film. Also duplicated are the juxtaposed shots of the drowned newlyweds and Ursula and Birkin in exactly the same positions, Birkin and Gerald's faces reflected in a mirror, and successive shots of Gerald lying over Gudrun on the first night he makes love to her.

Russell's film abounds in images that explicitly convey the eroticized subtext of Lawrence's prose. In keeping with the realism of the cinematic medium, however, Russell's sexual images are far more literal than Lawrence's suggestively sensual vocabulary. Some of them are drawn directly from the novel, such as Hermione crooning over catkins in Ursula's classroom, Gerald gouging the flanks of his horse, Birkin lying nude in tall grass, Gerald and Birkin wrestling, Birkin and Ursula frantically making love, and Gudrun writhing before horned bulls. Russell, however, adds his own eroticized images—Birkin transforming Hermione's quartered fig into a female sex organ and tasting his fingers provocatively, Hermione licking champagne off Birkin's chest and dancing provocatively around her salon in a clinging dress, the supine newlyweds kissing and caressing on a couch in the midst of Hermione's formal gathering, a drunken miner forcing himself on Gudrun after bumping into a dangling hunk of meat, and Gudrun writhing seductively on the ground before Gerald.

The diction in *Women in Love* is marked by quick shifts or gaps between an elevated and prosaic vocabulary; in the film, similar shifts occur both within and between shots. Throughout the opening sequence behind the credits, fashionably dressed Gudrun and Ursula clash sharply with drably attired laborers, wives, and children. The girls in their street clothes watching the Crich nuptials from the graveyard contrast sharply with the formally attired wedding guests; demure Ursula is contrasted with the flamboyant Hermione in the classroom scene; immaculately dressed Gerald and Mr. Crich are set off from a grubby crowd of miners. Birkin's provocative panegyric on a fig is immediately undercut by Hermione's invitation to take a walk, and Hermione's pretentious movements during her "Russian ballet" are similarly subverted by the playful 1920s popular dancing into which the party guests suddenly shift.

Shots contrasting Birkin's lofty sentiments and Ursula's domesticity abound. At a soldier's memorial service, Birkin pontificates about love, hate, humanity, and the end of the world; Ursula's housewifely putdown is to snatch the parcels he has been holding for her and flounce off. Similarly, Ursula and Birkin argue about the advantages of his being a lover or a husband as she hangs up the wash. In the final sequence of the film, Ursula and Birkin debate the possibilities of "two kinds of love" as she demurely darns a sock. Numerous shots contrast gritty reality and aesthetic beauty: Hermione's assault on Birkin is followed by his descent into Rousseau-esque vegetation, and the striking firelit nude wrestling scene is directly followed by Mrs. Crich setting her dogs on some charity-seeking miners. As Gudrun discusses the function of art and the life of the artist, Loerke rudely flicks ashes on Ursula's dessert.

Finally, the film includes just enough French, Italian, and German to preserve the Continental flavor of the text. The British slang of the World War I era, used mainly by Gudrun, is preserved analogously through the use of popular songs of the period, through authentic costumes and props, and through ragtime music and various types of dancing. The Midlands dialect used by the working-class characters in the novel is heard when Gudrun goes slumming in the miners' district.

Grammar and Syntax in the Novel

The diction in *Women in Love* is often idiosyncratic; the novel's syntax, too, is distinctive. Although the sentences in the extensive dialogue passages are short, averaging ten words, the sentences in the narrative and descriptive sections are consistently longer than in "The Rocking-Horse Winner" and *Sons and Lovers*, averaging 15.7 words—among the longest in all of Lawrence's novels.[118] Extremely lengthy sentences of up to 100 words are not unusual.

The majority of sentences in *Women in Love*, as in "The Rocking-Horse Winner" and *Sons and Lovers*, are simple (60 percent) and complex (24 percent); only 6 percent are compound and 2 percent compound/complex.[119] In almost all of the complex sentences, the subordinate clause follows the main clause. Such front-loaded sentences give the prose a pervasive fluidity and looseness that Richard Lanham categorizes as a "running style."[120] A similar effect is also produced by the extensive use of *parataxis* (the joining of sentences by a comma), one of the distinguishing hallmarks of prose style in *Women in Love*, accounting for 8 percent of all sentences in the novel. Indeed, although the majority of paratactic sentences contain two clauses, up to five main clauses are joined by a comma:

> They stopped, they discussed methods, they practiced grips and throws, they became accustomed to each other, to each other's rhythms, they got a kind of mutual physical understanding. (*5 main clauses*) (348)

The accretion of comma-linked main clauses gives the prose a rapidfire, pulsing, headlong quality that carries the reader along, barely conscious of the exact meaning of the words.

Because of the high incidence of intransitive verbs, including linking verbs—expletives (*it* and *there*) are used repeatedly in *Women in Love*—the characteristic subject-verb-object pattern that distinguishes simple sentences in "The Rocking-Horse Winner" and *Sons and Lovers* is atypical in *Women in Love*, and the passive voice is rarely used either. Main clauses in *Women in Love* are usually far more lengthy than in "The Rocking-Horse Winner" and *Sons and Lovers*, amplified by double and triple verbs, as well as by innumerable adjectival and adverbial words, and by phrases, both prepositional and participial. Indeed, Garrett Stewart suggests that Lawrence's "essential prose span," especially in *Women in Love*, "falls somewhere between the phrases and the sentence"; it is the phrase "echoing off the walls of the sentence."[121] The following participial phrases are typical:

> So she crept a few inches further, *proceeding* on her way to the back door, *crouching* in a wonderful, soft, self-obliterating manner, and *moving* like a shadow. (211)

A conspicuous element in the prose of *Women in Love* is the disjointedness of its syntax. In main clauses, a distinctive and recurring pattern is the separation of subject and verb by adjectives, relative clauses, or strings of modifiers, as well as the separation of other elements in the sentence by interrupting words or phrases. Also fairly common is the use of a delayed subject, following *it, there,* and *this*. The separation of elements in a sentence creates a sense of integration as well as of ambiguity:[122]

> Birkin, small and dark also, his hair tinged with moonlight, wandered nearer. (322)

> Hermione, who brooded and brooded till she was exhausted with the ache of her effort at consciousness, spent and ashen in her body, who gained so slowly and with such effort her final and barren conclusions of knowledge, was apt, in the presence of other women whom she thought simply female, to wear the conclusions of her bitter assurance like jewels, which conferred on her an unquestionable distinction, established her in a higher order of life. (372–373)

The splitting of the subjective appositive also evokes a sense of disharmony and fragmentation: "It was getting stronger, it was reasserting itself, the inviolable moon" (239). Sometimes syntactical elements vital to achieving clarity are omitted from the sentence, and on occasion it is difficult to tell which elements particular words and phrases refer back to, or indeed if they refer back to anything specific:

> It was in the curves of his brow and his chin, rich, fine, exquisite curves, the powerful beauty of life itself, something like laughter, invisible and satisfying. (458)

An aspect of "running style," the pervasive use of appositives noted by many critics, is one of the most distinctive features of syntax in *Women in Love*, indeed, in all of Lawrence's fiction.[123]

> It was the first great step in undoing, the first great phase of chaos, the substitution of the mechanical principle for the organic, the destruction of the organic purpose, the organic unity, and the subordination of every organic unit to the great mechanical purposes. (305)

Such series of syntactically similar or identical phrases, strung together one after another, suggest a fumbling or groping toward meaning, each phrase cubistically adding another angle or facet to the original idea, or repeating, with some variation, a previous phrase.

Closely allied with Lawrence's use of appositives, and contributing to the expansion and length of his sentences, is his frequent use of catalogues—"strings of words, phrases and clauses, usually minus coordinating conjunctions, that either precede, follow or interrupt sentences, to add additional material."[124] Quite frequently, these catalogues are series of nouns, verbs, and adjectives that resemble lists:

> The old grey managers, the old grey clerks, the doddering old pensioners he looked at them, and removed them as so much lumber. (302)

> There was a new world, a new order, strict, terrible, inhuman, but satisfying in its very destructiveness. (304)

> There he was, summed up, paid for, settled, done with. (342)

As in all of Lawrence's fictions, including "The Rocking-Horse Winner" and *Sons and Lovers*, outright or modified repetition of syntactic structures is a hallmark of the prose in *Women in Love*. As noted, Lawrence's use of syntactical repetition constitutes an eroticizing of language, or, as David J. Gordon terms it, the "sexualization of style."[125] Parallelism, a special form or repetition, appears frequently in *Women in Love*, as does anaphora, the repetition of a word or group of words at the beginning of successive clauses:

Parallelism

They stopped, they discussed methods, they practised grips and throws, they became accustomed to each other, to each other's rhythms, they got a kind of mutual physical understanding. (348)

Anaphora

She [Hermione] did not believe in her own universals—they were sham. She did not believe in the inner life—it was a trick, not reality. She did not believe in the spiritual world—it was an affectation. In the last resort, she believed in Mammon, the flesh and the devil—these at least were not sham. (373)

Lawrence's constant verbal and structural repetition in *Women in Love* creates a rhythmic, throbbing, incantatory prose that reaches beneath the level of ordinary mental consciousness and evokes often disturbingly primal emotions. As Jane Gurko observes:

The intricacy and power of Lawrence's repetitive style stems from a kind of *reculer pour mieux sauter*. He seems to want to turn every image over, every feeling, every word, so that nothing is left out, we get the fullest possible treatment of a psychological change or event, we have seen it from every angle; when we reach the end, the experience has not been disjointed or artificially suspenseful, it has been a slowly gathering wave.[126]

As in "The Rocking-Horse Winner" and *Sons and Lovers*, antithesis and paradox, which evoke, in Lawrence's terms, "a state of opposition," are found within and between sentences and paragraphs on almost every page of *Women in Love*. From the opening scene, in which Ursula and Gudrun discuss the advantages and disadvantages of marriage, the intellectual, highly articulate characters endlessly argue, debate, and contradict one another and themselves. Not surprisingly, the words *but* and *yet*, as in much of Lawrence's fiction, appear frequently. On occasion, so do coordinating conjunctions between main clauses, though far more often at the beginning of sentences. Oxymorons, or near-oxymorons, are also in evidence:

Still the faint *glamour of blackness* persisted over the fields and the wooded hills, and seemed *darkly to gleam* in the air. (59)

> In his clear northern flesh and his fair hair was a glisten like *cold sunshine* refracted through crystals of ice. (61)

Connected with antithesis and oxymoron is Lawrence's habit of indicating sudden, often violent shifts of feeling for which the reader is not prepared. In the opening scene, the sisters agree laughingly that they are strongly tempted not to marry. Without any warning, Lawrence follows their exchange with, "In their hearts they were frightened." (54) Likewise, when some working-class women call to the sisters in the first chapter, Lawrence writes of Gudrun, "A sudden fierce anger swept over the girl, violent and murderous. She would have liked them all to be annihilated, cleared away, so that the world was left clear for her." (59)

Finally, the use of mimetic sentences that, in terms of diction, sound, and structure imitate or evoke the experience they describe is far more prevalent in *Women in Love* than in "The Rocking-Horse Winner" or *Sons and Lovers*. A world dominated by machines is replicated in the measured repetitions of the following passage:

> Let them turn into mechanisms, let them. Let them become instruments, pure machines, pure wills, that work like clockwork in perpetual repetition. Let them be this, let them be taken up entirely in their work, let them be perfect parts of a great machine, having slumber of constant repetition. Let Gerald manage his firm. (566)

The sensation of delving deep into the subconscious is visualized and almost visceral in this sentence, in which repetition and parataxis create a sensation of fluid unfolding:

> It was as if she drew a glittering rope of knowledge out of the sea of darkness, drew and drew and drew it out of the fathomless depths of the past, and still it did not come to an end, there was no end to it, she must haul and haul at the rope of glittering consciousness, pull it out phosphorescent from the endless depths of the unconsciousness, till she was weary, aching, exhausted, and fit to break, and yet she had not done. (432-433)

Birkin's wrestling match with Gerald, during which their two bodies intertwine and fuse, is brilliantly evoked in the doubled nouns, adverbs, and adjectives, and repeated sounds of the following two sentences:

essential white figures working into a tighter, closer oneness of struggle, with a strange, octopus-like knotting and flashing of limbs in the subdued light of the room; a tense white knot of flesh gripped in silence between the walls of old brown books. . . . Often, in the white, interlaced knot of violent living being that swayed silently, there was no head to be seen, only the swift, tight limbs, the solid white backs, the physical junction of two bodies clinched into oneness. . . . (349)

A lengthy catalogue of participial phrases conveys the rapturous movements of Gudrun's dance before the bulls:

Gudrun, looking as if some invisible chain weighed to her hands and feet, began slowly to dance in the eurhythmic manner, pulsing and fluttering rhythmically with her feet, making low, regular gestures with her hands and arms, now spreading her arms wide, now raising them above her head, now flinging them softly apart, and lifting her face, her feet, all the time beating and running to the measure of the song. (231)

The circularity of a demented rabbit's movements is depicted in this sentence:

Round and round the court it went, as if shot from a gun, round and round like a furry meteorite, in a tense hard circle that seemed to bind their brains. (318)

Syntax in the Film

As in the screen adaptation of "The Rocking-Horse Winner," many of the effects produced by the distinctive syntax in Lawrence's *Women in Love* are replicated in Ken Russell's film. In contrast to the leisurely pace of *Sons and Lovers*, with its average shot length of 13 seconds, the pace of *Women in Love* is quite rapid, with an average shot length of just under 7 seconds (6.75), and many shots, often in quick succession, of ¼ to ½ second, particularly in those scenes depicting vigorous physical movement. However, despite the rapidfire straight cutting within and between shots, scenes, and sequences, the brevity of many shots, and the almost constant camera movement within shots, the overall pace of the film is considerably slower than the cutting technique and the average duration of shots would suggest. In part, this is because, like the vocabulary of the novel, the shots and images in the film are so eye-fillingly lush and arousing—in a word, so "purple"[127]—that Russell creates a sense of weightedness, density, and substantiality even when the shots are relatively brief and the cutting is rapid. It is also because in almost every scene, even those with series of extremely brief shots, one or more shots are comparatively lengthy,[128] up to 107 seconds, as, for example, in the pre-credits opening scene in which Ursula and Gudrun leave their home and start strolling to the Crich wedding. The film's tracking shots can be seen as corresponding to the numerous extremely lengthy sentences characteristic of the novel; they create a sense of fluidity at the same time as they sometimes retard the pace of the film. By maintaining a rapid pace tempered by at least one or two longer, more leisurely shots in each scene, Russell retains the considerable forward momentum characteristic of the prose in the novel, and also achieves a variety of tempos.

Although syntactic parallelism in prose strictly refers to consecutive phrases, clauses, or sentences that are repeated (with or without slight variation) in succeeding ones, parallelism in film can be used on many levels and is created not merely by juxtaposing shots but by mirroring entire scenes and sequences. In *Women in Love* Russell employs structural and syntactic parallelism to such an extent that it becomes a hallmark of the movie. Ana Laura Zambrano cites "the film's intricate parallel structure," which tightens "the parallels between the main characters,"[129] and Joseph Gomez notes the film's dance-like rhythms, produced partly by "parallel sequences and parallel shots with slight but meaningful variations."[130]

Many opportunities for cinematic parallels are offered by the contrasting love relationships between the principal characters. In the introductory wedding sequence, a series of closeups of Ursula and matching point-of-view closeups of Birkin is followed by closeups of Gudrun and point-of-view closeups of Gerald. Gudrun's dance before the bulls is succeeded by her rescue and Gerald's declaration of love; this sequence is crosscut with Birkin's breezy greeting to a terrified Ursula and his admission of love as they walk along the water's edge. Parallel scenes involving the two pairs of lovers are Ursula and Birkin's chance meeting at the soldier's memorial service followed, three scenes later, by Gudrun's providentially running into Gerald while being assaulted outside a tavern. The sequence in which Ursula and Birkin argue and then make love in lyrical slow motion is paralleled by one in which Gerald clashes with Gudrun at Shortlands on the eve of Mr. Crich's death, then sneaks into her bedroom the night of his father's funeral and makes love to her (the scene ends in a series of parallel dissolves as Gudrun awakens the next morning).

Scenes involving Gerald and Birkin are paralleled by scenes featuring Gudrun and Ursula. During the wedding sequence, just after Gerald and Birkin are shown walking to the church side by side, the sisters are filmed watching the proceedings from the cemetery. In a scene at Shortlands, Gerald and Birkin, separated by statues of women, discuss the possibilities of marriage. Two scenes later, as Gudrun works on a sculpture of Gerald, she and Ursula talk about a proposed trip to the Swiss Alps, and at the end of the film, Ursula is reunited with Gudrun in one scene and Birkin with the corpse of his would-be "blood brother" Gerald in another.

Throughout the film, actions or events are also paralleled. Gerald dives into Willey Pond as Gudrun and Ursula discuss their upcoming visit to Hermione's cottage; he dives again when Gerald attempts to rescue the drowning newlyweds. Hermione turns on the electric lights in Ursula's classroom, and Gerald switches on the light after his firelit wrestling match with Birkin. Gudrun observes a miner kissing his girlfriend in a tunnel; later, she stops to kiss Gerald in the same tunnel. Within scenes, events are also paralleled. During the outdoor luncheon at Breadalby, Birkin mimics Hermione's eating a quartered fig by vulgarly sucking on a fig slit down the middle. Hermione's solo dance is paralleled by the guests' ragtime dancing, and Tibby and Laura's nude swim is immediately echoed by Gudrun and Ursula's.

Like parallel phrases and clauses, types of shots are repeated consecutively, as in the blurred closeups of Birkin running into the forest, the series of lap dissolves of Gudrun writhing on the ground before Gerald, the three backward zooms of Gerald sleeping on top of Gudrun in her bedroom, and the numerous lap dissolves of Gerald wandering to his death in the snow. Throughout the film, series of closeups parallel those in the opening sequence. Five alternating closeups of Hermione and Birkin are insterspersed with pairs and single closeups of the other guests at Hermione's luncheon, tight reaction closeups of Gerald and Birkin that punctuate the "Russian ballet" sequence, and a series of medium closeups (two-shots) and tight individual closeups of the Brangwen sisters as they watch Gerald rein in his horse by a moving train. Parallel closeups of Loerke and Gudrun during their dressup games, a series of tight closeups of Gudrun as Gerald attempts to strangle her and of Birkin as he grieves over Gerald's corpse, and a series of extreme closeups of Birkin and Ursula as they talk by the fireside after their return to England, extend Russell's pervasive technique of repeating types of shots in sequence right through the final shots of the film.

Specialized types of shots and movements that appear in one sequence are paralleled in others. Tracking shots are used in many sequences: Ursula and Gudrun stroll through Beldover in the opening scene; Birkin dashes through the forest at Breadalby; and Ursula and Birkin walk through and away from the crowd at the old soldier's memorial service, and stroll beside the water in two different scenes. Panning shots recur during the outdoor luncheon and Mr. Crich's funeral. Gerald is repeatedly shot in rapid movement—running and diving into the water at Breadalby, galloping beside a moving train, dashing to the rescue of miners attacked by dogs, and skiing down on a slope in the Alps. Tibby and Laura, as well as Gudrun and Ursula, are photographed swimming. And of course, the numerous dance sequences repeat certain types of movements. Hermione's Isadora Duncan-like gyrations are paralleled by Gudrun's dance before her sister and the bulls, and later before Loerke in the snow. The Charleston performed poolside by a young couple is mirrored in the Charleston which interrupts Hermione's solo, and the waltz at the Crich picnic, danced to "I'm Forever Blowing Bubbles," is echoed in the waltz at the Alpine lodge.

Though Russell employs many visual parallels in *Women in Love*, verbal and musical echoes are even more pervasive, creating an intricate and unifying aural subtext. Through dialogue, as well as visuals, many of the film's recurring themes are introduced in the opening wedding sequence— the pros and cons of love and marriage, the value of spontaneity and unconventionality, the opposition between life and death as well as the presence of death in life, and the troubled relations between modern men and women.

The overriding theme of love is raised very early in the film by Gerald, who asks Birkin, "Have you ever *really* loved anybody?" In key scenes throughout the rest of the film, the meaning of love—carnal, spiritual, or communal, as in "love of humanity"—is argued and reargued, as is the question of whether any or all of the characters actually love each other or anybody else ("Say you love me," plead both Ursula and Gudrun to their respective lovers) or whether love as conventionally defined really does or ought to exist. The debate is carried on through the last scene of the film, in which Ursula insists that Birkin "cannot have two kinds of love" and that desiring the love of both a man and a woman is "an obstinacy, a theory, a perversity." The opposite emotion is also mentioned in a number of scenes, for example, by Birkin at a military memorial service ("What people want is hate, hate and nothing but hate!") and by Mr. Crich, who disapproves of Gerald's dismissing an aging miner ("They hate you. I'm glad I won't have to see it much longer!"). Just before Ursula and Birkin leave the Alps, Gerald says of Gudrun, "I hate her somewhere."

Like parallelism, antithesis in its many forms is pervasive in both the prose of *Women in Love* and the film. One sort of antithesis, of course, is thematic. The opposition between life and death in all their forms is a constant subtext in both the novel and the film. According to Joseph Gomez, "Russell seems to have pitted moments of vitality and spontaneity against episodes depicting death, both in literal and symbolic manifestations."[131] Russell translates Lawrence's thematic contrasts into syntactical antithesis within and between scenes. Hermione's self-indulgent dance of death is interrupted by the pianist playing ragtime music and her grateful guests gaily dancing the Charleston. Russell follows Hermione's attempt to kill Birkin with Birkin's healing flight into the woods, but—unlike the novel— immediately contrasts that scene with Birkin's disruption of a memorial service for the war dead. Birkin and Ursula's frantic love-making at the Crich picnic is preceded by the deaths of Tibby and Laura and immediately followed by Gerald's discovery of the drowned newlyweds.

Consistent with the antithetical life/death motif are sharp contrasts of mood and atmosphere within and between scenes and sequences. In the opening shots of the film, the quiet orderliness of the Brangwens' household is disrupted by the noisy intrusion of the sisters dressed in colorful, offbeat clothes. The relaxed scenes of Gudrun and Ursula swimming and Ursula singing with Gudrun's head on her lap are counterpointed in the tense succeeding scene with Gudrun's weird dance before the bulls. The calm beauty of the Criches' lake at night is disrupted by the subsequent frenzy of the drowning newlyweds and Gerald's subsequent futile attempt to save them. The discovery of the drowned lovers in the mud at the bottom of the lake and the removal of the bodies in a funeral procession at dawn is juxtaposed with the sensual wrestling match of Birkin and Gerald before a roaring fire. Also antithetical are Birkin and Ursula's lyrical lovemaking in a field, followed by the somber death and burial of Mr. Crich, and Loerke's verbal seduction of Gudrun in his bedroom as he shows her photographs of his sculpture, followed by Ursula and Birkin's abrupt decision to leave the "ghastly glamour" of the Alps.

Visual antithesis verging on oxymoron operates within many shots and scenes. Class differences are signaled by contrasting clothing. In a streetcar, the two fashionably clad sisters are hemmed in by laborers in somber clothes, while formally dressed Gerald Crich and his father, perched in a white automobile, are encircled by darkly clad miners trudging home from work. Russell also employs body language to indicate fundamental contrasts between characters—Gudrun's rigid, corpse-like pose on a tomb during the wedding sequence, contrasted with Ursula's upright but informal postures; Birkin running with Tibby juxtaposed with Gerald stiffly walking; Birkin lounging relaxed on the rug, while Gerald sits stiffly in a baronial chair before their wrestling match. Hermione's hyperactive solo dance contrasts with the frozen poses of the Brangwen sisters and the languidly reclining newlyweds on a couch. Birkin aggressively pushes his way through a silent and motionless crowd at the old soldier's memorial service. Russell counterpoints Gudrun's prancing before the bulls with the lumbering movements of the cattle and Ursula's panicky immobility. Opposing types of movement of actors and camera also create syntactic antithesis. In the "Russian ballet" scene, as Ken Hanke points out, the "heavily-choreographed camera movement and rhythmic editing," along with the angular gestures of Hermione's carefully staged dance, contrast markedly with "a series of freestyle pairs and infectiously jumbled editing"[132] when the pianist switches to ragtime music and the guests whirl about.

Another kind of counterpointing is created between shots, as in the intricate wedding sequence at the beginning of the film, with its crosscutting and flashbacks. Birkin and the groom's breakneck horse and buggy ride to the church is juxtaposed with the arrival of relatives, and the bride and groom's run to the church door is immediately succeeded by Ursula and Gudrun's brisk talk in the cemetery as they spy on the wedding. The rapid-cut Eisensteinian montage in which Gerald whips and kicks his horse beside a moving train is composed of contrasting low-angle zooms, closeups, and medium shots of Gerald, closeups of the horse's legs, feet, head, and flanks, and closeup reaction shots of Ursula and Gudrun. Other scenes and sequences involving visual counterpointing include Gudrun's dance before the bulls, the dance party in the Alps, and Hermione's "Russian ballet," as well as the rapid montages of Birkin and Ursula's frantic and somewhat comic lovemaking at the Crich picnic, and Gerald and Birkin's nude wrestling match, with its succession of long, medium, and closeup shots. Jarring montages that involve rapid cuts and clashing images include Gerald attempting to save the drowning newlyweds and Mrs. Crich letting loose dogs on charity-seeking miners. Several scenes are also punctuated by cutaways—a couple with a baby carriage, Mrs. Crich laughing at her husband's funeral, a man riding a bicycle past Ursula and Birkin during their quarrel, and Gudrun shaking her head in the sun.

Like the disjointed syntax that is a distinctive feature of the prose of *Women in Love*, the narrative structure of Russell's adaptation, in itself choppy and episodic, is punctuated by equally "disjointed" scenes. Frequent shifts of perspective mark one such scene in which Gerald and Birkin, sitting and standing in front of mirrors, discuss love, marriage, and the "additional perfect relationship between two men." "Shock editing" between shots also creates a type of disjointedness that jolts the viewer. The most calculated and controversial instance is the juxtaposition of the high-angle shot of the drowned newlyweds intertwined in a final embrace at the muddy bottom of the drained lake, and the contrasting yet nearly identical shots of Birkin and Ursula embracing after their frantic lovemaking.

Many other such jarring, often ironic contrasts between scenes and sequences are typical of *Women in Love*. A closeup of the bride and groom at the end of the Crich wedding is followed by an extra long shot of Gerald running and diving into the lake that will later kill them. An outdoor closeup of Birkin after he has told Gerald he wants to "sit in a field with my beloved" is ironically juxtaposed with an extreme low-angle shot of the door to Hermione's elegant salon. A shot of the high-key golden wheat field in which Birkin lies down to heal himself after Hermione's assault is followed by a closeup of Ursula at a memorial service for a World War I soldier. A long shot of Gudrun and Ursula walking behind the mourners of the Crich picnic is succeeded by an extreme closeup of Gerald in profile, backlit by a roaring fire, and a lingering closeup of Mr. Crich senior, blood oozing from his mouth, is cut short by a closeup of his young daughter Winnie sobbing at his funeral.

As in the film of *Sons and Lovers*, mimetic sentences that imitate, by means of syntax and rhythm, the experiences they describe are also replicated in a number of scenes and sequences of *Women in Love*. In the slow-motion pastoral lovemaking scene between Birkin and Ursula, for example, Russell attempts to encapsulate, through music and a mobile camera, the fluidity of the succeeding participial phrases that reproduce Ursula's "flooding" sensations as she is lifted into the transcendent realm of "star-equilibrium." The sentence describing Gudrun's dance before the bulls, constructed of another series of participial phrases, is also given its cinematic equivalent in a series of lap dissolves of Gudrun writhing on the ground before Gerald.

Paragraph Shape and Rhythm in the Novel

In general shorter than those in *Sons and Lovers*, the paragraphs in *Women in Love* range from 2 to 23 sentences. Although a significant number of paragraphs are over ten sentences, the average paragraph length in *Women in Love* is 5 sentences and 64 words, in comparison with 6 sentences and 94 words in *Sons and Lovers*. In only one chapter, "The Industrial Magnate" (Chapter XVII), are *Women in Love's* paragraphs exceptionally long, averaging 105 words.

The shape of paragraphs in *Women in Love* varies widely—indicative of the experimental nature of Lawrence's fifth novel. Mid-paragraph swelling, characteristic of "The Rocking-Horse Winner," and to a much lesser degree of *Sons and Lovers*, accounts for only 16 percent of the paragraphs in *Women in Love*. More paragraphs (22 percent) start with long sentences followed by shorter and shorter ones, and many more—37 percent—start with very short sentences (10 words and under) and gradually swell to longish sentences, sometimes followed by an abrupt falloff of one or two short ones. About half (52 percent) of the paragraphs end on an upsurge—the final sentence is longer than the penultimate one—and one quarter (25 percent) of last sentences are over 25 words long. Finally, 27 percent do not swell at the beginning, middle or end, but begin and end with sentences of similar lengths and alternate, wavelike, between shorter and longer sentences.

In dialogue passages, which are far longer and more numerous in *Women in Love* than in *Sons and Lovers*, the average length of quoted sentences, nearly half of which are questions, is nine words. Despite the fact that the principal characters are educated and articulate, speeches in the novel tend to be relatively brief—at most two short sentences. Gudrun and Ursula's terse conversation about marriage, which opens the novel and the film, is typical of Lawrence's use of "stychomythic" dialogue in *Women in Love*. Only Hermione and Birkin, regularly, and Ursula and Gudrun, in isolated, impassioned outbursts, speak in paragraphs. For all characters, conversations with Birkin turn into catechisms (Q & A) with his occasionally lengthy replies.

The insistent, often hypnotic and eroticized rhythms of the narrative and descriptive passages in *Women in Love*, even more striking than those in "The Rocking-Horse Winner" and *Sons and Lovers*, are achieved through repetition of metrical patterns and syntactical constructions as well as of words and sounds, as in the following prose passage, which includes many instances of parallel metrical and syntactical configurations:

> She sounded purely anxious. Nevertheless, Gudrun, *with her árms outspréad and her fáce uplífted, wént in a stránge* palpitating dance towards the cattle, lifting her body towards them as if in a spell, her feet pulsing as if in some little frenzy of unconscious sensation, *her árms, her wrísts, her hánds, strétching and héaving and fálling, her bréasts lífted and sháken towards the cáttle, her thróat expósed* as in some voluptuous ecstasy

towards them, whilst she drifted imperceptibly nearer, an uncanny white figure, towards them, *cárried awáy in its ówn rapt tránce, ébbing in stránge fluctuátions* upon the cattle, that waved, and ducked their heads a little in sudden contraction from her, watching all the time as if hypnotised, then bare horns branching in the clear light as the white figure of the woman ebbed upon them, in the slow, hypnotising convulsion of the dance. She could feel them just in front of her. It was as if she had the electric pulse from their breasts, running into her hands. *Soón she would toúch them, áctually toúch them.* A terrible shiver of fear and pleasure went through her. And all the while, *Úrsula, spéll-bound, képt up her hígh-pitched, thín, irrélevant sóng*, which pierced the fading evening like an incantation. (233)

Even more obvious than the metrical and syntactical repetition, and contributing significantly to the insistently rhythmic quality of the prose in the novel, is Lawrence's pervasive habit of modified and incremental repetition of words, noted in the section on diction, along with multiple instances of alliteration and assonance. Aural repetition creates the sensation of inexorable forward movement at the same time that the recursive echoing of words generates a semantic counter-movement—the eroticized frictional to-and-fro to which Lawrence referred in his preface to the American edition of *Women in Love*,[133] and which has been noted in analyses of diction and rhythm in "The Rocking-Horse Winner" and *Sons and Lovers*. The rhythmic rocking forward and backward, in *Women in Love*, produces not so much a wavelike as a circular or spiral effect, deepening and intensifying the portrayal of inner cognitive and emotional processes as the characters struggle toward awareness and resolution of tormenting conflict. Lawrence referred to this experimental method of portraying feelings through exploration and incremental repetition in *The Rainbow* and *Women in Love* as "the exhaustive method," in contrast to merely writing "a story with a plot . . . pure object and story." [134]

Even at the peak of an action or gesture, the rhythm and pace of the narrative usually slows to accommodate Lawrence's focus on the inner states of his characters. For example, a climactic moment in the narrative—Hermione smashing Birkin's skull with a paperweight—is prolonged and embellished by modified repetition of words, phrases, and clauses. In the six-paragraph passage, the emphasis is not on Hermione's assault but on her physical sensations and emotions as she anticipates and performs the acts:

Terrible shocks ran over her body, like *shocks* of *electricity*, as if many volts of *electricity* suddenly struck her down. She was aware of him sitting *silently* there, an unthinkable evil obstruction. Only this blotted out her mind, pressed out her very breathing, his *silent*, stooping *back*, the *back* of his head.

A *terrible voluptuous* thrill ran down her *arms*—she was going to know her *voluptuous* consummation. Her *arms* quivered and were *strong*, immeasurably and irresistably *strong*. What *delight*, what *delight* in strength, what delirium of pleasure! She was going to have her *consummation* of *voluptuous ecstasy* at last! It was coming! In utmost terror and agony, she knew it was upon her now, in extremity of bliss. Her hand closed on a blue, beautiful *ball* of lapis lazuli that *stood* on her desk for a paperweight. She rolled it round in her hand as she rose *silently*. Her heart was a *pure flame* in her breast, she was *purely unconscious* in *ecstasy*. She moved towards him and *stood* behind him for a moment in *ecstasy*. He closed within the spell, remained motionless and unconscious.

Then, swiftly, in a *flame* that drenched down her body like fluid lightning and gave her a perfect, *unutterable consummation*, *unutterable* satisfaction, she brought down the *ball* of jewel stone with all her force, crash on his head. . . . (162-163)

In the service of Lawrence's "exhaustive method," the prose of *Women in Love* moves sentences forward more slowly and less propulsively than it does in *Sons and Lovers*. The continuity and flow that typify *Women in Love* is produced not as much by the use of *and*, *but*, and conjunctive adverbs at the beginning of sentences as by the use of repetition of the same word at the beginning of sentences. On occasion, particularly in descriptive passages similar to those in *Sons and Lovers*, a slower rhythm and pace is also achieved by the use of numerous heavily accented syllables and the relative paucity of multiple unaccented syllables, as in the following paragraph, which contains 13 clusters of double or triple-accented syllables:

The *week passed* away. On the Saturday it rained, a *soft dazzling rain*, that *held off* at times. In one of the intervals Gudrun and Ursula *set out* for a walk, going towards Willey Water. The atmosphere was grey and translucent, the *birds sang sharply* in the *young twigs*, the earth would be quickening and hastening in growth. The *two girls walked swiftly*, gladly, because of the *soft, subtle* rush of morning that filled the *wet haze*. By the road the *blackthorn* was in blossom, white and wet, its tiny amber *grains burning* faintly in the *white smoke* of blossom. Purple twigs were darkly luminous in the *grey air*, *high hedges* glowed like living shadows, hovering nearer, coming into creation. (98)

Rhythm in the Film

Ken Russell went to considerable lengths to create visual and aural rhythms that in many respects approximate those of Lawrence's eroticized, rhythmic prose. Thomas Atkins notes the director's "restless rhythm in editing," which, combined with "movement, mass and color," creates "the visual equivalent of some aspect of sexual involvement."[135] Although Russell was apparently not familiar with Angus Wilson's observation that Lawrence's *Women in Love* "has a form as strict as a court dance,"[136] Russell also sensed the dancelike variations that served as the backbone of Lawrence's novel and, as Joseph Gomez notes, created a film "patterned after the structure of dance rhythms."[137] Entire sequences in the film are "choreographed,"[138] and the dancelike rhythms of *Women in Love* are also suggested in Russell's visual counterpointing, parallel sequences, and shots with "slight but meaningful variations," and in the film's complex use of mirrors and frequent repetition of objects, such as fireplaces, statues, and cups.[139]

With an average shot length of under seven seconds, and an average of 535 shots per hour (as opposed to 280 in *Sons and Lovers* and 305 in *The Rocking-Horse Winner*), the pace of Russell's adaptation of *Women in Love* is quite rapid. However, there are wide variations in speed throughout the film, and the overall pace perceived by the viewer, like the pace of the prose, seems somewhat slower than the brief average shot length would suggest. This effect is created by the elaborateness of the decor and costumes, the intensity of the color, the intellectually challenging Lawrentian dialogue, which forces viewer concentration, and the often abrupt shock editing, which disrupts the smooth progression of scenes and sequences. The choreographed movements of the characters and camera and the often lugubrious music also slow down the action in several scenes, as do several unusually long takes (often tracking shots) that parallel the novel's many exceptionally long sentences.

The generally brief paragraphs in *Women in Love*, as well as the novel's short chapters (20 out of 31 are under 20 pages long and about one third are 10 pages or under), are reproduced in the film's many short scenes. Approximately two thirds of them are under 100 seconds, and eight scenes are single takes, ranging from 14 to 56 seconds. Although the paragraphs in the novel are varied in shape, the "shapes" of the scenes in the film are far less diverse. Like Lawrence's "front-loaded" sentences (main clause followed by subordinate clause), almost all of them have longer shots at or near the beginning of each scene, yielding to much shorter shots and surging only at intervals—especially at or quite near the end of the scenes—to much longer shots.

In a very few action scenes featuring rapid montages, such as Gerald subduing his horse, Birkin and Gerald wrestling, and Birkin and Ursula making love at the Crich picnic, the pace is extremely rapid, with many shots of ¼ or ½ seconds. A few scenes, on the other hand, are quite slow paced, either because of slow-motion photography, as in the pastoral love-making scene between Birkin and Ursula, or because of consecutive long shots, in such scenes as Gerald and Mr. Crich riding in a white car through the miners and Gerald staggering to his death in the snow.

Most distinctive in many of the scenes in the film, as in more than half of the paragraphs in the novel, is the sexualization of the film's pace and rhythm. Even when dialogue is the only "action," most scenes build to a climax of psychological or physical conflict, or of physical movement, often accompanied by the accelerating pace and volume of the musical score; then they stop abruptly, shift to a different pace, and subside at the end of the scene. One instance is Hermione's Russian ballet, interrupted by guests doing the Charleston and followed by the slower confrontation between Hermione and Birkin. Another is Gudrun's dance before the bulls, terminated by the arrival of Birkin and Gerald, and followed by Gerald's halting, low-key declaration of love. A fierce row between Birkin and Ursula in field and forest builds to a loud and strident climax, followed by Ursula's quietly offering Birkin a flower. A final instance is the wrestling scene between Gerald and Birkin, which climaxes in an intense struggle captured in sweaty close-ups and then tapers off as the two men, glistening and exhausted, lie side by side, then slowly get dressed.[140]

Closely connected to the pattern of cinematic climaxes that suddenly taper off is the pattern of interrupted (or syncopated) rhythms created by sudden bursts of violent movement or gesture, which punctuate the film. One of many examples occurs during the opening scene of the film, in which Mr. Brangwen, steadily tapping nails into leather, is interrupted by Ursula and Gudrun thumping loudly and rapidly down the stairs.[141] The dignified arrival of the guests at the Crich wedding ends abruptly with the spontaneous, madcap race between the bridegroom and the bride, and in the classroom scene Hermione's pretentious crooning over catkins ("Aren't they *beau*tiful?") is silenced by Ursula's angrily ringing a bell behind her. Other instances include Hermione's smashing Birkin over the head with a paperweight, a tipsy miner's assaulting Gudrun outside a tavern, the sudden intrusion of horned cattle on Gudrun's dance, and Gerald's violently raping Gudrun in their bedroom in the Swiss lodge.

The driving, hypnotic rhythms created by repetition (with variation) of words, phrases, clauses, and sentences in Lawrence's novel are constantly replicated in Russell's adaptation. Types of shots as well as specific shots and variations of them are repeated throughout the film. For example, during the rapidfire montage of Gerald subduing his horse beside a moving train, repeated reaction shots of Ursula and Gudrun are interspersed with closeups of the sisters, creating a pulsating, dynamic rhythm. After Gudrun's dance before the bulls, repeated extreme low-angle closeups of Gerald are interspersed at regular intervals with high-angle dissolves of Gudrun writhing on the grass at Gerald's feet. In the wrestling scene, brief long shots of Gerald and Birkin, apart or grappling, are rhythmically intercut between medium shots, medium closeups, and closeups of the men embracing and straining against each other.

Certain *patterns* of rhythm are also repeated throughout the film. Some scenes accelerate in pace and then get slower, such as Gerald and Birkin's wrestling match and Gudrun's dance before the bulls. Others accelerate in speed and are succeeded by slower scenes. Hermione's solo dance, for example, is followed by the lively dancing of her guests and by Hermione's slower-paced confrontation with Birkin. Immediately afterward, Birkin rushes through the forest frantically shedding his clothes, then walks slowly through the foliage and lies down in it. Additional instances include the hectic drowning of the newlyweds followed by Birkin and Ursula's walking together and Mrs. Crich's setting dogs on the miners, succeeded by the far slower scene in which Gerald talks to Gudrun as she stands on a balcony above him.

The dialogue and delivery of four of the principal characters—Gerald, Birkin, Hermione, and Gudrun—also contain rhythmic repetition, exemplified by the constantly halting syncopation of Gerald's speeches gaspingly delivered by Oliver Reed, and in particular by the speech of Hermione and Birkin, who are given words and phrases to say over and over. "Hate, hate, hate," intones Birkin at the soldier's memorial; "Little red flames, aren't they beautiful!" croons Hermione repeatedly over catkins; and "Dreadful! Dreadful!" and "Only destroy!" she reiterates as Birkin lounges besides her at poolside. Interrogating Gerald in the Swiss Alps. Gudrun asks him how much he loves her, and in the ensuing conversation, the word "love" is repeated several times in a rhythmic pattern that builds up to a devastating moment in which Gudrun, after bullying Gerald into "admitting" he loves her, abruptly mocks him for it. Besides dialogue, many scenes incorporate rhythmically repetitive noises and sounds, as in Mr. Brangwen's previously noted tapping on nails in the opening shots of the film; Hermione clapping three times for silence in the ballet scene; or Loerke clapping compulsively to the beat of the dance music in the Alps. As Gerald wanders off into the snow, the rhythmic crunching of his boots is heard, as is the faint, repeated sound of church bells and handbells in many scenes.

The dancelike rhythms of the film are underscored in large part by the music. Besides the lilting songs "I'm Forever Blowing Bubbles" and "Oh, You Beautiful Doll," and the hymn "Jerusalem," music repeated throughout the film includes the lyrical score accompanying Birkin and Ursula's slow-motion lovemaking, heard again in their bedroom scene in the Swiss Alps. Ominously heavy music builds to a powerful climax in the wrestling scene between Birkin and Gerald. This musical motif recurs when Birkin and Gerald leave each other in the Alps, as well as later, when Gudrun, after tormenting and rejecting Gerald, makes aggressive overtures to him and is raped. The rhythm and pace of the score matches the rhythm of the action and cutting. The music gets repeatedly faster and louder in scenes that build to a noticeable climax, such as Hermione's bashing Birkin, Gerald's brutalizing his horse, Gudrun's dancing before the bulls, and Birkin and Ursula's making love at the picnic. The music rhythmically keeps pace with the action as Gerald and Birkin wrestle, Tibby and Laura drown, Gudrun and Gerald make love in various places, and Loerke and Gudrun cavort in costume.

Most remarkable is the way in which many key shots and scenes in the film capture almost exactly the rhythm and movement of the prose. Gerald's running dive into the water at Shortlands, photographed in an extra-long shot, parallels the description in the novel, in physical and emotional terms:

> Suddenly from the boat house a white figure ran out, frightening in its swift, sharp transit, across the old landing-stage. It launched in a white arc through the air, there was a bursting of water, and among the smooth ripples, a swimmer was making out to space, in a centre of faintly heaving motion. (96)

Hermione's smashing Birkin on the head, described in three longish paragraphs of slowed-down, highly rhythmic, repetitive prose (162-163), is replicated in the film by a blurry montage of off-angle shots which also prolong the violent act. After Birkin strips his clothes off in the forest and feels the white birch bark, his slow passage through the underbrush and tall grass mirrors the lengthy, repetitive, detailed description in the novel (164–165). The aurally repetitive passage depicting Gerald restraining his horse (108–109) is replicated in both visual and aural terms in the film. Russell attempts to reproduce the incredibly long, rhythmic, syntactically repetitive sentences in the paragraphs describing Gudrun's dance before the bulls (231–25) as well as those recounting the slow progress of the miners leaving work in Chapter XVII, "The Industrial Magnate" (295).

Also rhythmically analogous to passages in the novel are scenes depicting the guests dancing in the Swiss Alps (396), Gerald and Gudrun's sledding down a slope at a rapid clip (514), and most movingly, Gerald's trudging off to his death in the snow (573–575). The nine brief paragraphs describing Gerald's suicidal ascent contain many brief sentences or sentences with very short segments. The opening sentence of the passage, "Gerald stumbled on up the slope of snow, in the bluish darkness, always climbing, always unconsciously climbing, weary though he was" and the paragraph that follows are typical:

> He slithered down a sheer snow slope. That frightened him. He had no alpenstock, nothing. But having come safely to rest, he began to walk on, in the illuminated darkness. It was as cold as sleep. He was between two ridges, in a hollow. So he swerved. Should he climb the other ridge, or wander along the hollow? How frail the thread of his being was stretched! He would perhaps climb the ridge. The snow was firm and simple. He went along. There was something standing out of the snow. He approached, with dimmest curiosity. (574)

The film's rendition of Gerald's suicide, with its numerous consecutive dissolves and lap dissolves of Gerald aimlessly wandering to his death in the blue, snow-laden shadows of the glistening mountains, admirably mimics the short segments and sentences of the passage in the novel.

Metaphors in the Novel

The prose in *Women in Love* is distinctive, even idiosyncratic, for its pervasive use of figurative language, in particular a dense network of interlocking metaphors in both the narrative and dialogue passages.[142] Along with the frequent repetition of diction, syntax, and rhythm, Lawrence's pervasive use of metaphor and simile in *Women in Love* creates the evocative "purpleness" of the novel's prose that distinguishes it from the comparatively realistic and literal prose in *Sons and Lovers* and "The Rocking-Horse Winner." In *Metaphor and Meaning in D. H. Lawrence's Later Novels*, John Humma draws a distinction between "expansive or connective metaphors" and "local metaphors" which "do not exfoliate and interconnect throughout the text."[143] Humma's comments on Lawrence's "interpenetrating metaphors" in his last novel, *Lady Chatterly's Lover*, also apply to *Women in Love*:

> The figures of speech in the novel have a way of overlapping, of crossing boundaries, indeed of becoming at times cross-references taking us forward or backward from one scene or passage to another. They almost always make connections beyond themselves.[144]

As in many of Lawrence's novels and shorter fictions, including *Sons and Lovers*, metaphors in *Women in Love* are drawn from a variety of *non-human* sources, including the natural, the inorganic, and, as in "The Rocking-Horse Winner," the supernatural realms. Fairly early in the novel, Birkin regales Ursula with his vision of a Garden of Eden, a paradise entirely free of human beings:

> "Do you think that creation depends on man? It merely doesn't. There are trees and grass and buds. I much prefer to think of the lark rising up in the morning upon a humanless world. Man is a mistake, he must go."

And in a letter to his editor, Edward Garnett, on June 5, 1914, in which Lawrence expressed his interest in Futurism, the novelist wrote:

> That which is physic—non-human, in humanity, is more interesting to me than the old-fashioned human element. . . . Like as diamond and coal are the same pure single element of carbon. The ordinary novel would trace the history of diamond—but I say 'diamond, what! this is carbon.' And my diamond might be coal and soot, and my theme is carbon.[145]

In tracing and "bodying forth" the "carbon" in his principal characters, Lawrence employed imagery from a primeval world existing before human beings came into it as well as a medieval cosmos of earth, air, fire, and water, inhabited by angels and demons and by a bestiary of animals, birds, and insects. Although the events in *Women in Love* take place in pre-World War I England and the characters run the social gamut from untutored working-class provincials to cultivated upper-class sophisticates, the verbal subtext in the novel creates a mythical, dreamlike, and at times nightmarish landscape inhabited by creatures that might appear in a schizophrenic's hallucinations—"the real world falling into phantasmagoria."[146] The novel's metaphors and similes flicker like omnipresent Platonic shadows behind every person, place, and physical and psychological "event" in the novel.

Many of the metaphors and similes in *Women in Love* have their origin, literally and figuratively, in the first verses of Genesis, and fall into only a few categories, among them plants (including flowers, leaves, and fruit); animals (including insects and birds); water (including rivers, fountains, streams, waves, floods, and storms); snow and ice; light and fire; shadow and darkness; birth, life, and death; bondage and freedom; and demons, angels, and ghosts. In addition, quite a few figures of speech are drawn from religion, ancient history, and royalty, and from twentieth-century science and industry—chemistry, electricity, machines, and cutting tools. Striking are metaphors involving abstractions, such as, "he was an incarnation, a great phase of life" (249), "she is the flowering mystery of the death process" (239), "all life was a rotary motion, mechanised, cut off from reality" (262), "the terrible knot of consciousness . . . was broken, gone, his life was dissolved in darkness over his limbs and his body" (391), and "in the midst of this profound darkness, there seemed to flow on her heart the effulgence of a paradise unknown and unrealised" (478).

Whether clustered or separated by pages of narrative, the central metaphors and similes in the novel almost all appear in the first three chapters. The prevalence of figurative language is established in the opening scene, in which Gudrun declares, "Everything withers in the bud" (55), and Ursula is described as "having always that strange brightness and essential flame that is caught, meshed contravened" (55). When the sisters pass through the colliery town of Beldover on their way to the Crich wedding, Gudrun sees it as a "country in an underworld" (58) and the people, with their "watchful underworld faces" (59) having "the long unwearying stare of aborigines"(58). "Filled with repulsion," Ursula feels "like a beetle toiling in the dust." (57) After her first glimpse of Gerald Crich, Gudrun perceives "in his clear northern flesh and his fair hair . . . a glisten like cold sunshine refracted through crystals of ice"(61). Gerald is also described, through Gudrun's eyes, as a "young, good-humoured, smiling wolf" (61).

At Laura Crich's wedding, Gerald's father steps out of his carriage "like a shadow" (65); the groom races after his bride "like a hound" (65). Hermione Roddice is described as "almost drugged, as if a strange mass of thoughts coiled in the darkness within her"(62). During and after the wedding, Hermione's "rapt look" seems "spiritual like the angels" (69), yet "still subtly demoniacal" (69), while for Gerald, there is a "strange stealth glistening through his amiable, almost happy appearance" (70). Gerald and Birkin's unacknowledged "strange perilous intimacy" is described in quasi-sexual terms: ". . . the heart of each burned from the other" (83).

In Chapter III, "Class-Room," metaphors and similes from the first two chapters recur, in particular images of fire, light, darkness, fruits, snakes, insects, and demons. Birkin's face, "gleaming like fire" (84), encounters Ursula's, which has a "tender light of dawn shining" from it (84); together, they look at "the flickers of crimson that came from the female bud" of a catkin (85); "little red flames," murmurs Hermione (87). In the same scene Birkin accuses Hermione of making knowledge—"the eternal apple" (90)—her life. Hermione is "convulsed with fury and violation, speechless, like a stricken pythoness of the Greek oracle" (91). Considering Hermione's assault on Birkin with a paperweight in the chapter "Breadalby," Birkin's counterattack is ironic: "You want it all in that loathsome little skull of yours, that ought to be cracked like a nut. You'll be the same till it *is* cracked, like an insect in its skin" (92). Birkin prescribes knowledge in the blood: "Then you find yourself a palpable body of darkness, a demon" (93). When Hermione denounces Birkin as "such a *dreadful* satanist" (93), he accuses her of being "the real devil who won't let life exist" (93).

In succeeding chapters, the metaphors and similes that appear in the first three chapters are repeated, with variations. All of the negative, destructive characters (most of the characters in the novel, actually) are associated with darkness, the underworld, electricity, vermin, snakes, insects, and birds of prey; positive characters (Ursula and Birkin) are associated with flowers, birds, flame, light, shadow, rivers, floods, and stars. Images of fire, darkness, flood, and womb saturate the narrative, applying to all of the major characters.

The permutations of just two categories of metaphors and similes—fire and animals—exemplify the rich profusion of tropes in *Women in Love*. With its associated imagery of flames and burning, fire is one of the most pervasive metaphors in the novel. Besides Hermione's "little red flames" of the "pistillate flowers," Birkin excoriates her as "a bitterer red anger burned up to fury in him" (92). Gerald's desire for Pussum makes his back "tense like a tiger's with a slumbering fire" (129). As she was about to assault Birkin, Hermione's "heart was a pure flame in her breast" (163), and she brings down the ball of jewel stone on Birkin's head "in a flame that drenched down her body like fluid lightning" (163). When Birkin is becoming aware of Ursula, her face is "strangely enkindled, as if suffused from within by a powerful sweet fire" (190).

When they first become lovers, Birkin is "a perfect hard flame of passionate desire for her" (256). After Gudrun strikes Gerald across the face, "a dangerous flame darkened his eyes" (236). Later, when Gudrun asks Gerald not to be angry with her, "a flame flew over him" (237). During the stoning of the water in Chapter XIX ("Moony"), the moon flies asunder "in flakes of white and dangerous fire" (323). In Chapter XX ("Gladiatorial"), Gerald describes a Japanese wrestler as "quick and slippery and full of electric fire" (347). Awaiting Gudrun's arrival, young Winifred Crich is described as having "a strange new fire in her heart," and is "blinded for a moment with a flame of pleasure" (359). In the Alps, Gerald's heart goes up "like a flame of ice" as he enfolds Gudrun (493), while as Birkin dances with Ursula, there were "odd little fires playing in his eyes" (504). Tobogganing in the snow, Gerald and Gudrun fly down "through the white flame" (514). When Gudrun finally rejects an enraged Gerald near the end of the novel, his heart "burst into flame" (561).

Figures of speech involving animals, birds, and insects—often laden with sinister associations—are more numerous than any in the novel, intricately connecting seemingly dissimilar characters. Near the beginning of the book, Ursula, strolling through Beldover, feels "like a beetle toiling in the dust" (57). At the wedding, Gerald is seen by Gudrun as "a young good-humored smiling wolf" (61); at the wedding, Hermione is "convulsed with fury and violation, speechless, like a stricken pythoness of the Greek oracle" (91), and Birkin looks "like a deer." Ursula tells Gudrun, "One wants to strut, to be a swan among geese" (101), while Birkin declares that ". . . life is a blotch of labour like insects scurrying in filth" (106). In "Breadalby" (Chapter VIII) the guests at Hermione's estate are compared to aquatic or sewer animals—rats, lizards, sea lions, and water rats (157-159).

In Chapter XI, "Island," Birkin is sawing and hammering, fixing a boat "like a wild animal, active and intent" (183). "Strange as a bird of prey, with the fascinating beauty and abstraction of a hawk" (287), Mrs. Crich is described as pacing up and down "like a tiger" (284). Her daughter Winifred is a "soulless bird," (292) and Winifred's French governess is "like a little French beetle." (313) As his father lies dying, Gerald, like Hermione earlier, is portrayed as "convulsed. . . as in the coils of the great serpent Laocoon" (364). Bizarrely costumed, Gudrun is described as wearing a hat "brilliant green like the sheen of an insect" (476), although her sometime lover, Herr Loerke, is depicted with "quick full eyes like a mouse's" (497), and later as "a lop-eared rabbit or a troll" (516) and as a "bat." (517) Birkin sees Loerke as a "little obscene monster of the darkness" (522), and akin to the guests at Breadalby's, "like rats in the river of corruption" (522–523) and "the wizard rat that swims ahead" (523). Gerald denounces him as "vermin," "that little dry snake"and "that little insect" (553) with "the understanding of a flea" (554). Gudrun's final vision of Gerald is the one she first has of him: "She knew by the light in his eyes that she was in his power—the wolf" (553).

Metaphors in the Film

A film metaphor is an implied analogy, associating one visual image or sound "image" with the qualities of another.[147] Although Ken Russell made little attempt to create exact equivalents for Lawrence's abundant metaphors, he employed a variety of cinematic techniques to replicate the densely metaphorical texture of the novel's prose. In so doing, he managed to transcend the limitations on reproducing literary tropes in cinema identified by George Bluestone in *Novels Into Film: The Metamorphosis of Fiction Into Film* (1957).[148] Unlike Rudolph Arnheim, who claimed that the photographic literalness of film "makes metaphor impossible except in a highly restricted sense."[149] Bluestone allowed for the possibility of metaphor arising from a type of cinematic editing associated with Eisensteinian montage in which "two disparate elements, as in the trope, are linked together to create a *tertium quid*."[150]

In recent decades, film critics have explored alternative visual and aural means of creating metaphors in film.[151] One technique for suggesting resemblance within a single shot is the use of an area of the frame (often a window in the background, or the entire background itself) to portray an action that complements the main foreground action.[152] Other visual means of suggesting metaphor within shots include the use of objects, settings, natural phenomena, framing devices, camera movement, camera angles, movements of figures, space, color, and shadow. Aural techniques for creating metaphor include the use of artificial and natural sounds, music, and above all, dialogue.[153] Russell used all of these in *Women in Love*.

In the opening scenes of the film, sound and image combine to create abundant and pervasive interlocking metaphors and metonyms, some of them striking, others barely noticeable. As the Brangwen sisters, on their way to the Crich wedding, discuss marriage, Gudrun comments, "It is bound to be an experience of *some* sort." Eyeing a somber couple wheeling a fretful baby in a carriage, Ursula replies archly, "More likely to be the *end* of experience." The intercut long shot of the pair with their infant (Russell's invention) is a metonym for the stultifying effect of conventional wedlock, a theme that recurs throughout the film. In the following sequence, the sisters watch the Crich wedding from a graveyard opposite the church (in the novel, they sit on the low wall of the grammar school just outside the churchyard). As the sisters talk, Gudrun reclines on a tombstone. Admitting that she would consider marriage to "a highly attractive individual with sufficient means," she crosses her arms over her chest like a stone figure on a sarcophagus, and complains, "Everything fails to materialize. . . .

Everything withers in the bud." In the next breath, she pronounces marriage out of the question: "The man makes it impossible." The juxtaposition of the wedding scenes and the shots of Gudrun and Ursula in the graveyard creates a metaphor that equates traditional marriage with death ("the end of experience").

Words and image also establish the connection between Gerald and death in the scene in which he takes a running dive into the lake, while in the foreground Gudrun remarks that he is in charge of the mines, making all kinds of improvements ("He'll have to die soon when he's made all possible improvements. . . .") "He's got go, anyhow," observes Ursula. "Certainly he's got go," says Gudrun sardonically. "The unfortunate thing is, where does his go go to?" Gerald's metaphorical "go" that goes nowhere and ends in a "dead end" is imaged in his aggressive entry into the water for which he holds himself responsible and where he will be unable to save his newlywed sister and her husband from drowning.

Perhaps the most effective yoking of image and word is in the memorable outdoor luncheon scene in which Birkin, in borrowed words from a provocative Lawrence poem[154] dense with sexual innuendo, apostrophizes Hermione's quartered fig, shown in extreme closeup, and then eats one that he has cut down the center. By the time Birkin consumes the flesh from the "purple slit" of the fig and sucks the "sap" from his fingers, both the luncheon guests and movie audience perceive the fig as a "female part." The fruit becomes a verbal and visual metaphor for female sexuality associated, in Hermione's case (as in Gerald's), with death ("That's how women die too").

In a scene that is not in the novel, words underscore images to create a metaphor as Gudrun flirts with a miner outside a working-class pub in Beldover. "How are your thighs?" she taunts him. "Are they strong? Because I want to drown in flesh—hot, physical, naked flesh!" Surrounded by torches that suggest hellfire, the flustered miner bumps into a slab of raw meat, the equivalent of his "thighs" and a metaphor for the animalism that limits the relationship between Gudrun and Gerald. Encountering the mine owner leaving a pub with a prostitute on each arm, Gudrun shouts defensively after him, "Well, I was born here, and I'll die here until I fly away." Her identification with a bird on the wing is a metaphor for her inability to commit herself to a human relationship. At the Crich picnic, when Gerald rescues Gudrun from the bulls, he tells her that he cares about the animals because they are his. Mocking the metaphor of ownership, Gudrun replies, in dialogue borrowed from the novel, "How are they yours? You haven't swallowed them. Give me one of them now!" When Gudrun strikes him, Gerald retorts, "You struck the first blow," to which she replies meaningfully, "And I shall strike the last!" Gudrun's light slap on Gerald's cheek in both novel and film is thus verbally upgraded to a metaphor.

When Birkin and Ursula are boating at night, both are suffused in the glow of a hanging Chinese lantern. "There is a golden light in you which I wish you would give me," says Birkin, a statement both literal and figurative. In the aftermath of their nude wrestling match, Birkin and Gerald lie side by side, glistening with sweat, talking of their new communion: "We are mentally and spiritually close; therefore we should be physically close too. It's more complete," says Birkin, who asks Gerald to swear eternal love as medieval German knights did. In this sequence, the spiritual, emotional, and erotic aspects of the men's physical encounter are heightened by a fusion of image and dialogue; a wrestling match becomes, for Birkin at least, a metaphor for love-making on several levels.

In several scenes, the interplay of dialogue and visuals in the interaction between the characters is both allusive and metaphorical. Disgusted by Loerke's brutality and cynicism, Ursula persuades Birkin to travel to Verona, where they can, in Birkin's words, "find Romeo and Juliet and sit in the amphitheater." When Ursula lies on top of her husband on a mound in the snow, the two in fact resemble Romeo and Juliet, both in their wedding bed and in the tomb where they commit suicide, a further linkage of marriage and death. Finally, the scene in which Ursula and Loerke dress up in costumes and verbally roleplay Tchaikovsky and his nymphomaniac bride on their honeymoon is intrinsically metaphoric; the exotic game they play is emblematic of their superficial, exploitative, loveless relationship.

Many of the metaphors in the film are exclusively visual. A few are created by Eisensteinian cinematic editing, most striking among them the juxtaposition (technically a simile) of the drowned newlyweds at the bottom of the lake and a match cut of Birkin and Ursula, in exactly the same position after making love in the grass—an obvious equation of love and death.[155] The shot of Mrs. Crich maniacally laughing at her husband's graveside—intercut with the scene of Gerald's making love to Gudrun for the first time (here he is depicted literally, as he is figuratively in the novel, as a child at his mother's breast)—creates a metaphorical equivalence between his demented mother and Gudrun, further underscored by the Picassoesque painting of a witchlike female over Gudrun's bed.

The appearance and demeanor of a number of characters in the film are metaphorical. Although Lawrence's Gerald is associated with icy, arctic imagery and is pictured as tall, fair, and slender, actor Oliver Reed is burly, brooding and dark-haired, with a head described by critics as "pear-shaped"[156] or "massive" like an eggplant.[157] From a figurative standpoint, however, Gerald in the novel is depicted as "inhuman," "part of a machine," and "the God of the machine," and Oliver Reed does play Gerald as a sort of human robot—stiff, constrained, and poker-faced. His sculpturelike frozen corpse at the end of the film is a metaphor for a man already spiritually and emotionally dead. Lawrence also characterized Gerald as a "wolf" and as "an animal that is suffering," imagery suggested by Oliver Reed's troubled demeanor, as well as his slow, halting speech and deep, hoarse voice. Reclining on a gravestone, Glenda Jackson's Gudrun, as angular and hard-edged in her appearance as is Lawrence's psychological portrayal of her in the novel, metaphorically resembles a stone sculpture on a medieval sarcophagus. Mrs. Crich, who is depicted in the novel as "a hawk in a cage," looks exactly like that in the film as played by Catherine Wilmer, with her chiseled, bony face, beaked nose, bizarre manner, and high-pitched, shrieking laughter. Often she is photographed as a prisoner behind a gate, fence, or window. Loerke, often identified in the novel as some sort of repulsive animal (rat, lop-eared rabbit, mouse, beetle, bat, brown seal, snake, vermin) or as a troll, is played by Vladek Sheybal—a distinctively creature-like actor with large bulging eyes, a wide forehead, high cheekbones, a prominent nose, and a foreign accent.

Settings throughout the film are both metaphorical and symbolic. As the graveyard from which Ursula and Gudrun watch the Crich wedding becomes, by juxtaposition, a metaphor for conventional marriage, the open pastoral settings in which Birkin and Ursula commune and make spontaneous love—golden wheatfields, lush green grass, on the banks of lake and stream—are metaphors for the life-affirming wholesomeness and naturalness of their relationship. Indeed, in the sequence in which Birkin drives Ursula back to his millhouse and the two decide to marry, their kneeling kiss before a roaring fire is metaphorically shifted to an Edenic outdoor setting, a brilliantly golden wheat field.

Backgrounds also provide metaphors, as in the scene in which Birkin lounges next to Hermione beside her pool at Breadalby while a couple of youthful guests in the rear silently do the Charleston. The image of the dancing couple trivializes and also parallels Hermione and Birkin's corrupt relationship. In the wrestling scene between Birkin and Gerald, and the lovemaking scene between Ursula and Birkin in his cottage, the roaring fire, a traditional cinematic symbol, is a metaphor for emotional intensity and physical passion. In the final scene of the film, Birkin and Ursula clash before the bluish flames of a low-burning fire that hints of dimmed ardor.

Objects and natural phenomena, too, are metaphorical. Two extreme closeups of the three rings Birkin gives to Ursula, an image derived from the novel, can be interpreted as a metaphor for his ambivalence, torn as he is between Hermione and Ursula, on the one hand, and Gerald on the other. The flower Ursula brings Birkin after their quarrel is a metaphor for love, while the handful of mud that Gerald grabs in the cemetery where he has just buried his father is a metaphor for deathliness and spiritual inanition, as is the black mud at the bottom of the Criches' lake in which Gerald finds the drowned newlyweds. An extreme closeup of Loerke's cigarette ashes, which he has flicked onto Ursula's dessert, indicates the cynicism and scorn he directs at her. Throughout the film, statues and paintings are used as both metaphors and symbols, often providing ironic commentary.

Metaphors in *Women in Love* are created by cinematic techniques, such as camera movement. As Birkin and Ursula make love in the grass, the camera quivers and zooms in close on body parts; the continuous movement of the camera "comments metaphorically on the frenzied nature of their passion."[158] In the scene in which Gerald, lying on top of a just-awakened Gudrun, imprisons her with his body, the camera, in high-angle shots with different angles, zooms in and backward three times, with dissolves in between, ironically suggesting the emotional distance between the couple—a direct translation of Lawrence's description in the novel:[159]

> She could just distinguish his features, as he slept the perfect sleep. In this darkness, she seemed to see him so distinctly. But he was far off, in another world. Ah, she could shriek with torment, he was so far off, and perfected in another world. (432)

The technique of repeated backward zooms is similar to that used to convey resistance and separation in an earlier scene in which Gerald stops Gudrun from chasing bulls, and a series of rapid, pulsating zooms parallels the violence with which Gerald rapes Gudrun during their final night in the Swiss Alps. Another instance of metaphoric camera work that parallels the spontaneity Birkin insists he believes in is the chaotic shooting and jumbled editing of the ragtime dancing that interrupts Hermione's stagy, highly controlled "Russian ballet."[160] Birkin, along with Ursula, is often filmed in tracking shots, a metaphor for his protean personality and for the sort of "go" that actually goes somewhere, even if it is restless traveling.

The movement and positioning of figures within a frame is metaphorical. For example, in a highly stylized interior scene between Gerald and Birkin (a sharp contrast to their sensuous, firelit wrestling match), Gerald wonders whether he should follow Birkin's lead and marry

Gudrun, while Birkin proposes, beyond marriage, "the additional perfect relationship between man and man." Sitting in Gerald's gloomy study, the two formally dressed men are photographed in front of huge mirrors. In the opening shot, Birkin faces left, and Gerald, to his right, looks in the oppposite direction; it is difficult if not impossible to tell which image is of a real person and which one is merely a reflection in the mirror. In the next shot, the mirror, significantly, is cracked; the two men now "face" one another, but the image of one of them (again, it is not clear which one) is a mirror image. Although the two men continue to talk in succeeding shots, they do not face each other directly in any of them; instead, they are constantly photographed in front of or in mirrors, from various angles and in different positions. Near the end of the scene, the two men are filmed before mirrors so that there is an infinite regress of images of the two of them.

The positioning of the men in this strangely surrealistic succession of nearly static shots, as well as the series of shots itself, is a metaphor for the characters' narcissism; their ambivalence toward themselves, toward one another, and toward women; the indeterminate and shifting nature of their relationship; and above all, their inability truly to communicate or connect. The setting, filming and editing of the "mirror scene" suggest, more eloquently than the dialogue, why the relationship between the men is doomed.

Repeatedly throughout the film Gudrun and Gerald are shown walking or, in one scene, riding off with their backs to the viewer. Their movement away from the audience is a metaphor for rejection and alienation. Gudrun often moves against people who are walking toward the camera, as in the scene in which she pushes in the opposite direction through a group of miners moving forward within a narrow space. Filling the screen, Gerald often looms with his back to the camera—a metaphor for both rigidity and dominance. Similarly, Hermione often bursts into the frame—for example, near the beginning of the film when she accosts Birkin after the Crich wedding, aggressively entering from the right, and when she barges into Ursula's classroom.[161] Birkin, often with Ursula, is often filmed walking or running left or right across the screen. One of Ken Russell's directorial peculiarities throughout the film produces a surrealistic effect. His principal characters move, literally and metaphorically, although undifferentiated groups of people sit or stand virtually immobilized. Ursula and Gudrun chat in a streetcar, surrounded by mute, motionless miners and their women; Birkin and Hermione talk over the bowed heads of Ursula's pupils; Birkin and Ursula move as if invisible amid worshippers at the soldier's memorial.

Finally, Russell uses "running metaphors," which Roy Huss and Norman Silverstein define as "the repetition of an image throughout a sequence of shots, throughout several related sequences of shots, throughout several related sequences, or throughout the film as a whole."[162] One unified sequence consists of four consecutive, brief scenes containing repeated metaphors of masculine domination over human beings, animals, and machines. Gerald brutally subdues his horse, forcibly removes an aging worker from his mine, oversees his firing, and is driven from the mine through a crowd of workers in an oversized, luxurious white car, both literally and figuratively "part of a machine" and "God of the machine." Dance is also a recurring metaphor throughout the film, especially Hermione's and Gudrun's dances of domination and seduction.[163]

Symbolism in the Novel

A far more ambitious, original and intellectually challenging work than the realistic and relatively traditional *Sons and Lovers*, *Women in Love* is widely regarded as one of the greatest symbolist novels[164] whose complex meanings have been explicated and debated by more than six decades of critics since Lawrence's death in 1930. Symbolism in *Women in Love* is so pervasive and deliberate that almost all of the names, persons, animals, objects, natural phenomena, and locations, as well as encounters between individuals and between individuals and the environment, are imbued with mythic significance.

Symbolic names include Gudrun, in Teutonic legend a conniving, vengeful woman who kills her husband; Ursula, a virgin martyred saint; Loerke, named after Loki, a Norse giant or deity who murdered mortals and plotted against other gods; and Hermione of Greek myth and tragedy, who in Euripedes' *Andromache* is carried off by murderous Orestes and wed to him. All of the principal characters in the novel are symbolic on many levels[165]—the two pairs of lovers, their parents, Hermione Roddice ("the perfect totem of a deathly European culture"[166]), and Loerke. Also symbolic are various groups of characters, such as the bohemian set in London, the cultured intelligentsia at Breadalby, and the miners of Beldover. As in *Sons and Lovers*, the natural world is the source of many of *Women in Love's* symbols—animals, water, snow, fire, moon, and plant life. Much of the symbolism in *Women in Love* is also drawn from the realm of the inorganic—mechanical devices, houses, jewelry, furniture, art objects, and clothing. Locations, too, are symbolic—the mining town of Beldover;

London; Sherwood Forest; and the snowy mountains near Innsbruck. Particularly striking and characteristic of the novel are the many ritualistic or symbolic scenes, often uncanny and hallucinatory, always powerful and memorable, in which the characters engage in unconventional behavior.

Many of the symbols in *Women in Love* are esoteric and idiosyncratic, defying facile analysis. Eliseo Vivas calls the device Lawrence used in both *The Rainbow* and *Women in Love*, and his short stories, "the constitutive symbol"—a symbol that acquires significance cumulatively, works "below the level of consciousness," and whose referend cannot be fully exhausted by explication, because "that to which it refers is symbolized not only *through* it but *in* it."[167] Interpretation of Lawrence's symbols depends largely on context and on understanding his metaphysics. As Angelo Bertocci points out, in *Women in Love* "Lawrence uses not merely the symbols at hand which seem natural to all expression and which have been developed in social experience, but . . . strives to create new fusions of meaning and even to *enforce* new meanings based upon created premises."[168]

In *Women in Love*, as in *Sons and Lovers*, the duality of Lawrence's underlying dialectical metaphysic is reflected in seemingly antithetical imagery of darkness vs. light; creation vs. destruction; life vs. death or death-in-life; spontaneity and freedom vs. rigidity, domination, and imprisonment; the natural vs. the mechanical; sexuality vs. spirituality; private transactions between individuals vs. traditional social rituals. However, the polarities of *Women in Love* cannot be reduced simply to positives and negatives. In his essay "The Crown," written during the carnage and destructiveness of World War I, Lawrence developed his theory of the two parallel and simultaneous processes, creation and disintegration:

> Destruction and creation are the two relative absolutes between the opposing infinities. Life is in both. Life may even, for a while, be almost entirely in one, or almost entirely in the other. For life is really the two, the absolute is the pure relation which is both. If we have our fill of destruction, then we shall turn again to creation.[169]

Expounding a similar philosophy in *Women in Love*, Birkin contrasts "a river of darkness . . . the dark river of dissolution, of corruption" with "the silver river of life . . . flowing into a bright eternal sea," and suggests, apocalyptically, that the end of the world is as good as the beginning because "it means a new cycle of creation after . . . " (238).

Birkin's "two rivers of life" are embodied in one of the most pervasive and paradoxical symbols in *Women in Love* and the setting for many of its chapters—water.[170] Although a fluid medium ideal for spontaneous movement and self-expression, water in the novel is, ironically, most often associated with imprisonment, death, and destruction; it is Gerald's element right up to the final pages of the book. In "Water-Party" (Chapter XIV), Birkin pontificates about "a river of darkness putting forth lilies and snakes . . . the black river . . . the dark river of dissolution" (238). A festive boating party turns tragic when, despite Gerald's efforts to save them, his sister Diana (renamed Laura in the film) and a young doctor (Laura's newly wed husband in the film) drown and the water becomes a tomb. "If you once die," says Gerald, "then when it's over, it's finished. Why come to life again. There's room under that water for thousands" (251).

In the last three chapters of *Women in Love*, water turns to snow and finally into ice—the "inhuman abstraction of velocity and weight and eternal, frozen snow" (515) associated with Gudrun, who is mesmerized and transported by it, and with Gerald, who comes to dread it. From the first pages of the novel, Gerald is associated with arctic imagery—iciness, whiteness, northernness, cold—so it is fitting that he should die in the snow-laden Alps—"the frozen, mysterious navel of the world" (502). As Gerald is the representative and embodiment of a violent and dying civilization, his death by freezing symbolizes the spiritual bankruptcy of Western industrial society, dominated by the machine and mental consciousness and cut off from the primal source of life.

Birkin's "two rivers of life" are also reflected in clustered images of light and darkness that pervade *Women in Love*. Four kinds of light permeate the novel—most prevalent, blue or "white" light and flame associated with the moon and with the arctic light of the north and identified with mental consciousness, self-destructive exertion of the will, and death and destruction; a warm golden inner light or firelight associated with Ursula and Birkin and with "healthy" love and sexuality in general; yellowish light, usually associated with anger or other negative emotions; and artificial (or electric) light, connected with mechanization and industrialism.

In terms of light symbolism, one of the most striking and significant passages in *Women in Love* is the famous description of Birkin ritualistically stoning the moon ("Moony," Chapter XIX), while cursing Cybele (Syria Dea), an Asiatic goddess of fertility whose male devotees mutilated and even castrated themselves. As Ursula secretly looks on, Birkin unsuccessfully attempts to break up the cohesion of the moon's reflection in the water:

> Then again there was a burst of sound, and a burst of brilliant light, the moon had exploded on the water, and was flying asunder in flakes of white

and dangerous fire . . . at the centre, the heart of all, was still a vivid, incandescent quivering of a white moon not quite destroyed, a white body of fire writhing and striving and not even now broken open. . . . (323)

The moon in this passage has been variously interpreted, most often as a symbol of Ursula herself, and Birkin's attack on it as an assault on the matriarchal female. F. R. Leavis conceives of the moon as a symbol of the idealized love that Ursula demands and Birkin tries to destroy,[171] while Herman Daleski sees the moon "that is the planet of the self-assertive, sensual, devouring woman" as having a "symbolic value for Ursula as for Birkin . . ."[172]

Linked with the light of the moon, the arctic light that pervades the ice and snow in the Alps is also connected with the "cold fires of the marsh" in Breadalby's Willey Water. From the opening chapter of the novel, whiteness and iciness are associated with Gerald, and with the inhuman and mechanical. When Gudrun first sees Gerald at the Crich wedding, he is described in terms of arctic imagery: "There was something northern about him that magnetized her. In his clear northern flesh and his fair hair was a glisten like cold sunshine refracted through crystals of ice." (61) After the two men wrestle in "Gladiatorial" (Chapter XX), Birkin tells Gerald appreciatively, "You have a northern kind of beauty, like light refracted from snow" (352). As Gudrun becomes involved with Gerald, there seems "a faint white light emitted from him, a white aura . . . " (416). Although Ursula and ultimately Birkin reject the snowy Tyrol, Gerald and Gudrun embrace the icy wastes, Gudrun seeming "to pass altogether into the whiteness of the snow" (514). After Gerald dies, a grieving Birkin almost merges with him. "Again he touched the sharp, almost glittering fair hair of the frozen body. It was icy cold, hair icy-cold, almost venomous, Birkin's heart began to freeze" (579).

Golden light, always a spiritual phenomenon in *Women in Love*, is associated almost exclusively with Ursula and Birkin. After Birkin stones the moon, he tells Ursula, "There is a golden light in you, which I wish you would give me" (326), and when they seal their love in the chapter "Excurse," Ursula's face "was now one dazzle of released golden light, as she looked up at him. . . " (395). Firelight, on the other hand, is ironically connected with unfulfilled sensuality and love. Firelight casts a golden glow over Gerald and Birkin's wrestling match at Shortlands, and candle-flames flicker beside Gerald's frozen corpse as Birkin bitterly laments the failure of his relationship with his friend.

Artificial light is associated with soul-destroying mechanization. In

"Class-Room" (Chapter III), electric lights turned on by school-inspector Birkin make the room "distinct and hard" (85) and a perfect backdrop for Birkin's heated exchange with Hermione over mental consciousness, spontaneity, self-conscious sensuality, and exertion of the will, all of which Birkin denounces. At the end of the chapter, Ursula puts out the lights (95) and unaccountably weeps, suggesting a linkage between artificial light and the repression of primal emotions.

Associated with darkness and shadow in *Women in Love* are seduction, sexual passion, industrialization, and death. "The black look" of seductive Pussum's eyes "made Gerald feel drowned in some dreadful, potent darkness that almost frightened him" (130). After making love with Birkin, Ursula has "a full mystic knowledge of his suave loins of darkness, dark-clad and suave" (400), while Birkin accuses Hermione of not having "any real body, any dark sensual body of life" (92). Mechanization and industrialism are embodied in the coal mining town of Beldover, with its "dark air" and its "darkened dwellings with dark slate roofs . . . like a country in an underworld . . . a dark uncreated hostile world," and in the blackened miners, "powerful underworld men who spent most of their time in the darkness" (174). Death ("the great, dark, illimitable kingdom" 263), especially the deaths of Thomas Crich and Gerald, is also associated with darkness: "He [Thomas Crich] was only half-conscious—a thin strand of consciousness linking the darkness of death with the light of day" (401) and "Gerald stumbled up the slope of snow, in the bluish darkness . . ." (573).

Paradoxically, darkness suggests rebirth, as when Birkin and Ursula journey from England to the Tyrol: "To him [Birkin] the wonder of this transit was overwhelming. He was falling through a gulf of infinite darkness" (470). Decadence—the "mud" and "black river" of corruption and dissolution—is associated with the milieu of London bohemians, with the Thames mud in "Water-Party," and with Hermione's aristocratic world at Breadalby. Darkness also symbolizes the unconscious. Of Birkin, Lawrence wrote, "There was a darkness over his mind . . . his life was dissolved in darkness over his limbs and body" (391). Finally, according to R. E. Pritchard and others, darkness in *Women in Love* refers to excrement, and by extension, to anal sex.[173]

Symbolic images of freedom, spontaneity, and physical movement are frequently contrasted with images of rigidity, imprisonment, and domination associated with mechanization and industrialism, and ultimately with death, both physical and spiritual. Indeed, most of the symbols in the novel fall into these opposing categories. All of the major characters seek "freedom" and often claim to have found it, even when they haven't. Mark Schorer sees only four of them as being in any sense "free":

> We have a group of "free" characters, and a group of "bound" characters. The free characters are limited to four, the four who actively seek out their fate, through the plot movement; the rest are all fixed in their social roles, and in rigid social scenes, and except perhaps for Hermione and the elder Criches, are caricatures whose fate is sealed before the outset. These have all taken the way of death, and therefore they exist at the level of the social personality alone.... But the free characters, the four, are compounded of a double drive.... As two take the way of death, their social role becomes more and more important.... And as the two others take the way of life, their social role becomes less important, ceases, in fact, to exist....[174]

In fact, only Birkin and Ursula emerge into true "freedom," in Lawrentian terms; the other characters remain trapped in so-called civilized society, the "social mechanism," and are doomed to live unfulfilled, even tragic, lives.

Spontaneity in *Women in Love* is portrayed as both positive and negative. In the first chapter, "Sisters," Laura Crich suddenly bolts from her pursuing bridegroom, Tibby Lupton, and ironically races him to the church door, which symbolizes conventional marriage. Birkin defends the impromptu race as "a masterpiece in good form . . . it's the hardest thing in the world to act spontaneously on one's impulses—" (81-82). In "Diver" (Chapter IV), under the jealous gaze of Gudrun, who envies "the freedom, the liberty, the mobility" of being a man (98), Gerald dives into Willey Water, "thrusting his legs and all his body, without bond or connection anywhere" (97). In "Water-Party" (Chapter XIV), Ursula and Gudrun joyfully shed their clothes, run in the grass, and swim together. Similarly, in "Gladiatorial" (Chapter XX), without forethought or preparation Gerald and Birkin strip and do free-form Japanese wrestling.

Paradoxically, "spontaneous" gestures in *Women in Love* are also depicted as seductively manipulative, sadistic, and destructive, such as Gudrun's gyrating before the Highland bulls, Pussum's stabbing a young man's hand with a knife in London's Café Pompadour, Hermione's smashing Birkin on the head with a paperweight, and Gerald's nearly strangling Gudrun in the Alps before he commits suicide. In numerous symbolic scenes in the novel, characters act "spontaneously" to prevent others from exercising their own freedom. In "Class-Room" (Chapter III), for example, Birkin viciously attacks Hermione, who tries to exercise her will over him and everyone else. "You and spontaneity! You, the most deliberate thing that ever walked or crawled!" (92).

Nudity is a major symbol of spontaneity and freedom in *Women in Love*; however, Lawrence distinguishes between deliberate, self-conscious nakedness—a symbol of decadence and corruption exemplified by Hermione's watching herself making love in mirrors or the bohemians' lounging around nude in Halliday's London flat—and the nakedness associated with spiritual openness and communion, as when Ursula and Birkin throw off their clothes in Sherwood Forest and transcend the purely sensual to achieve a mystical "star-equilibrium":

> Quenched, inhuman, his fingers upon her unrevealed nudity were the fingers of silence upon silence, the body of mysterious night upon the body of mysterious night, the night masculine and feminine, never to be seen with the eye, or known with the mind, only known as a palpable revelation of mystic otherness. (403)

Birkin seeks another kind of separateness and fusion with Gerald. The nascent homoerotic relationship between the two men, which Gerald finally rejects, is symbolized by the highly charged nude wrestling scene in "Gladitorial." Although Gerald is the aggressor with women, in this memorable scene it is slender Birkin who "seemed to penetrate into Gerald's solid, more diffuse bulk, to interfuse his body through the body of the other, as if to bring it subtly into subjection . . . (348).

In connection with nudity, body parts are both metonymic and symbolic for Lawrence—in particular fingertips and hands that sensitively seek mystical communion with other beings, as well as men's thighs, loins, and flanks and women's breasts, wombs, and navels. In "Death and Love" (Chapter XXIV), a grieving Gerald sneaks into Gudrun's bedroom, and seeking solace like a child, suffuses himself in "the miraculous, soft effluence of her breast" (430). In "Excurse," Birkin thinks angrily of Ursula as "the perfect Womb, the bath of birth, to which all men must come!" (391) but after surrendering to his love for her, he feels as if "newly born out of the cramp of a womb" (393), as does Ursula. In the final chapters of the novel, the valleys and slopes of the Swiss Alps are described as female body parts associated with childbirth, like "the navel of the earth," or "the unfolded navel of eternal snow" (502).

One of the most pervasive and paradoxical symbols involving spontaneity in *Women in Love* is travel—the excursion or journey by foot, tramcar, railroad, boat, or automobile. It is not accidental that six of the chapters bear the titles "In the Train," "Threshhold," "Excurse," "Flitting," "Continental," and "Exeunt." The constant, often restless movement of characters through a pastoral or urban landscape is symbolic of dissatisfaction with the status quo and a quest for a more fulfilled life. For those characters in the novel who use travel as a temporary escape, movement takes them spiritually nowhere, except round and round in circles; all of the locales in *Women in Love*, in England or otherwise, are in effect prisons. Only for Birkin and Ursula, who cut themselves off from their families and from society, is movement truly liberating.

Lawrence uses animals—horses, bullocks, rabbits, snakes—as symbolic and mythic surrogates for powerful, unconscious psychic states, and for the passional self.[175] In "Coal-Dust" (Chapter IX) a fascinated, swooning Gudrun and a horrified Ursula are forced to watch as Gerald digs his spurs into his horse's side, attempting to force the balky red Arabian mare (a white horse in the film) to stand still as a noisy locomotive passes close by. Gerald's sadistic torture of the animal, suggestive of his brutal treatment of the miners, draws him and Gudrun together in obscene mutual recognition, with Gudrun nearly swooning in erotic arousal. In a famous symbolic scene that parallels Gerald's brutal subjugation of his horse. Gudrun mesmerizes a herd of horned bulls with her "strange palpitating dance" (233) ("Water-Party," Chapter XIV). The cattle, which belong to Gerald and are symbolic of his intimidating masculinity, scatter when Gudrun defiantly rushes at them. Gudrun's attempt to dominate Gerald's herd is symbolic of her ultimately successful effort to exert her will over him.

In another symbolic scene in the novel, Gudrun and Gerald subdue Bismarck, a frightened but powerful rabbit ("a long, demon-like beast . . . looking something like a dragon" (315–316), which, in its frantic efforts to get free, gashes both of their forearms in a grotesque parody of the *Blutbrüderschaft* Birkin has unsuccessfully sought with Gerald. The rabbit, like the horse and the Highland cattle, symbolizes instinctual life, the "id" that must be suppressed or harnessed in civilized society. The demonic rabbit is also reminiscent of infant Gerald, who would "kick and struggle like a demon." "Many's the time I've pinched his little bottom for him," declares his nurse, an agent of repression (284).

Besides animals, Lawrence uses plant life in *Women in Love* to symbolize male and female eroticism and the instinctual life. In "Class-Room" (Chapter III), Birkin, Ursula, and Hermione focus on catkins, to which Hermione has an "almost mythic-passionate attraction" (87): "Red sticky little stigmas of the female flower, dangling yellow catkin, yellow pollen flying from one to the other," muses Birkin provocatively (87–88). In "Sketch-Book" (Chapter X), Gudrun stares at the phallic water plants "that rose succulent from the mud of the low shores. . . thick and cool and fleshy, very straight and turgid, thrusting out their leaves at right angles, and having dark lurid colours, dark green and blotches of black-purple and bronze" (178). Vegetation is also associated with sexuality, as in the scene in the chapter "Breadalby" (Chapter VIII) in which Birkin, after getting bashed on the head by Hermione, wanders to a "wild valley-side" and amid "thickets of hazel, many flowers, tufts of heather, and little clumps of fir-trees" (164), removes his clothes and lies down "naked among the primroses," finding freedom and "his marriage place...." (166) In "Excurse" (Chapter XXIII), Birkin and Ursula achieve sexual and spiritual consummation in a mythical Sherwood Forest, among "great old trees, with dying bracken undergrowth ... the fern rose magical and mysterious" (402).

As in *Sons and Lovers*, flowers in *Women in Love* are often associated with budding female sexuality, spontaneity, love, and death. Both Gudrun and Ursula (more often Ursula) are described as flowers—"just opened," "fresh, luminous," "just unfolded." In "Excurse," when Ursula and Birkin fight over Hermione, Ursula's gesture of reconciliation is to offer Birkin "purple-red bell-heather": "See what a flower I have found you" (392). Gudrun, Pussum, and the London bohemians, on the other hand, are associated with corruption symbolized by "flowers of mud," or with dissolution. White flowers—chrysanthemums, as in *Sons and Lovers*—are associated with death. After his father's funeral, Gerald stumbles through a graveyard toward Gudrun's house: "Even in this darkness he could see the heaped pallor of old white flowers at his feet. This then was the grave.... There was a raw scent of chrysanthemums and tube-roses, deadened" (424).

Houses in *Women in Love* are symbolic of conventional love and marriage, which Lawrence regards as a form of spiritual bankruptcy leading to imprisonment within the social mechanism—"each couple in its own little house watching its own little interests, and stewing in its own little privacy" (439). Throughout the novel, Lawrence also uses houses to symbolize England's stultifying aristocratic past. Eighteenth-century Shortlands, "a long, low old house, a sort of manor form ... protected by an iron fence" (79), is the home of the mine owner Thomas Crich and his large family. Despite its benign, pastoral setting, it is also the scene of the accidental drownings in "Water-Party," of the death of Mr. Crich, and it is the command center of the industrial dynasty described in "The Industrial Magnate" (Chapter XVII). For matriarch Christiana Crich, Shortlands is a prison, and in her husband's last months, it is his prison too. For Gerald, who installs electricity in the mansion as he modernizes the mines, it is a mausoleum. Efficiency and technology render both him and the past (symbolized by the house and estate) irrelevant; the machine runs itself.

Like Shortlands, Hermione's Breadalby is "a very quiet place . . . unchanged and unchanging," a "Georgian house with Corinthian pillars" that looks over "a lawn, fish ponds, and a park. . ." (139). Like Gudrun, who sees Breadalby as "'final as an old aquatint,'" Birkin views it as "the lovely accomplished past" and concludes that Breadalby is "a horrible dead prison . . . an intolerable confinement" (154). In his sparsely furnished millhouse, Birkin alone resists the sense of imprisonment that pervades all the other homes in *Women in Love*.

In *Women in Love*, clothes are symbolic of imprisonment within the self as well as within the social system. "Bounded" characters—static, rigid, incapable of inner growth and change, and therefore doomed to isolation, frustration, and spiritual death—are depicted chiefly in terms of their attire—expensive, made of distinctive fabrics, unusual, and often colorful. Indeed, colors are symbolic throughout *Women in Love*, especially the metallic blues and greens typical of Gudrun's and Hermione's clothing and of the iridescent colors of the marsh or the wings and carapaces of insects.[176]

For Gudrun and Hermione, clothing is a brittle shell that shuts out the world; it establishes social and cultural superiority, protests against the ordinary, and asserts separateness and uniqueness. In the opening chapter, Gudrun's outfit, in characteristic blues and greens, is described in specific detail, with special emphasis on her stockings:

> Gudrun was very beautiful, passive, soft-skinned, soft-limbed. She wore a dress of dark-blue silky stuff, with ruches of blue and green linen lace in the neck and sleeves, and she had emerald-green stockings. (54)

At the Crich picnic, she wears a white dress, like Ursula, but also "a sash of brilliant black and pink and yellow colour wound broadly round her waist," and "pink silk stockings. . ." (219). Toward the end of the novel, an iridescent and almost hallucinatory Gudrun, "fashionably dressed in blackish green and silver," sweeps triumphantly out of London's Cafe Pompadour with Birkin's letter. Hermione Roddice wears even more outlandish getups. Her typically yellow costume at the Criches' wedding is described in vivid detail:

> Now she came along with her head held up, balancing an enormous flat hat of pale yellow velvet, on which were streaks of ostrich feathers, natural and grey. . . . She wore a dress of silky, frail velvet, of pale yellow colour, and she carried a lot of small rose-colored cyclamens. Her shoes and stockings were of brownish grey, like the feathers on her hat. . . . (62)

In Ursula's classroom, where she is bizarrely out of place, she wears "a large old cloak of greenish cloth . . . lined with dark fur" (86-87). Like Hermione, Gerald, "almost exaggeratedly well-dressed," wears elegant, expensive, formal clothing—in "Gladiatorial," "a gown of broad-barred, thick, black-and-green silk, brilliant and striking" as well as expensive "silk socks and studs of fine workmanship, and silk underclothing, and silk braces" (352).

Birkin and Ursula, on the other hand, are rarely depicted in terms of their clothing or physiognomy. Being "immanent," neither of them fully awakened or "born" in a spiritual sense, both are represented as pictorially vague and unfinished, without the defined boundaries that clothing creates. For the truly evolved in *Women in Love*, clothing becomes an impediment, as symbolized by Birkin and Ursula "throwing off their clothes" in Sherwood Forest (403).

Probably because of Lawrence's animus against modern technology, concrete images of industrialism are scarce in *Women in Love*, limited almost entirely to trains, automobiles, the cinema, an electric generator, Gudrun's imaginary eternally ticking clock, Gerald's hand badly injured when it is caught in a machine, streets and roads covered with coal-dust, and streams of sullen, blackened miners. Throughout the novel, however, the aura of the coercive, repressive machine, and the word "machine" or "mechanical," extend to all interpersonal relationships as well as to the entire social, economic, and political order, so that every act of domination and victimization—and they are legion in *Women in Love*—is symbolic of the destructive effects of machines and of the mental consciousness that produces them.

In allowing themselves to be mastered by others or by their own lust for material goods, power, or control, individuals transform themselves into inhuman machinelike creatures. Gerald ruthlessly subjugates his willing instruments—"the half-automised colliers" (174)—in the process of rebuilding the antiquated mines. In one of the novel's more striking symbolic images, Gerald drives his motor car almost phallically through the miners and their families, "a solid mass of human beings," who make way for their masters "automatically, slowly" (295). Hermione's attempted mastery over Birkin constitutes an effort to make him part of "the social machine" which he, Ursula, and Gudrun try to escape, while Gerald, "God of the machine," is trapped and destroyed by it.

Keith Alldritt contends that "works of art play a more crucial role in this novel than in any other of Lawrence's fictions. . . ."[177]

Most obviously, each painting or sculpture serves to reveal something about character. It tells us something of the nature and the mode of perception of the character who created it or the quality of response in the person who admires it.[178]

Symbolic artworks in *Women in Love* that reveal the characters of their creators, or their admirers or detractors, include the West African statuettes of nude women that Birkin contemplates in Halliday's flat in the chapter "Totem VII"; Loerke's "great granite frieze for a granite factory in Cologne" of peasants at a fair in "a frenzy of chaotic motion" (517); Hermione's Chinese drawing of geese "in the flux of cold water and mud" (145) that Birkin pays homage to by copying; Loerke's green bronze statue of a naked girl on a horse to which Ursula objects because the animal is "as stiff as a block . . . stock and stupid and brutal" (524); and Gudrun's small models of animals, birds, and people in everyday dress. Another art object that represents "a pitch of culture" is the "armchair of simple wood . . . of the purest, slender lines" (443) which Birkin gives to a young working-class couple at a jumble market. The beautiful antique chair (443), in which the mechanical has not yet triumphed, is also a symbol of conventional marriage. The "great carven statues of real Egypt" (400) to which Lawrence compares Birkin driving the car after he has made love to Ursula also epitomize an ancient culture and suggest an eternality that transcends time and place. Finally, the half-buried Crucifix that Gerald finds in the snow just before he lies down to die ironically represents the Christianity which his father has fruitlessly tried to practice as a mine owner and which Gerald, "God of the machine," has essentially rejected, adhering to it in form only.

References to mirrors, suggestive of narcissism and decadence, recur in *Women in Love*. Birkin denounces Hermione, accusing her of being pornographic: "Watching your naked animal actions in mirrors, you can have it all in your consciousness, make it mental" (92). The sophisticated café-goers in London are "reflected more simply and repeated ad infinitum in the great mirrors on the walls" (114); Gerald stands behind Gudrun as she gazes at herself in the mirror in their room in the Tyrol while brushing her hair, and Gudrun is subsequently terrified by seeing her face in the mirror "like a twelve-hour clock-dial" (565).

Symbolism in the Film

In adapting Lawrence's *Women in Love*, Ken Russell made a concerted effort to replicate the symbolist texture of the novel within the limitations imposed by an essentially realistic medium. As almost every page of the novel resonates with thematic and symbolic overtones, nearly every shot and scene in the film is also imbued with symbolic significance—far too heavy-handedly, in the view of some of the movie's less enthusiastic reviewers. The symbolic significance of much of the film's imagery is created not only through repetition and exaggeration, two common cinematic techniques for conveying symbolism, but also through the use of a distinctive mise-en-scène and framing, lighting, camera angles, editing, music, and sound effects. The strictures of a commercial feature-length movie, however, compelled Russell to omit, modify, and condense key symbolic elements in the novel.

As noted, some memorable and thematically significant symbolic scenes were omitted entirely, including Birkin's stoning of the moon and Gudrun and Gerald's victory over a berserk rabbit. Key images of symbolic objects and artworks, such as the African statuettes in Halliday's flat and Loerke's granite frieze for a factory, were also left out. Russell altered several symbolic episodes, such as the drowning at the Criches' picnic, Hermione's Russian ballet, and Mrs. Crich's fantasy of setting dogs on charity-seeking miners. He invented a number of overtly symbolic images and scenes, including a couple wheeling a baby carriage, Hermione eating a fig, Gudrun reclining on a tombstone during the Crich wedding, the Criches' white automobile moving slowly among a crowd of miners, Mrs. Crich acting bizarrely at her husband's funeral, and Loerke and Gudrun role-playing Tchaikovsky and Cleopatra. In addition, he incorporated images of objects and works of art that convey themes or comment on characters and their relationships, such as a broken photographic plate at the Crich wedding, a Picassoesque painting of a woman over Gudrun's bed, a chalice on the mantlepiece between Gerald and Birkin after their wrestling match, and Gudrun's unflattering bust of Gerald.

Russell also altered, expanded, or condensed certain symbolic events in *Women in Love*. In the novel, Hermione merely presides over a briefly mentioned impromptu "Russian ballet"; in the film she is portrayed as the pretentious star of Russell's overly long and often laughable Isadora Duncanesque parody. The pair who drown during the Criches' water party are Gerald's sister Diana Crich and a young doctor who have no relationship, not, as in the film, the newlywed couple of Gerald's sister Laura Crich and Tibby Lupton. As a consequence, Russell's parallel match cuts of the drowned couple and of similarly intertwined Birkin and Ursula after they have made love at the picnic are not derived from the novel. Lawrence's Mrs. Crich merely fantasizes setting dogs on charity-seeking minters; in Russell's version, Gerald's demented mother actually does it.

Russell did not modify events alone. One of the major changes in the film, for which the filmmaker was taken to task by many critics, was the casting of major symbolic characters, notably dark-haired, stocky Oliver Reed as slender, blonde-haired Gerald,[179] and perky, Debbie Reynolds lookalike Jennie Linden as soft-limbed, sensuous Ursula.[180]

Despite Russell's omissions and modifications, and in a few instances because of them, however, the filmmaker preserved the sort of symbolic and thematic counterpoint and interconnectedness characteristic of the novel's organization and texture. As in the novel, contrasts as well as ironic parallels between light and darkness, spontaneity and rigidity, and love and death permeate the imagery of the film.

Where Lawrence uses images of light and darkness, both literally and figuratively, to depict realistic experiences as well as inner states and metaphysical concepts, Russell employs imagery of light and darkness to convey contrasting moods and to affect the viewers' perceptions of the characters and their contrasting relationships. In the novel, Gerald's blondness, his "northern kind of beauty" (352), is associated with the arctic snow-world, a deathly, inhuman environment that symbolizes the sterility of modern industrial society. Although Lawrence's persistent symbolic identification of Gerald with icy, snow-reflective white light is absent from the film, mainly because of Russell's choice of dark-haired, swarthy Oliver Reed to play the role of the young mine owner, the frigid spiritual and emotional atmosphere of the Alps is alluded to in the film's dialogue.[181] In bed with Ursula, Birkin tells her, "I couldn't bear this cold eternal place without you," and Ursula later exclaims, "Oh, I *hate* the snow and the unnatural light it throws on everybody. Oh the ghastly glamour of it all, and the unnatural feelings it makes everybody have." In scenes showing the lovers sledding and skiing, the coldness and icy whiteness of the snow is highlighted, and in the sequence in which Gerald climbs to his final resting place in the Alps, the bluish expanse of snow that envelopes him becomes a potent symbol for spiritual and physical death.

Russell uses high-key lighting throughout the film to indicate states of spiritual and emotional intensity and romantic communion, specifically in scenes involving Birkin and Ursula. Merging with nature, a naked Birkin lies down in high, sun-bleached grass. Shot in medium closeups, Birkin and Ursula, in light-colored clothing, picnic amid tall, pale-golden wheat. In the slow-motion lovemaking scene between the couple, the light is so high-key that the lush vegetation is pastel-colored.

Like Lawrence, Russell connects diffused golden light, generated in the film by candles and flame, with Birkin and Ursula. As in the novel, a Chinese lantern illuminates Birkin and Ursula as they row across the candlelit lake during the water-party. "There is a golden light in you which I wish you would give me," says Birkin,[182] suggesting that Ursula's radiant spirituality is represented by the lantern itself. Many indoor locations are candlelit—Hermione's salon, the dancehall of the Alpine lodge, Loerke's bedroom, and the room where Gerald's frozen corpse is laid out.

More significantly, firelight, associated with unfulfilled sensuality and love in the novel, is both a positive and a negative symbol of sexual passion that links many scenes in the film. A romantic fire blazes in the grate in Birkin's cottage the afternoon he and Ursula agree to marry and seal their vows by making love on the hearth. However, flickering torches that light the miners' marketplace and the gritty exterior of the pub where Gerald rescues Gudrun from being sexually assaulted conjure up a hellish underworld. Even as Gerald leaves the pub with a prostitute on each arm, Gudrun reveals a desire to indulge in "hot naked flesh." Although this scene is not in the novel, it implies, as does Lawrence's commentary, the corruptness of Gudrun and Gerald's doomed relationship.

Fire also provides a backdrop for many scenes involving Gudrun and Gerald together and separately. At Shortlands, on the eve of Mr. Crich's death, formally dressed Gudrun and Gerald play billiards while a fire burns in the background. Pacing before a roaring fire on the night of Mr. Crich's funeral, Gerald bolts and makes his way through the graveyard to Gudrun's bedroom where, true to form, he overpowers her. The most memorable fire in the film (not in the novel) is the one that burns throughout the homoerotic wrestling scene. Stripped of formal clothing, Birkin and Gerald, bathed in reddish golden light, glisten with perspiration. The stunningly sensual physical encounter ends in frustration when Birkin's plea to Gerald that they swear eternal love for each other is rejected. Fire is not mentioned during the wrestling match in the chapter "Gladiatorial," nor is Birkin denied blood-brotherhood by Gerald. By using fire symbolically in the film, however, Russell heightens the scene's erotic implications and also stresses the ironic thwarting of Birkin's illusions about a love between men parallel or even superior to the love between a man and a woman.

More obviously than Lawrence, Russell uses electric lighting symbolically. In Chapter XVII, "The Industrial Magnate," Lawrence is critical of Gerald's "great reform" of the mines, in which he installs an enormous electric plant both for lighting, haulage underground, and power; the novelist portrays the use of electricity as destructive. In Chapter III, "Class-Room," Birkin, in his official capacity as school inspector, is described as turning on the lights, which makes the room "distinct and hard, a strange place after the soft, dim magic that filled it before he came" (85). (Just after Birkin leaves, Ursula turns the lights off, promptly bursting into tears.) In the classroom scene in the film, it is Hermione, disrupting Birkin and Ursula's budding intimacy, who noisily turns on the overhead light, a gesture Russell undoubtedly meant to indicate her artificiality and her need to dominate. After Gerald and Birkin's wrestling match, it is Gerald who dramatically throws on the light switch, an action symptomatic of his will to control and dominate through the use of technology, as well as a repudiation of the men's physical and emotional closeness.

Although darkness in the novel is positive as well as negative, in the film darkly lit scenes, nighttime, and dark clothes are associated with unhealthy emotions and with negative concepts and experiences. In contrast to Birkin and Ursula, Gerald and Gudrun, dressed mainly in dark or deep-colored clothes, are usually photographed together in low-lit indoor or outdoor scenes, or in nighttime scenes lit by candlelight or fire. Even in daylit natural surroundings, Gudrun's clothes are dark blue or mustard, and Gerald's clothes are mostly black. In an outdoor landscape, the vegetation surrounding the doomed lovers is a velvety green or dark brown, or the pair are photographed in shadowy silhouette in the gritty, soot-covered alleys of Beldover's working-class district. Indoors, they are shot amidst dark, formal furnishings and decor in Victorian rooms cluttered with art objects.

Gerald, alone and with Gudrun, is depicted in a number of dark environments, symbolizing Lawrence's "dark river of dissolution" and the darkness of death. In a sequence of scenes following Gerald's subduing of his horse, we see him with his workers in a dimly lit mine, with a coal-besmeared pit worker in his father's office, amidst miners trudging home at the end of a gray day in a cloud of steam, and rescuing Gudrun at night from sexual assault. As it does in the novel, symbolic darkness pervades the scene in which Gerald walks at night through the graveyard in which his father has just been buried and in which he grabs a handful of black mud. In a sequence near the end of the film that closely parallels the passage in the novel, extreme long shots of Gerald wandering off into the vast Alpine drifts reduce him to a smaller and smaller dark oval in a deeply shadowed bluish landscape. Visually shrinking, Gerald becomes part of the "abyss" or "bottomless void" into which, according to Lawrence, the young industrialist is fated to fall.

Like Lawrence, Russell repeatedly juxtaposes contrasting symbolic images of apparent vitality, spontaneity, and freedom with images of constraint, domination, and imprisonment. As in the novel, spontaneity is depicted as both positive and negative. Although all of the principal characters in both the novel and the screen adaptation seek freedom from whatever oppresses them and attempt to escape their bonds through impulsive action in love, sport, dance, and travel, none of them in the film appears to be liberated or liberating. That none of the characters in the film version of *Women in Love*, including Birkin and Ursula, are shown to achieve the sort of "freedom together" or apart that Lawrence seems to have had in mind constitutes Russell's critique of the novelist's central themes and, despite many instances of sudden, rapid movement, underlines the prevalence in the film of symbols of restraint, restriction, and confinement.

In the early scenes of the film, spontaneous motion or action is abruptly cut off or terminated by both a literal and figurative dead-end. As Gudrun laments in the graveyard scene, "Nothing materializes. Everything withers in the bud." In the second scene in the movie, Gudrun and Ursula, disregarding their mother's protest, noisily depart for the Crich wedding, a contrast to the novel's opening scene, in which the sisters chat quietly in the window-bay of their home and leave for the wedding unnoticed. Although Gudrun and Ursula in the film, jauntily strolling through Beldover, seem to be exercising their freedom as modern, independent women, they end up, not on a low wall opposite the church, as in the novel, but ironically, hemmed in by tombstones in a cemetery, watching the members of the wedding party as they exit the church.

In the film, as in the novel, Birkin and the tardy groom rush to the church in a horse-drawn wagon, and the groom spontaneously races the bride to the church door. In the film, however, when Tibby unceremoniously kisses Laura, the moment is cut off by a tracking shot of Gerald, disgusted by the young man's breach of decorum, striding beside an amused Birkin. In the classroom scene, a medium close-up of Hermione exclaiming over catkins disrupts the interactions between Birkin and Ursula, and holds the actors and movie audience at bay until Ursula suddenly and angrily shakes her school bell.

The scene after the wedding sequence opens with an extreme long shot of Gerald, naked, running and diving into the Criches' lake, then swimming and waving at Gudrun and Ursula in the foreground. In the film, Gerald's swim is intercut by an extreme long shot, a medium shot, and finally a close-up of the two sisters, who discuss Hermione's weekend invitation to her "country cottage" and Gerald's takeover of the mines. "Certainly he's got go," archly observes Gudrun of Gerald's swimming. "The unfortunate thing is, where does his go go to?" The sisters' skepticism makes Gerald's splashing in the background seem futile, which it clearly turns out to be when he tries to save his sister from drowning.

The cutting off of spontaneous action or gesture is a pattern obsessively repeated throughout the rest of the film. In a scene invented by Russell, with dialogue drawn, in part, from a Lawrence poem,[183] Birkin puts an end to conversation at Hermione's outdoor luncheon by "spontaneously" delivering his embarrassing yet amusing monologue on Hermione's method of eating a fig. When she attempts to counter his attack by archly "inviting" her guests for a walk, Birkin thwarts her by refusing to go. Throughout the rest of this sequence, and many others in the film, acts of control alternate with gestures of defiance. Hermione's pretentious "Russian ballet," danced to Liszt's "Marche Funèbre," is disrupted by ragtime music and the Charleston. Birkin's flow of invective, in which he accuses Hermione of not being able to "bear anything to be spontaneous" is cut off by her sudden smashing of his skull with a paperweight.

In a number of symbolic scenes, genuine spontaneity in humans and animals is shown to be suppressed by acts of domination that are either calculated or impulsive. Such scenes include Gerald racing alongside a moving train, then forcing his terrified mare to halt at a crossing gate by whipping and bloodying its flanks with spurs; Gudrun's frenzied rout of horned cattle, cut off by Gerald trapping her in his arms; and Gerald's frantic, failed attempt to rescue the drowning newlyweds. Other instances include Gerald's impromptu rescue of the miners from Mrs. Crich's ferocious dogs, and his sudden ghostlike appearance in the Alps, when he knocks a flask out of Loerke's hand and tries to strangle Gudrun.

In terms of cinematic technique, Russell used composition and editing literally and symbolically both to convey and contrast spontaneity and rigidity. For example, in the Russian ballet sequence, although shots of Hermione's dance are photographed in a formal, stylized, calculated way, the cinematography and editing give the impression of being speeded up, blurred and jumbled in keeping with the impulsiveness and randomness of the action. Birkin's dash through the forest, Gerald's brutal subjugation of his horse, and Birkin and Gerald's wrestling match are also scenes in which cinematography and editing mirror experiences depicted.

As in the novel, the characters' spontaneous acts, most of them Russell's additions, are depicted as bizarre, disturbing, ominous, or antagonistic. Russell calls attention to their symbolic nature by means of staging, closeups, prolonged shots, camera movements, costuming, and editing. Such acts include Mrs. Crich dropping a trowel onto her husband's coffin, Birkin pushing his way through the crowd at the memorial service for a World War I soldier, and Gerald hurling an object into the fire on the night of his father's funeral. Other spontaneous gestures that are ominous or hostile include Gudrun thrusting a tool into the mouth of her bust of Gerald, Loerke preventing Herr Leitner from dancing with Gudrun, banging his boots on a table and flicking ashes in Ursula's dessert, and Gudrun and Loerke play-acting their fantasies.

Throughout the film, spontaneous activities are performed against a symbolic backdrop of imprisonment. In the scene in which Gudrun and Loerke first talk, Gudrun peers from behind the prominently featured "bars" of a bulstrade. When they act out the fantasy of being Tchaikovsky and his ill-fated bride, Loerke is also repeatedly photographed "behind bars"—in this instance, the footboard of his bed. In many scenes, one or more characters move while the rest sit or stand motionless. For example, expressionless mourners at the funeral service for Mr. Crich stand totally still although Mrs. Crich giggles hysterically, and Hermione prances while Ursula and Gudrun awkwardly freeze. This repeated visual motif suggests (and critiques) the notion that the world is a prison and that the "freedom" of a few is too often achieved by the subjugation of others.

Like Lawrence, Russell repeatedly uses nudity as a symbol of spontaneity and freedom, though not always with the same positive connotations. For example, when Gerald is shown diving and swimming in the nude in the film, Ursula and Gudrun comment on his reported domination of the mines, not, as they do in the novel, on his enviable freedom and mobility. However, in general, nudity in the film, as in the novel, suggests a stripping away of so-called civilized obstacles and restraints, a merging with nature and with another human being. This notion is conveyed in the swimming scenes involving Tibby and Laura as well as Ursula and Gudrun (while the sisters splash gaily, Gudrun cries, "Ursula, I'm utterly, utterly happy!"); in Birkin's shedding his clothes in the forest; in the wrestling match between Birkin and Gerald; and in the pastoral love-making of Birkin and Ursula.

Not surprisingly, Russell depicted nudity in *Women in Love* more concretely than the philosophical and sometimes rhapsodic novelist. For example, in the climactic love-making scene between Ursula and Birkin in the novel's "Excurse" (Chapter XXXI), when the couple shed their clothes at night in Sherwood Forest, Lawrence's description of their union is far more metaphysical and metaphorical than literal ("He gathered her to him, and found her, found the pure lambent reality of her forever invisible flesh") (403). Stuck with real people in a real forest, however, Russell unimaginatively filmed Birkin and Ursula's coming together as a choreographed slow-motion interlude of barely touching nude bodies, drifting together and apart sideways in a pastel landscape, accompanied by a lush, romantic, Elvira-Madigan-like score.[184] The prettified scene, to some reviewers a cynical and even comic commentary on romantic illusions, is scarcely the transcendent epiphany evoked in the novel. The sensuous, golden nudity in Gerald and Birkin's homoerotic wrestling scene is far more powerful as a symbol of freedom from the repressive conventions of civilization and of the essential beauty of the human form than any other in the film—and possibly in all of film literature.

Like Lawrence, Russell uses parts of the body symbolically as well as metonymically. For example, in the film a shot of Gerald burying his head between Gudrun's breasts is symbolic of her maternality, especially so when intercut with a closeup of his mother laughing at his father's funeral. Although the novel does not focus on smaller parts of the body, extreme closeups of hands, often holding symbolic items, are featured as both metonyms and symbols several times in the film. Birkin's bloodied hand inches up a white birch tree, a metonym and symbol suggesting crucifixion or the purification of a blood ritual and paralleling shots of the bloodied flank of Gerald's white horse at the railroad crossing. Ursula's hand holds Birkin's gift of three rings, and when she later throws them down in a rage, Birkin's hand holds the retrieved rings and a flower that an unseen Ursula has silently placed alongside them, symbolic of reconciliation. In a closeup, Hermione holds a quartered fig, a symbol (in this context) of female sexuality. Mrs. Crich drops a garden trowel onto her husband's coffin, symbolizing both life and death, and Hermione seizes a paperweight, a symbol of her cultured, acquisitive lifestyle, and ironically tries to kill Birkin with it. Gudrun's hands, crossed over her chest as she lies on a tomb, signify death. In an extreme closeup, Birkin and Ursula's entwined hands as they lie in bed together in the Swiss Alps symbolize their union.

The symbolic journeys and excursions of Lawrence's principal characters—Ursula and Birkin's boat trip from Dover to Ostend, for example—are not shown in the film; a major symbol in the novel is almost entirely eliminated. On the other hand, there is much locomotion in Russell's adaptation. From the start of their relationship, Birkin and Ursula are repeatedly seen moving in unison, whether walking, dancing, riding in a tiny car, or frolicking in the snow, suggesting their aliveness and the openess and flow between them. In contrast, Gerald and Gudrun together most often stand, sit or lie stiffly in fixed positions, symbolic of their relationship as a dead end. Alone, Gerald most often moves aggressively and compulsively, even frantically. His final slow, tortured ascent to his death in the snowy Alps is symbolic of his "go" going nowhere.

In both the novel and the film, animals, often surrogates for human beings, represent unselfconscious aliveness, raw libido, and on a metaphysical and mythical plane, the mysterious core of life itself. Russell brilliantly replicates the scene in the chapter "Coal-Dust" in which Gerald, flaunting his male potency, subjugates his terrified red mare before the closed railroad-crossing gate. In the novel, the bleeding female horse is likened to a woman being battered and raped, "the strong, indominable thighs of the blond man clenching the palpitating body of the mare into pure control" (172). Ursula responds to Gerald by passionately demanding that the animal be set free, while Gudrun goes numb and quickly detaches herself. In the film, the red mare is white, and the "quivering delicacy" and femaleness of the animal is all but lost; the fragmented closeups of the horse's head and flanks suggest a monumentality which Lawrence certainly did not intend. However, as in the novel, Gerald's brutality and mastery, as well as his sadism, is strongly conveyed in the rapid-fire montage of spurs digging repeatedly into his horse's side and blood running down.

The long-horned cattle before which Gudrun does her rapturous dance are anthropomorphized in the novel. Gudrun feels a mystical, hypnotic connection between herself and the bullocks, who breathe heavily "with helpless fear and fascination" (233), and, terrified, gallop away from her when she rushes after them. In his awkwardly staged version of this bizarre episode, Russell attempts to "personify" the bulls by positioning the camera in their midst, but he captures the animals' massive shagginess and dumb stolidity rather than their "dark wicked eyes" watching "as if hypnotized" (233). As a result, Gudrun's rapt expressions, caught in closeups and medium closeups, look rather foolish,[185] and the cinematographer could not create the mutuality of communion between the bulls and Gudrun that

Lawrence clearly had in mind.[186] However, the closeups of the massive horned cattle, along with the weird music that accompanies Gudrun's writhing movements, create a suitably menacing effect.

While Lawrence's Mrs. Crich merely fantasizes setting dogs on the workers who regularly petition her husband for alms, in the film she viciously lets loose a pack of dogs on a group of unsuspecting miners, and is thus revealed as a major instigator of her son's brutality. To his mother's evident disgust, Gerald subdues the dogs as he restrained his horse. The demonic, screaming rabbit overpowered by Gerald in the novel is transformed in the film into a tame rabbit, gently held by Winifred and then by Gerald, who stands beneath a balcony looking up at Gudrun. The only line of dialogue retained from Lawrence's scene is that of Winifred, Gerald's younger sister. As Gerald holds and rhythmically strokes her black and white rabbit while gazing seductively up at Gudrun, Winifred, close beside him, croons, "Let its mother stroke its fur then, darling, because it's so mysterious" (319). Gerald's stroking of the rabbit, like his subjugation of his horse, conveys his possessiveness and need to dominate.

Aware that some critics had faulted him for omitting the bloody episode in the novel, Russell noted that he had filmed the scene with the rabbit as Lawrence wrote it, but ultimately omitted the footage because he felt that he had already made the same point with Gerald's mastery of his horse.[187] Reference to rabbits is repeated at the soldier's memorial service when Birkin yearns for the destruction of humanity—"a world empty of people, just uninterrupted grass and a rabbit sitting up." As in the novel, the rabbit is seen as a primal form of life, both pre- and post-human.

One of the structural patterns in the film, as in the novel, is a repeated contrast or analogy between love and death. In the film, Russell simplifies Lawrence's rather complex taxonomy of love, constantly juxtaposing and linking symbolic images of love and death, most notably in the opening sequence when Ursula, seeing a somberly dressed couple with a baby carriage, glumly characterizes marriage as "the end of experience." The love-and-death equation continues in the next scene, with crosscutting from the sisters' discussion of marriage to the tombstone on which Gudrun reclines back to the glowing bride and groom and the wedding party.

In symbolic scenes invented by Russell, sex and death are symbolically linked. Discussing the origin of her name at Hermione's luncheon, Gudrun says ominously, "In a Norse myth, Gudrun was a sinner who murdered her husband." Birkin's monologue on "the proper way to eat a fig in society" compares the death of the "bursten" fruit, which resembles an exposed female organ, to the death of a prostitute, and implies that sex with Hermione is a kind of death. (Birkin admits as much when he describes his love affair with Hermione as "a deathly process.") Draped in black, Hermione drones on about the tragic widowhood of the three biblical characters in her "Russian ballet" (including Ruth and Naomi) while on a couch, the reclining newlyweds embrace and kiss.

At the Criches' water-party, the symbolic center of both the novel and the film, love and death, represented by the two principal couples and by newlyweds Tibby and Laura, intersect with an un-Lawrentian neatness and symmetry criticized by a number of critics.[188] As Birkin courts Ursula in a canoe, newlyweds Tibby and Laura drown, despite the frantic efforts of Gerald to save them. A montage of shots of half-clothed Birkin and Ursula making passionate love in the grass is symbolically juxtaposed with a shocking closeup of the entwined bodies in the blue-black mud that backward zooms to an extra-long high-angle shot of Gerald walking over to them and staring down. A close-up of the naked drowned lovers embracing, shot from the waist up, is abruptly matched by one of Birkin and Ursula in exactly the same position as, sated yet seemingly full of self-disgust, they separate and lie side by side in the grass. The visual equation between love and death, symbolized by the memorable match cuts of the two couples, is emphasized by Gerald's comment as the dead are carried away: "*She* killed him," implying that the bride's helpless clutching and, by extension, all women's, dragged the groom down to his death. In the novel, Gerald makes the same accusation against his sister Diana, who is discovered to have "had her arms tight around the neck of the young man [the doctor], choking him" (258). The newlyweds' drowning foreshadows Gerald's suicide, prompted in the film by Gudrun's rejection of him.

Love and death are again linked in Mr. Crich's death and burial, followed by Gerald's quest for refuge in Gudrun's arms, and even in Birkin and Ursula's decision to leave the Alps for Verona to "find Romeo and Juliet," the ultimate symbols of the yoking of love and death. Gerald's final bedroom scene with Gudrun turns into a rape ("Shall I die?" she cries), and during his last encounter with her, he tries to strangle her. While Loerke persuades Gudrun to live with him in Dresden, Gerald climbs to his death in the snow. "He should have loved me, I offered him," says Birkin over the frozen corpse of Gerald, implying that his love would have saved the young industrialist from spiritual and emotional, if not physical, death.

In the film, however, the sort of love and rebirth that Birkin seeks is illusory and never materializes. For Russell, love between men and women is, in fact, reduced to settled domesticity, as symbolized by scenes of Ursula and Birkin after they marry. The last scene of the film, in which the two sit quietly by the fireside in Birkin's cottage, suggests they are stuck there for life. In Russell's version, Birkin's (and Lawrence's) quest for emotional and spiritual transcendence is shown to be as futile as most of the novelist's characters insist it is; if conventional marriage is indeed a form of death, there doesn't seem to be any other kind.

Although the scene-painting and sensuous, concretely detailed descriptions of nature typical of Lawrence's *Sons and Lovers* are not a prominent feature of *Women in Love*, Russell repeatedly uses natural settings symbolically throughout the film, and reserves the lushest, most aesthetically beautiful landscapes for scenes involving Birkin and Ursula, who are most closely identified with naturalness and spontaneity. In the opening sequences of the film, Birkin and the bridegroom Tibby Lupton are photographed in a carriage against the velvety green midlands countryside; in contrast, we first see Gerald against the backdrop of a stone church. When Birkin sheds his clothes in a tangle of ferns, or drifts with Ursula in a forest setting, the images of nature are primeval and unspoiled, exemplifying Birkin's vision, in both novel and film, of "a world empty of people, just uninterrupted grass and a hare sitting up" (188).

In the film, fields as well as forests are symbolic of nature at its purest and most unsullied. Russell's Birkin tells Gerald that he wants to "sit with my beloved in a field with daisies growing all around us," and a key sequence in the film begins with a high-key shot of Birkin and Ursula in light clothing sitting in a stunning platinum gold wheat field. The impression created by the wind-blown field is sensuous, flowing, and romantic, even if the ensuing lovers' quarrel about Hermione propels them from the idyllic field into the jungle-like forest. In the next scene, we see a long shot of Birkin's cottage in a lushly bucolic setting, and after Birkin and Ursula agree to marry, they appear to make love in a forest, bringing the sequence full-circle.

More specifically than Lawrence, Russell uses trees to symbolize emotional sustenance, stability, and strength. Birkin steadies himself on the trunk of a nurturing white birch during his flight through the forest; Ursula weeps against a tree trunk during her passionate outburst at Birkin. When Birkin "rescues" Ursula from the routed cattle, he runs up to a tree and, in a playful gesture, half climbs it; the trunk appropriately curbs his insouciance. By way of contrast, Gerald declares his love for Gudrun against a tree, pinning her with his arms. For the doomed pair, nature is either a snare or something to be used, mastered, and controlled.

Like Lawrence, Russell uses plant life symbolically. In the classroom scene, Birkin and Hermione converge on the catkins, symbolic of human sexuality. In the outdoor luncheon scene, Birkin verbally transforms a quartered fig into a female sexual organ, and in the next scene, as Birkin tells Gerald of his desire for love, Gerald picks some grapes from a symbolic bowl of fruit that sits on the table between them. As in the novel, flowers too are symbolic—the wildflower Ursula puts into Birkin's hand after their battle royal over Hermione and a large cluster of white chrysanthemums, symbolic of death, that are featured prominently in a shot of Gerald passing through the graveyard the night after his father's funeral.

One of the most pervasive natural images in both the novel and the film is water, and its frozen form, ice. As the chapter "Water-Party" is the symbolic center of the novel, water also links many sections of the film. Gerald's first dive, the newlyweds' nude swim, Gerald's attempted rescue of the drowning couple, and the draining of the lake to reveal the corpses in the mud, are visually and symbolically connected. As G. B. Crump points out, in the outdoor scene in which Gerald confesses his love to Gudrun, the darkened silhouettes of the couple, shot against a white expanse of pond which resembles the deadly snow, show them "symbolically sunk in the death-dealing element, trapped in a foredoomed relationship where one must kill the other in an attempt to survive...."[189]

Indeed, as the film unfolds, water becomes less and less benign; a medium of freedom and gaiety is transformed into a destructive element that draws the young lovers to their deaths and renders Gerald as helpless as a child. The bluish black mud at the bottom of the lake through which Gerald stumbles toward the drowned couple is echoed in the handful of wet clay that he grabs in the graveyard and carries on his shoes into Gudrun's bedroom ("You're very muddy," she observes, as he takes off his clothes.) The mud and clay in the film suggest the deathly "river of darkness" or "the black river of corruption" (238) of which Birkin speaks to Ursula in "Water-Party" (238), or the mud from Willey Water in "Sketch-Book" out of which Gerald emerges (179).

The complex symbolism of snow and ice, which represents, for Lawrence, not merely absence of love and connectedness but the demise of an entire cycle of Western civilization, is lost in the postcard picturesqueness of the film's Alpine snowscape. However, to some extent Russell uses the Alps symbolically. The phallic peak of the Matterhorn that fills the screen as Gudrun lifts her arms ecstastically on her arrival at

Zermatt appears to symbolize the masculine power she admires and envies. Her dizzy descent with Gerald on a sled and her romp in the snow with Loerke suggest that the "ice-built mountain tops" (530) are her element; in the novel Lawrence writes of her, "She wanted to gather the glowing, eternal peaks to her breast, and die" (594). For Ursula, on the other hand, the Alpine mountains represent doom (530). In the film, as in the novel, Ursula tells Birkin she "hates the snow and the unnatural light it throws on everybody" (530). Gerald's death in the snow is meant to symbolize the emotional and spiritual "death" that has reduced him to hopelessness and driven him to suicide. However, the meanings and motivations behind Gerald's self-murder in the novel are more complex than in the film, which simplifies matters by implying that Gudrun's rejecting him for Loerke is the immediate cause of his depression and suicide.

Though not nearly as pervasively as in the novel and film of *Sons and Lovers*, natural imagery, both in Lawrence's and Russell's *Women in Love*, is contrasted with images drawn from the realm of the urban, industrial, and mechanical. As Candace Kasper Brand points out, Russell takes advantage of the visual powers of cinema to portray the ravages of industrialism lamented by Lawrence.[190] In the opening sequence in which the sisters stroll through the gritty streets of Beldover, the black clothes of men and women rummaging for coal, and the soot on the faces of those in the bus suggest the ugly imprisonment from which both women will try to escape. Allusions to World War I, deliberately omitted by Lawrence[191] but unobtrusively planted throughout the film—the uniformed soldiers and the little girl begging with the "Somme" sign around her neck—are explicitly linked with the blackened miners and their sullen oppression, suggesting that World War I was an inevitable outcome of the sort of industrialization that Lawrence attacks in the novel.

Several times during the rest of the film, Russell visually juxtaposes the natural and the mechanical, as in the scene in which Gerald subdues his horse beside the moving locomotive or the scene in which Gudrun and Ursula drive up to Breadalby in a royal blue convertible. He also portrays machinery, or the products of machines, as a symbol of capitalistic power, greed, and inequality. This is shown when Gerald and his father ride among the miners in their pristine white automobile. However, Lawrence's notions of the complex connections between industrialization, the abuse of the will characteristic of modern society, and the death of Gerald on the nonhuman "static ice-built mountain top" are not conveyed by Russell's picturesque Alpine setting nor by the frozen corpse of Gerald.

Symbolic in both the novel and film of *Women in Love* are houses and rooms, and the furnishings and artworks that adorn them. Lawrence's Birkin rejects houses and possessions as a form of imprisonment and keeps his quarters as sparsely furnished as possible. In the film, Birkin's cluttered and cheerfully sloppy cottage, which Ursula finds "perfectly lovely," matches his mischievous impulsiveness and at the very least symbolizes his indifference to bourgeois pretentiousness. In both novel and film, Birkin buys and, at Ursula's instigation ("I don't want old things!"), gives away a beautiful hand-made antique chair to a working-class couple; "The truth is, we don't want things at all," Birkin cries. "The thought of a house and furniture of my own is hateful to me." In Chapter XXVII, "Flitting," Lawrence depicts the Brangwens' emptied home, "a little grey home in the west" (464), as "an enclosure without substance" (462); in the opening scene of the film, the Brangwens' parlor symbolizes lower-middle-class order and respectability. At the other extreme, Breadalby is a far more palatial mansion in the film than in the novel, in which "the pillared front of the house," redolent of the past, is described as "sunny and small like an English drawing of the old school" (137). Almost vulgarly lavish, Russell's Breadalby represents the unearned wealth as well as the cultivation and social dominance of the British aristocracy, to which Gudrun cynically refers when she and Ursula drive to the palatial house. "Oh, so this is Hermione's country cottage," says Ursula. "Well, there's one reason why Ruppert is attracted to her," replies Gudrun. "Lovers have sold their souls for far less, my dear." Shortlands, with its manicured grounds, long driveway, and dark, ornate interiors symbolizes the exploitative wealth of the industrial magnate. The somber, formal billiard room and the rococo, high-ceilinged, baronial chamber in which Birkin and Gerald wrestle suggests the heaviness of Gerald's brooding spirit, as well as the deathliness of his family's way of life. Similarly, Gudrun's claustrophobic, cluttered, bohemian bedroom where she and Gerald first make love, as well as the narrow dark tunnel where they stop to kiss, are symbolic of the emotional and spiritual limitations of their affair.

As Lawrence does in the novel, Russell uses art in the film as an expression of the characters' personalities, as a commentary on their illusions about themselves and others, and as an ironic counterpoint to their ideas and perceptions. Although Russell omitted significant works of art that Lawrence described in detail, he substituted or invented other symbolic works of art that both convey and contradict some of Lawrence's themes and characterizations. In the classroom scene, for example, Birkin dashes off an unflattering cartoon of a man's face on Ursula's blackboard, expressing his misanthropy but also a playfulness and insouciance that is far from evident in the novel. Indeed, Birkin's crude caricature would probably be anathema to Lawrence's high-minded savior of mankind. On the other hand, a voluptuous nineteenth-century female nude hanging over Hermione's couch suggests a self-portrait as she would like to be seen, even as Birkin denounces Hermione for her pornographic desire to watch herself having sex in mirrors. Similarly, the Picassoesque head of a crone-like woman with angular, primitive features that hangs on the wall behind Gudrun as she sits bare-breasted on her bed awaiting her would-be lover implies an identity between the subject and its owner, a liberated "New Woman" whose cool detachment contributes to Gerald's destruction.

Although Russell omits the African statuettes in Halliday's flat and Gudrun's small wooden sculptures of animals and birds, sculptures are repeatedly used as symbols in the film. The Grecian-style nude statues in Hermione's salon and the nude statues in Gerald's study represent the classical ideal of female beauty and in Hermione's case, homage to the "high culture" of Western civilization. As Birkin and Gerald discuss marriage in his library, the statue of a dancing woman in the foreground separates the two men, and in the background, mirrors reflect a woman's portrait and the sculpture of a woman's head. As Joseph Gomez points out, the presence of the female images suggests the impossibility of the sort of extra-marital, man-to-man relationship that Birkin seeks.[192] In contrast, the photo of a classical Greek male nude that hangs on Loerke's bedroom wall in the Alps suggests the sculptor's bisexuality.

As in the novel, Loerke's bronze sculpture of a horse, which Ursula attacks for being so "stiff," is predictably praised by Gudrun, who thinks it "beautiful"; for both Lawrence and Russell, the rigidity of the sculpture symbolizes death as well as Loerke's coldness, manipulativeness, corruptness, and sadism. At the World War I memorial service, the bronze statue of a soldier with bayonet drawn (Russell's invention) represents the violence and death that is a constant visual and verbal motif in both the novel and the film. Gudrun's unflattering Neanderthal-looking bust of Gerald, with its Mongolian cheekbones and slanted eyes—another of Russell's contributions—is, significantly, made of clay like that which Gerald grasps in his fist the night of his father's funeral. Gudrun ominously thrusts a wooden sculpting tool into the mouth of the portrait head, reflecting her hostile attitude toward her lover and revealing that she is as amateurish an artist as Loerke accuses her of being. (Lawrence's view of

Gudrun's artistry is a good deal more charitable.)

In a narrative that downplays the importance of appearances, the particulars of some of the characters' clothing are recorded in vivid detail, suggesting symbolic significance. Throughout the novel, Lawrence reminds us of Gudrun's penchant for striking, bold colors (especially in stockings) and idiosyncratic fashions, and describes her, like Ursula, as soft-skinned and soft-limbed. In the opening sequence of the film, however, Glenda Jackson's Gudrun, soft neither in appearance nor manner, wears a chic narrow-cut, high-necked royal blue coat-dress, green stockings and a matching blue cloche hat. Her outfit in this and other scenes conveys a hard-edged toughness and definition that Lawrence attributes only to Gudrun's personality, not her appearance.

In the novel, Ursula's clothing and physiognomy are barely described. "I don't want to *see* you," Birkin says to Ursula irritatedly, and we do not really "see" Ursula, who transcends her body and her clothing. In the film, however, Russell dresses Ursula even more garishly than Gudrun, at least in the opening sequence, when she wears a boldly patterned, colorful coat of orange and yellows with a white fur collar. On their stroll through Beldover, the sisters' fashionable attire contrasts strikingly with the black apparel and dirty faces of the townfolk—symbolic of class and cultural divisions but also of the young women's arrogance, egocentricity, and social isolation. In the rest of the film, in keeping with Lawrence's vision, Ursula's clothing is for the most part neutral in color (pale yellow, ivory, and beige), and not nearly as distinctive and sophisticated as Gudrun's. Her wardrobe includes a beaded black evening gown, an exotic Cleopatra veil, a fur hat, and a black-and-white striped fur cape.

If Lawrence's Hermione, a symbol of spiritual excess, is described as wearing eccentric but chic clothing, Russell's Hermione, a comic and frankly ridiculous figure who symbolizes upper-class pretentiousness and decadence, wears several bizarre outfits—a long velvet cloak, an ugly, flowered turban and awkward bathing costume, and a black shroud in the "Russian ballet" scene. Finally, as in the novel, the clothing of Birkin and Gerald symbolizes their contrasting personalities and destinies. Birkin, the more casual of the two, often appears in light jackets, shirts, and pants, while Gerald, as in the novel almost always dressed formally, usually wears dark or black clothes.

Russell's transposition of Lawrence's symbolism in *Women in Love* has been dismissed for being too facile and obvious (Gerald and his father in their white Rolls-Royce among pit-blackened miners; the criss-cross between the drowned newlyweds and Birkin and Ursula),[193] as well as crude, ponderous, and heavy-handed (Gerald restraining his horse).[194] Aside from being taken to task for leaving out key symbolic scenes (e.g., Birkin's stoning of the moon and Gerald's taming of a demented rabbit),[195] Russell has been faulted for simplifying Lawrence's complexities (the image of Mrs. Crich laughing intercut with Gerald making love to Gudrun; Gudrun's mocking profile, head thrown back, intercut with Birkin and Ursula's leave-taking in the Alps and Gerald's suicide). Finally, critics have complained about Russell's inventing overly long, self-indulgent extravaganzas (Hermione's Russian ballet), injecting tasteless advertisements for previous or upcoming film projects (*Isadora Duncan* and *The Music Lovers*),[196] and in general for attempting too strenuously to reproduce in a realistic medium the essentially surrealistic quality of the novel.

As Joy Gould Boyum persuasively argues, however, Russell's cinematic hyperbole is the equivalent of Lawrence's and is "a crucial source of the power of both the novel and the film."[197] The novelist's "faults" are mirrored in Russell's baroque imagery. Gerald brutalizing his horse or Gudrun dancing before bulls may look and sound overwrought in the film, but descriptions of these events read that way in the novel too. If Russell's symbolic images are not exact duplicates of Lawrence's, or as nuanced and complex, the requirements and limitations of commercial cinema, as well as the filmmaker's satirical bent, baroque and sometimes vulgar tastes and sensibilities, and above all, his characteristic urge to transform, must be held accountable.

Tone in the Novel

One of the truly distinctive features of Lawrence's story-telling technique in *Women in Love* is the way the narrator, by turns, enters the consciousness of each of the principal characters, assuming the language appropriate to his or her experience of the physical and emotional events described. In effect, the narrator merges with and is carried away by his creations, so much so that, at peak moments, the reader often loses the sense of an omniscient storyteller and seems to become one with the character, even if the characters sometimes seem interchangeable, as early reviewers complained. At times, the voice of the narrator seems neutral and objective, but it quickly shifts into an evaluative mode; Lawrence makes little effort to remain detached.

Although the "voices" of the narrator in *Women in Love* are quite varied, the overall tone of the novel is extremely serious, quite often urgent, and melodramatic. Frequently, the narrator seems agitated and sadly angry. Although the narrator's attitude is sometimes sarcastic and mocking, Lawrence never for a moment slackens his gravity by injecting lightness or humor. The narrator's impassioned earnestness remains a constant throughout.

This intensity often creates jarring effects. On the upbeat end of the spectrum, the tone is alternately trancelike, philosophical and meditative, quietly conversational, tender and compassionate, religiously reverent and awed, hushed and gentle, calm and serene, seductive, lyrical and gushing, and exultant. On the down side, the tone is by turns resigned and depressed, mechanical, condescending and judgmental, dismissive and ironical, mocking and sardonic, shrill and dissonant, hateful and outraged, repelled and disgusted, anguished and tormented, alarmed and horrified, hysterical, and gothic romantic (Poe-like). Throughout the entire novel, there is little traditional storytelling; the narrative is continuously infused with a kaleidoscope of weirdly high-pitched emotions that create dissonant, unsettling effects.

Tone in the Film

Considering the unusual tonal effects generated by Lawrence's novel, it seems fitting that the aspect of Russell's film that received the most critical attention, both positive and negative, was its overall tone. In a film, tone is generally defined as the filmmaker's attitude towards the characters and events—conveyed by a range of cinematic techniques, including camera angles and shots, composition, film editing, color, lighting, settings, and costumes, as well as the casting of roles and actors' performances. Although the majority of commentators praised Russell's faithfulness to the spirit of the text embodied in Lawrence's lush, overblown language, the film's detractors attacked Russell's "purple style" of filmmaking as equivalent to the worst excesses of Lawrence's "purple prose." John Simon, for example, mocked the slow-motion lovemaking interlude in which Birkin and Ursula are "surrounded by enough pink and gold flora to make it all look like two stripped dress-shop dummies accidentally dumped in the middle of a florist's window" as conveying Lawrence's "purple prose of physical fulfillment…in the most horrible way conceivable."[198]

Although many scenes and sequences in the film project an exaggerated intensity strongly reminiscent of the novel, the "purpleness" of Russell's cinematic style in *Women in Love* does not consistently replicate the many intense tones of the text. Indeed, the overall "tone" of the film, which often shifts as abruptly as it does in the novel, is markedly different in certain respects from that of the original, and it is this crucial difference, more than any other, that makes Russell's adaptation an original interpretation of and commentary on the work rather than a literal rendition of it. Paradoxically, many of the alterations in tone are a direct consequence of the extravagantly "purple" cinematography, in conjunction with George Delerue's musical score and idiosyncratic performances by some of the offbeat cast members. Tonal changes also result from significant changes in and additions to material drawn from the text.

The main difference between Lawrence's *Women in Love* and Russell's is that the novelist seems to empathize with the intense feelings of his principal characters in a way that Russell and his co-screenwriter, Larry Kramer, clearly do not. As a consequence, the emotions of the novel's narrator, replicated in Lawrence's often hyperbolic prose, are muted, neutralized, or deliberately undercut by the filmmaker's cool, detached, ironic and at times critical stance. Minimized or ignored in the screenplay are Lawrence's urgent sociopolitical concerns, leaving the relationships between and among the principals as the film's primary focus. Yet Russell portrays most of these tormented characters, whose actions and destinies originate in the novelist's bitter, apocalyptic post-World War I malaise, with a bemused condescension that trivializes them and invites the audience to view their behavior as eccentric or ridiculous. Although a reader of *Women in Love* might agree with a number of Lawrence's early critics that most of the characters in it are slightly mad, Lawrence himself certainly did not consider them so. Russell clearly did, however, and depicted nearly all of them, except for Ursula—consistently the voice of wholesomeness, common sense, and sanity—as perverse (if charming) misfits.

Despite the lush, pictorial effects of the settings, costumes, and cinematography, and reasonably faithful renditions of a handful of the more dramatic and memorable scenes in the novel, Russell sustains a flippant and detached stance throughout much of the film. The director's ironic distance from the characters and events of *Women in Love*, manifested in the film's many mildly amusing moments and flourishes, is signaled in the opening sequence, which includes much of the dialogue of the novel's first few pages but offers marked contrasts in location, action, and mood.

In the novel, Ursula and Gudrun, sitting in the bay window of their home, draw, stitch, and discuss the pros and cons of marriage, then stroll through Beldover to the Crich wedding, which they observe from a low fence opposite the church. Their conversation is punctuated by ominous and disturbing comments like "she darkened slightly" (53), "a shadow came over Ursula's face" (53), "in their hearts they were frightened" (54), and "the sisters found themselves confronted by a void, a terrifying chasm, as if they had looked over the edge" (59). In the film, however, no ominous undertones disturb Ursula and Gudrun's animated dialogue. Having dismissed their mother's pleas to stay home, the ostentatiously dressed sisters walk through the drab, working-class town, ironically oblivious to signs of social and economic decay and of the aftermath of World War I, represented by a soldier in uniform playing a clarinet for money and a girl begging with a sign reading "Somme" around her neck. Along with the two women, we grimace at a couple with a yowling infant in a baby carriage and tap our feet in waltz time as a bassoon plays a lilting rendition of "I'm Forever Blowing Bubbles." We empathize as Ursula trips on a cobblestone and grabs her twisted foot, and we are equally disdainful as the smirking sisters stare down a working-class woman. We are also amused as Gudrun hangs on a pole while she hops off a tram and lighthearted as the sisters trip off into the graveyard.

In an upbeat, comical scene during the following wedding sequence, Birkin rushes to the carriage with a flustered Tibby, who is still dressing for his wedding. As they speed toward the church, Birkin airily reassures the groom,"Oh, don't worry! A little unconventionality will do that family good!" and when the groom chases the bride to the church door (an episode drawn from the text), Birkin applauds their spontaneity. As in the novel, Gerald asks, "Do you expect me to take you seriously?" Birkin replies, "Yes, Gerald, you're one of the very few people I do expect that of," but the very lightness of his response keeps us from doing so. An impatient Hermione encounters Birkin in front of the church. "You're late!" she mildly reproves him, whereupon he wisecracks about the groom detaining him with talk about "the immortality of the soul." By way of contrast, in the novel, Hermione waits for Birkin at the altar, in the depths of despair:

> . . . . he was not there. A terrible storm came over her as if she were drowning. She was possessed by a devastating hopelessness, and she approached mechanically to the altar. Never had she known such a pang of utter, final hopelessness. It was beyond death, so utterly null, desert. (65)

When Gudrun, reclining on a tombstone intones with mock seriousness, "Nothing materializes," Ursula responds, "Frightening!" an echo of the novel's "In their hearts they were frightened." Her tone of voice is so casual and insincere, however, that it makes a mockery of the word.

The tone of the classroom scene in the film differs from the novel's. In the text, after Ursula's pupils leave, a rancorous argument between Hermione and Birkin erupts. Hermione delivers herself of "queer rhapsodies" about the corrupting effects of "mental knowledge" on children and adults, and Birkin denounces her *to* in a vehement personal attack that leaves Ursula out in the cold. Although Russell shot the quarrel scene, it is not included in the film; instead Birkin suggestively lectures Ursula on the reproductive process of catkins and draws a smiley cartoon face on her blackboard. Lawrence takes Hermione seriously when she croons over Ursula's catkins: "Her absorption was strange, almost rhapsodic" (87). In the film, however, Hermione exclaims, "Aren't they *beau*tiful!" in such a pretentious, affected tone that Ursula frowns, and as Birkin snickers appreciatively, she cuts Hermione off by angrily ringing her schoolbell.

All of the semi-comical touches in the densely textured first sequence of the film—the sisters' saucy putdown of their stodgy parents, their sarcastic reaction to the couple with the wailing baby, Ursula's tripping on a cobblestone, the sisters' impudent disdain toward the working-class women who stare at their colorful getups, Birkin and the half-dressed bridegroom's dash to a carriage, Birkin's crack about Tibby's worrying over the immortality of the soul while being unable to find a buttonhook, and Hermione's paeans to catkins cut off by Ursula's bell ringing—create a lightness, flippancy, even gaiety that is entirely nonexistent in the narrative.

Throughout the rest of the film, but most especially in the first two thirds of it, touches of wit, humor, and insouciance lighten many scenes. How else to characterize the sisters' response to Gerald's diving into his own lake ("Where does his go go *to*?" asks Gudrun archly) and the luncheon guests' embarrassed reactions as Birkin verbally transforms a fig into a sexual organ? Other diverting moments include Hermione's "Russian ballet" undercut by the grimacing of Ursula and Gudrun, Birkin's muffled laughter, and by Tibby and Laura's furtive lovemaking on a couch; and the chaotic ragtime dancing that follows Hermione's solo. Indeed, there's more: Gudrun's slapstick encounter with a half-drunk miner, her dance before the bulls interrupted by Birkin's light-footed rescue of Ursula, the drive-by of an extraordinarily polite cyclist during the lovers' knock-down, drag-out fight over Hermione, Ursula's twitting Birkin about wanting a lover instead of a husband as she hangs the wash, and the two couples arriving in the Alps, dancing at the ski lodge, and frolicking in the snow. All of these entertaining scenes evoke a cynical amusement totally inconsistent with Lawrence's intense solemnity.

A number of critics have singled out two scenes—Ursula and Birkin's frantically groping at each other's clothing as they make love on the night of the Crich picnic, and the vertical images printed sideways of Ursula and Birkin's pastoral lovemaking in a field—as comical, or at very least ironic, though it is by no means obvious that Russell intended audiences to perceive them so.[199] However, irony is certainly generated throughout the film by Russell's use of background music. The recurring tunes "I'm Forever Blowing Bubbles" and "Oh, You Beautiful Doll" are played in situations diametrically opposed to the implications of the lyrics. For example, "I'm Forever Blowing Bubbles," according to Russell the most popular British song of 1920,[200] is sung by Ursula as Gudrun launches into her Dalcroze movements before the bulls.[201] The song accompanies the sisters' walk through the gritty streets of Beldover and is raucously belted out in the working-class tavern as Gudrun is accosted by a miner outside. It is also heard in snatches throughout the film—on the piano at the end of the ragtime dance that cuts off Hermione's solo, during the Crich picnic, and finally, when Gudrun, frolicking with Loerke in the snowy Alps, repeats her Dalcroze movements. In each of these situations, the images on the screen, juxtaposed with the sardonic words of the post-World War I song, suggest the loss of illusions and the anomie experienced by all of the characters in the novel and film.[202]

Another popular song of the period, "Oh, You Beautiful Doll," is used as an ironic backdrop for Gudrun's encounter with a lecherous miner, as well as for Tibby and Laura's nude swim and drowning. We hear it as Gudrun and Ursula beg Gerald to let them explore the Criches' lake in a canoe, and Birkin belts it out as he rushes up to Ursula, who is cringing from possible attack by the horned cattle. In each of these instances, the misogynistic vulgarity of the song provides an ironic commentary on the action. In Gudrun's encounter with a miner, she is the sexual predator momentarily turned victim, rescued by the equally predatory Gerald, who exits the pub with a prostitute on each arm. Russell's Tibby drowns because he is sexually besotted by his bride; in effect, she lures him to his death. Russell mocks Birkin's quest for a transcendent kind of love with Ursula ("I want to be gone out of myself. I want you to be lost to yourself, so we are found different") when he shows Birkin impulsively giving in to his physical passion for her; his comic surrender is echoed by the carnal desire celebrated by the song.

Russell's selection and direction of the cast, as well as some of the behavior he invents for them, also significantly alters the tone of the novel. Several of the performances caricature or trivialize the angst of the principal characters. Although Lawrence satirizes and exaggerates Hermione, he also takes her intellectually more seriously and treats her role as a *kultur-träger* with greater respect than does Russell, who makes Eleanor Bron, with her outlandish costumes, theatrical makeup, and self-conscious speech and movements, unappealing and obnoxious—"an insufferable, Pre-Raphaelite lady" [203] and a campy figure of fun. In the novel, Hermione merely presides over her guests' "Russian ballet" rather than participating in it, and Birkin actually approves. In the film, however, Hermione's embarrassing solo evokes contempt in both the onlookers in the film and in the movie audience.

Like Hermione, Lawrence's "caged hawk," Mrs. Crich, is an embattled eccentric, but Russell makes her dangerously pyschotic, repelling us with her icy and bizarrely dissociated behavior. In the novel, she daydreams about setting dogs on charity-seeking miners. In the film, she actually does it, to the dismay of John Weightman, who points out that such behavior in a mining community would have set off a riot.[204] Lawrence says nothing about Mrs. Crich's acting weirdly at her husband's funeral and next to nothing about the funeral itself. In the film, however, she laughs maniacally over her husband's coffin, an act that is shown to haunt Gerald when he first makes love to Gudrun, and becomes the psychological motivation for his tortured relationship with Gudrun.

A character whose physical appearance and behavior in the film are quite different from those in the novel is Gerald, played by dark-haired, squat, brooding Oliver Reed, a Jerry Colonna look-alike whose head shape has been variously compared to a pear[205] and an eggplant.[206] Oddly, Reed's portrayal of the tortured, self-defeating industrialist, with his stiff carriage and halting, syncopated speech punctuated by sharp, idiosyncratic intakes of breath, is a more compassionate, sympathetic portrayal than any other in the film, with the possible exception of Mr. Crich. At the same time, however, Russell diminishes and trivializes Gerald by making him appear awkward, helpless, and clumsy as he is cuckolded by Loerke. In the sequence showing Gerald's suicidal trek into the snow, the final shot, instead of being a closeup as it would have been if faithful to the novel, is an extreme long shot of Gerald as a tiny dark spot in the snow, a poignant image of cosmic and personal insignificance.

Although visually undefined in the novel, Lawrence's Ursula is psychically a more substantial figure in the novel than in the film, a voluble and feisty foil for Birkin's passionate rant. Throughout much of the narrative, she struggles against the domination of her lover and her father until she finally surrenders to Birkin and becomes a mouthpiece for his metaphysic. On the whole, however, Lawrence's Ursula is a serious, thoughtful adult capable of profound spiritual and emotional transformation. Russell's Ursula, on the other hand, is a pretty, practical-minded, conventional, and rather shallow young woman with a pert, chirpy manner. Although capable of jealous rage, Russell's Ursula is portrayed as far too down-to-earth, level-headed, and skeptical to be carried away by Birkin's high-flown attitudinizing. Indeed, Russell, unlike Lawrence, usually gives her the last, dismissive word in her conflicts with Birkin, an indication of his critical attitude toward the novel's protagonist. In the final shots of the film, as in the novel, the couple debate the possibility of Birkin's having an "eternal" relationship with a man. When Ursula declares it "impossible," Birkin replies, "I don't believe that," but the final, lingering freeze-frame close-up of Ursula's solemn, doubting face, which remains on the screen through the end credits, gives the lie to Birkin's denial.

With the exception of Mr. Brangwen, who is depicted as a fiercely patriarchal bully in the novel and as a testy nonentity in the film, Birkin undergoes the most change in Russell's adaptation, not only in the ingratiating performance of bearded Lawrence look-alike Alan Bates but also because Birkin is portrayed as far more high-pitched, aggressive, dominating, explosive, and noisily long-winded in the novel than he is in the film. "He sounded as if he were addressing a meeting" (94), Ursula and Hermione muse after a long series of denunciatory outbursts from Birkin. In Chapter III, "Class-Room," Lawrence describes Birkin as "exasperated" (90), "irritable" (90), "satirical" (91), in "a silent fury" (89), "starting violently" (104), "overpowering" (108), "violent" and "cruel" (162), and filled "with an insane fury" (270). To Ursula, he seems "almost a monster of hateful arrogance" (203).

Instead of being overbearing, contemptuous, hateful, infuriated, despairing, and hopeless—and overall, an unlikable visionary—Alan Bates's Birkin is mellow, self-mocking, playful, boyish, full of charm, and nimble-footed. As G. B. Crump points out, Bates's performance is meant "to reduce Lawrence's hero to a human scale, to make him more sympathetic dramatically."[207] When Russell's Birkin pontificates, he knows he probably won't be taken seriously. Even when he is at his loudest and most obnoxious, during the memorial service for the World War I soldier, none of the members of the crowd even give him a sidelong glance. In the fig scene, Birkin roguishly humiliates his mistress and discomforts her guests. Afterward, when he tells Gerald that he wants "to sit with my beloved in a field with daisies growing all around us," he waves away a fly with a grin. According to G. B. Crump, "This is a Birkin who knows that the daisies may be full of bees and that his wish may seem sentimental or too wildly visionary." [208] In the absence of Birkin's high seriousness and passionate vehemence, a mirror of Lawrence's, the tone of the film is far milder than the novel's—a major alteration that challenges and undermines some of the author's basic beliefs expressed through the work.

The intermittent serio-comic flippancy of the film, along with the satirical, caricatured portrayals of several of Lawrence's characters, certainly undercuts and critiques the portentousness of the novel. Like early detractors of Lawrence, Russell recognized the hyperbolic excesses of *Women in Love* and clearly did not take the themes and ideas of the work as seriously as did F. R. Leavis, who denounced the filming of the novel as "an obscene undertaking."[209] In adapting *Women in Love*, however, Russell's ironic and somewhat irreverent take on Lawrence's overwrought extravagances did not prevent him from identifying and appreciating the stylistic effects the novelist was trying to achieve and finding effective cinematic analogues for them. About the passage in which Gudrun dances before the bulls, for example, Russell mused, ". . . though I don't know if Lawrence meant the scene on the island to be slightly comic, I always saw it as romanto-comic and slightly ridiculous." [210] Yet Glenda Jackson's gyrations in front of bulls in the film have an undeniably menacing, hypnotic power reminiscent of the sacred and mysterious rite depicted in the novel; almost in spite of himself, one might say, Russell felt driven to be faithful to the text. Thus, although his adaptation of *Women in Love* may fall short of the power, profundity, and grandeur of Lawrence's masterpiece, it brings us, through a dazzling profusion of bold and original cinematic strategies, as close to the spirit and substance of Lawrence's novel as we are ever likely to get, apart from the printed page.

79. Sculptress Gudrun Brangwen (Glenda Jackson) and sister Ursula (Jennie Linden), right, a schoolteacher in the English Midlands mining town of Beldover, leave their parents' home to attend the wedding of Laura Crich and Tibby Lupton.

80. On their way to the Crich wedding, fashionably dressed Brangwen sisters, Ursula (Jennie Linden), left, and Gudrun (Glenda Jackson), stroll through the working class district of Beldover. (Museum of Modern Art/Film Stills Archive)

Women in Love 245

81. Discussing the "experience of marriage," Ursula and Gudrun eye a couple wheeling a baby carriage (above): "More likely the *end* of experience," quips Ursula.

82. At the Crich wedding, wealthy arts patron Hermione Roddice (Eleanor Bron) adjusts cravat of lover Rupert Birkin (Alan Bates).

83. As guests at the Crich wedding pose for a group photograph, one of the glass "films" ominously breaks.

84. "Nothing materializes; everything withers in the bud," muses Gudrun Crich (Glenda Jackson) as sister Ursula watches the Crich wedding from the graveyard opposite the church.

85. In Ursula's classroom, school inspector Rupert Birkin (Alan Bates) examines catkins as unwelcome guest Hermione (Eleanor Bron) exclaims, "Little red flames—aren't they beautiful!" (Museum of Modern Art/Film Stills Archive)

86. Hermione Roddice's "country cottage" Breadalby, where Ursula and Gudrun are invited for the weekend.

Women in Love

87. Hermione's weekend guests assemble for outdoor luncheon.

88. Lecturing embarrassed guests on the "proper way to eat a fig in society," Birkin (Alan Bates) transforms the fruit Hermione (Eleanor Bron) is eating into a woman's sexual organ: ". . . a glittering, rosy, moist, honeyed, heavy-petaled, four-petaled flower."

89. Hermione (Eleanor Bron), Ursula (Jennie Linden), and Gudrun (Glenda Jackson) perform a dance in "the style of the Russian ballet," with Hermione as the widow, Orpah; Ursula as Naomi; and Gudrun as Ruth. (Museum of Modern Art/Film Stills Archive)

90. Hermione (Eleanor Bron) strikes a provocative pose.

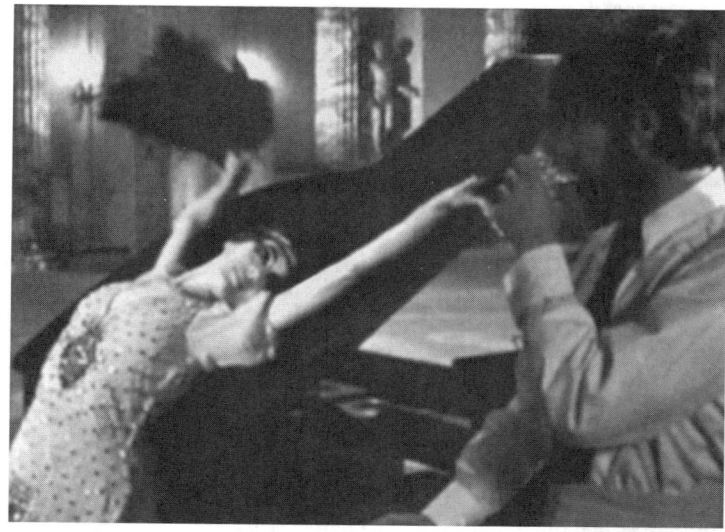

91. After a time-consuming costume change, Hermione (Eleanor Bron) throws herself into a seductive solo that annoys Birkin.

92. Birkin (Alan Bates) and Ursula (Jennie Linden) unceremoniously interrupt Hermione's Isadora-Duncanesque "ballet" by leading guests in a spontaneous ragtime dance.

Women in Love 251

93. Rupert Birkin (Alan Bates) denounces Hermione's (Eleanor Bron) lust for power and her lack of real sensuality and spontaneity; the female nude behind them is ironic decor.

94. In a rage, Hermione (Eleanor Bron) bashes Rupert Birkin (Alan Bates) on the head with a paperweight. (Museum of Modern Art/Film Stills Archive)

95. Fleeing Hermione's wrath, bloodied Birkin (Alan Bates) sheds his clothes as he runs through lush green forest, leaning momentarily on the trunk of a birch tree. (Museum of Modern Art/Film Stills Archive)

96. At a funeral for a World War I soldier, a minister extols the virtues of love while Rupert Birkin rants to Ursula about hate, death, and violent destruction.

97. Gerald Crich (Oliver Reed) races his horse beside a speeding train.

98. In a rapid montage, Gerald Crich (Oliver Reed) whips his rearing horse to make it stand still.

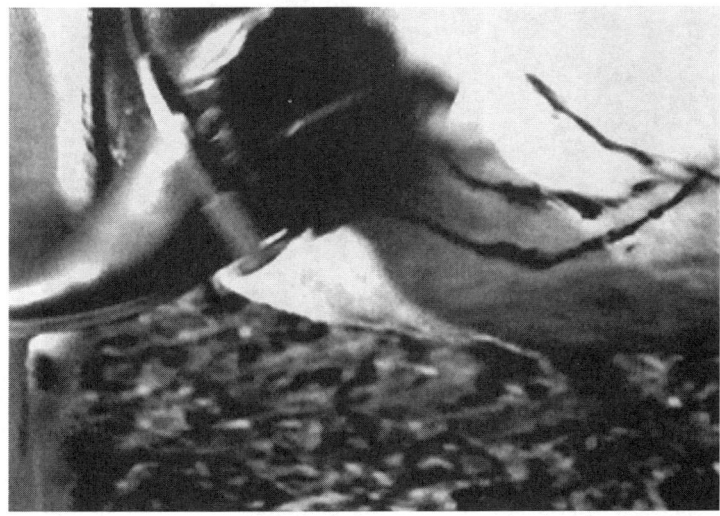

99. Forcibly restraining his mount, Gerald Crich (Oliver Reed) draws blood with his spurs.

100. Ursula (Jennie Linden) and Gudrun (Glenda Jackson) react to Gerald's brutal treatment of his horse with shock and anger.

Women in Love 255

101. In the coal mine, Gerald (Oliver Reed) confronts an aging worker whom he later fires. (Museum of Modern Art/Film Stills Archive)

102. Gerald (Oliver Reed) and his father, colliery owner Thomas Crich (Alan Webb), drive home in luxury amidst the departing miners.

103. How are your thighs?" Gudrun (Glenda Jackson) teases a miner who accosts her in the working class district of Beldover. "I want to drown in flesh—hot, physical, naked flesh!"

104. Rupert Birkin (Alan Bates) and Gerald Crich (Oliver Reed) greet Ursula Brangwen's parents (Michael Gough, Norma Shebeare) at the Criches' yearly picnic.

105. Half-mad Georgiana Crich (Catherine Wilmer), Gerald's mother, remains indoors behind a barred window during the festivities.

106. In an idyllic interlude with Gudrun (Glenda Jackson) at the Criches' picnic, Ursula sings "I'm Forever Blowing Bubbles," a song popular in England in 1920. (Museum of Modern Art/Film Stills Archive)

107. Seductive Gudrun (Glenda Jackson) dances fearlessly before the horned bulls. (Museum of Modern Art/Film Stills Archive)

108. Rescuing Gudrun (Glenda Jackson) from her bizarre dance before the bulls, Gerald (Oliver Reed) tells her he is in love with her; she responds enigmatically, "Well, that's one way of putting it." (Museum of Modern Art/Film Stills Archive)

109. On the Crich's lake at night, Birkin (Alan Bates) tells Ursula (Jennie Linden), "There is a golden light in you which I wish you would give me."

110. Drowned newlyweds Laura (Sharon Gurney) and Tibby Lupton (Christopher Gable) are found in a fatal embrace.

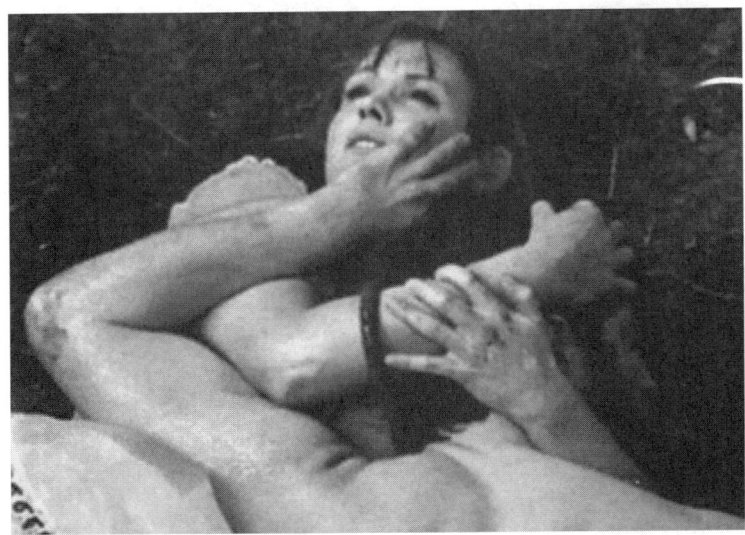

111. Match cut of Ursula (Jennie Linden) and Birkin (Alan Bates) in an embrace nearly identical to Laura and Tibby Lupton's (See Figure 110).

112. Rupert Birkin (Alan Bates) and Gerald Crich (Oliver Reed) in their memorable and controversial Japanese-style wrestling match, notable for its sensuality, frontal nudity, and stunning cinematography. (Museum of Modern Art/Film Stills Archive)

Women in Love 261

113. Birkin (Alan Bates) and Gerald Crich (Oliver Reed) in a strenuous clinch during their free-form encounter.

114. As the two men rest after their match, Birkin (Alan Bates) proposes to Gerald (Oliver Reed) that they swear blood brotherhood and eternal love.

115. Gerald (Oliver Reed) responds evasively to Birkin's offer of blood brotherhood. (Museum of Modern Art/Film Stills Archive)

116. Birkin (Alan Bates) and Gerald (Oliver Reed) end their wrestling match with a symbolic chalice between them

117. To her husband's dismay, Georgiana Crich (Catherine Wilmer) lets their dogs loose on petitioning miners.

118. Stroking Winifred Crich's pet rabbit, Gerald Crich (Oliver Reed) asks Gudrun to visit his younger sister again.

119. After agreeing to marry, Ursula (Jennie Linden) and Rupert (Alan Bates) driftsideways in slow-motion, choreographed lovemaking. (Museum of Modern Art/Film Stills Archive)

120. To son Gerald's (Oliver Reed) dismay, Georgiana Crich (Catherine Wilmer) drops a trowel on her husband's coffin lid and laughs hysterically at his graveside.

121. After his father's funeral, Gerald (Oliver Reed) stumbles through the graveyard where Thomas Crich has just been interred.

122. On the night of his father's burial, muddy-booted Gerald (Oliver Reed) sneaks into Gudrun's (Glenda Jackson's) bedroom. (Museum of Modern Art/Film Stills Archive)

123. Under a symbolic modern painting of a woman, Gudrun (Glenda Jackson) awaits Gerald's embrace.

124. Literally pinned down, Gudrun (Glenda Jackson) urges Gerald (Oliver Reed) to leave before daylight when her parents awaken. (Museum of Modern Art/Film Stills Archive)

125. Multiple images reflected in mirrors, Birkin (Alan Bates) and Gerald (Oliver Reed) discuss marriage and "the additional perfect relationship between man and man."

126. Newly married Rupert Birkin (Alan Bates) tells amused Ursula (Jennie Linden), hanging out the wash, that all women are either wives or mistresses. (Museum of Modern Art/Film Stills Archive)

127. The four lovers enjoy winter sports in the Swiss Alps. (Museum of Modern Art/Film Stills Archive)

128. Gerald Crich (Oliver Reed) in a tense moment with Gudrun (Glenda Jackson) during their tryst in the Swiss Alps. (Museum of Modern Art/Film Stills Archive)

Women in Love 269

129. Birkin (Alan Bates) confesses to Ursula (Jennie Linden) that without her, he couldn't bear the snow in "this cold eternal place." (Museum of Modern Art/Film Stills Archive)

130. Her interest piqued, Gudrun, symbolically "behind bars," learns that Loerke (Vladek Sheybal) is a sculptor who has had a hard life.

131. In the bedroom they share, Loerke (Vladek Sheybal), with his "friend" (Richard Heffer), defends his sculpture of a young girl on a horse from Ursula Brangwen's attack.

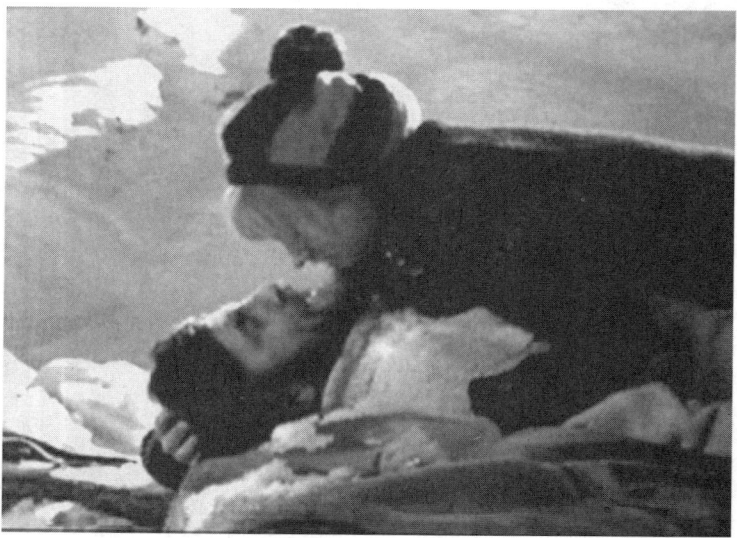

132. Renouncing the "ghastly glamour" of the snow, Ursula (Jennie Linden) enthusiastically agrees to Birkin's (Alan Bates) proposal that they travel to Italy "to find Romeo and Juliet."

133. Gudrun (Glenda Jackson) provocatively reveals to Loerke (Vladek Sheybal) that she and Gerald (Oliver Reed) are not married. (Museum of Modern Art/Film Stills Archive)

134. Gudrun (Glenda Jackson) plays Cleopatra in a perverse dress-up game with Loerke (Vladek Sheybal).

272 *Women in Love*

135. Loerke (Vladek Sheybal), "behind bars" like Gudrun (see Figure 130), pretends to be homosexual Tchaikovsky on his honeymoon.

136. As Gudrun (Glenda Jackson) cavorts in the snow, Loerke proposes that she live and work with him in Dresden, Germany.

137. In a poignant series of lap dissolves, rejected Gerald (Oliver Reed) climbs to his icy death in the snow.

138. Home in Beldover after Gerald's suicide, Birkin (Alan Bates) tells Ursula that in addition to the love of a woman, he needs "a man friend as eternal as you and I are eternal."

139. Just before the film's final freeze frame, above, Ursula (Jennie Linden) insists that Birkin can't have two kinds of love "because it's impossible."

140. D. H. Lawrence (rear) and bearded look-alike Alan Bates, who plays Lawrence's alter ego Rupert Birkin in the film of *Women in Love*. (Museum of Modern Art/Film Stills Archive)

Chapter 5

Conclusion

The Three Adaptations

In writing this book, I set myself a surprisingly difficult task. Identifying and describing the multi-faceted aspects of D.H. Lawrence's prose style in three markedly different works turned out to be a far more subtle, complicated, and time-consuming process than I expected it to be. Yet through such close analysis, I was able to move well beyond the subjective impressionism of most other studies of Lawrentian prose and to discover exactly how the novelist achieved his strangely powerful, often poetic effects. I was able to pinpoint how Lawrence conveyed eroticism through suggestive diction, parallel syntax, and repetitive rhythms; how he conveyed a mystical sense of the ineffable through his use of abstract, multisyllabic words; or how he created paradox and antithesis through compound sentences joined by the coordinating conjunctions *and* and *but*.

The precision of such analysis proved crucial to identifying equivalences between specific elements of Lawrence's prose and the corresponding cinematic effects achieved by the three filmmakers of *The Rocking Horse Winner*, *Sons and Lovers*, and *Women in Love*. Indeed, examining the films for cinematic analogues of such stylistic elements as abstract diction, incantatory rhythm, interlocking metaphor, and ironic tone proved to be even more revealing and rewarding than analyzing Lawrence's prose. Such an examination made it clear to me just how creatively and intelligently certain filmmakers manage to reproduce the aspects of prose style, even while others fail or do not bother to try. I also discovered that, when successful, the directors' efforts at transposing Lawrence's unique prose style to film enhanced each of the three film adaptations far more than I supposed they would.

Precisely because two of the three Lawrence adapters felt compelled to invent innovative cinematic strategies for replicating key aspects of Lawrence's distinctive prose style, the films they made are rich and complex in ways that do justice to the novelty, intricacy, subtlety, and profundity of the originals. Any aesthetic evaluation of a work of art is, of course, subjective, yet I believe that my study, based on objective criteria, conclusively demonstrates that a film adaptation which analogously reproduces the unique properties of a superb writer's literary style is immeasurably superior, as an adaptation, to one that does not. Not only that: such an adaptation is almost certain to be a far better film in its own right. Thus, despite their flaws, *The Rocking Horse Winner* and *Women in Love*, independent of their sources, are dramatically enhanced by their filmmakers' willingness to seek and devise stylistic equivalences that preserve the unique characteristics of Lawrence's prose style, for it is Lawrence's remarkable prose itself—terse and ironic in "The Rocking-Horse Winner," heightened and hyperbolic in *Women in Love*—that generates the powerful impact of both works. By the same token, Jerry Wald's *Sons and Lovers*, though an appealing film in certain respects, ultimately fails to move us or to capture the greatness of the novel, not only because of its foreshortened, schematic, and simplified narrative structure but, more importantly, because it simply does not re-create the propulsiveness, rhapsodic passion, sensuous immediacy, and eroticism—nor the tensions and ambivalence—inherent in the language of the original.

In spite of its slow pace and gloomy atmosphere, Pelissier's adaptation of "The Rocking-Horse Winner" is greatly enhanced by its confined, theatrical sets, moody *film noir* lighting, extreme camera angles, deep-focus photography, zoom and tracking shots, parallel cut and climactic sequences, montages and superimpositions, eerie soundtrack, and symbolic images of horses, money, stairs, doors, and windows. The film achieves a power and expressiveness that is attributable to the director's originality in creating equivalents for the story's blend of fairytale and realistic aspects as well as for the principal elements of Lawrence's prose style—its fairytale atmosphere and its realistic, simple diction, insistent repetitiveness, rocking sentence and paragraph rhythms, pervasive parallelism and antithesis, multiple paradoxes and ironies, and symbolic use of images of the rocking horse, the whispering house, and money.

The best of the three, both as an adaptation and as a film, Ken Russell's version of *Women in Love*—remarkably restrained compared with most of his other extravagances—captures the lush texture of the novel's prose so superbly that, apart from some of the excellent films of Jane Austen's novels produced in the mid-nineties, it is hard to think of many screen adaptations of literary works that equal it. A visual and verbal feast, the film artfully reproduces the opulence of Lawrence's highly figurative, rhythmic prose, embodying and celebrating the novelist's rhapsodic writing and making style, in every sense of the word, its centerpiece. That some critics faulted the film for being *too* stylish, and for thereby failing adequately to convey the novel's serious (if not readily comprehensible) philosophical themes, suggests the difficulty of transposing abstract ideas to the screen. But the film of *Women in Love* is distinctive and memorable precisely because of the dazzling cinematic pyrotechnics that mirror the stylistic peculiarities and excesses of Lawrence's experimental novel. Lush indoor and outdoor settings—ornate marble salon, multi-mirrored baronial library bathed in golden firelight, subtropical forests, wind-swept fields, velvety green lawns, candle-lit lake, and snowy Alpine peaks—along with vivid colors, sensuous textures, and striking costumes and artwork, re-create a stunning visual opulence drawn directly from the overblown language and evocative passages of the text.

The idiosyncratic syntax of the sentences in the novel, and the eroticized, often syncopated rhythms of many of its paragraphs, are replicated in the film's artful editing, with its dancelike rhythms and choreographed scenes, recurring visual counterpoint, numerous parallel cut sequences, abrupt shifts and contrasts, speeded-up montage, and slow-motion photography. The syntax and rhythms of the text are also mirrored in the film's unusual series of shots, such as repeated pulsating zooms, overlapping dissolves, horizontal images printed vertically, hand-held camera shots, eye-catching closeups, high- and low-angle shots, intercut shots, and match cuts. Of the three adaptations I studied, *Women in Love* comes closest to replicating the pace of the work in transposing it to film. Lawrence's relatively short paragraphs and chapters are mirrored in the film's overall fast pace as well as in the rapid cutting, brief shots, and short scenes. However, there are wide variations of speed throughout the movie, and some unusually long takes that parallel the very long sentences in the novel.

The symbolism that permeates every detail of the novel and the density of its metaphorical language are brilliantly embodied in the film's eye-filling, richly suggestive imagery, symbolic indoor and outdoor settings, and unforgettable scenes—Gudrun lying on a tombstone with her hands crossed over her breasts, Gerald subduing his bloodied white horse with a whip, Gudrun hynotizing a herd of horned bulls with her Isadora Duncanesque dance, Birkin transforming Hermione's quartered fig into a woman's genitals, Gerald seductively stroking a rabbit as he gazes up at Gudrun or clenching a handful of mud in the graveyard on the night of his father's funeral, Birkin and Gerald in the naked embrace of "Japanese wrestling" on a white fur rug in front of a blazing fire, and the drowned newlyweds in the mud of the Criches' lake juxtaposed with Birkin and Ursula entwined after making love.

And finally, the lilting musical score, with its 1920s popular songs, reproduces the disillusionment and malaise implied in the novel, written mostly during the carnage of World War I.

Critics have attacked Russell's *Women in Love* for its extravagantly "purple" style, with its facile symbolism, overripe color, too obvious symmetries, eccentric camera angles and editing, as well as its sensational scenes, unlikely casting, exaggerated performances, altered characterizations, and flippant tone. But some of the most often cited faults of the film are also its greatest strengths. Russell's overstatement parallels Lawrence's, and it is Lawrence's hyperbolic, overheated prose in *Women in Love* that, despite its insistent repetitiveness and jargon, creates the powerfully mesmerizing effects that Russell so brilliantly captured in his film.

Unlike Pelissier's *The Rocking Horse Winner* and Russell's *Women in Love*, Jerry Wald's abridged and censored version of *Sons and Lovers*, regardless of critical acclaim, commercial success, and seven Academy Award nominations,[1] for the most part fails to capture "the spirit and essence" of the original that Wald promised Frieda Lawrence he would preserve. For despite the authentic industrial midlands locales, picturesque wide-screen black-and-white photography, fine performances by seasoned British actors Trevor Howard, Wendy Hiller, and Mary Ure, and a few outstanding scenes and sequences, the film has few of the stylistic felicities that enrich Lawrence's novel and transform it into a powerful and deeply affecting work of art.

Almost entirely missing from the film, which omits all of Paul's youth and adolescence, are the concrete, sensory details of the Morels' domestic life and of the midlands landscape lovingly described in the text—a drop of blood on a baby's glistening hair, a broken wax doll burned as a sacrifice, the hiss of a ball of spit on a hot iron, a miner's pit trousers drying on the hearth, a big black saucepan simmering on the stove, a hammered piece of red-hot iron, the nocturnal shriek of a wind-swept ash tree, tall white lilies reeling in the moonlight, and a red mooon slowly rising "like a great bird" (77). Cinematographer Freddie Francis was rarely permitted to linger over ordinary objects or to create extreme closeups or slow pans of natural phenomena—trees, birds, sunsets, and most especially the colorful profusion of emblematic flowers that permeate the novel and are almost totally absent from the film. Typical of most Hollywood producers with chiefly commercial interests, Wald converted the work into a superficial drama, sacrificing the wealth of visual particulars without which the novel would have been a mere shadow of itself.

Conclusion 279

Because of the surgical removal of Part One of the novel and further plot simplification, almost all of the quintessentially Lawrentian scenes depicting symbolic mystical communions with nature and the cosmos or the enactment of some sort of primitive rite are also missing from the film—Mrs. Morel, pregnant with Paul and locked out by her drunken husband, sniffing "a deep draught of the scent of lilies" in "the mysterious out of doors" (27), thrusting her newborn baby Paul upwards towards "the crimson throbbing sun" (37) and impulsively naming him, Paul's ritual burning of his sister Annie's doll as a sacrifice, and Paul and Miriam's communion in the darkness over a white rose bush.

The film's temperate rhythms, symmetrical and predictable, conform to the norms of classical Hollywood style and are weak echoes of the propulsive, climactic rhythms of the text. The longish takes, stately transitions, relatively static scenes with lengthy closeups at the end of them, and absence of parallel-cut sequences fail to convey the rapidfire pace of the novel or the pervasive parallelism and antithesis of its syntax. Subtle and contextual in the novel, the symbolism of the film is clichéd and heavy-handedly explicit. Above all, with the exception of an arousing shot of Paul gazing amorously at the nape of Clara's neck, the electrifying sequence in which he stays overnight at her house, and a restrained bedroom scene between the lovers at a seaside rendezvous (added to the American version), the filmmakers took few opportunities to eroticize the cinematic imagery and rhythms, stripping the film of Lawrence's sexual and spiritual intensity. What remains of the novel is slick and conventional, lacking in texture, and far less emotionally involving and visually exciting than it might have been in the hands of more daring and imaginative filmmakers.

Only one aspect of style—tone—was not faithfully reproduced in any of the screen versions, though *Sons and Lovers* comes closest to the novel in the overall seriousness of its mood. In fact, it may well be that even when plot and prose style are reproduced in a film adaptation—and that happens seldom enough—tone is the element of a literary work that usually undergoes the greatest change from page to screen. Film adapters frequently use changes in tone both to interpret and to comment on the writer's attitude toward his material—as did Ken Russell. Tonal changes may also be made for commercial rather than intellectual or artistic reasons, and may be necessary to increase box office appeal.

The unsentimental, coolly ironic detachment of the narrator in "The Rocking-Horse Winner" becomes portentously melodramatic in Pelissier's film, and the film's atmosphere, lightened only by some wittily sarcastic dialogue and interchanges between Uncle Oscar and his sister and brother-in-law, is relentlessly gloomy and ominous. Indeed, the anxiety, melancholy, and malaise that suffuses the film virtually ensured its short run in England, even though it starred renowned British actors John Mills and Valerie Hobson. The urgent seriousness of Lawrence's *Women in Love*, on the other hand, gives way to flippancy, comic flourishes, and high camp in Russell's adaptation, and the passionate earnestness of *Sons and Lovers* is lightened by humor and satire in a number of scenes in the film. Not surprisingly, both films were box office winners.

Auteur theory holds that a major factor in establishing the tone of a film is the controlling sensibility behind it. In *The Rocking Horse Winner* and *Women in Love* there is clearly only one controlling sensibility, but in *Sons and Lovers* there are a number of key players, any combination of whom may have a profound effect on the atmosphere and mood of the film. When a filmmaker controls nearly all aspects of a film version of a literary work, then the film truly bears the stamp of its creator, and the adaptation is, as Joy Boyum argues in *Double Exposure: Fiction into Film*, an interpretation rather than a mere facsimile of the original. British director-screenwriter Pelissier's seriousness of purpose and reverence for Lawrence's text, suggested in comments he wrote about his earnest efforts to be faithful to the nuances of Lawrence's story,[2] are enshrined in the film's rather heavy-handed musical score, its weird sound effects, its expressionistic lighting, and the disturbing morbidity and angst pervading the entire production. Russell's brash irreverence, his un-British extravagance, and his skepticism about Lawrence's apparent absurdities—shared, it would seem, by co-writer/co-producer Larry Kramer—are also responsible for the often satirical and essentially critical attitude conveyed in many scenes of the adaptation, and in the excesses of staging, acting, decor, costume, cinematography, and editing that strongly affect the overall tone of the production.

General Conclusions

My examination of the three adaptations has led me to a number of other conclusions, not only about the translation of style to films but about the process of adapting literary works to the screen in general. It's apparent that the transformation into film of literary works is a complex, often lengthy process involving many players, and that, as my discussion of tone in the three Lawrence adaptations indicates, the number of parties involved and the period of time it takes to produce a film adaptation can profoundly affect its fidelity to both the letter and spirit of the source.

Although the screenplay for almost any feature film, particularly one produced in Hollywood, passes through many stages, often with the involvement of several writers and screen doctors, and usually undergoes changes even during filming, the collaborative process typical of film has special implications for the adaptation of classic literary works, especially those with a distinctive narrative or prose style. It would seem that the greater the number of successive participants involved in composing the final screenplay of an adaptation, the likelier it is that both the narrative and prose styles of the work will be either misrepresented or essentially ignored, which is undoubtedly why *The Rocking Horse Winner*, scripted and directed by Pelissier, and *Women in Love*, co-scripted and directed by Ken Russell, are stylistically more evocative of their originals than *Sons and Lovers*. (Russell rejected Larry Kramer's earlier screenplay as "a tawdry piece of sensationalizing.")[3]

Jerry Wald's film of *Sons and Lovers*, on the other hand, went through many phases before it was produced in 1960. In addition to an early script—approved, ironically, by Frieda Lawrence—the screenplay for the adaptation went through seven rewrites and a change in studios from Columbia Pictures to Twentieth Century Fox until veteran British screenwriters Gavin Lambert and T. E. B. Clarke co-wrote a commercially viable but un-Lawrentian script. It was former screenwriter Wald, producer of the scandalous *Peyton Place* and a bastardized version of William Faulkner's *The Sound and the Fury*, who was responsible for directing the screenwriters and cinematographer to downplay the literary qualities of the episodic novel, deemphasizing the natural settings saturated with Lawrentian sensuality and symbolism in favor of a much-reduced and simplified storyline and a focus on human drama.[4]

Besides the apparently negative impact of successive script revisions on a film adaptation's stylistic fidelity to the text, it's evident that the films that most imaginatively and accurately reproduce the style of the works upon which they are based—in this instance, *The Rocking Horse Winner* and *Women in Love*—are those written and directed by a "hyphenate," one individual wearing two hats. Clearly, when the director has a major role in writing the screenplay, or actually writes it—a common practice in European, British, and Commonwealth film adaptations of literary works—innovative cinematic techniques for replicating elements of narrative prose style are far more likely to be conceived, tried out, and ultimately incorporated into the film adaptation than in the typical Hollywood production. As Andre Bazin pointed out, "The more important and decisive the literary qualities of the work . . . the more it needs a creative talent to reconstruct it on a new equilibrium, not indeed identical with but the equivalent of the old one."[5] Certainly, when a director controls film production, more attention seems to be paid to the purely aesthetic qualities of both the fiction and the film simply because the director is much closer than any hired screenwriter to the actual shooting and editing process, and consequently more aware of what can be done to re-create the style of the original. This presupposes, of course, that the director-writer in question is sufficiently literate and zealous enough about preserving the unique qualities of his source to recognize, identify, and replicate its stylistic properties.

The production history of the screen adaptations reveals that the overall cinematic style of each film, whether controlled by an individual or a Hollywood combine, was as much influenced by the style and conventions of films produced during the same period as it was by the style of its fictional source. The impact of contemporary cinematic style is evident in all film adaptations and limits the filmmakers' capacity to translate freely and imaginatively elements of prose and narrative style into cinematic terms. Indeed, it appears that whatever degree of technological sophistication has been reached at the point a particular film adaptation is undertaken, the extent to which filmmakers can violate, circumvent, or transcend the cinematic codes and conventions of their time determines to a significant degree their ability to approximate a truly distinctive literary style.

As I noted earlier, *The Rocking Horse Winner* was one of a number of literate, well-crafted, dialogue-centered adaptations of British novels, stories, and plays, including *Oliver Twist, The Fallen Idol, Brighton Rock, Black Narcissus, Hamlet, Richard III*, and *Henry V*, that were made in post-World War II Great Britain between 1945 and 1950. In fact, several reviewers contended that Pelissier's film was stylistically similar to David Lean's adaptation of Dickens's *Great Expectations*, in which John Mills, who produced and played the role of Bassett in *The Rocking Horse Winner*, excelled in the role of Pip, and Valerie Hobson, who played Hester in Pelissier's film, triumphed as Estelle. In Pelissier's black-and-white film, the expressionistic lighting, claustrophobic sets and decor, and often half-lit, deep-focus photography are also reminiscent of techniques associated with *film noir*. And, as Julian Smith pointed out, the open traveling shot that zeroes in on the Grahame house, the first view of Paul playing in the snow, the use of distorting lenses and camera angles, and the burning of the rocking-horse at the end—like the burning of Orson Welles's legendary Rosebud—are reminiscent of *Citizen Kane*.[6] Despite the film's stylistic affinities with productions of its time, however, Pelissier made imaginative use of varied offbeat cinematic techniques to reproduce Lawrence's style and substance, and, as a result, *The Rocking Horse Winner* is a strikingly original adaptation.

The location shots contrasting the urban and the pastoral, the distinctive black-and-white cinematography, and the gritty portrayal of working-class life in the industrial midlands, key aspects of *Sons and Lovers*, are features typical of a number of candid films of social realism made in Great Britain during the late fifties and early-to-mid sixties. Not surprisingly, Freddie Francis, the cinematographer of *Sons and Lovers*, was also the lensman for *Room at the Top* and *Saturday Night and Sunday Morning*, both highly successful British "New Wave" films. However, the classical Hollywood style of filmmaking that was superimposed over British "neorealism" resulted in a picturesque but curiously restrained, hybrid cinematic style lacking in inventiveness and daring.

The most experimental and original of the three adaptations, *Women in Love*, owes much to the radical stylistic cinematic conventions of the French New Wave and to the innovative work of a more visually oriented generation of British film directors who appeared in the late sixties. However, Russell had already evolved a unique style in his television biopics before he turned to feature-film making, and his stylistic allusions in *Women in Love* owe as much to his own films for the BBC program *Monitor*, in particular, *Isadora Duncan: The Biggest Dancer in the World* (1966), and to his film *The Music Lovers* (1970), as they do to the work of contemporaneous filmmakers. In any case, it is precisely Russell's individualistic and iconoclastic approach to filmmaking that enabled him to transpose Lawrence's stylistic quirks and excesses to the screen with such empathy and panache.

Not only the style of movies made in the same time frame but also the prevailing social, political, and religious norms of the period—expressed in and through the events, characterizations, and dialogue of the adaptations—can markedly affect a filmgoer's perception of whether the film version is stylistically faithful to its source. Thus, the anti-gambling sentiments imposed on *The Rocking Horse Winner* by British censors and conveyed in the maudlin, melodramatic denouement tacked on at the end were more appropriate in pietistic nineteenth-century fiction than to the works of D. H. Lawrence or to the year in which the film was made, and contributed to the impression of several reviewers that the style of the film was distinctly un-Lawrentian.[7] So also did the considerably expanded role of Bassett, transformed in the film from an unwitting catalyst of doom to a surrogate father, moral tutor, and genial spokesperson for solid British working-class virtues and values. The softening of the mother's image at the end of the movie, a tribute to reverential notions of maternity prevalent at the time the film was made, was clearly out of keeping with the harsh, dry-eyed view of Paul's mother in Lawrence's story. The deemphasis on the sexual implications of Paul's frenzied rides on his rocking-horse, noted by many post-World War II interpreters, reflects the restraint and puritanism of the late forties in Great Britain and further detracts from the audience's perception of the film as Lawrentian.

Controversial aspects of the novel *Sons and Lovers* were also omitted or muted in the film version, which was made just prior to the advent of true sexual candor in both British and American feature films. The absence of these elements accounts, in part, for the impression that the film is fundamentally un-Lawrentian both in substance and style. Almost all of the erotic scenes in *Sons and Lovers*, unlike those in the novel, are lacking in passion and are decorously prim; the women are clothed or draped and nothing much happens between the lovers, either in the scene of Clara and Paul half-dressed before the fireplace (they are nude in the novel) or in the seaside bedroom scene showing Clara covered by a sheet. Clara's feminism, taken somewhat seriously in the novel, is treated humorously and satirically in the film, as one might expect in a movie made a few years before the second wave of twentieth-century feminism.

In accord with Frieda Lawrence's contention, in a letter to Jerry Wald, that her late husband had regretted his harsh portrayal of his father in the novel,[8] but also undoubtedly because support for a patriarchal family structure was widespread in the 1950s, the character of Mr. Morel is toned down and made more appealing. Some of the dialogue spoken by Mr. Morel in the film is distinctly un-Lawrentian, in particular his incongruously sophisticated speech denouncing his wife's Oedipal attachment to Paul and insisting on the importance of his son's separation from her so that he would be able to love an appropriate woman. The speech reflects Freudian theories of psychosexual developments to which Lawrence did not subscribe and which, in any case, he would never have put into the mouth of his barely literate, uneducated, dialect-spouting character.

The mercy-killing of long-suffering Mrs. Morel, carried out in the novel by Paul and his sister with an overdose of morphine, was omitted from the film, obviously because of the taboo against euthanasia. Instead, Mrs. Morel dies a quick, peaceful, un-Lawrentian death. Almost all of Paul's decidedly rough edges are smoothed out, both in the script and in Dean Stockwell's bland, inexpressive, mechanical portrayal. In keeping with the upbeat finale of most Hollywood movies, the film, unlike the novel, ends with the hopeful implication that Paul and Miriam, both going to London, will meet again and unite.

In the case of *Women in Love*, the growing acceptance of unconventional attitudes and behavior, as well as the lifting of censorship that resulted in the sexual frankness and controversial themes tackled in films of the late sixties and early seventies, enabled Ken Russell to transpose to the screen a daring novel that was in many respects ahead of its time. Russell's adaptation creates the impression of fidelity to its source not only because of its analogous style but because it advocates or at least accepts free love, bohemianism, women's independence, nontraditional marriage, and anti-capitalist and anti-war sentiments. The film also outdoes Lawrence in its unblinking portrayal of homosexuality and bisexuality, as well as its explicit full-frontal male and female nudity.

Whatever their flaws and limitations, the adaptations analyzed in this study, each produced during successive decades by different filmmakers, demonstrate conclusively that almost all of the unique features of Lawrence's distinctive prose are cinematically reproducible and have in fact been rendered in at least one of the adaptations. For even though film is primarily a visual medium, it is clearly possible through a fusion of shot and word, as well as through a combination of contemporary movie technology and sophisticated composition, shooting, lighting, editing, acting, costumes, and decor, to create facsimiles of just about any stylistic element of prose or the effects created by them, no matter how "literary," if a filmmaker is imaginative and original enough to discover analogous means and take the risk of using them.

The ability of filmmakers to transpose a distinctive prose style has important and far-reaching consequences for the future of adaptation and for film itself. Despite a lingering prejudice against adaptations, more and more of them are being made for mass audiences. As a result of the current deemphasis on reading the classics of Western literature, even among undergraduate majors in English and American literature, film adaptations, whether commercial feature-length or television mini-series, may become the main source of exposure to outstanding and definitive works of fiction. In the future, how many students, except possibly for those who attend elite prep schools, will ever read Jane Austen's *Pride and Prejudice, Sense and Sensibility, Persuasion,* or *Emma*? Yet in 1995 and 1996, superb films or television series based on all of these works were released, to great fanfare, and did remarkably well in television ratings and at the box office. And according to a survey in *The Chronicle of Higher Education,* Austen's *Sense and Sensibility* was ranked among the 10 most popular books read by U.S. undergraduates in January and February 1996.[9]

Film critics generally continue to insist that filmmakers cannot truly reproduce the nuances of a distinctive prose style. Dave Kehr in his review of the BBC's film of Jane Austen's *Persuasion* (1995), for example, argued that "no film could reproduce the subtle beauties of Austen's narration, which magically manages to suggest every shade of perception (and misperception) and every shift of understanding (and misunderstanding) that crosses her heroines' fine, lucid minds." He further warned that "few filmmakers are imaginative enough to find the small variations—the shift in camera position, the change in lighting, that convey the dawning of a fresh perspective." However, he allowed that director Robert Michell, through a variety of cinematic techniques, does convey "the inner workings of Austen's prose," and concluded that his version of *Persuasion* is therefore an "unusually successful and seductive example of the art of literary adaptation."[10] The fact that filmmakers may find it quite difficult to reproduce the unique qualities that enthrall readers of D. H. Lawrence or Jane Austen, or any other outstanding stylist, doesn't mean that such cinematic transposition shouldn't be undertaken. Increasingly, imaginative and innovative filmmakers, with new technologies and strategies at their disposal, are successfully bringing established literary classics to the screen and in the process developing and refining the art of adaptation as well as enriching the art of film.

Notes

Chapter 1: Introduction: Literature on Film

1. Morris Beja, *Film and Literature* (New York: Longman, 1979), 78.
2. Linda Segar, *The Art of Adaptation: Turning Fact and Fiction into Film* (New York: Henry Holt, 1992), xi.
3. Joy Gould Boyum, *Double Exposure: Fiction into Film* (New York: New American Library, 1985), 77.
4. Martin Battestin, "Osborne's *Tom Jones*: Adapting a Classic," in *Film and/as Literature*, ed. John Harrington (Englewood Cliffs, N.J.: Prentice-Hall, 1977), 38.
5. Among others, a film based on Lawrence's novel *The Plumed Serpent*, directed by Christopher Miles (c. 1974) was shot in Mexico but was apparently never released. See Harry T. Moore, "D. H. Lawrence and the Flicks," *Literature/Film Quarterly* 1 (January 1973), 11.
6. Ibid., 3.
7. Charles Eidsvik, "Toward a Politique des Adaptations," in *Film and/as Literature*, ed. John Harrington (Englewood Cliffs, N.J.: Prentice-Hall, 1977), 32.
8. Harry T. Moore, *The Priest of Love* (Rev. ed.; N. Y.: Penguin, 1974), 572.
9. Quoted in Joseph Gomez, "The Elusive Gold at the End of the Rainbow: Russell's Adaptation of Lawrence's Novel," in *Literature/Film Quarterly* 18, 2 (1990), 134–136.
10. Quoted in Harry T. Moore, "D.H. Lawrence and the Flicks," *Literature/Film Quarterly* 1 (January 1973), 3.
11. D. H. Lawrence, "Let Us Be Men," in *Selected Poems* (London: Penguin, 1968), 146.
12. D. H. Lawrence, *Phoenix: The Posthumous Poems of D. H. Lawrence*, ed. Edward D. McDonald (New York: Penguin, 1978), 325.
13. D. H. Lawrence, "Sex Versus Loveliness," in *Phoenix II: Uncollected, Unpublished and Other Prose Works*, eds. Warren Roberts and Harry T. Moore (New York: Viking, 1970), 529.
14. Moore, "D. H. Lawrence and the Flicks," 3.
15. Brenda Mattox, *D. H. Lawrence: The Story of a Marriage* (New York: Simon and Schuster, 1994), 498.
16. Moore, "D. H. Lawrence and the Flicks," 5–6.
17. Moore, *The Priest of Love*, 645–646.
18. Robert Murphy, *Sixties British Cinema* (London: British Film Institute, 1992), 261.
19. A relatively tame black-and-white Gallicized version of *Lady Chatterly's Lover*, *L'amant de Lady Chatterly*, directed by Marc Allegret and based on a stage play by Gaston Bonheur and Philippe de Rothschild, was produced in France in

1956. It starred Danielle Darrieux as Lady Chatterly, Leo Genn as Lord Chatterly, and Italian actor Erno Crisi as Mellors.

20. Moore, "D. H. Lawrence and the Flicks," 5–6.

21. S.E. Gontarski, "Christopher Miles on the Making of *The Virgin and the Gypsy*," *Literature/Film Quarterly* 11, 4 (1983), 250.

22. See Barry Salt, "Statistical Style Analysis of Motion Pictures," in *Movies and Methods*, vol. V, ed. Bill Nichols (Berkeley, Los Angeles, and London: University of California Press, 1985), 691–703. See also Barry Salt, *Film Style and Technology* (London: Starword, 1983; 2nd ed., 1992).

Chapter 2: "The Rocking-Horse Winner"

1. D.H. Lawrence, "The Rocking-Horse Winner," in *The Portable D.H. Lawrence*, ed. Diana Trilling (New York: Penguin Books, 1981), 147–166. All future references are to this edition.

2. See Rosemary Reeves, "Lawrence, Lady Cynthia Asquith and 'The Rocking-Horse Winner,'" *Studies in Short Fiction*, 20 (1983), 121–126. See also Jeffrey D. Meyers, *D.H. Lawrence: A Biography* (New York: Knopf, 1990), 123: "Lawrence's famous story 'The Rocking-Horse Winner' was inspired by the desperate unhappiness of the Asquith family; by the parents' remoteness from each other (because of the war and its aftermath) as well as from the children, by Cynthia's obsession with more money, by John's autistic frenzy and by the impossible demands she made on him."

3. "Three stories, all relatively late fictions—'The Rocking-Horse Winner,' 'The Lovely Lady,' and 'Mother and Daughter'—show the modern matriarch turning sons, lovers and self into things"—Kingsley Widmer, *The Art of Perversity* (Seattle: Univ. of Washington Press, 1962), 92. "Quite simply, the theme of 'The Rocking-Horse Winner' (as of Lawrence's equally satirical 'Mother and Daughter') is that matriarchy is the devil-man's just punishment for failing to assert his phallic dignity ... the discrediting of the real father ... precipitates the tragedy."—W.S. Marks III, "The Psychology of the Uncanny in Lawrence's 'The Rocking-Horse Winner,'" *Modern Fiction Studies*, II (Winter 1965), 389.

4. "'The Rocking-Horse Winner'... utilizes, in a Balzacean sense, a money plot and theme. In a letter written about the time of the writing of this story, Lawrence said, 'Perhaps it's really true, lucky in money, unlucky in love.' This old adage, with its antithesis of love and money, which so appealed to Lawrence, appears to be the literal source of the sardonic fairy-tale theme"—Widmer, 92.

5. Harry T. Moore, *The Life and Works of D. H. Lawrence* (New York: Twayne, 1951), 278–279.

6. W.S. Marks III, "The Psychology of the Uncanny in Lawrence's 'The Rocking-Horse Winner,'" *Modern Fiction Studies*, II (Winter 1965), 391.

7. "Like all good fairy tales, this one has several complementary levels of reference: social, familial, psychological. . . .If one takes these three levels of reference and seeks out their complementarity, one sees the rich logic of the tale."—Janice Hubbard Harris, *The Short Fiction of D.H. Lawrence* (New Brunswick, N.J.: Rutgers University Press, 1984), 225–226.

8. Besides the well-known versions of Shakespeare by Laurence Olivier (*Hamlet, Henry V,* and *Richard III*), and of Dickens by David Lean (*Great Expectations*, 1946; *Oliver Twist*, 1948), as well as the adaptations of Grahame Greene's novels and scripts by director Carol Reed (*The Fallen Idol*, 1948 and *The Third Man*, 1949), there were adaptations of many other literary genres and authors, including plays by George Bernard Shaw, Oscar Wilde, and Noel Coward. See Roy Armes, *A Critical History of British Cinema* (New York: Oxford University Press, 1978), 198.

9. See, for example, Myro, "The Rocking-Horse Winner": *Variety*, 21 December 1949, 8; Otis L. Guernsey, "The Rocking-Horse Winner," *The New York Times*, 9 June 1950, 29, col. 3; T.M.P., Review of "The Rocking-Horse Winner," *New York Times Reviews*, 9 June 1950, 2; John McCarten, "The Current Cinema: Small Handicapper," *The New Yorker*, 10 June 1950, 90.

10. See, for example, Robert Lewis Shayon, "The Rocking-Horse Winner," *Saturday Review*, 24 June 1950, 34–35; Henry Becker III, "'The Rocking-Horse Winner': Film as Parable," in *From Fiction to Film: D.H. Lawrence's "The Rocking-Horse Winner,"* Gerald R. Barrett and Thomas L. Erskine, eds. (Encino & Belmont, Calif.: Dickinson, 1974), 204–213.

11. T.M.P., Review of "The Rocking-Horse Winner," *New York Times Reviews*, 9 June 1950, 2.

12. British film critic Margaret Tarratt found the forced conclusion to *The Rocking Horse Winner* inimical to Lawrence's intentions: "The leaden scene which Mills subsequently praised destroyed the sharp unacceptable irony of Lawrence's own ending in which there is no hint of the mother's repentance, no sign that the money will not be used as Paul had intended"—Margaret Tarratt, "An Obscene Undertaking," *Films and Filming*, 17 (Nov. 1970): 17.

13. "A filmed classic, at this time [1940s], was not intended to disturb but rather to consolidate the national heritage after the upheaval of the Second World War. Lawrence's story was given an ending appropriate to some of the more pietistic nineteenth-century fictions"—Tarratt, 27.

14. Pauline Kael, *Kiss Kiss Bang Bang* (Boston and Toronto: Little Brown, 1968), 339.

15. Anthony Pelissier, "Lawrence on Film: The Problem of Adapting 'The Rocking-Horse Winner,'" *The New York Times*, 25 June 1950, II, 1, col. 8.

16. Hester's financially and emotionally unrewarding stint as a fashion illustrator, and the incident in which she coldly receives the birthday letter informing her of her £1,000-a-year windfall are both omitted in the film. However, the original shooting script, 20 percent longer than the final film version, contains

the incidents from the story omitted in the finished product, as well as additional scenes not in the text, including an extremely unflattering one in which a manipulative Hester confronts the family lawyer demanding the £5,000 all at once, and another, again uncomplimentary, in which Hester argues with and is fired by the tough-minded head of the dress-making establishment for which she briefly works. The film script is reprinted in its entirety in *From Fiction to Film: D.H. Lawrence's "The Rocking-Horse Winner,"* eds. Gerald R. Barrett and Thomas L. Erskine (Encino and Belmont, Calif.: Dickinson, 1974), 75–202.

17. John Mills, who played the good-hearted gardener, was also the film's producer.

18. The script instructs the actress who plays Hester that "her grief and remorse are too great to bear." Quoted by Joan Mellon in "'The Rocking-Horse Winner' as Cinema," 221.

19. Pelissier, 2.

20. Julian Smith, "The Social Architecture of 'The Rocking-Horse Winner,'" in *From Fiction to Film: D.H. Lawrence's "The Rocking-Horse Winner"*, eds. Gerald R. Barrett and Thomas L. Erskine (Encino and Belmont, Calif.: Dickinson, 1974), 227.

21. Ibid.

22. Ibid., 224.

23. A British film historian notes Welles's impact on Desmond Dickinson, the cinematographer of *The Rocking Horse Winner*, who also shot Laurence Olivier's *Hamlet*: "Its [*Hamlet's*] style was compelling, with deep focus camera work by Desmond Dikinson, recalling the work of Gregg Toland in *Citizen Kane*"—George Perry, *The Great Picture Show* (London: Pavilion Books, 1985), 132.

24. Jack L. Ellis, *A History of Film* (Englewood Cliffs, N.J.: Prentice-Hall, 1985), 218–219.

25. "While the direction is sensitive, imaginative, as well as characteristically understated in the British manner, it [*The Rocking Horse Winner*] lacks the thrust and impact of *The Asphalt Jungle*. And yet in terms of A. N. Whitehead's 'fertilization of the soul,' his criterion for a work of art, *The Rocking Horse Winner* may be a better film . . . . The picture, as the copy-writer put it, 'haunts you'"— Shayon, 35.

26. David A. Cook, *A History of Narrative Film* (New York: W.W. Norton, 1961), 404.

27. Ibid., 404–405.

28. Ibid., 404.

29. The story's parallels with other fairy tales and myths have been explored by several critics, among them W.D. Snodgrass, who compares it to many well-known tales in which "the hero bargains with evil powers for personal advantages of forbidden knowledge." The bargains are always rigged "so that the hero, after his apparent triumphs, will lose in the end—this being, in itself, the standard moral"—"A Rocking-Horse: The Symbol, The Pattern, The Way to Live," *Hudson*

Review 11 (Summer 1958): 192–193. Robert Gorham Davis focuses on the occult elements in the story, pointing out that many witches presumably rode hobby-horses of one type or another (witches' brooms) to rock themselves into a magical and prophetic trance—"Observations on 'The Rocking-Horse Winner,'" in *Instructor's Manual for Ten Modern Masters: An Anthology of the Short Story,* 2d ed. (New York: Harcourt, Brace & World, 1959), 49–50. Frederick W. Turner III views Paul's death as a sacrifice resembling the mythical horseman Bellerophon— "Prancing to a Purpose: Myths, Horses, and True Selfhood in Lawrence's 'The Rocking-Horse Winner,'" in *D.H. Lawrence: "The Rocking-Horse Winner,"* ed. Dominick Consolo (Columbus, Ohio: Charles E. Merrill, 1969), 95–106, while W.S. Marks sees Paul as, among other things, "an Oedipal hero of Greek tragedy and as the hero of an Arthurian family romance"—"The Psychology of the Uncanny in Lawrence's 'The Rocking-Horse Winner,'" *Modern Fiction Studies* 11 (Winter 1965), 383. Links to medieval literature are drawn by S.A. Cowan, who explores the traditional connotations of the color green and of the goddess of fortune and compares Paul's mother, Hester, with Mala Fortuna, the Roman goddess of fortune or chance, indifferent to the fate of humanity—"Lawrence's 'The Rocking-Horse Winner,'" *Explicator* 28 (October 1969), item 29. The strong influence exerted on Lawrence by Sir James Frazer's *The Golden Bough*, "a definitive work of magic," is cited by L. T. Fitz, who notes that the riding of a rocking horse to acquire secret information about real horses is an instance of what Frazer calls "homeopathic magic." Further connection to *The Golden Bough* is evidenced by Lawrence's use of the name Malabar for the Derby winner, a word repeated 13 times in the story; "Malabar" is the name of an area in India in which a king exercised godlike power for 12 years, at the end of which he was expected to cut his own throat. "It is quite possible," argues Fitz, "to see the relevance of this custom to the story of Paul, who is allowed to exercise his magical powers for a time but must finally (in the Faustian tradition) pay for his powers with his life"—L. T. Fitz,"'The Rocking-Horse Winner' and *The Golden Bough*," *Studies in Short Fiction* 11 (1974), 199–200.

30. Because of its supernatural elements and its simplified, cadenced language, the opening of "The Rocking-Horse Winner" has also led a few critics to view the story as a biblical parable with some of the same allegorical overtones. Noting "the same succinctness, the same tendency to short, clipped clauses, and the same reliance on coordination," Charles Koban compares the introductory lines to the beginning of the parable of the Good Samaritan from the King James Bible:

> A certain man went down from Jerusalem to Jericho, and fell
> among thieves, who stripped him of his raiment, and wounded
> him, and departed, leaving him half dead. [Luke 10:30]

Charles Koban, "Allegory and Death of the Heart in 'The Rocking-Horse Winner,'" *Studies in Short Fiction* 15, no. 4 (1978): 396.

31. Jess Stein and Lawrence Urdang, eds., *The Random House Dictionary of the English Language* (New York: Random House, 1967), 1539.

32. "The Psychology of the Uncanny in Lawrence's 'The Rocking-Horse Winner,'" *Modern Fiction Studies* 11 (Winter 1965): 383. According to Marks, aspects of the uncanny implicit in the story include the unknown; withheld secrets, divination; Paul's animistic belief that the rocking-horse is a real horse; his omnipotence of thought in predicting the winners; and his fatalistic belief (which he shares with his mother) in the existence of lucky and unlucky thought.

33. See Jeannine Basinger, *American Cinema: One Hundred Years of Filmmaking* (New York: Rizzoli International Publications, 1994), 215–217.

34. Pelissier gives the family a last name (Grahame) and Hester's husband a first name (Richard); he also names the daughters Matilda and Joan and gives Oscar Creswell a different last name—Nethersoll.

35. Barrett and Erskine, 130.

36. Joan Mellen, "'The Rocking-Horse Winner' as Cinema," in *From Fiction to Film: D.H. Lawrence's "The Rocking-Horse Winner"*, eds. Gerald R. Barrett and Thomas L. Erskine (Encino and Belmont, Calif.: Dickinson, 1974), 218.

37. Ibid., 215.

38. Ibid., 214.

39. Gordon Hendricks, "Film Music Comes of Age," *Films in Review* 4 (January 1952): 23.

40. Maryanne Felter, "Verbal Analysis and Fantasia of the Unconscious: Style in the Short Stories of D.H. Lawrence" (Ph.D. diss., University of Delaware, 1982).

41. D.H. Lawrence, *Women in Love* (New York: Penguin Books, 1980), viii.

42. Herbert Read, *English Prose Style* (New York: Henry Holt, 1928), 151.

43. Ibid.

44. Ibid., 163.

45. Ibid., 165.

46. Ibid., 175.

47. Anthony Pelissier, *The Rocking-Horse Winner* (shooting script) in *From Fiction to Film: D.H. Lawrence's "The Rocking-Horse Winner,"* eds. Gerald R. Barrett and Thomas L. Erskine (Encino and Belmont, Calif.: Dickinson, 1974), 100.

48. Ibid., 121.

49. Ibid.

50. Ibid., 122.

51. Lawrence, *Women in Love*, viii.

52. Thomas M. McCabe, "Rhythmic Form in Lawrence: 'The Horse Dealer's Daughter,'" *PMLA* 67 (January 1972), 64.

53. Daniel J. Schneider, *D.H. Lawrence: The Writer as Psychologist* (Lawrence, Kans.: University Press of Kansas, 1984), 103.

54. F. R. Leavis, *D. H. Lawrence: Novelist* (Chicago: University of Chicago Press, 1955), 113, 183, 187, 189.

55. In *The House of Fiction: An Anthology of the Short Story* (New York: Scribners, 1960) Caroline Gordon and Allen Tate astutely point out the key role that

sound plays in "The Rocking-Horse Winner," even in the choice of horses' names, many of them foreign (Singhalese, Mirza)— in particular, the Derby-winner Malabar. "Let the student substitute a name like 'Little Andy' or 'Sea Biscuit' for the winner and see what a difference such a substitution will make in the story. The combination of short a's and broad a's has a tragic sound and the word 'Malabar' itself strikes one's ear strangely" (351).

56. David Lodge, *The Modes of Modern Writing: Metaphor, Metonymy, and the Typology of Modern Literature* (London: Edward Arnold, 1977), 167.

57. Mark Schorer, *The World We Imagine* (New York: Farrar, Straus and Giroux, 1968), 135.

58. Joseph M. Boggs, *The Art of Watching Films*, 2nd ed. (Palo Alto, Calif.: Mayfield, 1985), 46–51.

59. Marks, 383.

60. Ibid., 392.

61. Kingsley Widmer, *The Art of Perversity* (Seattle: U. of Washington Press, 1962), 93.

62. Marks, 391.

63. Caroline Gordon and Allen Tate, eds., "'The Rocking-Horse Winner': Commentary," in *The House of Fiction: An Anthology of the Short Story* (New York: Scribners, 1950), 350.

64. Michael Goldberg, *Modern Fiction Studies*, 15 (Winter, 1969), 530.

65. Snodgrass, 196. Significantly, in his landmark essay, "Pornography and Obscenity," Lawrence condemns masturbation because it always carries "a secret feeling of futility and humiliation" and because, unlike intercourse, which involves "give and take," in masturbation "there is nothing but loss. . . and deadening"—*The Portable D. H. Lawrence*, ed. Diana Trilling (New York: Viking Press, 1981), 659–660.

66. Goldberg, 535.

67. Snodgrass, 192.

68. According to one of Lawrence's biographers, the novelist's friend Catherine Carswell noted "a fine, rare beauty in Lawrence, with his deep-set, jewel-like eyes . . ." (Niehls I, 227). Indeed, he claims that it was the author's eyes that *all* of his friends remembered. Richard Aldington, for instance, recalled his first sight of Lawrence:

> A tall slim young man with bright red hair, and the most brilliant blue
> eyes, came in with a lithe, springing step. As a rule, I don't remember
> people's eyes, but I shall not forget Lawrence's—they showed such a
> vivid flame-like spirit (Niehls I, 236).

Quoted in Keith Sagar, *The Life of D.H. Lawrence* (New York: Pantheon Books, 1980), 74.

69. Gordon and Tate, in *The House of Fiction: An Anthology of the Short Story*, sum up the essence of the story in one sentence: "The boy Paul has invoked strange gods and pays the penalty with his death," 49–50.

70. Margaret Tarratt, "An Obscene Undertaking," *Films and Filmmaking* 17 (November 1970): 27.

71. In one scene, according to Pelissier's shooting script, the two girls also hear the whisper, but in the final version there is no sense of complicity among the siblings. See Barrett and Erskine, 105.

72. "The staircase becomes a central symbol of the false values of this family, with its endless climbing. Most frightening moments for Paul in the film have occurred when he is on the stairs"—Joan Mellen, "'The Rocking-Horse Winner' as Cinema," in Barrett, 221.

73. Henry Becker III, "'The Rocking-Horse Winner': Film as Parable," in *From Fiction to Film: D.H. Lawrence's "The Rocking-Horse Winner,"* eds. Gerald R. Barrett and Thomas L. Erkine (Encino & Belmont, Calif.: Dickinson, 1974), 212.

74. Ibid.

75. J.A. Cuddon, *A Dictionary of Literary Terms*, rev. ed. (New York: Penguin Books, 1984), 479.

76. Wayne Booth, *The Rhetoric of Fiction* (Chicago and London: University of Chicago Press, 1961), 74.

77. Fred B. Millett, *Reading Fiction: A Method of Analysis with Selections for Study* (New York: Harper, 1950), 11.

78. Benet's *Reader's Encyclopedia*, 3rd ed. (New York: Harper & Row, 1987), 486.

79. Ibid.

80. Daniel J. Schneider, *D.H. Lawrence: The Artist as Psychologist* (Lawrence, Kans.: University Press of Kansas, 1984), 105.

81. Lawrence frequently starts sentences with *and*, *but*, or *yet*, though technically, the coordinating conjunction would merely link two clauses of a compound sentence.

82. *Base* is defined as: starting point; fundamental principle; center of organization; lowest part of a structure; of low birth, rank or position; servile, menial; proceeding from low moral standards; treacherous, contemptible; corrupted by extraneous elements; short in stature—*The American Heritage Dictionary of the English Language* (N. Y.: American Heritage and Houghton-Mifflin, 1973), 110.

Chapter 3: *Sons and Lovers*

1. *D.H. Lawrence and "Sons and Lovers": Sources and Criticism*, ed. E. W. Tedlock, Jr. (New York: New York University Press, 1965), 30. *Sons and Lovers* was written and rewritten four times between 1910 and the end of 1912. In the initial version of the novel, Miriam is brought up as foster child in a bourgeois family and Willey Farm does not exist. Brother Ernest is absent. Paul plans to

murder his hated father by slowly poisoning his tea, but is spared from having to carry out the crime when Walter Morel accidentally stabs and kills his son Arthur, goes to jail, and dies soon after. William, the oldest son, goes off to London and instead of dying at 23, as he did in real life and in the final version of the novel, gets married, has a prosperous career, and lives happily every after. See Keith Sagar, *D.H. Lawrence: Life into Art* (New York: Viking Penguin Books, 1985), 95.

2. Anthony Burgess, *Flame into Being: The Life and Work of D.H. Lawrence* (New York: Arbor House, 1985), 65–66.

3. Sagar, 95.

4. Ibid., 96.

5. Ibid.

6. Lawrence's first two novels were *The White Peacock* (1911) and *The Trespasser* (1912).

7. Mark Schorer, "Technique as Discovery," in Tedlock, 168.

8. "In *Sons and Lovers* Lawrence's intention and the intention of the novel are disparate. But I should add that in this case, the disparity does not constitute an artistic defect: it merely gives the novel qualities that Lawrence did not see were there and that, within my knowledge, have not been generally noticed"—Eliseo Vivas, *D.H. Lawrence: The Failure and the Triumph of Art* (Evanston, Ill.: Northwestern University Press, 1960), 180. See also Barbara Hardy, *The Appropriate Form* (London: The Athlone Press, 1964); George Ford, *Double Measure: A Study of the Novels and Stories of D.H. Lawrence* (New York: W.W. Norton, 1965), 74; Louis L. Martz, "Portraits of Miriam: Study in the Design of *Sons and Lovers*," in *Imagined Worlds: Essays on Some English Novels and Novelists in Honour of John Butt*, eds. Maynard Mack and Ian Gregor (London: Methuen, 1968), 343–369.

9. Dorothy Van Ghent, "On *Sons and Lovers*," in *The English Novel: Form and Function* (New York: Holt, Rinehart and Winston, 1953), 247.

10. Schorer, 167.

11. Julian Moynihan, ed., *D. H. Lawrence: Sons and Lovers: Text, Background and Criticism* (Westford, Mass.: Viking Press, 1979), 561.

12. "Introduction," in Judith Farr, ed., *Twentieth Century Interpretations of Sons and Lovers* (Englewood Cliffs, N.J.: Prentice-Hall, 1970), 14–16.

13. "Counterfeit Loves" in Tedlock, 201—202. Although Lawrence became familiar with the Freudian concept of the Oedipus complex secondhand, through conversations with his wife Frieda (Burgess, 60), he wrote the better part of the novel in ignorance of Freudian doctrine. Later, he rejected key Freudian concepts of childhood sexuality, the libido, and the unconscious and strongly resisted the reduction of *Sons and Lovers* to an instance of psychosexual disturbance (Moynahan, 570). *Sons and Lovers* as a modern exemplum of the Oedipus complex is analyzed with considerable depth and insight by Daniel Weiss in *Oedipus in Nottingham* (Washington: University of Washington Press, 1962). See also Frederick J. Hoffman, "Lawrence's Quarrel with Freud," in *The Achievement of*

D.H. Lawrence, eds. Frederick J. Hoffman and Harry Moore (Norman, Okla.: University of Oklahoma Press, 1953), 106–127; Louis Fraiberg, "The Unattainable Self: D.H. Lawrence's *Sons and Lovers*," in Tedlock, 217–237; and Seymour Betsky, "Rhythm and Theme: D.H. Lawrence's *Sons and Lovers*," in Hoffman and Moore, 131–143.

14. Prior to 1960, as a screenwriter Jerry Wald adapted *Brother Rat*, and as a film producer was responsible for the adaptations of many plays, including *The Man Who Came to Dinner*, *Key Largo*, *Johnny Belinda*, *Clash by Night*, and *Picnic*. Among other literary adaptations Wald produced were *Peyton Place*, *The Sound and the Fury*, and Hemingway's *Adventures of a Young Man*. After producing *Sons and Lovers*, Wald purchased the screen rights to James Joyce's *Ulysses*, for which he planned to use Jack Cardiff as director. However, Wald died before he was able to complete the project.

15. Jerry Wald, "Scripting *Sons and Lovers*" in *Sight and Sound* 29 (Summer 1960), 117.

16. Although she approved of Gavin Lambert's first draft of the screenplay of *Sons and Lovers*, completed in March 1956, Frieda Lawrence was to have no influence over the final product; she died in 1957, before the film version was released in 1960.

17. A one-hour-and-39-minute version of the film was shown in English movie theaters because of the omission of a scene unacceptable to British censors.

18. "Prize-Copping *Sons and Lovers* Cost $350,000," *Variety,* October 1960.

19. Cardiff had photographed *Caesar and Cleopatra* (1946), *The Red Shoes* (1948), and *The African Queen* (1951), and had won an Academy Award for the color cinematography of *Black Narcissus* (1947). He had previously directed only two other films, *William Tell* (1953) and the low-budget *Intent to Kill* (1958). After *Sons and Lovers,* Cardiff directed *Young Cassidy* (1964), based on the early life of playwright Sean O'Casey, and *The Girl on the Motorcycle* (1968), an exercise in visual style.

20. Several American critics did find fault with Dean Stockwell's acting, if not his accent. Whitney Balliet judged him the weakest actor in the cast, "looking and behaving like an edgy pre-school boy"—"The Current Cinema: An Embarrassment of Talk," *The New Yorker*, 3 August 1960, 56; the critic in *The Saturday Review* felt that Stockwell was miscast, "not quite on home ground as the mother-sickened Paul Morel" (6 August 1960, 28); and Bosley Crowther described Stockwell condescendingly as "a model of filial devotion who seldom raises his libidinous voice" (*New York Times*, 3 August 1960, 35).

21. Mary Ure, wife of playwright John Osborne, played the role of the protagonist's wife in her husband's successful play *Look Back in Anger*, and played the same role in Tony Richardson's film version (1958). Heather Sears played the role of ingenue Susan Brown in Jack Clayton's adaptation of John Braine's novel *Room at the Top* (1959).

22. In Great Britain, an X-certificate meant that only adults could attend, while an A-certificate meant a film was deemed suitable for adolescents accompanied by an adult. *Sons and Lovers* received a coveted A-certificate because of the deletion of a bedroom scene involving candid dialogue between Mary Ure, nude under a sheet, and Dean Stockwell, bare to the waist (Peter Evans, "The Scene of the Censor Cut from *Sons and Lovers*," *Daily Express*, 22 June 1960, 6).

23. John Hill, *Sex, Class and Realism: British Cinema, 1956–1963* (London: British Film Institute, 1986), 127.

24. Clancy Sigal turned both thumbs down: "Not to mince words, the film version of D.H. Lawrence's *Sons and Lovers* is something of an act of desecration. It is Lawrence not only de-gutted, but stuffed and mounted. It is Lawrence pre-packaged—in the usual, time-encrusted Hollywood tradition of 'shooting the classics'"—"Shooting the Classics," *Time and Tide* 41, 2 July 1960, 759.

25. Along with *The Apartment*, *Sons and Lovers* won the New York Film Critics' Award as well as the National Board of Review's award as best film of the year (1960).

26. The film broke the Beekman Theater's house record on opening day, and did even better the second and third day.—*Variety*, 6 August 1960, 9.

27. "Tender and Terrible: *Sons and Lovers*," *Newsweek*, 1 August 1960, 80.

28. Neil Sonyard contended that the film is "more a paraphrase than an adaptation" ("Another Fine Mess: D.H. Lawrence and Hardy on Film," in *Filming Literature: The Art of Screen Adaptation* (New York: St. Martin's Press, 1986, 52), and John Gillett took issue with the brevity of the movie, claiming that it is simple enough to maintain a coherent story-line and yet "miss the essence":

> Curiously enough, the film is not really long enough; a span of three hours might have encompassed the story's incidental riches (such as the description of the early life of the Morel family) but a hundred minutes reduce the story to the unhappy life of a talented boy from the pits.

Film Quarterly 14 (Fall 1960), 42.

29. Sagar, 91.

30. In adapting *Sons and Lovers* for the screen, Gavin Lambert found the 25-year narrative, which "unfolds episodically, sometimes fitfully" with relationships that "explode and then subside again," impossible to squeeze into the 100 minutes of screen time available. However, he concluded that the "marvelous interior force of Lawrence is far more important than its external plot construction. Its continuity, in fact, is poetic rather than narrative." In seeking a "simpler, more condensed dramatic structure that could still contain the poetically charged atmosphere of Lawrence's novel," Lambert and Wald saw parallels between Eugene Gant in Thomas Wolfe's *Look Homeward, Angel* and Paul Morel, both of whom have delayed adolescences, experiencing teenage *angst* in their twenties. "Exploring this line of approach, we found it was possible to open the story with Paul on the threshold of becoming a man, and to pick out at once the two main threads of his life: the vivifying and yet binding closeness to his mother, and his desire to establish

himself as a painter. From this, all the rest could open out — the relationships with Miriam, his childhood friend, and with Clara, the suffragette; the alienation from his father, which turns at last into a kind of piety; and interwoven throughout enough reminiscence from Mrs. Morel to convey the progress of her marriage from youthful passion to bitter disillusionment. . . . It meant, of course, being faithful to the spirit rather than the letter of the original: sometimes, even *at the expense of the original.*" Gavin Lambert, "The Script [of *Sons and Lovers*]" *Films and Filming* 6 (May 1960), 9.

31. "The screen adapter must perform the thankless task of 'tampering with,' 'altering,' 'scissoring,' and 're-writing' recognized classics. . . .The two key problems in adaptation are length, and changes. Screen writers *must* select, picking out the main thread, the most important characters, the central theme, and the best excerpts of dialogue in order to make a story of 'suitable' length, generally not more than 110 to 120 minutes. . . . Screen adapting involves translating ideas from one *medium* to another. The novelist can spend a chapter, or more, to describe what is going on in the mind of his hero. He can spend paragraphs to create mood, or merely to tell his reader that the hero is making up his mind. . . . The screenwriter enjoys no such luxury. He cannot dwell on a single thought too long; he cannot pause to reflect; he should rarely if ever use dialogue to tell part of his story as narrative. The watchword of all screenwriters is 'economy' —in dramatic interpretation, and in costs. . . . Above all the responsibility of a screenwriter is the one to the original author — to keep the faith. The screen adapter may have to delete a favorite passage or character, but he does not do so in ignorance, nor through lack of judgment, and certainly not from lack of respect for the original. He does it for creative economy" —Jerry Wald, "Screen Adaptation," in *Films in Review,* ed. Henry Hart (New York: National Review of Motion Pictures, 1954), 62–67.

32. Frank Baldanza, "*Sons and Lovers*: Novel to Film as a Record of Cultural Growth," *Literature/Film Quarterly* 1 (Winter 1973), 68–69.

33. Lambert, 9.

34. Baldanza, 65–66.

35. Arnold Bennett (1867–1931), born and raised in the English midlands, is best known for realistic novels set in his native region—*Anna of the Five Towns* (1902); *The Old Wives' Tale* (1908); The Clayhanger series: *Clayhanger* (1910); *Hilda Lessways* (1911), among others. Aspects of *Sons and Lovers* have also evoked comparisons with material in the works of British novelists George Meredith, Thomas Hardy, George Eliot, and James Joyce, as well as lesser known novelists Richard Jeffries and Mark Rutherford (William Hale White). The realism of style and subject matter in *Sons and Lovers* also links Lawrence strongly to the nineteenth-century tradition of literary realism exemplified by French writers Flaubert, Balzac, and Zola; Russians Turgenev, Tolstoy, Dostoyevsky, Chekhov, and Gorky; Scandinavians Brandes, Bjornson, and Ibsen; and Americans Howells, Norris, Garland, and Crane. Although these authors vary widely in techniques and themes, certain features characterize much of their work. These include a focus on

the lives of ordinary lower - or middle-class people, neither heroic nor idealized but possessed of many human weaknesses and complexities; an almost scientific, impersonal objectivity in presenting characters and events; minimal intrusion of authorial philosophizing or moralizing; avoidance of artfully contrived or constructed plots full of melodrama and "miracles"; dramatic presentation of episodes, with almost phonographic accuracy in reproduction of speech; and pervasive emphasis on recording minute details of the observable, external world. Quite a few novels in the realist tradition were characterized by frank treatment of material excluded from "genteel" Victorian fiction. See George L. Becker, *Realism in Modern Literature* (New York: Frederick Ungar, 1980), 40–103, 132–193.

36. Lawrence's prose style became even more idiosyncratic and pronounced in two subsequent, innovative novels, *The Rainbow* (1915) and *Women in Love* (1920).

37. See Alfred Kazin, "Sons, Lovers and Mothers," in *D.H. Lawrence: A Collection of Criticism*, ed. Leo Hamalian (New York: McGraw-Hill, 1973), 28; and Mark Schorer, "Poste Restante: Lawrence as Traveler," in *The World We Imagine* (New York: Farrar, Straus & Giroux, 1968), 152–153.

38. A number of critics have noted an unusual fusion of realistic and romantic elements in *Sons and Lovers*. Herbert Lindenberger suggests that *Sons and Lovers* "was not so far removed from the romantic tradition as Lawrence seems to have planned" and that, in fact, Lawrence's contribution to the history of the novel was "his success in instilling the dominant strain of English fiction with the romantic tradition"—"Lawrence and the Romantic Tradition," in *A D.H. Lawrence Miscellany*, ed. Harry T. Moore (Carbondale, Ill.: Southern Illinois University Press, 1959), 337. "He [Lawrence] is a romantic," writes Alfred Kazin. "The effect of his prose is always to heighten our consciousness of something, to relate it to ourselves"—"Sons, Lovers and Mothers," in *D.H. Lawrence*: Sons and Lovers: *Text, Background and Criticism*, ed. Julian Moynahan (New York: Viking Press, 1968), 605. Despite Lawrence's refusal in *Sons and Lovers* "to retreat from tough realities into attitudes of escape," Ronald Draper argues that in this novel "romance penetrates to the humblest details of life" and that "the romantic element in *Sons and Lovers* has an intricate relationship with character"—especially the character of Miriam, who loves Wordsworth and whose "peculiar way" of responding to flowers "communicates the quality of her romantic sensibility": "In *The Trespasser*, realism and romance had split the novel into two parts, but in *Sons and Lovers*, they come much nearer to coalescing. At the very least, the novel moves between the two easily, without a jolting change of gear"—Ronald Draper, *D. H. Lawrence* (New York: St. Martin's Press, 1974), 49.

39. Tedlock, 13.
40. Tedlock, 31.
41. Ibid.
42. *Vers libre*, according to *The Oxford Companion to English Literature*, is "a term used to describe many forms of irregular, syllabic, or unrhymed verse, in

which the ordinary rules of prosody are disregarded: Whitman pioneered a form of *vers libre* in America, and its independent evolution in France and Belgium (in the works of Laforgue, Maeterlinck, and others in the 1890's) had a great influence on the early Modernists such as T.S. Eliot and Pound"—Margaret Drabble, ed., *The Oxford Companion to English Literature* (Oxford: Oxford University Press, 1985), 1027.

43. See Frank Baldanza, "D.H. Lawrence's Song of Songs," *Modern Fiction Studies* (Summer 1961), 106–114.

44. "The first mature signs of the symbolic mode appear in *Sons and Lovers*. That novel reveals the deeper necessities of its author's imagination, those which demanded a mode that could effectively handle the not-so-obvious, 'invisible' aspect of things and situations. . . . Here, as elsewhere in Lawrence, the symbolic mode refers to the vital relationship existing between the human and the natural as between single individuals and the circumambient universe. During those times when Lawrence uses the symbolic mode of style successfully, we become aware of a magic of suggestion behind every action and utterance"—Bibhu Pahdi, *D.H. Lawrence: Modes of Fictional Style* (Troy, N.Y.: The Whitston, 1989), 3–4.

45. Eliseo Vivas has called such symbols "constitutive" as opposed to "quasi-symbols" or "pseudo-symbols." Vivas defines "constitutive symbol" in relation to *Sons and Lovers* as "a complex situation or scene. . . which gathers the significance of events preceding it and illumines the scenes or situations that follow it"—*D. H. Lawrence, The Failure and Triumph of Art* (Evanston, Ill.: Northwestern University Press, 1960), 281, 284. Keith Sagar has termed Lawrence's symbols "organic": "He creates numerous scenes and incidents which are perfectly realistic, natural and appropriate, on the surface, but are rendered in such a way that, without our realizing it, they reverberate, open out into large significance, and link up with other such symbols to provide a matrix of images and resonances which is both a formal grid for the novel and often a source for its value judgements"—Sagar, 95.

46. Sagar, 96.

47. Bosley Crowther, "Tepid Passions," *New York Times*, 3 August 1960, 35.

48. Paul Buckley, "*Sons and Lovers*," *New York Herald Tribune*, 3 August 1960, 11.

49. "*Sons and Lovers*: Lawrence's Novel on the Screen," *London Times*, 21 June 1960, 4.

50. C. A. Jejeune, "At the Films: The Artist as a Young Man," *London Observer*, 26 June 1960, 15.

51. Margaret Tarratt, "An Obscene Undertaking," *Films and Filming*, 17 (November 1970), 28.

52. Sinyard, 52.

53. Crowther, 35.

54. Pauline Kael, *I Lost It at the Movies* (Boston: Little Brown, 1965), 72.

55. See John Hill, *Sex, Class and Realism: British Cinema 1956–1963*, 58; and Hill, "Working-Class Realism and Sexual Reaction," in *British Cinema History*, eds. James Curran and Vincent Porter (Totowa, N.J.: Barnes & Noble, 1983), 303–311.

56. See "Return to Lawrence Country," *Manchester Guardian*, 20 November 1959, 8; Tarratt, 38.

57. Louis Giannetti, *Understanding Movies*, 4th ed. (Englewood Cliffs, N.J., 1987), 468.

58. Both the exceptionally fast Tri-X black-and-white film and the extreme close-up CinemaScope lens were innovations introduced just at the time of the filming of *Sons and Lovers*. See Jack Cardiff, 9.

59. Cardiff, 9.

60. Maryanne Felter, "Verbal Analysis and Fantasies of the Unconscious: Style in the Short Stories of D.H. Lawrence" (Ph.D. diss., University of Delaware, 1982), 60. Felter found that in 10 stories by D.H. Lawrence, 21.4 percent of his words were nouns, and 11.58 percent verbs. In descriptive passages, the percentage of nouns is higher—24 percent nouns, 10.33 percent verbs; and even in passages involving conflict, in which one might expect a preponderance of active verbs, the proportion is heavily weighted toward nouns—18.8 percent nouns, 12.8 percent verbs.

61. John Russell, *Style in Modern Fiction: Studies in Joyce, Lawrence, Forster, Lewis, and Green* (Baltimore and London: Johns Hopkins University Press, 1978), 70–78. In *Sons and Lovers*, examples of nouns ending in *ity* are *intensity, triviality, virginity, perversity*; nouns ending in *ness* include *consciousness, nothingness, seriousness, awkwardness, relentlessness, vastness*; nouns ending in *ion* include *obstruction, renunciation, apprehension, temptation, vibration,* and *extinction.*

62. References to *bondage* or *imprisonment* appear on 89, 145, 160, 278, 296, 345, 359; to *battle* or *struggle*, on 14, 114, 173, 197, 215, 219, 250, 256, 257, 258, 276, 278, 297, 360, 411; to *sacrifice*, on 58, 171, 215, 222, 279, 282, 286, 289, 290, 384, 417, 418.

63. The exact matching of gesture and music is called *mickey-mousing*.

64. Verbal references to bondage and freedom abound. Mrs. Morel and Paul repeatedly allude to being "dragged down," Mrs. Leivers accuses Miriam of smothering her brother, and Paul chides Miriam for wanting to put him in her pocket, where he would "die... smothered." Similarly, Walter Morel castigates his wife for trying to smother her eldest son, William, who escapes by going to London, and for keeping Paul "in chains all his life." When Paul breaks off with Miriam for the second time, she bitterly challenges him: "Will you *ever* be allowed to feel free?" At the suffragette rally in which the word *liberty* is prominently displayed, the group's spokeswoman proclaims, "Freedom is what we must have." Near the end of the film, Paul tells Miriam, who is escaping her bondage by going to London to become a teacher, "I want to be free. I don't ever want to belong to anyone again."

65. Noting the crackling intensity of the scene in the novel in which Paul returns after an evening out with Clara and waits angrily and impatiently for Mrs. Radford to go to bed so that he can make love to her daughter, Kenneth Arthur MacKinnon observes: "I do not suggest that this scene is an example of the hard violent style because a character like Clara has eyes 'hard as steel' or because Paul is full of suppressed violence. The hardness is seen rather in the unadorned explicitness of the narrative: the short, declarative sentences, the decisively clear actuality of each observed feeling, the persistence in pursuing the feeling through the various stages of its intensity. The violence is simply the unabashed presentation of strong feeling . . ."—"Stylistic and Narrative Techniques in the Early Novels of D. H. Lawrence" (Ph.D. diss. University of Toronto, 1976), 159.

66. "Mother Love," *The New York Times Review of Books*, 21 September 1913, 479.

67. "Notes on D.H. Lawrence," in *Twentieth Century Interpretations of* Sons and Lovers, ed. Judith Farr (Englewood Cliffs, N.J.: Prentice-Hall, 1970), 25.

68. Felter, 76.

69. According to Marion Smith McKeown, all of her "control" authors—Arnold Bennett, Thomas Hardy, Joseph Conrad, and Virginia Woolf—had a higher incidence of passive constructions than D.H. Lawrence—"Patterns of Stylistic Change in the Novels of D.H. Lawrence," (Ph.D. diss., McGill University, 1974), 15–16.

70. Comparing Lawrence's sentences with those of four of his contemporaries, McKeown found Lawrence's to be the shortest. According to McKeown, Bennett averaged 14 words per sentence, Conrad 15.6, Hardy 21.2, and Woolf 24.3 (12).

71. According to Maryanne Felter, Lawrence's appositives are used for four purposes: to repeat key words, to expand or amplify parts of "kernel" sentences, to vary sentence structure for rhetorical effect, and to create distinctive sentence and paragraph rhythms. Felter found that 16 percent of the sentences in her sample of 20 pages from ten short stories contained appositives (86).

72. Felter found that of 482 sentences in her 20-page sample of 10 short stories by Lawrence, 20 percent began with a coordinating conjunction (78).

73. Associated with Augustan poets such as Pope and Dryden, antithesis in literary style refers to "contrasts or opposition in the meaning of contiguous phrases or clauses, emphasized by parallelism—that is, a similar order and structure in the syntax"—M.H. Abrams, *A Glossary of Literary Terms*, 5th ed. (Fort Worth, Texas: Holt, Rinehart and Winston, 1988), 10. It has also been defined as "contrasting ideas sharpened by the use of opposite or noticeably different meanings"—A. Cuddin, *A Dictionary of Literary Terms*, rev. ed. (Harmondsworth, Middlesex, England: Penguin Books, 1984), 49—and "the placing of a sentence or one of its parts against another to which it is opposed . . . the second sentence or part thus set in opposition"—*The Random House Dictionary of the English Language*, Unabridged ed. (New York: Random House, 1967), 67.

74. In the film as a whole, shots range from only one or two seconds to nearly 70 seconds, with many shots approximately 30 seconds long and an average shot length of just under 13 seconds; in contrast, the average length of a shot (ASL) in a classic non-widescreen Hollywood film of the period was 11 seconds, and most shots ranged in length from 10 to 15 seconds—David Bordwell, Janet Staiger, and Kristin Thompson, *The Classical Hollywood Cinema: Film Style & Mode of Production to 1960* (New York: Columbia University Press, 1985), 361.

75. Jerry Wald's decision to use the popular wide-screen process of Cinemascope, introduced in 1953, influenced the shooting techniques and editing of the film. Since any shot could easily include two or three characters, or even a cast of thousands, there was far less need to shoot solo figures in the shot/reverse shot technique typical of the classical Hollywood film. Instead, realism was enhanced by having the characters move within the frame, or by having a character's movement followed with a moving camera to achieve relatively lengthy two- or three-shots rather than cutting from one character to another. By 1959, when *Sons and Lovers* was produced, filmmakers had discovered that traditional Hollywood shooting techniques could, in fact, be aptly translated to the wide screen.

76. The average shot length (ASL) in *Sons and Lovers*, just under 13 seconds, is a bit longer than the ASL of 11 seconds in other widescreen films of the period but far slower than the 6-second ASL of typical films of the 1930's.

77. An exception to the tendency of critics to generalize about the rhythm of Lawrence's prose is Maryanne Felter, 104–134. Frank Baldanza, in "D. H. Lawrence's Song of Songs," *Modern Fiction Studies* 7 (Summer, 1961), 106–114, also characterizes the rhythms of Lawrence's sentences as derived from various types of parallelism typical of the King James version of the Bible. Some attempt to describe Lawrence's rhythms in two novels, *The Lost Girl* and *Kangaroo*, is made by John Russell in *Style in Modern British Fiction: Studies in Joyce, Lawrence, Forster, Lewis and Green* (Baltimore and London: Johns Hopkins University Press, 1978), 44–50.

78. Anais Nin, *D.H. Lawrence: An Unprofessional Study* (Denver: A Swallow Press, 1964), 121.

79. Post-1955 widescreen films had generally fewer shots per hour than the common Academy-ratio norm, which fell between 100 and 500 shots per hour, but by 1959, it was feasible to cut a widescreen film as rapidly as earlier non-widescreen films. The number of shots in Cinemascope films ranged from 200 to 600 per hour, with 300 to 400 shots per hour being most common. (Bordwell et al., 361) *Sons and Lovers*, on the other hand, has about 280 shots per hour, on the low end of the scale.

80. D.H. Lawrence, *Phoenix: The Posthumous Papers of D.H. Lawrence: 1936*, ed. Edward D. McDonald (New York: Viking Press, 1980), 295.

81. Van Ghent, 247.

82. Farr, 9.

83. Daniel Schneider, *D. H. Lawrence: The Artist as Psychologist* (Lawrence, Kansas: University Press of Kansas, 1984), 134.

84. For her comprehensive exploration of nature symbolism and other types of symbolism in *Sons and Lovers, Women in Love*, and films based on these novels, I am indebted to Candace Brand Kaspers' dissertation, Symbolism in the Film Adaptations and Novels of D. H. Lawrence's *Sons and Lovers, Women in Love*, and *The Virgin and the Gypsy*. (Ph.D. diss., University of Michigan, 1976, 31–88, 133–185). With regard to insights drawn from her study, page numbers will be cited.

85. Kazin, 248.

86. See Mark Spilka, "How to Pick Flowers," in *D.H. Lawrence and* Sons and Lovers: *Sources and Criticism*, ed. E.W. Tedlock, Jr. (New York: New York University Press, 1965), 188–199.

87. Mark Spilka explores the nature and significance of various characters' attitudes towards flowers in *The Love Ethic of D. H. Lawrence* (Bloomington, Ind.: Indiana Unversity Press, 1955), 39–59.

88. Kaspers, 35–37.

89. Ibid.

90. Ibid., 66.

91. Ibid., 65.

92. Ibid., 56.

93. Sagar, 98.

94. Tedlock, 183.

95. Schneider, 134.

96. Daniel Weiss, "The Mother in the Mind," in *Twentieth Century Interpretations of* Sons and Lovers, ed. Judith Farr (Englewood Cliffs, N.J.: Prentice-Hall, 1970, 39.

97. The almost total lack of flowers was probably necessitated by a low budget and an extremely tight, 45-day, on-location shooting schedule, which spanned early autumn in 1959 to early spring of 1960. During most of the film's production, there were undoubtedly few real-life flowers to shoot.

98. Kaspers, 62.

99. Ibid.

100. Ibid., 54.

101. Ibid., 67.

102. Ibid., 80.

103. Ibid.

104. Ibid., 79.

105. Ibid., 78.

106. Ibid.

107. The script emphasizes the theme of imprisonment. When Paul swings high in Miriam's swing and disappears into the hayloft, Miriam cries, "Come down, Paul." Reluctantly complying, Paul grumbles, "Women are all the same. They all want to drag a man down to their own level."

108. The relative sexual candor of the film version of *Sons and Lovers*, emphasized in advertisements, was undoubtedly responsible for its large audience, particularly in the United States, where the brief X-rated bedroom scene between Clara and Paul, not shown in England, was included.

109. "When Lawrence wrote his novel, he was himself treating autobiographical experiences which have since become cultural commonplaces under the category of the Freudian Oedipus complex. We now approach *Sons and Lovers* with a wealth of cross-cultural developments that have burgeoned since the day on which the novel was published. . . .The voice of Mr. Morel in this scene has no counterpart in the novel because it is the voice of a culture that was produced at least in part by Lawrence's own novel, itself a naïve early stimulant for precisely this cultural development. And the speech also constitutes a strong shift in point of view, since Lawrence was far too preoccupied by Paul's dilemma to be able to stand off from it and make this kind of judgment on Mrs. Morel" (Baldanza, 69).

Chapter 4: *Women in Love*

1. Harry T. Moore, ed., *The Collected Letters of D. H. Lawrence*, vol. I (London: Heinemann, 1977), 519.
2. Ibid., 484.
3. Julian Moynahan, *The Deed of Life: The Novels and Tales of D. H. Lawrence* (New Jersey: Princeton University Press, 1963), 72.
4. Rebecca West, *New Statesman*, 9 July 1921, 388.
5. Review of *Women in Love*, *The Observer*, 26 July 1921, quoted in Introduction to David Farmer, et al., eds., *Women in Love* (Cambridge: Cambridge University Press, 1987), liv.
6. E. Shanks, Review of *Women in Love*, *London Mercury* (17 September 1921), 433.
7. W.C. Pilly, *John Bull* (17 September 1921), 4.
8. John Middleton Murry, "A Review of *Women in Love*, in *D. H. Lawrence: The Rainbow and Women in Love*, ed. Colin Clarke (Nashville and London: Aurora, 1970), 68.
9. Mark Schorer, "*Women in Love* and Death," in *D.H. Lawrence: A Collection of Critical Essays*, ed. Mark Spilka (Englewood Cliffs, N.J.: Prentice-Hall, 1963), 50–60.
10. F.R. Leavis, *D.H. Lawrence: Novelist* (Chicago: University of Chicago Press, 1955), 5.
11. Ibid., 183.
12. Ibid., 9.
13. Ibid., 179.
14. Ibid., 272.

15. Ibid., 235.

16. In *D. H. Lawrence* (N. Y.: The Viking Press, 1973), Frank Kermode cites various influences on Lawrence during the time he wrote *The Rainbow* and *Women in Love*, including Joachitism, a Protestant doctrine of history that prophesied increasing corruption until, at the climax, the anti-Christ would appear in the last days; Dostoevski and Thomas Mann, both of whom perceived civilization as "swirling away with the stream of corruption" (38); Cambridge anthropology, so important to T.S. Eliot; works on occult symbolism that contributed to Lawrence's system building; racialist theories, probably derived from Houston Steward Chamberlain, whose *The Foundations of the Nineteenth Century* was an important source of Nazi thought; and Edward Carpenter, Yorkshire sage and socialist who wrote *Civilization: Its Cause and Cure* (1889), *Love's Coming of Age* (1895), and *The Intermediate Sex* (1908). Carpenter was the first English writer on sex and a sexual reformer concerned with theosophy and yoga. He had inclusive theories of history and spoke of the desirability of non-intellectual "blood knowledge."

17. Frank Kermode, "The Novels of D. H. Lawrence," in *D. H. Lawrence: Novelist, Poet, Prophet*, ed. Stephen Spender (N. Y.: Harper & Row, 1973), 85.

18. R. E. Pritchard, *D.H. Lawrence: Body of Darkness* (Pittsburgh: University.of Pittsburgh Press, 1971), 85.

19. Schorer, 44–45.

20. H.M. Daleski, *The Forked Flame: A Study of D.H. Lawrence* (Evanston, Ill.: Northwestern University Press, 1967), 127–128.

21. Moynahan, 88.

22. Schorer, 58–59.

23. Keith Sagar, *D.H. Lawrence: Life into Art* (Harmondsworth, Middlesex, England: Viking/Penguin Books, 1985), 193.

24. Ronald P. Draper, *D. H. Lawrence* (N. Y.: St. Martin's Press, 1964), 76.

25. Joseph Gomez, *Ken Russell: The Adaptor as Creator* (New York: Pergamon Press, 1976), 79.

26. Ibid.

27. Gene D. Phillips, *Ken Russell* (Boston: Twayne, 1979), 27–33.

28. Phillips, 75–81.

29. See Gomez, 208–209. For the BBC, Kramer produced films on Marie Rambert (1960), John Cranko (1960), Sergei Prokofiev (1961), Antonio Gaudi (1960), Edward Elgar (1962), Bela Bartok (1964), Claude Debussy (1965), Henri Rousseau (1965), Isadora Duncan (1966), Dante Gabriel Rossetti (1967), Frederick Delius (1968), and Richard Strauss (1970)—Diane Rosenfeldt, *Ken Russell: Guide to References and Resources* (Boston: G.K. Hall, 1978), 121–124.

30. United Artists Corp., "Production Notes on *Women in Love*," promotional brochure, 16 September 1969, 12.

31. John Baxter, *An Appalling Talent/Ken Russell* (London: Michael Joseph, 1973), 168–169.

32. Anthony Holden, *Behind the Oscar: The Secret History of the Academy Awards* (New York: Penguin Books, 1993), 543.

33. Ibid., 497.

34. "I knew, for instance, that in *Women in Love* Birkin was based on some things Lawrence saw in himself, and that Gerald was in fact someone he knew who owned the local mine, and that he knew two school teachers in Nottingham on whom he based Gudrun and Ursula, and Hermoine [sic] was Lady Ottoline Morrell. This gave me a sort of factual foundation on which I could build the script"— Gomez, 86.

35. Baxter, 169–170.

36. Quoted in Phillips, 83.

37. Baxter, 171.

38. Joseph Gomez notes that in the film, Oliver Reed wears a mustache like that of Sir Thomas Philip Butler, the Eastwood mine owner upon whom Lawrence partly based his characterization of Gerald Crich—Gomez, 86.

39. Ian Woodward, *Glenda Jackson: A Study in Fire and Ice* (New York: St. Martin's Press, 1985), 66. See also Ken Russell, *Altered States: The Autobiography of Ken Russell* (New York: Bantam Books, 1991), 63–64.

40. Baxter, 174.

41. Baxter, 170–171.

42. Baxter, 170–171.

43. Ibid., 181–182.

44. Anthony Slade, *Fifty Classic British Films, 1932–1982: A Pictorial Record* (New York: Dover Publications, 1965), 133.

45. In 1970, for her performance in *Women in Love*, Glenda Jackson also received awards from the New York Film Critics, the National Society of Film Critics, and the Variety Club of Britain—Woodward, 66.

46. Ken Hanke, *Ken Russell's Films* (Metuchen, N.J. and London: The Scarecrow Press, 1984), 51.

47. "Nude Male Wrestlers Draw British Trade," *Variety* 28 January 1970, 7.

48. Arthur Knight, "SR Goes to the Movies: Liberated Classics," *Saturday Review*, 21 March 1970, 50.

49. Tarratt, 29.

50. Richard Schickel, "A Past Master in the Hands of a Future One," *Life*, 6 March 1970, 14.

51. Judith Crist, "Love Is a Many-Splendored Thing," *New York*, 30 March 1970, 54.

52. Kathleen Carroll, "*Women in Love* Is Stunning Film," *New York Daily News*, 26 March 1970, 79.

53. Penelope Mortimer, "Passion Triumphantly Translated," *The Observer Review*, 16 November 1969, 28.

54. Harry T. Moore, "D.H. Lawrence and the Flicks," *Film/Literature Quarterly* 1 (January 1973), 9.

55. Quoted in Tarratt, 29.
56. John Simon, "Lawrence on Film," *The New Leader*, 13 April 1970, 27.
57. Pauline Kael, "Lust for Art," *The New Yorker*, 28 March 1970, 97.
58. Elliot Sirkin, *"Women in Love," Film Quarterly*, 24 (Fall 1970), 44.
59. Neil Sinyard, "Another Fine Mess: D.H. Lawrence and Thomas Hardy in Film," in *Filming Liberature: The Art of Screen Adaptation* (New York: St. Martin's Press, 1986), 50–51.
60. Leavis, 179.
61. Ibid., 183.
62. Frank Kermode, "The Novels of D.H. Lawrence," in *D.H. Lawrence: Novelist, Poet, Prophet*, ed. Stephen Spender (New York: Harper & Row, 1973), 85.
63. Eliseo Vivas, *D.H. Lawrence: The Failure and the Triumph of Art* (Evanston, Ill.: Northwestern University Press, 1960), 225.
64. Graham Holderness, *Women in Love* (Milton Keynes, England; Philadelphia: Open University Press, 1986), 21.
65. Angus Wilson, review of F. R. Leavis, *D.H. Lawrence: Novelist*, quoted in George Ford, *Double Measure: A Study of the Novels and Stories of D.H. Lawrence* (New York: W.W. Norton, 1965), 208.
66. Keith Aldritt, *The Visual Imagination of D.H. Lawrence* (London: Edward Arnold, 1971), 162, 164.
67. Gene D. Phillips, "An Interview with Ken Russell," *Film Comment* 6 (Fall 1970), 12.
68. Ken Russell, *The Lion Roars: Ken Russell on Film* (Boston and London: Faber and Faber, 1993), 73.
69. Baxter, 181–182.
70. Russell, 73.
71. Baxter, 176.
72. See conversations between Birkin and Mrs. Crich (Chapt. II, "Shortlands"), Gerald and Birkin (Chapt. XI, "In the Train" and Chapt. XVI, "Man to Man"), Birkin and Ursula (Chapt. XI, "An Island" and Chapt. XIII, "Mino") and Ursula and Hermione (Chapt. XII,"Carpeting" and Chapt. XII, "Woman to Woman").
73. D.H. Lawrence, *Women in Love* (New York: Penguin Books, 1980), vii.
74. "We set the film in 1920, which was a time of disillusionment, of change, when it was difficult to tell where one was as far as fashion was concerned. The girls' clothes were neither Edwardian nor what most people think of as 'Twenties' but something in between"—Baxter, 176.
75. Baxter, 176.
76. D.H. Lawrence, 148.
77. Gomez, 90.
78. John Weightman, "Trifling with the Dead," *Encounter* 34 (Jan. 1970), 52.
79. Gomez, 83.

80. D. H. Lawrence, *Birds, Beasts and Flowers* (New York: Thomas Seltzer, 1923), 5–9.

81. Imagism was a movement of English and American poets in revolt against Romanticism, which flourished from 1910 to 1917, and derived in part from the aesthetic philosophy of T.E. Hulme. Imagism's first anthology, edited by Ezra Pound, included poems by Richard Aldington, Hilda Doolittle, Amy Lowell, James Joyce, and Ezra Pound. Some of the Lawrence's poems of this period have been described as imagist. Characteristic products of the movement tend to be brief; to be composed of short lines of musical cadence rather than metrical regularity; to avoid abstraction; and to treat the image with a hard, clear precision rather than overt symbolic intent. See Margaret Drabble, ed., *The Oxford Companion to English Literature*, 5th ed. (Oxford: Oxford University Press, 1985), 492.

82. Henry Schvey, "Lawrence and Expressionism," in *D.H. Lawrence: New Studies*, ed. Christopher Heywood (New York: St. Martin's Press, 1987), 104–123, 125–127.

83. Ibid., 127.

84. Vorticism was an aggressive literary and artistic movement that flourished from 1912 to 1915 and was dominated by Wyndham Lewis, Ezra Pound, and Gaudier-Brzeska. It attacked the sentimentality of nineteenth-century art and celebrated violence, energy, and the machine. The Vorticist style, with its abstract compositions of bold lines, sharp angles, and planes, was indebted to Cubism and Futurism, although Lewis derided the Futurist obsession with speed. *Blast: The Review of the Great English Vortex*, published in June 1914 and edited by Lewis, was an attempt to establish in England a magazine dedicated to the modern movement and to draw together artists and writers of the avant-garde. The movement petered out after the Vorticist exhibition held at the Dore Gallery in 1915. See Drabble, 1035.

85. Futurism originated in some Italian artists' revolt against the Academy, spearheaded by F. T. Marinetti in a manifesto published in Milan in 1909 and taken up in France and England, where it spread to the literary world. The fundamental premise of Futurism was that modern communication and machinery had produced a radical change in twentieth-century sensibilities, and this change had to be recorded in Futurist art. "What was new . . . and what created the most unsettling effects on early readers, was that fierce language, abrupt tone, rapid changes in imagery, deliberate exaggerations and insult, all of which were permeated with a sense of dynamic vitality"—Kim A. Herzinger, *D. H. Lawrence in His Time: 1908–1915* (Louisburg, Pa.: East Brunswick, N.J.: Associated University Presses, 1982), 127.

86. Ibid., 133.

87. Sagar, 193.

88. Hanke, 7.

89. Gomez, 43.

90. Vincent Canby, "Screen: *Women in Love* Done as Torrid Romance: Lawrence's Philosophy in Subordinate Role," *New York Times,* 26 March 1970, 58.

91. Thomas R. Atkins, *Ken Russell* (New York: Simon & Schuster, 1976), 43.

92. Mortimer, 28.

93. Crist, 54.

94. Sinyard, 51.

95. Sirkin, 47.

96. Stanley Kauffmann, "*Women in Love*,"*The New Republic,* 18 April 1970, 20.

97. Hanke, 51.

98. Kael, 97.

99. Quoted by Mary Blume, "Director Russell with 'Boyfriend': Ogre in a Nursery," *Los Angeles Times,* 19 September 1971, *Calendar Magazine,* 18.

100. Kael, 97.

101. Gomez, 40.

102. Joy Gould Boyum, *Double Exposure: Fiction Into Film* (New York: New American Library, 1985), 125.

103. Maryanne Felter, "Verbal Analysis and Fantasia of the Unconscious: Style in the Short Stories of D.H. Lawrence" (Ph.D. diss., University of Delaware, 1982), 60.

104. Based on quantitative analysis of the first four narrative/descriptive paragraphs of each of 31 chapters of *Women in Love.*

105. Harry T. Moore, ed., *Collected Letters of D.H. Lawrence,* vol. I (New York: Viking Press, 1962), 259.

106. D. H. Lawrence, *Women in Love,* viii.

107. Michael Ragussis, *The Subterfuge of Art: Language and the Romantic Tradition* (Baltimore and London: The Johns Hopkins University Press, 1978), 179.

108. Ibid., 191.

109. "The basic paradoxes of the novel's theme are presented through the interaction of the ambiguities and connotations of its words. The symbolist novel (and this is one of the greatest) works by the absolute organisation of its basic material: language. The multiple meanings of the words coalesce in characters, scenes and incidents that are not simply set in the novel like plums in a pudding, but grow out of it and are an intensification of their medium; characters, events, and scene are completely fused"—E. Pritchard, *D.H. Lawrence: Body of Darkness* (Pittsburgh, Pa.: University of Pittsburgh Press, 1971), 86.

110. Garrett Stewart, "Lawrence, 'Being' and the Allotropic Style," in *Towards a Poetics of Fictions: Essays from Novel: A Forum on Fiction 1967–1976,* ed. Mark Spilka (Bloomington, Ind., and London: Indiana University Press, 1977), 332.

111. John Russell, *Style in Modern British Fiction* (Baltimore and London: Johns Hopkins University Press, 1978), 71–76.

112. The exact meaning of these phrases is, of course, unspecified and cannot really be deduced from their context, although many of Lawrence's critics have attempted to provide a gloss by referring to material on metaphysics and psychology in Lawrentian essays written during the period in which *Women in Love* was composed, such as "A Study of Thomas Hardy" (1914), "The Crown" (1915), "The Reality of Peace" (1917), and "Fantasia of the Unconscious" (1921).

113. Derek Bikerton, "The Language of *Women in Love*" *A Review of English Literature*, 8 (1967), 60.

114. Ibid., 61.

115. Diane Bonds, *Language and the Self in D.H. Lawrence* (Ann Arbor, Mich.: UMI Research Press, 1987), 96.

116. Leo Barsani, *A Future for Astynax: Character and Desire in Literature* (Boston and Toronto: Little, Brown, 1976), 168.

117. Kael, 174.

118. Marion Smith McKeown, *Patterns of Stylistic Change in the Novels of D.H. Lawrence* (Ph.D. diss., McGill University, 1974), 12–13.

119. These conclusions are based on an analysis of 552 sentences from the first four narrative paragraphs of each of the novel's 31 chapters.

120. Lanham identifies two categories of prose style—periodic, which is tightly structured and based on subordination, and running. "The running style is basically paratactic, incremental, shapeless. It just goes on . . . . The serial syntax registers first the first thing and then the second thing second, simple chronological sequence always calling the tune and beating the tempo."—Richard A. Lanham, *Analyzing Prose* (New York: Charles Scribner's Sons, 1963), 53–54.

121. Stewart, 335.

122. "At times these ambiguities enrich the texture of the novel by reflecting the ambiguities and uncertainties of the world which the novel portrays. After all, it is a world of frustrated potential, of certainties which are incomplete, and perfections which must disintegrate, and the syntax reflects the complexities of such a world with suggestive richness"—McKeown, 39.

123. According to Maryanne Felter, in a sample of 20 pages from ten of Lawrence's short stories, 16 percent of all the sentences contain appositives, and stories that are emotionally intense have a higher proportion of appositives than stories that are ironical in tone—"Verbal Analysis and Fantasia of the Unconscious: Style in the Short Stories of D.H. Lawrence" (Ph.D. diss., University of Delaware, 1982), 85. According to Marion McKeown, the number of appositives is greatest in *Women in Love* (McKeown, 40).

124. Felter, 93.

125. David J. Gordon, "Sex and Language in D.H. Lawrence," *Twentieth Century Literature* 27 (Winter 1981), 366.

126. Jane Gurko, "The Flesh Made Word: A Study of Narrative and Stylistic Techniques in Five Novels by D.H. Lawrence" (Ph.D. diss., University of California, 1971), 131.

127. Kael, 97.

128. In *Women in Love*, 20 shots are between 20 and 30 seconds long, 18 shots last between 30 and 50 seconds, and 10 shots last well over 50 seconds, whereas in *Sons and Lovers* the longest shot in the film is 50 seconds.

129. Ana Laura Zambrano, "*Women in Love*: Counterpoint on Film," *Literature/Film Quarterly*, I (January 1973), 47; Gomez, 85.

130. Gomez, 85.

131. Gomez, 88–89.

132. Hanke, 58.

133. Figures based on a sample of 248 paragraphs, 8 from each of 31 chapters.

134. D.H. Lawrence, *Women in Love*, viii.

135. Thomas R. Atkins, *Ken Russell* (New York: Monarch Press, 1976), 39.

136. Quoted in Gomez, 82.

137. Ibid.

138. Hanke, 58.

139. Gomez, 85.

140. See Candace Brand Kaspers, "Symbolism in the Film Adaptation and Novels of D. H. Lawrence's *Sons and Lovers*, *Women in Love*, and *The Virgin and the Gypsy*" (Ph.D. diss., University of Michigan, 1976), 143.

141. See Hanke, 52.

142. Lawrence portrays the characters in *Women in Love* as self-consciously using figurative language. "There is only one tree, there is one tree, there is only one fruit in your mouth, the eternal apple," exclaims Birkin, "hating his own metaphors" (89–90).

143. John Humma, *Metaphor and Meaning in D.H. Lawrence's Later Novels* (Columbia, Missouri, and London: University of Missouri Press, 1990), 6.

144. Ibid., 86.

145. *The Collected Letters of D.H. Lawrence*, ed. Harry T. Moore, 281–282.

146. John Worthen, *D.H. Lawrence and the Idea of the Novel* (Totowa, N.J.: Rowman and Littlefield, 1979), 104.

147. John Harrington, *The Rhetoric of Film* (New York: Holt, Rinehart and Winston, 1973), 148.

148. George Bluestone, *Novels into Film* (Berkeley: University of California Press, 1973).

149. Ibid., 19.

150. Ibid., 22.

151. See Roy Huss and Norman Silverstein, *The Film Experience* (New York: Harper & Row, 1982), 81–104; Trevor Whittock, *Metaphor and Film* (Cambridge: Cambridge University Press, 1990); John Harrington, *The Rhetoric of Film* (New York: Holt, Rinehart & Winston, 1973).

152. Huss and Silverstein, 82.

153. See Trevor Wittock, *Metaphor and Film* (Cambridge, New York, Melbourne: Cambridge University Press, 1990), 49–69.

154. "Fig," in D. H. Lawrence, *Birds, Beasts and Flowers* (New York: Thomas Selzer, 1923), 5–9.

155. G.B. Crump, *"Women in Love:* Novel and Film," *D.H. Lawrence Review* 4 (Spring 1971), 35. "Russell unites the love and death themes by cutting from the nude lovers, drowned but still intertwined in the black mud, to Birkin and Ursula, stirring fretfully after their first love scene. . . the crosscutting visually dramatizes the author's point that Ursula's emotional possessiveness would drag Birkin to his psychic death in the same way Laura dragged her unfortunate husband to his actual death."

156. Simon, 28.

157. Elliot Sirkin, *"Women in Love," Film Quarterly* 24 (Fall 1970), 46.

158. Stuart Y. McDougal, *Made into Movies: From Literature to Film* (New York: Holt, Rinehart & Winston, 1985), 283.

159. Ibid., 285.

160. Hanke, 58.

161. Hanke, 53–54.

162. Roy Huss and Norman Silverstein, *The Film Experience: Elements of Motion Picture Art* (New York: Harper & Row, 1982), 93.

163. "It takes the actual sight of the black-robed Hermione bounding and posturing as 'Orpah, vivid, sensational, subtle widow,' of Birkin scampering gaily through a fox-trot, or of Gudrun twisting and flaunting her body at Gerald's feet, to show how much the dances are the proper objective correlative for the flickering and glowing of the 'single radically unchanged element' in man, the fire that radiates from personality"—Crump, 33.

164. See R.E. Pritchard, *D.H. Lawrence: Body of Darkness* (Pittsburgh: University of Pittsburgh Press, 1971), 86; Angelo P. Bertocci, "Symbolism in *Women in Love,*" in *A D.H. Lawrence Miscellany*, ed. Harry T. Moore (Carbondale, Ill.: Southern University Press, 1959), 83–102; Keith Sagar, *D.H. Lawrence: Life into Art* (Harmondsworth, Middlesex, England: Viking Penguin Books, 1985), 159.

165. Kim A. Herzinger, *D.H. Lawrence in His Time: 1908–1915* (Lewisberg, Pa.: East Brunswick, N.J.: Associated University Presses, 1982), 140. "Each of the major characters in *Women in Love* is rendered in symbolic and imagistic terms suggested by one radical element: for Ursula, earth; for Rupert, air; for Gudrun, fire; for Gerald, water. The impulse which led Lawrence to define his characters symbolically this way was the impulse to find the 'unchangeable,' 'the carbon'— which is the elemental force prior to character."

166. Gary Adelman, *Snow of Fire* (New York and London: Garland, 1991), 65.

167. Eliseo Vivas, *D. H. Lawrence: The Failure and the Triumph of Art* (Evanston, Ill.: Northwestern University Press, 1960), 208.

168. Angelo Bertocci, "Symbolism in *Women in Love,*" in *A D. H. Lawrence Miscellany*, ed. Harry T. Moore (Carbondale, Ill.: Southern Illinois University Press, 1959), 86–87.

169. D. H. Lawrence, "The Crown," in *Phoenix II: Uncollected Writings*, ed. Warren Roberts and Harry T. Moore (New York: The Viking Press, 1970), 404.

170. See Chapt. IV ("Diver"); Chapt. VIII ("Breadalby"); Chapt. XI ("An Island"); Chapt. X ("Sketchbook").

171. Leavis, 220.

172. H.M. Daleski, *The Forked Flame: A Study of D. H. Lawrence* (Evanston, Ill.: Northwestern University Press, 1965), 166–167.

173. R.E. Pritchard, *D. H. Lawrence: Body of Darkness* (Pittsburgh, Pa.: University of Pittsburgh Press, 1971), 101.

174. Mark Schorer, *"Women in Love* and Death," in *D. H. Lawrence: A Collection of Critical Essays*, ed. Mark Spilka (Englewood Cliffs, N.J.: Prentice-Hall, 1963), 44–45.

175. Charles L. Ross, *Women in Love: A Novel of Mythic Realism* (Boston: Twayne, 1991), 68.

176. Keith Sagar, *D. H. Lawrence: Life into Art* (Harmondsworth, Middlesex, England: Penguin Books, 1985), 160.

177. Keith Alldritt, *The Visual Imagination of D.H. Lawrence* (London: Edward Arnold, 1971), 189.

178. Ibid.

179. "Gerald changes from a Teutonic hero-figure into a squat, brooding, unfathomable neurotic. . . ."—Penelope Mortimer, "Passions Triumphantly Translated," *The Observer Review*, 16 November 1969, 18.

180. "Oliver Reed . . . although not physically ideal for Gerald, sports a mustache just as did Sir Thomas Philip Barber, the Eastwood mine owner whose experience contributed to the characterization of Gerald"—Joseph Gomez, *The Adaptor as Creator*, (New York: Pergamon Press, 1977), 86.

181. Larry Kramer said of his screenplay, "I believe in film as a medium for words and ideas. . . .I don't agree with the directors who say everything in the film must be expressed visually. If film is to be a serious art form, it has to deal with abstract ideas and deal with them in words." Quoted by Wilfred Bevins, "Lawrence's *Women in Love*: Word to Image," *Los Angeles Herald Examiner*, 12 April 1970, Sec. G, 4.

182. This piece of dialogue is excerpted from Chapt. XIX, "Mooney" (326).

183. "Fig" in D.H. Lawrence, *Birds, Beasts and Flowers* (New York: Thomas Selzer, 1923), 5–9.

184. "His [George Delerue] best moments in *Women in Love* came from the waltz he composed for the naked lovers floating up to heaven in clouds of pink flowers—the schmaltziest moment in the film that would have made Lawrence turn in his grave . . ."—Ken Russell, *The Lion Roars* (Boston and London: Faber & Faber, 1993), 73.

185. "Gudrun's dance before the cattle in Russell's film not only looks ridiculous but reverses the meaning of the scene in the novel: Gudrun appears stupid rather than rapt . . ."—Neil Sinyard, "Another Fine Mess: D.H. Lawrence

and Thomas Hardy on Film," in *Filming Literature: The Art of Screen Adaptation* (New York: St. Martin's Press, 1986), 45.

186. See Kaspers, 157–158.

187. John Baxter, *An Appalling Talent/Ken Russell* (London: Michael Joseph, Ltd., 1973), 175.

188. John Simon, for example, characterizes the paired shots as "misleading" and "sinister nonsense," arguing that Lawrence avoided "such obvious symbolism." See "On Screen: Lawrence in Print and on Film," *The New Leader* 53, 13 April 1970, 28.

189. G.B. Crump, "*Women in Love*: Novel and Film," *D. H. Lawrence Review* 4 (Spring 1971), 35.

190. Brand, 168 ff.

191. Although Lawrence deliberately avoided mentioning World War I or specifically dating the events in the novel, he claimed in his preface that the "bitterness caused by the war may be taken for granted in the characters"—*Women in Love*, vii.

192. Gomez, 92.

193. Simon, 28.

194. Sinyard, 45.

195. Simon, 28.

196. Tarratt, 30.

197. Boyum, 125.

198. Simon, 27.

199. In describing "the naked lovers floating up to heaven in clouds of pink flowers" as "the schmalziest moment in the film that would have made Lawrence turn in his grave had his wife, Frieda, not thoughtfully buried his ashes in a ton of concrete," Ken Russell indicated that he did not intend the scene to be comical, although he acknowledged its excess—Russell, *The Lion Roars: Ken Russell on Film,* 73–74.

200. Baxter, 176.

201. The lyrics sung by Ursula in the film are as follows: "I'm forever blowing bubbles,/Pretty bubbles in the air/They fly so high/Nearly reach the sky/Then like my dreams/They fade and die/Fortune's always hiding/I've looked everywhere/For I'm forever blowing bubbles/Pretty bubbles in the air."

202. "We set the film in 1920, which was a time of disillusionment, of change . . . . I wanted to give a feeling of disillusionment right form the beginning . . . since the whole film is about illusion, about love and the hopes of love that aren't returned or requited or fulfilled . . ."—Baxter, 176.

203. John Weightman, "Trifling with the Dead," *Encounter*, 34 (January 1970), 52.

204. Ibid., 51.

205. Simon, 28.

206. Sirkin, 46.

207. Crump, 30.
208. Ibid.
209. Ken Russell, *The Lion Roars: Ken Russell on Film*, 175.
210. Quoted in Tarratt, "An Obscene Undertaking," *Films and Filming*, 17 (November 1970), 26.

Conclusion

1. Academy Award nominations for *Sons and Lovers* included Best Picture; Trevor Howard for Best Actor; Mary Ure for Best Actress; Jack Cardiff for Best Director; Gavin Lambert and T. E. B. Clarke for Best Screenplay Based on Material from Another Medium; Freddie Francis for Best Cinematography (Black and White); and Tom Morahan and Lionel Couch for Art Direction-Set Direction. Only Freddie Francis won the 1960 New York Film Critics Award for Best Film and Best Director, tying with *The Apartment*.
2. Anthony Pelissier, "Lawrence on Film: The Problem of Adapting 'The Rocking-Horse Winner,'" *New York Times,* June 25,1950, II, 1, Col. 8.
3. Quoted in John Baxter, *An Appalling Talent/Ken Russell* (London: Michael Joseph, 1973), 169.
4. Allen Rivkin and Laurie Kerr, *Hello Hollywood!* (New York: Doubleday, 1962), 19-20.
5. André Bazin, *What Is Cinema?* I (Berkeley: University of California Press, 1967), 68.
6. Julian Smith, "The Social Architecture of 'The Rocking-Horse Winner,'" in *From Fiction to Film: D.H. Lawrence's "The Rocking-Horse Winner,"* eds. Gerald R. Barrett and Thomas L. Erskine (Encino-Belmont, Calif.: Dickinson, 1974), 224.
7. Margaret Tarratt, "An Obscene Undertaking." *Films and Filming* 17 (November 1970), 26-27.
8. Jerry Wald, "Scripting *Sons and Lovers,"* *Sight and Sound* 29 (Summer 1960), 117.
9. *Sense and Sensibility* ranked tenth place in January and eighth place in February—*Chronicle of Higher Education,* March 8, 1996, A34; April 5, 1996, A36.
10. Dave Kehr, "Austen's *Persuasion* Adeptly Adapted," *Daily News*, September 27, 1995, 35.

Filmography

The Rocking Horse Winner (1949), Two Cities Films, Ltd.

Producer: John Mills *Production Manager*: Andrew Allan *Director*: Anthony Pelissier *Screenplay*: Anthony Pelissier, based on the story by D. H. Lawrence *Photography*: Desmond Dickinson *Editor*: John Seaborne *Art Direction*: Carmen Dillon *Music*: Composed by Willliam Alwyn, played by the Royal Philharmonic Orchestra.
With: Valerie Hobson (Hester Grahame), John Howard Davies (Paul Grahame), John Mills (Bassett), Hugh Sinclair (Richard Grahame), Ronald Squire (Uncle Oscar), Susan Richards (Nannie), Charles Goldner (Mr. Tsaldouris), Cyril Smith (The Bailiff), Anthony Holles (Bowler Hat), Melanie McKenzie (Matilda), Caroline Steer (Joan.)
Released by Universal-International.
Running time: 91 minutes.

Sons and Lovers (1960), Two Cities Films, Ltd.

Producer: Jerry Wald *Associate Producer and Production Designer*: Tom Morahan *Production Managers*: Teddy Joseph and Geoffrey Haine
Director: Jack Cardiff *Assistant Director*: Peter Yates *Screenplay*: Gavin Lambert and T. E. B. Clarke, based on the story by D. H. Lawrence. *Photography*: Freddie Francis, B.S.C. *Camera Operator*: Denys Coop *Editor*: Gordon Pilkington *Music*: Composed by Mario Nascimbene, conducted by Lambert Williamson; "Orpheus in the Underworld" arranged by Lambert Williamson *Costume Designer*: Gordon Pilkington *Sound Mixer:* Peter Handford *SoundEditor*: Don Challis *Make-up*: Harold Fletcher *Continuity*: Angela Martella *Art Director*: Lionel Couch *Casting Director*: Nora Roberts Cinemascope lenses by Bausch & Lomb.
With: Wendy Hiller (Gertrude Morel), Trevor Howard (Walter Morel), Dean Stockwell (Paul Morel), Mary Ure (Clara Dawes), Heather Sears (Miriam), William Lucas (William Morel), Conrad Phillips (Baxter Dawes), Ernest Thesiger (Mr. Hadlock), Donald Pleasance (Mr. Pappleworth), Rosalie Crutchley (Mrs. Leivers), Sean Barrett (Arthur Morel), Rosalie Ashley(Louisa), Elizabeth Begley (Mrs. Radford).
Released by Twentieth-Century Fox.
Running time: British version, 99 minutes; American version, 100 minutes.

Women in Love. (1969), Brandywine Productions.

Producers: Larry Kramer and Martin Rosen *Associate Producer*: Roy Baird.
Production Controller: Harry Benn *Director*: Ken Russell
Screenplay: Larry Kramer from the D. H. Lawrence novel *Photography*: Billy Williams *Editor*: Michael Bradsell *Set Designer*: Luciana Arrighi *Costume Designer*: Shirley Russell *Music*: Georges Delerue *Unit Manager*: Neville C. Thompson *Camera Operator* David Harcourt *Assistant Director*: Jonathan Benson *Continuity*: Angela Allen *Choreographer*: Terry Gilbert *Sound Recordist*: Brian Simmons *Dubbing Editor*: Terry Rawlings *Dubbing Mixer*: Terry Rawlings *Dubbing Mixer*: Maurice Askew *Assistant Cameraman*: Stephen Claydon *Location Manager*: Lee Bolon.
With: Alan Bates (Rupert Birkin), Oliver Reed (Gerald Crich), Glenda Jackson (Gudrun Brangwen), Jennie Linden (Ursula Brangwen), Eleanor Bron (Hermione Roddice), Alan Webb (Mr. Crich), Vladek Sheybal (Loerke), Catherine Wilmer (Mrs. Crich), Sarah Nicholls (Winifred Crich), Sharon Gurney (Laura Crich), Christopher Gable (Tibby Lupton), Michael Gough (Mr. Brangwen), Norma Shebeare (Mrs. Brangwen), Nike Arrighi (Contessa), James Laurenson (Minister), Michael Graham Cox (Palmer), Richard Heffer (Loerke's friend), Michael Garratt (Maestro).
Released by United Artists.
Running time: 129 minutes.

Bibliography

Prose Style, Narrative Technique,
and Aesthetic Theory

Abrams, M. H. *A Glossary of Literary Terms*. 5th ed. Fort Worth, Texas: Holt, Rinehart & Winston, 1988.

Armes, Roy. *Patterns of Realism*. South Brunswick, N.J. and New York: A. S. Barnes, 1971; London: Tantivy Press, 1971.

Anderson, Linda R. *Bennett, Wells and Conrad: Narrative in Transition*. New York: St. Martin's Press, 1988.

Barthes, Roland. "Style and its Image." In *Literary Style: Symposium*, ed. Seymour Chatman, 3–15. Oxford: Oxford University Press, 1971.

Baum, Paull Franklin. *The Other Harmony of Prose . . . an Essay in English Prose Rhythm*. North Carolina: Oxford University Press, 1952.

Beardsley, Monroe C. *Aesthetics From Classical Greece to the Present: A Short History*. New York: Macmillan, 1966.

Becker, George J. *Realism in Modern Literature*. New York: Frederick Ungar, 1980.

Bersani, Leo. *A Future for Astynax: Character and Desire in Literature*. Boston and Toronto: Little Brown, 1976.

Booth, Wayne C. *The Rhetoric of Fiction*. Chicago: University of Chicago Press, 1961.

Chatman, S. B., ed. *Literary Style: A Symposium*. Oxford and New York: Oxford University Press, 1971.

Clayton, Jay. *Romantic Vision and the Novel*. Cambridge: Cambridge University Press, 1987.

Daiches, David. *The Novel and the Modern World*, rev. ed. Chicago and London: University of Chicago Press, 1960.

Dobree, Bonamy. *Modern Prose Style*. Oxford: Oxford University Press, 1934.

Drabble, Margaret, ed. *The Oxford Companion to English Literature*. Oxford: Oxford University Press, 1985.

Earle, John. *English Prose*. New York: G. P. Putnam's Sons; London: Smith, Elder, 1891.

Ellis, John. *The Theory of Literary Criticism: A Logical Analysis*. Berkeley: University of California Press, 1974.

Enkvist, Nils Erik. "On Defining Style." In *Linguistics and Style*, ed. John Spencer, 30–31. Oxford: Oxford University Press, 1964.

———. "On the Place of Style in Some Linguistic Theories." In *Literary Style: A Symposium*, ed. Seymour Chatman, 47–64. Oxford: Oxford University Press, 1971.

Fish, Stanley. *Is There a Text in This Class?* Cambridge, Mass.: Harvard University Press, 1980.

Forster, E. M. *Aspects of the Novel.* New York: Harcourt, Brace, Jovanovich, 1975.

Fowler, Roger, ed. *Style and Structure in Literature: Essays in the New Stylistics.* Ithaca, N.Y.: Cornell University Press, 1975.

Freeman, P. C., ed. *Linguistics and Literary Style.* New York: Holt, Rinehart & Winston, 1970.

Gadamer, Hans-Georg. *Philosophical Hermeneutics.* Translated and edited by David E. Linge. Berkeley: University of California Press, 1976.

Gardner, John. *The Art of Fiction: Notes on Craft for Young Writers.* New York: Random House, 1985.

Gibson, Walker. *Tough, Sweet and Stuffy: An Essay on Modern Prose Style.* Bloomington: Indiana University Press, 1966.

Gombrich, E. H. *Art and Illusion: A Study in the Psychology of Pictorial Representation.* Princeton, N.J.: Princeton University Press, 1972.

Goodman, Nelson. *The Language of Art.* Indianapolis, Ind.: Hackett, 1976.

Gordon, Ian A. *The Movement of English Prose.* Bloomington and London: Indiana University Press, 1966.

Hyman, Stanley Edgar. *The Armed Vision.* New York: Vintage Books, 1955.

Kawin, Bruce F. *Telling it Again and Again: Repetition in Literature and Film.* Ithaca, N.Y.: Cornell University Press, 1972.

Kenney, William. *How to Analyze Fiction.* New York: Simon and Schuster, 1966.

Kiely, Robert. *The Romantic Novel in England.* Cambridge: Harvard University Press, 1972.

Lakoff, George, and Mark Johnson. *Metaphors We Live By.* Chicago and London: University of Chicago Press, 1980.

Langer, Susanne K. *Philosophy in a New Key: A Study in the Symbolism of Reason, Rite and Art.* 3d ed. Cambridge: Harvard University Press, 1980.

———. *Problems of Art.* New York: Scribner's, 1959.

Lanham, Richard A. *Analyzing Prose.* New York: Scribner's, 1963.

Leech, Geoffrey N. and Michael H. Short. *Style in Fiction: A Linguistic Introduction to English Fictional Prose.* New York: Longman, 1981.

Lodge, David. *Language of Fiction: Essays in Criticism and Verbal Analysis of the English Novel.* London: Routledge & Kegan Paul, 1966; reprint, 1984.

———. *The Modes of Modern Writing: Metaphor, Metonymy, and the Typology of Modern Literature.* Chicago: University of Chicago Press, 1977.

Martin, Harold C., ed. *Style in Prose Fiction: English Institute Essays.* New York: California University Press, 1967.

Milic, Louis T. *A Quantitative Approach to the Style of Jonathan Swift.* The Hague: Mouton, 1967.

Millet, Fred B. *Reading Fiction: A Method of Analysis with Selections for Study.* New York: Harper, 1950.

Murry, J. Middleton. *The Problem of Style*. Oxford: Oxford U. Press, 1922.
Myers, Walter L. *The Later Realism: A Study of Characterization in the British Novel.* Chicago: University of Chicago Press, 1927.
Ohmann, Richard. "Prolegomena to the Analysis of Prose Style." In *Style in Prose Fiction: English Institute Essays, 1958*, ed. Harold C. Martin, 1–24. New York: Columbia University Press, 1967.
———. "Speech, Action and Style." In *Literary Style: A Symposium*, ed. Seymour Chatman, 241–259. Oxford: Oxford University Press, 1971.
———. *Shaw: The Style and the Man*. Middletown, Conn.: Wesleyan University Press, 1962.
Ragussis, Michael. *The Subterfuge of Art: Language and the Romantic Tradition.* Baltimore and London: Johns Hopkins University Press, 1978.
Read, Herbert. *English Prose Style*. N. Y.: Henry Holt, 1928; rpt, Pantheon, 1980.
Richards, I. A. *Principles of Literary Criticism*. N. Y.: Harcourt, Brace & World, 1925.
Riffaterre, Michael. "Criteria for Style Analysis." *Word* 15 (1959): 154–74.
Saintsbury, George. *A History of English Prose Rhythm*. London: Macmillan, 1912.
Schlueter, Paul and June, eds. *The English Novel: 20th Century Criticism*, Vol. 2, *20th Century Novelists*, by Paul and June Schlueter. Athens, Ohio: Ohio University Press, Swallow Press, 1982.
Scholes, Robert and Robert Kellog. *The Nature of Narrative*. New York: Oxford University Press, 1981.
Selden, Raman. *A Reader's Guide to Contemporary Literary Theory*. Lexington: University Press of Kentucky, 1985.
Seobok, Thomas A. *Style in Language*. London and New York: Longman, 1981.
Smith, Barbara Herrnstein. *On the Margins of Discourse: The Relation of Literature to Language*. Chicago and London: U. of Chicago Press, 1983.
Sontag, Susan. *Against Interpretation*. New York: Dell, 1966.
———. "Godard." In *Styles of Radical Will*, 147–89. New York: Dell, 1969.
———. "On Style." In *Against Interpretation and Other Essays*, 24–45. New York: Dell, 1966.
Spitzer, Leo. *Linguistics and Literary History*. New York: Russell & Russell, 1948.
Sypher, Wylie. *Four Stages of Renaissance Style: Transformations in Art and Literature 1400–1700*. Garden City, N.Y.: Doubleday, 1955.
Thorpe, James. *The Sense of Style: Reading English Prose*. Hamden, Conn.: Archon Books, 1987.
Tufte, Virginia. *Grammar as Style*. New York: Holt, Rinehart & Winston, 1971.
Turner, G. W. *Stylistics*. Baltimore: Penguin Books, 1973.
Van Ghent, Dorothy. *The English Novel: Form and Function*. New York: Holt, Rinehart & Winston, 1965.

Wellek, Rene and Austin Warren. *Theory of Literature.* 2d ed. New York: Harcourt, Brace & World, 1956.
Williams, Joan. *The Realist Novel in England: A Study in Development.* Pittsburgh: University of Pittsburgh Press, 1975.

Film Style, Technique, and History

American Film Institute. *Guide to College Courses in Film and Television.* 8th ed. New York: Prentice-Hall, 1990.
Andrew, Dudley. *Concepts in Film Theory.* Oxford: Oxford University Press, 1984.
―――. *The Major Film Theories.* New York: Oxford University Press, 1976.
Armes, Roy. *A Critical History of British Cinema.* New York: Oxford University Press, 1978.
―――. *Film and Reality: An Historical Survey.* Harmondsworth, England: Penguin Books, 1974.
Arnheim, Rudolf. *Film as Art.* Berkeley: University of California Press, 1957.
Aumont, Jacques, et al. *Aesthetics of Film.* Translated and revised by Richard Neupert. Austin: University of Texas Press, 1994.
Balazs, Bela. *Theory of Film.* Translated by Edith Bone. London: Dobson, 1952; reprint, New York: Dover, 1970.
Barr, Charles. "Cinemascope: Before and After." In *Film Theory and Criticism.* 2d ed., eds. Gerald Mast and Marshall Cohen, 140–168. New York and Oxford: Oxford University Press, 1974.
Basinger, Jeannine. *American Cinema: One Hundred Years of Film-making.* New York: Rizzoli International, 1994.
Bazin, Andre. "In Defense of Mixed Cinema." In *What is Cinema?*, ed. Hugh Gray, 53–75. Berkeley: University of California Press, 1967.
―――. *What is Cinema?* 2 vols. Translated by Hugh Gray. Berkeley: University of California Press, 1967–1971.
Belton, John. *Cinema Stylists.* Metuchen, N.J.: Scarecrow Press, 1983.
Boggs, Joseph. *The Art of Watching Films.* 2d ed. Palo Alto, Calif.: Mayfield, 1985.
Bordwell, David, Janet Staiger, and Kristin Thompson. *The Classical Hollywood Cinema: Film Style and Mode of Production to 1960.* New York: Columbia University Press, 1985.
Cook, David A. *A History of Narrative Film.* New York: W. W. Norton, 1981.
Curran, James and Vincent Porter, eds. *British Cinema History.* Totowa, N.J.: Barnes & Noble, 1983.
Dent, Ian. "The World of the Cinema." *The Illustrated London News*, 9 July 1960, 74.
DeNitto, Dennis. *Film: Form and Feeling.* New York: Harper & Row, 1985.

Dick, Bernard F. *Anatomy of Film*. New York: St. Martin's Press, 1978.
Durgnat, Raymond. *A Mirror for England: British Movies From Austerity to Affluence*. London: Faber and Faber, 1970.
Ellis, Jack L. *A History of Film*. 2d ed. Englewood Cliffs, N.J.: Prentice-Hall, 1985.
Giannetti, Louis. *Understanding Movies*. 4th ed. Englewood Cliffs, N.J.: Prentice-Hall, 1987.
Hale, Clarence Benjamin. "The Application of Linguistic Principles to the Analysis of Film Surface-Structure." Ph.D. diss., University of North Texas, 1980.
Harrington, John. *The Rhetoric of Film*. New York: Holt, Rinehart & Winston, 1973.
Hill, John. *Sex, Class and Realism: British Cinema, 1956–1963*. London: British Film Institute, 1986.
——. "Working-Class Realism and Sexual Reaction." In *British Cinema History*, eds. James Curran and Vincent Porter, 303–11. Totowa, N.J.: Barnes & Noble, 1983.
Holden, Anthony. *Behind the Oscar: The Secret History of the Academy Awards*. New York: Simon & Schuster, 1993; reprint, Penguin Books, 1994.
Huss, Roy and Norman Silverstein. *The Film Experience: Elements of Motion Picture Art*. New York: Dell, 1968.
Jacobs, Lewis. *The Movies as Medium*. New York: Farrar, Straus and Giroux, 1970.
Jinks, William. *The Celluloid Literature*. 2d ed. Beverly Hills, Calif.: Glencoe Press, 1974.
Knight, J. Wilson. *The Liveliest Art: A Panoramic History of the Movies*. rev. ed. New York: New American Library, 1979.
Kolker, Robert Phillip. *The Altering Eye: Contemporary International Cinema*. New York: Oxford University Press, 1960.
Krakauer, Siegfried. *Theory of Film: The Redemption of Physical Reality*. New York: Oxford University Press, 1960.
MacCann, Richard Dyer, ed. *Film: A Montage of Theories*. New York: E. P. Dutton, 1966.
Mast, Gerald. *Film Cinema Movie*. Chicago and London: University of Chicago Press, 1983.
——. *A Short History of the Movies*. 4th ed. New York: Macmillan, 1986.
——, and Marshall Cohen, eds. *Film Theory and Criticism*. 2d ed. New York: Oxford University Press, 1979.
Metz, Christian. *Film Language: A Semiotics of the Cinema*. Translated by Michael Taylor. New York: Oxford University Press, 1981.
Monaco, James. *How to Read a Film*. Rev. ed. New York: Oxford University Press, 1981.
Murphy, Robert. *Sixties British Cinema*. London: British Film Institute, 1992.
Nathan, David. *Glenda Jackson*. New York: Hippocrene Books, 1984.

Oakey, Virginia. *Dictionary of Film and Television Terms.* New York: Harper & Row, 1983.

Panofsy, Erwin. "Style and Medium in the Motion Pictures." In *Film Theory and Criticism*, ed. Gerald Mast and Marshall Cohen, 243–263. New York: Oxford University Press, 1979.

Perry, George. *The Great Picture Show.* London: Pavilion Books, 1985.

Salt, Barry. "Film Style and Technology in the Thirties." *Film Quarterly* 31 (Fall 1977): 19–32.

———. "Film Style and Technology in the Forties." *Film Quarterly* 30 (Fall 1976): 46–57.

———. *Film Style and Technology.* London: Starword, 1983. 2d ed., 1992.

———. "Statistical Style Analysis of Motion Pictures." In *Movies and Methods*, ed. Bill Nichols, 692–703, 2 vols. Vol. II. Berkeley: University of California Press, 1985.

Sharff, Stefan. *The Elements of Cinema: Toward a Theory of Cinesthetic Impact.* New York: Columbia University Press, 1982.

Sitney, P. Adams. *Visionary Film: The American Avant-Garde.* New York: Oxford University Press, 1974.

Slide, Anthony. *Fifty Classic British Films: 1932–1982: A Pictorial Record.* New York: Dover Publications, 1985.

Spottiswoode, Raymond. *A Grammar of the Film: An Analysis of Film Technique.* Berkeley: University of California Press, 1973.

Stephenson, Ralph and J. R. Debrix. *The Cinema as Art.* 2d ed. Harmondsworth, Middlesex, England: Penguin Books, 1976.

Talbot, Daniel, ed. *Film: An Anthology.* Berkeley: University of California Press, 1975.

Vermilye, Jerry. *Great British Films.* Secaucus, N.J.: Citadel Press, 1978.

Wiley, Mason and Damien Bone. *Inside Oscar: The Unofficial History of the Academy Awards.* New York: Ballantine Books, 1993.

Withers, Robert S. *Introduction to Film.* New York: Harper & Row; Barnes & Noble Books, 1983.

Wollen, Peter. *Signs and Meaning in the Cinema.* Bloomington: Indiana University Press, 1969.

Woodward, Ian. *Glenda Jackson: A Study in Fire and Ice.* New York: St. Martin's Press, 1985.

Theory and Practice of Film Adaptation

Allen, Boo. "A Study of Evelyn Waugh's *Brideshead Revisited* as Compared to the Telefilm Version." Ph.D. diss., East Texas State University, 1990.

Asheim, Lester. "From Book to Film: A Comparative Analysis of the Content of the Novels and the Motion Pictures Based Upon Them." Ph.D. diss., University of Chicago, 1950.

Baines, Arthur. "Aspects of Language in Literature and Film." Ph.D. diss., University of Texas, Austin, 1993.

Bates, H. F. "When the Cinematographer Complains That — 'It Isn't Like the Book' — Who's to Blame?" *Films and Filming* 5 (May 1959): 7.

Battestin, Martin. "Osborne's *Tom Jones*: Adapting a Classic." In *Film and/as Literature*, ed. John Harrington, 38–44. Englewood Cliffs, N.J.: Prentice-Hall, 1977.

Bluestone, George. *Novels Into Film: The Metamorphosis of Fiction Into Cinema.* Berkeley: University of California Press, 1973.

Bodeen, Dewitt. "The Adapting Art." *Films in Review* 14 (1963): 349–56.

Boyum, Joy Gould. *Double Exposure: Fiction Into Film.* New York: New American Library, 1985.

Bradt, David Richard. "From Fiction to Film: An Analysis of Aesthetics and Cultural Implications in the Adaptations of Two American Novellas." Ph.D. diss., Washington State University, 1974.

Burgess, Anthony. "On the Hopelessness of Turning Good Books Into Films." *New York Times*, 20 April 1975, 2: 1, 15.

Chatman, Seymour. *Story and Discourse: Narrative Structure in Fiction and Film.* Ithaca: Cornell University Press, 1978.

Cohen, Keith. *Film and Fiction: The Dynamics of Exchange.* New Haven: Yale University Press, 1979.

Conger, Sydney and Janice Welsch, eds. *Narrative Strategies: Essays in Film and Prose Fiction.* Macomb, Ill.: Western Illinois University Press, 1981.

Cooper, Stephen Philip. "Towards a Theory of Adaptation: John Huston and the Interlocutive." Ph.D. diss., University of Southern California, 1991.

Crump, G. B. "Lawrence and *The Literature/Film Quarterly.*" *D. H. Lawrence Review* 6 (Fall 1973): 326–332.

———. "Lawrence's *Rainbow* and Russell's *Rainbow.*" *The D. H. Lawrence Review* 21 (Summer 1989): 187–201.

———. "Gopher Prairie or Papplewick: *The Virgin and the Gypsy* as Film." *D. H. Lawrence Review* 4 (Summer 1971): 142–153.

Eidsvik, Charles. "Soft Edges: The Art of Literature, the Medium of Film." *Literature/Film Quarterly* 2 (Winter 1974): 16–21.

———. "Towards a 'Poetiques des Adaptations.'" In *Film and/as Literature*, ed. John Harrington, 31–32. Englewood Cliffs, N.J.: Prentice-Hall, 1977.

Eisenstein, Sergei. "From Dickens, Griffith, and the Film Today." In *Film Theory and Criticism*, eds. Gerald Mast and Marshall Cohen, 394–405. New York: Oxford University Press, 1979.

Fell, John. *Film and the Narrative Tradition.* Norman: University of Oklahoma Press, 1974.

Godfrey, Lionel. "It Wasn't Like That in the Books." *Films and Filming* 13 (April 1967): 12–15.

Gontarski, S. E. "*The Virgin and the Gypsy*: An English Watercolor." In *The English Novel and the Movies*, eds. Michael Klein and Gillian Parker, 257–267. New York: Frederick Ungar, 1981.

Gow, Gordon. "Novel Into Film." *Films and Filming* 12 (May 1966): 19–22.

Graham, John. "Fiction and Film: An Interview with George Garrett." *The Film Journal* 1 (1971): 22–25.

Harrington, John. *Film and/as Literature*. Englewood Cliffs, N.J.: Prentice-Hall, 1977.

Hartley, Dean Wilson. "How Do We Teach It?" A primer for the Basic Literature/Film Course. *Literature/Film Quarterly* 3 (Winter 1975): 60–68.

Horton, Andrew S. and John Magretta, eds. *Modern European Film Makers and the Art of Adaptation*. New York: Frederick Ungar, 1981.

James, Jo Ann and William J. Cloonan. *Apocalyptic Visions Past and Present: Selected Papers from the Eighth and Ninth Annual Florida State University Conferences on Literature and Film*. Tallahassee, Fla.: Florida State University Press, 1988.

Jinks, William. *The Celluloid Literature*. 2d ed. Beverly Hills: Glencoe Press, 1974.

Kael, Pauline. *Deeper Into Movies*. New York: Warner Books, 1973.

———. *Going Steady*. New York: Warner Books, 1970.

———. *I Lost It At the Movies*. Boston: Little, Brown, 1965.

———. *Kiss Kiss Bang Bang*. Boston: Little, Brown, 1968.

Kauffmann, Stanley. "Adaptations." In *A World on Film*, 70–137. New York: Harper & Row, 1966.

Kawin, Bruce F. *Faulkner and Film*. New York: Frederick Ungar, 1977.

———. "Fiction and the Camera Eye." *Film Quarterly* 30 (Summer 1977): 44–45.

Kinney, Judy Lee. "Text and Pretext: Stanley Kubrick's Adaptations." Ph.D. diss., University of California, Los Angeles, 1982.

Kittredge, William and Steven M. Krauzer, eds. *Stories Into Film*. New York: Harper & Row, 1979.

Klein, Michael and Gillian Parker, eds. *The English Novel and the Movies*. New York: Frederick Ungar, 1981.

Lawrence, Frank M. *Hemingway and the Movies*. Jackson, Miss.: University of Mississippi Press, 1981; reprint, New York: DaCapo Press, 1981.

Macdonald, George B. "An Application of New Critical Methodology to the Study of the Narrative Fictional Film." Ph.D. diss., Lehigh University, 1972.

Magill, Frank N., ed. *Cinema: The Novel Into Film*. Pasadena, Calif.: Salem Press, 1980.

Marcus, Fred H., ed. *Film and Literature: Contrasts in Media*. Scranton: Chandler, 1971.

Marcus, Millicent. *Film-making by the Book: Italian Cinema and Literary Adaptation*. Baltimore and London: Johns Hopkins University Press, 1993.

McDougal, Stuart T. *Made Into Movies: From Literature to Film*. New York: Holt, Rinehart & Winston, 1985.

McFarlane, Brian. *Words and Images: Australian Novels Into Film*. Richmond, Va.; Victoria, Australia: Heinemann, 1983.

Mellen, Joan. "Outfoxing Lawrence: Novella into Film." *Literature/Film Quarterly* 1 (January 1973): 17–27.

Miller, Gabriel. *The Classic American Novel and the Movies*. New York: Frederick Ungar, 1977.

———. *Screening the Novel: Rediscovering American Fiction in Film*. NewYork: Frederick Ungar, 1981.

Millichap, Joseph R. *Steinbeck and Film*. New York: Frederick Ungar, 1963.

Moore, Harry T. "D. H. Lawrence and the Flicks. "*Film/Literature Quarterly* 1 (January 1973): 3–11.

Morrissette, Bruce. *Novel and Film: Essays in Two Genres*. Chicago and London: University of Chicago Press, 1985.

Murray, Edward. *The Cinematic Imagination: Writers and the Motion Pictures*. New York: Frederick Ungar, 1972.

Nicoll, Allardyce. "Literature and Film." *English Journal* 26 (1937): 7–9.

Peary, Gerald and Roger Shatzkin, eds. *The Classic American Novel and the Movies*. New York: Frederick Ungar, 1977.

———. *The Modern American Novel and the Movies*. New York: Frederick Ungar, 1978.

Phillips, Gene D. *Grahame Greene: The Films of His Fiction*. New York: Teachers College Press, 1974.

———. *Hemingway and Film*. New York: Frederick Ungar, 1980.

Rentschler, Eric, ed. *German Film and Literature: Adaptations and Transformations*. New York and London: Methuen, 1986.

Richardson, Robert. *Literature and Film*. Bloomington: Indiana University Press, 1969.

Rollins, Janet Buck. "Stephen Crane on Film: Adaptation as Interpretation." Ph.D. diss., Oklahoma State University, 1983.

Ross, Harris Edward. "Some Aspects of the Relationship of Film to Literature." Ph.D. diss., University of Arkansas, 1979.

Ruhe, Edward. "Film: the 'Literary' Approach." *Literature/Film Quarterly* 1 (January 1973): 76–83.

Ruppert, Peter, ed. *Ideas of Order in Literature and Film. Selected Papers from the 4th Annual Florida State University Conference on Literature and Film*. Tallahassee, Fla.: University Presses of Florida, 1980.

Schneider, Harold W. "Literature and Film: Making Out Some Boundaries." *Literature/Film Quarterly* 3 (Winter 1975): 30–44.

Scholes, Robert. "Narration and Narrativity in Film." In *Film Theory and_Criticism*, ed. Gerald Mast and Marshall Cohen, 417–433. New York: Oxford University Press, 1979.

Seger, Linda. *The Art of Adaptation: Turning Fact and Fiction Into Film*. New York: Henry Holt, 1992.

Sigal, Clancy. "Shooting the Classics." *Time and Tide*, 2 July 1960, 759.

Simon, John. *Movies Into Film: Film Criticism 1967–70*. New York: Dell, 1971.

Sinyard, Neil. "Another Fine Mess: D. H. Lawrence and Thomas Hardy on Film." Chapter in *Filming Literature: The Art of Screen Adaptation*. New York: St. Martin's Press, 1986.

Smith, Julian. "Vision and Revision: *The Virgin and the Gypsy* as Film." *Literature/Film Quarterly* 1 (January 1973): 28–36.

Sobchack, Thomas. "*The Fox*: The Film and the Novel." *Western Humanities Review* 23 (1964): 73–78.

Solecki, Sam. "D. H. Lawrence's View of Film." *Literature/Film Quarterly* 1 (January 1973): 12–16.

Sontag, Susan. "A Note on Novels and Films." In *Against Interpretation*. New York: Dell, 1972.

Spiegel, Alan. *Fiction and the Camera Eye: Visual Consciousness in Film and the Modern Novel*. Charlottesville, Va.: University of Virginia Press, 1975.

Vick, Christina. "Cinematic Aspects and Film Adaptations of Selected Works by Thomas Hardy." Ph.D. diss., Texas A & M University, 1990.

Wagner, Geoffrey. *The Novel and the Cinema*. Cranbury, N.J.: Associated University Presses; London: Tantivy Press, 1971.

Wald, Jerry. "Screen Adaptation." In *Films in Review*, ed. Henry Hart, 62–67. New York: National Review of Motion Pictures, 1954.

Weinberg, Herman G. "Novel into Film." *Literature/Film Quarterly* 1 (April 1973): 99–102.

Whittock, Trevor. *Metaphor and Film*. Cambridge: Cambridge U. Press, 1990.

Zambrano, A.L. *Dickens and Film*. New York: Gordon Press, 1976.

D. H. Lawrence: Primary Sources

Lawrence, D. H. *Birds, Beasts and Flowers*. New York: Thomas Seltzer, 1923.

———. *The Collected Letters of D. H. Lawrence*. 2 vols. Edited and with an Introduction by Harry T. Moore. London: William Heinemann, 1962; reprint, 1977.

———. *The Letters of D. H. Lawrence: Vol. l: Sept. 1901–May 1913*. Edited by James T. Boulton. Cambridge: Cambridge University Press, 1979.

———. *The Letters of D. H. Lawrence*. Edited and with an Introduction by Aldous Huxley. London: Heinemann; New York, Viking Press, 1932.

———. *Phoenix: The Posthumous Papers of D. H. Lawrence: 1936.* Edited by Edward D. McDonald. New York: Viking Press, 1980.

———. *Phoenix II: Uncollected Writings.* Edited by Warren Roberts and Harry T. Moore. New York: Viking Press, 1970.

———. *The Portable D. H. Lawrence.* Edited and with an Introduction by Diana Trilling. New York: Viking Press; reprint, New York: Penguin Books, 1981.

———. "The Rocking-Horse Winner." In *The Portable D. H. Lawrence.* Edited by Diana Trilling, 147–165. New York: Viking Press, 1947; reprint, NewYork: Penguin Books, 1981.

———. *The Selected Letters of D. H. Lawrence.* Edited and with an Introduction by Diana Trilling. New York: Farrar, Straus and Cudahy, 1958.

———. *Sons and Lovers.* London: Duckworth & Son, 1913; reprint, New York: Penguin Books, 1983.

———. *Studies in Classic American Literature.* New York: Viking Press, 1964.

———. *Women in Love.* New York: Thomas Seltzer, 1920; reprint, New York: Penguin Books, 1980.

D. H. Lawrence: Secondary Sources on His Life And Works in General

Adelman, Gary. *Snow of Fire: Symbolic Meaning in "The Rainbow" and "Women in Love."* New York and London: Garland, 1991.

Alcorn, John. *The Nature Novel from Hardy to Lawrence.* New York: Columbia University Press, 1977.

Alden, Patricia. *Social Mobility in the English Bildungsroman: Gissing, Hardy, Bennett, and Lawrence.* Ann Arbor, Mich.: UMI Research Press, 1986.

Aldington, Richard. *Portrait of a Genius, But . . .: The Life of D. H. Lawrence: 1885–1930.* London: Heinemann, 1950.

Amon, Frank. "D. H. Lawrence and the Short Story." In *The Achievement of D. H. Lawrence*, ed. Frederick J. Hoffman and Harry T. Moore, 222–234. Norman: University of Oklahoma Press, 1953.

Aldritt, Keith. *The Visual Imagination of D. H. Lawrence.* London: Edward Arnold, 1971.

Appleman, Philip. "D. H. Lawrence and the Intrusive Knock." *Fiction Studies III* 3 (Winter 1957): 328–332.

Balbert, Peter and Phillip L. Marcus, eds. *D. H. Lawrence: A Centenary Consideration.* Ithaca: Cornell University Press, 1985.

Baldanza, Frank. "D. H. Lawrence's Song of Songs." *Modern Fiction Studies* 7 (Summer 1961): 106–114.

———. "*Sons and Lovers*: Novel to Film as a Record of Cultural Growth." *Film/Literature Quarterly* 1 (Winter 1973): 64–70.
Becker, George L. *D. H. Lawrence*. New York: Frederick Ungar, 1980.
Bell, Michael. *D. H. Lawrence: Language and Being*. Cambridge: Cambridge University Press, 1992.
Bertocci, Angelo P. "Symbolism in *Women in Love*." In *A D. H. Lawrence Miscellany*, ed. Harry T. Moore, 83–102. Carbondale, Ill.: Southern Ill.: Southern Illinois University Press, 1959.
Betsky, Seymour. "Rhythm and Theme. D. H. Lawrence's *Sons and Lovers*." In *The Achievement of D.H. Lawrence*, ed. Frederick J. Hoffman and Harry Moore, 131–143. Norman: University of Oklahoma Press, 1953.
Bickerton, Derek. "The Language of *Women in Love*." *A Review of English Literature* 8 (1967): 56–67.
Black, Michael. *D. H. Lawrence: The Early Fiction.* Cambridge: Cambridge University Press, 1986.
Bloom, Harold, ed. *D. H. Lawrence's "Women in Love."* New York, New Haven, Philadelphia: Chelsea House, 1988.
Bonds, Diane. *Language and the Self in D. H.Lawrence*. Ann Arbor, Mich.: UMI Research Press, 1987.
Burgers, Anthony. *Flame Into Being: The Life and Work of D. H. Lawrence*. New York: Arbor House, 1985.
Burroughs, William D. "No Defense for 'The Rocking-Horse Winner.'" *College English* 24 (1963): 323.
Cavitch, David. "On *Women in Love*." In *D. H. Lawrence: A Collection of Criticism*, ed. Leo Hamalian, 54–64. New York: McGraw-Hill, 1973.
Chambers, Jessie. *D. H. Lawrence: A Personal Record*. Cambridge: Cambridge University Press, 1980.
Clark, L. D. "Immediacy and Recollection: The Rhythm of the Visual in D. H. Lawrence." In *D. H. Lawrence: The Man Who Died*, eds. Edward B. Partlow, Jr. and Harry T. Moore, 121–138. Carbondale, Ill.: Southern Illinois University Press, 1980.
Clarke, Colin, ed. *"The Rainbow" and "Women in Love."* Nashville and London: Aurora, 1970.
———. *River of Dissolution: D. H. Lawrence. D. H. Lawrence and English Romanticism*. London: Routledge & Kegan Paul; New York: Barnes & Noble, 1969.
Consolo, Dominic P., ed. *D. H. Lawrence: "The Rocking-Horse Winner."* Columbus, Ohio: Charles E. Merrill, 1969.
Cowan, James C., ed. *D. H. Lawrence: An Annotated Bibliography of Writings About Him (1982, 1985)*. 2 vols. Dekalb, Ill.: Northern Illinois University Press, 1982–1985.
———. *D. H. Lawrence and the Trembling Balance*. University Park and London: The Pennsylvania State University Press, 1990.

Cowan, S. A. "Lawrence's 'The Rocking-Horse Winner.'" *The Explicator* 28 (October 1969), item 9.

Daiches, David. "Lawrence and the Form of the Novel." In *D. H. Lawrence: Sons and Lovers*, ed. Gamini Salgado, 164–170. Casebook Series. Nashville: Aurora, 1970.

———. *The Novel and the Modern World: Joseph Conrad, James Joyce, D. H. Lawrence, Virginia Woolf.* Chicago: University of Chicago Press, 1960.

Daleski, H. M. *The Forked Flame: A Study of D. H.Lawrence.* Evanston, Ill.: Northwestern University Press, 1965.

Davis, Robert Gorham. "Observations on 'The Rocking-Horse Winner." In Instructor's Manual for *Ten Modern Masters: An Anthology of the Short Story*, 49–50. 2d ed. New York: Harcourt, Brace & World, 1959.

Dataller, Roger. "Elements of D. H. Lawrence's Prose Style." *Essays in Criticism* 8 (Oct. 1953): 413–24.

DeBattista, Maria. "*Women in Love*: D. H. Lawrence's Judgment Book." In *D. H. Lawrence: A Centenary Consideration*, eds. Peter Balbert and Phillip L. Marcus, 67–90. Ithaca, N.Y.: Cornell University Press, 1985.

Delany, Paul. *D. H. Lawrence's Nightmare; The Writer and His Circle in the Years of the Great War.* New York: Basic Books, 1978.

Delavenay, Emile. *D. H. Lawrence and Edward Carpenter: A Study in Edwardian Transition.* London: Heinemann, 1971.

———. "Lawrence, Otto Weininger and 'Rather Raw Philosophy.'" In *D. H. Lawrence: New Studies*, ed. Christopher Heyood. New York: St. Martin's Press, 1987.

deSola Pinto, V. "Lawrence and the Non-Conformist Hymns." In *A D. H. Lawrence Miscellany*, ed. Harry T. Moore, 103–113. Carbondale, Ill.: Southern Illinois University Press, 1959.

Donaldson, George. "Men in Love? D. H. Lawrence, Rupert Birkin and Gerald Crich." In *D. H. Lawrence: Centenary Essays*, ed. Mara Kalnins, 41–68. Bristol, England: Bristol Classical Press, 1986.

Draper, Ronald P. *D. H. Lawrence.* New York: St. Martin's Press, 1964.

Ebbatson, Roger. *Lawrence and the Nature Tradition: A Theme in English Fiction, 1859–1914.* Atlantic Highlands, N.J.: Humanities Press, 1980.

Englander, Anne. "Technique as Evasion." Ph.D. diss., Northwestern University, 1966.

Farmer, David, Lindeth Vasey and John Worthen, eds. *D. H. Lawrence: Women in Love.* Cambridge: Cambridge University Press, 1987.

Farr, Judith, ed. *Twentieth Century Interpretations of Sons and Lovers: A Collection of Critical Essays.* Englewood Cliffs, N.J.: Prentice-Hall, 1970.

Felter, Maryanne. "Verbal Analysis and Fantasia of the Unconscious: Style in the Short Stories of D. H. Lawrence." Ph.D. diss.,University of Delaware, 1982.

Fitz, L. T. "'The Rocking-Horse Winner' and *The Golden Bough*." *Studies in Short Fiction*, 11 (1974), 199–200.

Ford, George. *Double Measure: A Study of the Novels and Stories of D. H. Lawrence.* New York: Holt, Rinehart & Winston, 1965.
Fraiberg, Louis. "The Unattainable Self: D. H. Lawrence's *Sons and Lovers.*" In *D. H. Lawrence and "Sons and Lovers": Sources and Criticism,* ed. E. W. Tedlock, Jr., 217–237. New York: New York University Press, 1965.
Freeman, Mary. *D. H. Lawrence: A Basic Study of His Ideas.* New York: Grosset & Dunlap, 1955.
Friedman, Alan. "The Other Lawrence." *Partisan Review* 37 (1970): 239–253.
———. *The Turn of the Novel.* New York: Oxford University Press, 1966.
Goldberg, Michael. "Dickens and Lawrence: More on Rocking Horses." *Modern Fiction Studies* 17 (1971–72): 574.
———. "Lawrence's 'The Rocking-Horse Winner': A Dickensian Fable?" *Modern Fiction Studies* 15 (Winter 1969): 525–536.
Gomme, A. H., ed. *D. H. Lawrence: A Critical Study of the Major Novels and Other Writings.* New York: Barnes & Noble; Hassocks: Harvester Press, 1978.
Goodheart, Eugene. *The Utopian Vision of D. H. Lawrence.* Chicago: University of Chicago Press, 1963.
Gordon, Caroline and Allen Tate, eds. "'The Rocking-Horse Winner': Commentary." In *The House of Fiction: An Anthology of the Short Study.* 2nd ed. New York: Scribner's, 1960.
Gordon, David J. *D. H. Lawrence as a Literary Critic.* New Haven: Yale University Press, 1966.
———. "*Women in Love* and the Lawrencean Aesthetic." In *Twentieth_Century Interpretations of "Women in Love,"* ed. Stephen J. Miko, 50–60. Englewood Cliffs, N.J.: Prentice-Hall, 1969.
———. "Sex and Language in D. H. Lawrence." *Twentieth Century Literature* 27 (Winter 1981): 362–75.
Gregory, Horace. *D. H. Lawrence: Pilgrim of the Apocalypse.* New York: Grove Press, 1957.
Gurko, Jane. "The Flesh Made Word: Study of Narrative and Stylistic Techniques in Five Novels by D. H. Lawrence." Ph.D. diss., University of California, Berkeley, 1971.
Hamalian, Leo., ed. *D. H. Lawrence: A Collection of Criticism.* New York: McGraw-Hill, 1973.
Hardy, Barbara. *The Appropriate Form.* London: Athlone Press, 1964.
Harris, Janice Hubbard. *The Short Fiction of D. H. Lawrence.* New Brunswick, N.J.: Rutgers University Press, 1984.
Heilbut, Anthony Otto. "The Prose of D. H. Lawrence." Ph.D. diss., Harvard University, 1966.
Hepburn, James G. "Disarming and Uncanny Visions: The Uncanny with Regard to Form and Content in Stories by Sherwood Anderson and D. H. Lawrence." *Literature and Psychology* 9 (Winter 1959), 9–12.

Herzinger, Kim A. *D. H. Lawrence in His Time: 1908–1911*. Louisburg, Pa.: East Brunswick, N.J.: Associated University Presses, 1982.

Heywood, Christopher, ed. *D. H. Lawrence: New Studies*. New York: St. Martin's, 1987.

———. "'Blood-Consciousness' and the Pioneers of the Reflex and Ganglionic Systems." In *D. H. Lawrence: New Studies*, ed. Christopher Heywood, 104–123. New York: St. Martin's Press, 1967.

Hobsbaum, Philip. *A Reader's Guide to D. H. Lawrence*. London: Thames and Hudson, 1981.

Hoffman, Frederick and Harry T. Moore, eds. *The Achievement of D. H. Lawrence*. Norman: University of Oklahoma Press, 1953.

———. "Lawrence's Quarrel with Freud." In *The Achievement of D. H. Lawrence*, eds. Frederick J. Hoffman and Harry Moore, 106–127. Norman: University of Oklahoma Press, 1953.

Holderness, Graham. *Women in Love*. Milton Keynes, England; Philadelphia: Open University Press, 1986.

Hough, Graham. *The Dark Sun: A Study of D. H. Lawrence*. New York: Macmillan, 1957.

Humma, John B. *Metaphor and Meaning in D. H. Lawrence's Later Novels*. Columbia, Mo., and London: University of Missouri Press, 1990.

Ingram, Allan. *The Language of D. H. Lawrence*. New York: St. Martin's Press, 1990.

Kalnins, Mara, ed. *D. H. Lawrence: Centenary Essays*. Bristol: Bristol Classical Press, 1986.

Kay, Ian Arthur. "Rotary Image-Thought: A Study of D. H. Lawrence's Prose Style." Ph.D. diss., London, Ontario: University of Western Ontario, 1978.

Kazin, Alfred. "Sons, Lovers and Mothers." In *Twentieth Century Interpretations of "Sons and Lovers,"* ed. Judith Farr, 74–84. Englewood Cliffs, N.J.: Prentice-Hall, 1970.

Kermode, Frank. *D. H. Lawrence*. New York: Viking, 1973.

———. "The Novels of D. H. Lawrence." In *D. H. Lawrence: Novelist, Poet, Prophet*, ed. Stephen Spender, 77–89. New York: Harper & Row, 1973.

Kinkead-Weeks, Mark. "The Marble and the Statue: The Exploratory Imagination of D. H. Lawrence." In *Imagined Worlds: Essays on Some English Novels and Novelists in Honour of John Butt*, ed. Maynard Mack and Ian Gregor, 371–418. London: Methuen, 1968.

Kittner, Alfred Booth. "*Sons and Lovers*: A Freudian Appreciation." *The Psychoanalytic Review* 3 (July 1916): 295–317.

Koban, Charles. "Allegory and the Death of the Heart in 'The Rocking-Horse Winner.'" *Studies in Short Fiction* 15 (1978): 391–96.

Leavis, F. R. *D. H. Lawrence: Novelist*. Chicago: University of Chicago Press, 1955.

———. "Mr. Eliot and Lawrence." In *The Achievement of D. H. Lawrence*, eds. Frederick J. Hoffman and Harry T. Moore, 95–105. Norman: University of Oklahoma Press, 1979.

———. *The Great Tradition: George Eliot, Henry James, Joseph Conrad.* London: Chatto and Windus; New York: Stewart, 1948.

———. *Thought, Words and Creativity: Art and Thought in Lawrence.* New York: Oxford University Press, 1970.

Lindenberger, Herbert. "Lawrence and the Romantic Tradition." In *A D. H. Lawrence Miscellany*, ed. Harry T. Moore, 326–341. Carbondale, Ill.: Southern Illinois University Press, 1959.

Mack, Maynard and Ian Gregor, eds. *Imagined Worlds: Essays on Some English Novels and Novelists in Honour of John Butt.* London: Methuen, 1968.

Mackinnon, Kenneth Arthur. "Stylistic and Narrative Techniques in the Early Novels of D. H. Lawrence." Ph.D. diss., University of Toronto, 1976.

Marks, W. S. III. "The Psychology of the Uncanny in Lawrence's 'The Rocking-Horse Winner.'" *Modern Fiction Studies* 11 (Winter 1965): 381–392.

Martin, W. R. "Fancy of Imagination? 'The Rocking-Horse Winner.'" *College English* 24 (1962): 64–65.

Martz, Louis L. "Portrait of Miriam: Study in the Design of *Sons and Lovers*." In *Imagined Worlds: Essays on Some English Novels and Novelists in Honour of John Butt*, eds. Maynard Mack and Ian Gregor, 343–369. London: Methuen, 1968.

McCabe, Thomas H. "Rhythm as Form in Lawrence: 'The Horse-Dealer's Daughter.'" *PMLA* 87 (Jan. 1972): 64–68.

McKeown, Marion Smith. "Patterns of Stylistic Change in the Novels of D. H. Lawrence." Ph.D. diss., McGill University, 1974.

Melchior, Barbara. "Objects in the Powerful Light of Emotion." *Ariel* (Leeds) 1 (1970): 21–30.

Meyers, Jeffrey. *D. H. Lawrence: A Biography.* New York: Alfred A. Knopf, 1990.

———. *D. H. Lawrence and Tradition.* Amherst: University of Massachusetts Press, 1985.

———. *The Legacy of D. H. Lawrence: New Essays.* New York: St. Martin's Press, 1987.

Miko, Stephen J. *Toward "Women in Love": The Emergence of a Lawrentian Aesthetic.* New Haven and London: Yale University Press, 1971.

Moore, Harry T. *D. H. Lawrence: His Life and Works.* New York: Twayne, 1964.

———. *The Priest of Love: Life of D. H. Lawrence.* rev. ed. New York: Penguin Books, 1954.

———, ed. *D. H. Lawrence: His Life and Works.* New York: Twayne, 1964.

———, ed. *A D. H. Lawrence Miscellany.* Carbondale, Ill.: Southern Illinois University Press, 1959.

"Mother Love." Rev. of *Sons and Lovers* (the novel). *New York Times*, 21 Sept. 1913, 479.

Moynahan, Julian. *The Deed of Life: The Novels and Tales of D. H. Lawrence*. Princeton, N. J.: Princeton University Press, 1963.

———, ed. *D. H. Lawrence: "Sons and Lovers": Text, Background, and Criticism*. New York: Penguin Books, 1968.

Murry, John Middleton. "A Review of *Women in Love*." In *D. H. Lawrence: "The Rainbow" and "Women in Love,"* ed. Colin Clarke, 67–72. Nashville and London: Aurora, 1970.

———. *Son of Woman: The Story of D. H. Lawrence*. London: Jonathan Cape, 1939; reprint, *D. H. Lawrence: Son of Woman*. London: Jonathan Cape, 1954.

Nehls, Edward, ed. *D. H. Lawrence: A Composite Biography*. 3 vols. Madison: University of Wisconsin Press, 1957–59.

Nicholes, E. L. "The 'Symbol of the Sparrow' in *The Rainbow* by D. H. Lawrence." In *The Achievement of D. H. Lawrence*, eds. Frederick J. Hoffman and Harry T. Moore, 159–62. Norman: University of Oklahoma Press, 1953.

Nin, Anaïs. *D. H. Lawrence: An Unprofessional Study*. Chicago: Swallow Press, 1964.

Niven, Alastair. *D. H. Lawrence: The Novels*. Cambridge: Cambridge University Press, 1978.

Oates, Joyce Carol. *The Hostile Sun: The Poetry of D. H. Lawrence*. Los Angeles: Black Sparrow Press, 1973.

Padhi, Bibhu. *D. H. Lawrence: Modes of Fictional Style*. Troy, N.Y.: Whitston, 1989.

Partlow, Robert B. Jr. *D. H. Lawrence: The Man Who Lived*. Carbondale and Edwardsville, Ill.: Southern Illinois University Press, 1979.

Pilly, W. C. Review of *Women in Love*. *John Bull*, 17 Sept. 1921, 4.

Potter, Stephen. *D. H. Lawrence: A First Study*. London: Jonathan Cape, 1930.

Pritchard, R. E. *D. H. Lawrence: Body of Darkness*. Pittsburgh: University of Pittsburgh Press, 1971.

Pritchett, V. S. "*Sons and Lovers*." In *The Living Novel*, 131–138. London: Chatto and Windus, 1946.

Ragussis, Michael. "D. H. Lawrence: The New Vocabulary of *Women in Love*: Speech and Art Speech." In *The Subterfuge of Art: Language and the Romantic Tradition*, 172–225. Baltimore: Johns Hopkins, 1978.

Reddick, Bryan D. "Point of View and Narrative Tone in *Women in Love*: The Portrayal of Interpsychic Space." *D. H. Lawrence Review* 7 (Summer 1974): 156–171.

Reeves, Rosemary. "Lawrence, Lady Cynthia Asquith and 'The Rocking-Horse Winner.'" *Studies in Short Fiction* 20 (1983): 121–126.

Ross, Charles L. *The Composition of "The Rainbow" and "Women in Love": A History*. Charlottesville, Va.: University Press of Virginia, 1979.

———. *"Women in Love": A Novel of Mythic Realism*. Boston: Twayne, 1991.

Ruderman, Judith. *D. H. Lawrence and the Devouring Mother: The Search for a Patriarchal Ideal of Leadership.* Durham, N.C.: Duke University Press, 1984.

Russell, John. *Style in Modern British Fiction: Studies in Joyce, Lawrence, Forster, Lewis, and Green.* Baltimore and London: Johns Hopkins University Press, 1978.

Sagar, Keith, *The Art of D. H. Lawrence.* Cambridge: Cambridge University Press, 1960; reprint, 1975.

———. *D. H. Lawrence: Life Into Art.* New York: Viking Penguin Books, 1985.

———. *The Life of D. H. Lawrence.* New York: Pantheon, 1980.

———, ed. *A D. H. Lawrence Handbook.* Manchester, Eng.: Manchester University Press; New York: Barnes & Noble, 1982.

Salgado, Gamini, ed. *D. H. Lawrence: "Sons and Lovers."* (Casebook series) Nashville: Aurora, 1970.

———. *A Preface to Lawrence.* London and New York: Longmans, 1982.

Sanders, Scott. "D. H. Lawrence and the Resacralization of Nature." In *D. H. Lawrence: The Man Who Lived*, ed. Robert B. Partlow, Jr. and Harry T. Moore, 159–167. Carbondale and Edwardsville, Ill.: Southern Illinois University, 1980.

San Juan, E., Jr. "Theme Versus Imitation: D. H. Lawrence's 'The Rocking-Horse Winner.'" *D. H. Lawrence Review* 3 (1971): 136–40.

Schneider, Daniel J. *The Consciousness of D. H. Lawrence: An Intellectual Biography.* Lawrence: University Press of Kansas, 1986.

———. *D. H. Lawrence: The Artist as Psychologist.* Lawrence: University Press of Kansas, 1984.

Schorer, Mark. "Poste Restante: Lawrence as Traveler." Chapter in *The World We Imagine.* New York: Farrar, Straus & Giroux, 1968, 147–161.

———. "Technique as Discovery." *Hudson Review* 1 (Spring 1948): 67–87.

———. "*Women in Love* and Death." *Hudson Review* 6 (Spring 1953): 34–37; reprinted in *D. H. Lawrence: A Collection of Critical Essays*, ed. Mark Spilka, 50–60. Englewood Cliffs, N.J.: Prentice-Hall, 1963.

———. *The World We Imagine.* New York: Farrar, Straus & Giroux, 1968.

Schvey, Henry. "Lawrence and Expressionism." In *D. H. Lawrence: New Studies*, ed. Christopher Heywood. New York: St. Martin's Press, 1987.

Shanks, E. Review of *Women in Love. London Mercury*, 17 Sept. 1921, 433.

Slade, Tony. *D. H. Lawrence.* New York: Arco, 1970. Snodgrass, W. D. "A Rocking-Horse; The Symbol, The Pattern, The Way to Live." *The Hudson Review*, 11 (Summer 1958): 191–200.

Spender, Stephen, ed. *D. H. Lawrence: Novelist, Poet, Prophet.* New York: Harper & Row, 1973.

Spilka, Mark. "How to Pick Flowers." In *D. H.Lawrence and "Sons and Lovers": Sources and Criticism*, ed. E. W. Tedlock, Jr., 188–199. New York: New York University Press, 1965.

———. *The Love Ethic of D. H. Lawrence*. Bloomington and London: Indiana University Press, 1955.
Squires, Michael and Keith Cushman. *The Challenge of D. H. Lawrence*. Madison: University of Wisconsin Press, 1990.
Steinmann, Martin, Jr. "The Old Novel and the New." In *From Jane Austen to Joseph Conrad*, ed. R. C. Rathburn and Martin Steinmann, Jr., 214–243. Minneapolis: University of Minnesota Press, 1958.
Steward, J. I. M. *Eight Modern Writers*. Oxford: Clarendon Press, 1963.
Stewart, Garrett. "D. H. Lawrence and the Allotropic Style." *Novel* 9 (1976): 217–42.
Stoll, John E. *The Novels of D. H. Lawrence: A Search for Integration*. Columbia: University of Missouri Press, 1971.
Tedlock, E. W., Jr., ed. *D. H. Lawrence and "Sons and Lovers": Sources and Criticism*. New York: New York University Press, 1965.
Tindall, William York. *D. H. Lawrence and Susan His Cow*. New York: Cooper Square. 1972.
Tiverton, Father William. *D. H. Lawrence and Human Existence*. New York: Philosophical Library, 1951.
Trilling, Diana. "A Letter of Introduction to Lawrence." In *A D. H. Lawrence Miscellany*, ed. Harry T. Moore, 114–30. Carbondale, Ill.: Southern Illinois University Press, 1959.
Turner, Frederick W. III. "Prancing to a Purpose: Myths, Horses, and True Selfhood in Lawrence's 'The Rocking-Horse Winner.'" In *D. H. Lawrence: The Rocking-Horse Winner*, ed. Dominick Consolo, 95–106. Columbus, Ohio: Charles E. Merrill, 1969.
Urang, Sarah. *Kindled in the Flame: The Apocalyptic Scene in D. H. Lawrence*. Ann Arbor, Mich.: UMI Research Press, 1982.
Van Ghent, Dorothy. "On *Sons and Lovers*." In *D. H. Lawrence and "Sons and Lovers": Sources and Criticism*, ed. E. W. Tedlock, Jr., 170–187. New York: New York University Press, 1965.
Vivas, Eliseo. *D. H. Lawrence: The Failure and the Triumph of Art*. Evanston, Ill.: Northwestern University Press, 1960.
Wallace, Douglas, Roy Lamson and Hallett Smith. Commentary on "The Rocking-Horse Winner." In *The Critical Reader*, Douglas Wallace et al., eds., 416–21. New York: Norton, 1949.
Wayland, James Ward. "D. H. Lawrence: A Study of His Prose Style." Ph.D. diss., University of California, Los Angeles, 1972.
Weiss, Daniel. "The Mother in the Mind." In *Twentieth Century Interpretations of "Sons and Lovers,"* ed. Judith Farr, 51–63. Englewood Cliffs, N.J.: Prentice-Hall, 1970.
———. *Oedipus in Nottingham*. Washington: University of Washington Press, 1962.

West, Anthony. "The Short Stories." In *The Achievement of D. H. Lawrence*, eds. Frederick J. Hoffman and Harry T. Moore, 202–21. Norman: University of Oklahoma Press, 1953.

West, Rebecca. Review of *Women in Love*. *New Statesman*, 9 July 1921, 388.

Widmer, Kingsley. *The Art of Perversity*. Seattle: University of Washington Press, 1962.

Woolf, Virginia. "Notes on D. H. Lawrence." In *Twentieth Century Interpretations of "Sons and Lovers,"* ed. Judith Farr, 24–27. Englewood Cliffs, N.J.: Prentice-Hall, 1970.

Worthen, John. *D. H. Lawrence and the Idea of the Novel*. Totowa, N.J.: Rowman & Littlefield, 1979.

Articles and Books on the Film Adaptations of D. H. Lawrence's Fictions

"The Rocking Horse Winner"

Becker, Henry III. *"The Rocking Horse Winner*: Film as Parable." In *From Fiction to Film*, eds. Gerald R. Barrett and Thomas L. Erskine, 204–213. Encino and Belmont, Calif.: Dickinson, 1974.

Guernsey, Otis L. "The Rocking-Horse Winner." *New York Times*, 9 June 1950, 29.

Hartung, Philip. Review of *The Rocking Horse Winner*. In *Commonweal*, 23 June 1950, 272.

Hendricks, Gordon. "Film Music Comes of Age." *Films in Review*, 3 January 1952, 23.

McCarten, John. "The Current Cinema: Small Handicapper." *The New Yorker*, 10 June 1950, 90.

Mellen, Joan. "'The Rocking-Horse Winner' as Cinema." In *Fiction to Film: D. H. Lawrence's 'TheRocking-Horse Winner,'* eds. Gerald R. Barrett and Thomas L. Erskine, 214–223. Encino and Belmont, Calif.: Dickinson, 1974.

"Movies: The Good with the Bad." (Review of *The Rocking Horse Winner*) *The New Republic*, 26 June 1950, 22.

M. Y. "*The Rocking Horse Winner*." *The Christian Century*, 4 Oct. 1950, 1183.

Myro. "The Rocking Horse Winner." *Variety*, 21 December 1949, 8.

Pelissier, Anthony. *The Rocking Horse Winner* (shooting script). In *From Fiction to Film: D. H. Lawrence's "The Rocking-Horse Winner,"* eds. Gerald R. Barrett and Thomas L. Erskine. Encino and Belmont, Calif.: Dickinson, 1974.

———. "Lawrence on Film: The Problem of Adapting 'Rocking-Horse Winner.'" *New York Times*, 11 June 1950, II, 5, 1.

Review of *The Rocking Horse Winner*. *Newsweek*, 19 June 1950, 90.

Review of *The Rocking Horse Winner*. *New York Times*, 9 June 1950, 23.

Review of *The Rocking Horse Winner*. *Time*, 26 June 1950, 96.

Shayon, Robert Lewis. "*The Rocking Horse Winner.*" *Saturday Review*, 24 June 1950, 34–35.

Smith, Julian. "The Social Architecture of *The Rocking Horse Winner.*" In *From Fiction to Film: D. H. Lawrence's "The Rocking Horse Winner,"* eds. Gerald R. Barrett and Thomas L. Erskine, 224–30. Encino and Belmont, Calif.: Dickinson, 1974.

Tarratt, Margaret. "An Obscene Undertaking." *Films and Filming* 17 (November 1970): 26–30.

T.M.P. Review of *The Rocking Horse Winner. New York Times Film Reviews*, 9 June 1950, 2.

Whitebait, William. "*The Rocking Horse Winner* at the Marble Arch Odeon." *New Statesman and Nation*, 24 Dec. 1949, 756.

Sons and Lovers

Alpert, Hollis. "The Classic Novel: *Sons and Lovers.*" *Saturday Review*, 6 August 1960, 68.

Baldanza, Frank. "*Sons and Lovers*: Novel to Film as a Record of Cultural Growth." *Literature/Film Quarterly* 1 (Winter 1973): 68–69.

Balliet, Whitney. "The Current Cinema: An Embarrassment of Talk." *The New Yorker*, 13 August 1960, 56.

Beckley, Paul. "*Sons and Lovers.*" *New York Herald Tribune*, 3 August 1960, 11.

Cameron, Kate. "Two Films Tie for Critics' Award." *The New York Daily News*, 30 Dec. 1960, 38.

Cardiff, Jack. "Lawrence . . . and the Camera." [*Sons and Lovers*] *Films and Filming* 6 (May 1960): 9.

Cavander, Kenneth. "*Sons and Lovers.*" In *Sight and Sound* 29 (Summer 1960): 145.

Crowther, Bosley. "Tepid Passions." *The New York Times*, 3 August 1960, 35.

Dent, Alan. "The World of the Cinema." *The Illustrated London News*, 9 July 1960, 74.

DeNitto, Dennis. "*Sons and Lovers*: All Passion Spent." In *The English Novel and the Movies*, eds. Michael Klein and Gillian Parker, 235–247. New York: Frederick Ungar, 1981.

Evans, Peter. "The scene the censor cut from *Sons and Lovers* . . ." *Daily Express* (London), 22 June 1960, 6.

Gibbs, Patrick. "A Superficial *Sons and Lovers.*" *Daily Telegraph and Morning Post* (London), 16 May 1960, 14.

Gillet, John. "*Sons and Lovers.*" *Film Quarterly* 14 (Fall 1960): 41–42.

Hartung, Philip T. "The Screen: All That a Mother Can Mean." *Commonweal*, 9 September 1960, 469.

Kael, Pauline. "Commitment and the Straitjacket." [*Sons and Lovers*] In *I Lost It at the Movies*, Little, Brown, 1965.

Kauffmann, Stanley. "Several Sons, Several Lovers." *New Republic*, 29 August 1960, 21–22.
Lambert, Gavin and Jack Cardiff. "Lawrence: The Script . . . and the Camera." *Films and Filming* 6 (May 1960): 9.
Lejeune, C. A. "At the Films: The Artist as a Young Man." *London Observer*, 26 June 1960, 25.
Powell, Dilys. *Sunday Times* (London). 26 June 1960, 35.
"Prize-Copping *Sons and Lovers* cost $535,000." *Variety*, c. Oct. 1960. (exact d. and p. not avail.)
Quigley, Isabel. "*Sons and Lovers*." *Spectator* (London). (July 1960): 21, 24.
"Return to Lawrence Country." *Manchester Guardian*, November 20, 1959, 8.
Review of *Sons and Lovers*. *Saturday Review*, 6 August 1960, 28.
Review of *Sons and Lovers*. In *Sight and Sound* 29 (Spring 1960): 54–55.
Review of *Sons and Lovers*. *Time*, 1 Aug., 1960, 58.
"*Sons and Lovers*: Lawrence's Novel on the Screen." *Times* (London), 21 June 1960, 4.
"Tender and Terrible: *Sons and Lovers*." *Newsweek*, 1 August 1960, 80.
Tarratt, Margaret. "An Obscene Undertaking." In *Films and Filming* 17 (November 1970): 26–30.
Wald, Jerry. "Scripting *Sons and Lovers*." In *Sight and Sound* 29 (Summer 1960): 17.
Walsh, Moira. "*Sons and Lovers*." *America*, 13 August 1960, 542.

Women in Love

Armstrong, Marion. "Spirited Creatures." *Christian Century*, 16 September 1970, 1099.
Bahrenburg, Bruce. "Lawrence Novel Too Complex for Film." *Newark Sunday News*, 30 August 1970, Sec. 6, 85.
Billington, Michael. "With Lawrence in Derbyshire." *Illustrated London News*, 22 November 1969, 24.
Bevins, Wilfred. "Lawrence's *Women in Love*: Word to Image." *Los Angeles Herald Examiner*, 12 April 1970, Sec. G, 4.
Boyum, Joy Gould. "*Women in Love*: Style as Daring." In *Double Exposure: Fiction into Film*. New York: New American Library, 1985.
Canby, Vincent. "Screen: *Women in Love* Done as Torrid Romance." *The New York Times*, 26 March 1970, 58.
———. Review of *Women in Love*. *New York Times*, 29 March 1970, Sec. 2, 33.
Carroll, Kathleen. "*Women in Love* Is Stunning Film." *New York Daily News*, 26 March 1970, 79.
Christie, Ian Leslie. "*Women in Love*." *Sight and Sound* 39 (Winter 1969/70): 49–50.

Coleman, John. "Writing It Again." *New Statesman*, 14 November 1969, 704.
Crist, Judith. "*Love* Is a Many-Splendored Thing." *New York*, 30 March 1970, 54–55.
Crump, G. B. "*Women in Love*: Novel and Film." *D. H. Lawrence Review* 4 (Spring 1971): 28–41.
Dooley, Roger. "*Women in Love*." *The Villager*, 26 March 1970, 9.
Frederick, Robert B. "Larry Kramer Touts *Women in Love*." *Variety*, 1 April, 1970, 13.
Gerard, Lillian N. "Of Lawrence and Love." *Film/Literature Quarterly* 3 (Fall 1970): 6–12.
Gow, Gordon. "*Women in Love*." *Films and Filming* 16 (January): 49–50.
Kael, Pauline. "Lust for Art." *The New Yorker*, 28 March 1970, 97–101.
Kauffmann, Stanley. "Stanley Kauffmann on Films. Rev. of *Women in Love*." *The New Republic*, 18 Apr. 1970, 20.
Knight, Arthur. "SR Goes to the Movies: Liberated Classics." [Rev. of *Women in Love*] *Saturday Review*, 21 March 1970, 97–98.
Knoll, Robert F. "*Women in Love*." *Film Heritage* 6 (Summer 1971): 1–6.
Kuhn, Helen Weldon. "*Women in Love*." *Films in Review* 21 (April 1970): 241–242.
"Larry Kramer Touts *Women in Love*." *Variety*, 1 April 1970, n. p.
L. Sw. "Lawrence's 'Women' Novel as a Film." *Christian Science Monitor*, 13 April 1970, 4.
"The Making of *Women in Love*." *Observer Review* (London), 2 Sept. 1973, 25.
Morgenstern, Joseph. "Body and Soul." *Newsweek*, 16 April 1970, 97.
Mortimer, Penelope. "Passions Triumphantly Translated: Lawrence's *Women in Love*." *Observer Review* (London), 16 November 1969, 28.
Phillips, Gene D. "An Interview with Ken Russell." *Film Comment* 6 (Fall 1970): 10–17.
"Quartet of Soloists." *Time*, 13 April 1970, 103, 106, 109.
Review of *Women in Love*. *Observer Review* (London) 2 September 1973, 25.
Rich, J. "*Women in Love*." *Variety*, 19 November 1970, 14.
Schickel, Richard. "A Past Master in the Hands of a Future One." *Life* 63, 6 March 1970, 14.
Schlesinger, Arthur Jr. "*Women in Love*." In *Film 70/71*, ed. David Denby, 215–17. New York: Simon and Schuster, 1971.
Simon, John. "On Screen: Lawrence in Print and on Film." *The New Leader*, 13 April 1970, 26–28.
Sirkin, Elliot. "*Women in Love*." *Film Quarterly* 24 (Fall 1970): 43–47.
Sweeney, Louise. "Lawrence's 'Women': Novel as a Film." *Christian Science Monitor*, 13 April 1970, 4.
Tarratt, Margaret. "An Obscene Undertaking." *Films and Filming* 17 (November 1970): 26–30.
Tucker, Martin. "Lawrence's Women: The Screen." *Commonweal*, 15 May 1970, 223–224.

United Artists Corp., "Production Notes on *Women in Love*." Promotional and informational brochure, 26 September 1969, 12.

Walsh, Moira. "*Women in Love*." *America*, 25 April 1970, 456.

Warga, Wayne. "Kramer Scripts Thinking Man's *Women in Love*." *Los Angeles Times*, 3 May 1970, *Calendar* Magazine, 1, 12–13.

Weightman, John. "Trifling with the Dead." *Encounter* 34 (January 1970): 50–53.

Westerbeck, Colin I., Jr. "Movies: Why Do They Love?" *Manhattan Tribune*, 28 March 1970, 6.

Winsten, Archer. "*Women in Love* Unreels D. H. Lawrence Sex Tale." *New York Post*, 21 March 1970, 53.

"*Women in Love*." *Films and Filming* (Nov. 1970), 29.

Woodward, Ian. *Glenda Jackson: A Study in Fire and Ice*. New York: St. Martin's Press, 1985.

Zambrano, Ana Laura. "*Women in Love*: Counterpoint on Film." *Film/Literature Quarterly* 1 (January 1973): 46–54.

Articles and Books on Director Ken Russell

Atkins, Thomas R. *Ken Russell*. New York: Simon and Schuster, 1976.

Baxter, John. *An Appalling Talent/Ken Russell*. London: Michael Joseph, 1973.

Flatley, Guy [and Ken Russell.] "'I'm Surprised My Films Shock People.'" *The New York Times*, 15 Oct. 1972, 15.

Gomez, Joseph A. Jr. *Ken Russell: The Adaptor as Creator*. New York: Pergamon Press, 1977.

———. "The Sources and Films of Ken Russell: The Adaptor as Creator." Ph.D. diss., University of Rochester, 1975.

Hanke, Ken. *Ken Russell's Films*. Metuchen, N.J., and London: Scarecrow Press, 1984.

Phillips, Gene D. "An Interview with Ken Russell." *Film Comment* 6 (Fall 1970): 10–17.

———. *Ken Russell*. Boston: Twayne, 1979.

Rosenfeldt, Diane. *Ken Russell: A Guide to References and Resources*. Boston: G. K. Hall, 1978.

Russell, Ken. *Altered States: The Autobiography of Ken Russell*. New York: Bantam Books, 1991.

———. *The Lion Roars: Ken Russell on Film*. Boston and London: Faber & Faber, 1993.

Index

A

Abstract nouns, 28, 89, 162, 167–9, 171, 275
Academy Awards, 1, 154–5, 278
Adaptations, cinematic, 1–12, 15, 18 20, 77, 85, 106, 124, 155–6, 158, 163–4, 166, 170, 181, 191, 193, 222, , 237, 242–3, 275–86,
African statuettes, 158, 217–18, 233
Aldritt, Keith, 157, 216
Alliteration, 35, 83, 189
Alwyn, William, 25
Amelia and the Angel, Ken Russell's film, 154
Anaphora, 35, 178–9
Anglo–Saxon, 27, 83, 89, 106, 166
Animals, images of, 36, 158, 162–3, 165, 196–7, 199, 203, 206, 213, 217, 223, 226
Antithesis, 12, 18, 30–1, 48, 52, 57, 83, 88, 99–100, 103–4, 157, 162, 165, 180, 184–6, 276–7
Appositives, use of, 98, 178
Arnheim, Rudolph, 200
ASL (average shot length), 11, 32–3, 107–8, 181–2, 191
Asphalt Jungle, 19
Asquith, Lady Cynthia, 13–14
Assonance, 35, 83, 189
A Taste of Honey, 85
Atkins, Thomas R., 163, 191
Atlee, Clement, 14
Austen Jane, 1, 5, 286

B

Baldanza, Frank, 81
Bars, as symbol, 37, 44, 96, 122, 171, 174, 224, 269
Bates, Alan, 155, 242, 245, 247–8, 250–2, 256, 259–62, 264, 267, 269–70, 273–4
Battestin, Martin, 4
Bazin, Andre, 282
Becker, Henry III, 46
Beckley, Paul, 84
Ben–Hur, 5
Bennett, Arnold, 82, 97
Bersani, Leo, 170
Bertocci, Angelo, 207
Bickerton, Derek, 168
Billion Dollar Brain, film by Ken Russell, 154
Biopics, 5, 154, 165, 283
Black Narcissus, 282
Blake, William, 115
Bluestone, George, 9, 200
Bondage, images of, 76, 92, 96, 114, 119, 121–2, 163, 197
Booth, Wayne, 47
Boyum, Joy Gould, 4, 9, 166, 235, 280
Braine, John, 85
Branagh, Kenneth, 5
Brand, Candace Kasper, 231
Brighton Rock, 282
Bron, Eleanor, 240, 245, 247–51
Bronte, Charlotte, 1
Bronte, Emily, 1, 8
Bulls, Gudrun's dance before, 171, 173, 175, 181–2, 184–7,

188–9, 192–5, 201, 204, 211, 213, 226, 235, 239–40, 243

C

Caine, Michael, 154
Camera angles, 11, 19, 38, 47, 88, 105, 163, 172, 194, 200, 218, 236, 277–8, 283
Canby, Vincent, 163
Cardiff, Jack, 47, 77, 84, 88, 92, 101–2, 108
Carroll, Kathleen, 156
Chaplin, Charlie, 6
Chiasmus, 18, 48
Chronicle of Higher Education, 286
CinemaScope, 77, 86–7, 92, 101
Citizen Kane, 19, 283
Clarke, T.E.B., 79, 281
Clothes, imagery of, 16, 26, 28, 56, 70, 114–5, 122, 172, 174–5, 185–6, 193–4, 212, 214–16, 221, 229, 231, 233–4, 284
Coal mines, 79, 112, 115, 117, 122 201, 210, 216–17, 221, 223, 231
Conrad, Joseph, 97–8
Cook, David, 19
Coordinating conjunctions, use of, 29–30, 98, 101, 178–9, 275
Crist, Judith, 156, 163
Crowther, Bosley, 84
Crump, G. B., 230, 242–3
Curtiz, Michael, 19

D

Daleski, H.M., 153, 209
Dance
    in *Sons and Lovers,* 94, 96, 125
    in *Women in Love,* 159–60, 165–6, 171, 173, 175–6, 181, 183–7, 189, 191–5, 199, 206, 222–4, 226, 233, 235, 239–40, 243, 277
Davies, John Howard, 14, 18, 26, 60–7, 69, 71, 73
Death, as motif, 21, 25, 44, 46, 50, 56, 73, 80, 99–100, 110–113, 116, 118–9, 121, 152–3, 163, 170, 183–4, 197, 200–4, 207–15, 219–20, 222, 226–33, 238, 240
Decadence, 211–12, 217, 234
Deep focus photography, 20, 22, 86 276, 282
Delaney, Shelagh, 85
Delerue, George, 237
Dialect, 89, 93, 170, 176
Dialogue, changes in, 15, 18, 26–9, 31–3, 54–7, 81, 93–4, 96, 98–100, 104, 106, 117, 120, 157–62, 166, 176, 184, 188, 191–3, 196, 201–2, 205, 219, 223, 227, 237, 238, 280, 283
Dickens, Charles, 1, 18–20, 39, 44, 282
Diction, 3, 9, 10–11,18, 27–8, 57, 82–3, 88–9, 99–100, 154, 162, 166–76, 180, 189, 195, 275–6
DosPassos, John, 6
Draper, Ronald, 154
Duncan, Isadora, 160, 184, 218, 235, 250, 277, 283

E

Eastwood, 77, 86, 155
Eisenstein, Sergei, 163, 186, 200, 202
Eliot, George, 1
Eroticized prose, 83, 90–1, 93–4, 115–6, 127, 161, 175, 178, 188–9, 191, 275–7

Index

Euripides' *Andromache*, 206
Expressionism, 19, 88, 161

F

Fairy tale effects, 18, 21, 22, 27, 276
Fallen Idol, The, 282
Farr, Judith, 76, 109
Faulkner, William, 5, 281
Fielding, Henry, 4
Felter, Maryanne, 27–8, 97
Fig, as symbol, 161, 173, 175, 183, 201, 218, 223, 225, 227, 229, 239, 242
Figurative language, 4, 9, 12, 18, 44–5, 195–9, 202, 205–6, 218, 222
Film noir, 19, 20, 22, 85, 277, 282
Fitzgerald, F. Scott, 1, 5
Fire, symbolism of, 41, 90, 95, 113, 118, 120–1, 123, 163, 197–9, 203–204, 206, 209, 220–1, 224
Flowers, images of, 28, 78–9, 89–90, 94, 110, 113, 115–7, 123–4, 192, 197–8, 204, 214, 225, 230
Food, images of, 111–2, 119, 121
Ford, George, 157
Ford, John, 163
Francis, Freddie, 77, 84, 278, 283
Frank, Waldo, 151
French Dressing, film by Ken Russell, 154
Freudian analysis, 10, 21–2, 40–1, 43, 76, 111, 126, 284
Futurism, 161–2, 196

G

Galsworthy, John, 1
Garnett, Edward, 75, 82, 196
Georgie Girl, 154

Goldberg, Michael, 39
Goldner, Charles, 26, 28
Gomez, Joseph, 160, 182, 185, 191, 233
Gordon, Caroline, 39
Gordon, David J., 178
Grammar, 10, 88, 100, 176–81
Graves, Robert, 1
Griffith, D.W., 87
Gurko, Jane, 179

H

Hamlet, 43, 282
Hanke, Ken, 164, 186
Hardy, Thomas, 97–8
Hawthorne, Nathaniel, 3
Hemingway, Ernest, 5
Hendricks, Gordon, 25
Henry V, 24, 282
Hiller, Wendy, 77, 87, 127–8, 130–3, 137, 140, 147, 149, 278
Hitchcock, Alfred, 19
Hobson, Valerie, 14, 18, 26, 47, 58–9, 63–5, 67–73, 280, 282
Holderness, Graham, 157
Hollywood, 1, 6, 8, 19, 77, 85, 88, 92, 101–2, 106–7, 117, 123, 154, 279–81, 282–5
Homoeroticism, 79, 160, 202, 212, 220, 225, 285
Houses, imagery of, 16, 21–3, 25, 35, 38, 44, 49, 52–3, 58, 64, 165, 206, 214, 231–2
Howard, Trevor, 77, 87, 126–8, 131–3, 135, 137, 140–1, 150, 278
Humma, John, 195–6
Huss, Roy, 206
Huxley, Aldous, 6
Hyperbole, 91, 172, 235, 243, 278

I

Imagery, 27, 56, 88, 109–24, 162, 196, 198, 202–3, 207–9, 216–19, 222, 227, 229–31, 233, 235, 239–40
Industrialism, 6, 13, 76, 117–8, 128, 152, 163, 165, 197, 208–11, 214, 216, 219, 221–2, 228, 231–2, 241
Intensifiers, 162, 169, 172
Irony
  In "The Rocking-Horse Winner," 18, 27, 47–8, 50, 52–7, 84
  in *Sons and Lovers,* 114, 116, 125
  in *Women in Love,* 166, 187, 204, 209, 211, 217, 219, 222, 225, 232, 236–40, 243

J

Jackson, Glenda, 155, 203, 234, 243–6, 249, 254, 256–8, 265–6, 268–9, 271–2
Jackson, Shirley, 20
James, Henry, 1, 5
John Bull, 151
Joyce, James, 5
Jungian analysis, 39

K

Kael, Pauline, 15, 85, 156, 164, 174
Kaufmann, Stanley, 164
Kazin, Alfred, 110
Keats, John, 115
Kehr, David, 286
Kermode, Frank, 152, 157
King James Bible, 83, 105
Knight, Arthur, 156
Kramer, Larry, 154–6, 159–61, 237, 280–1

L

Lacanian analysis, 10
Lambert, Gavin, 79–81, 281
Landscape, 87, 92, 107, 110, 116, 125, 162, 165, 196–7, 213, 219, 221–2, 225, 229
Lang, Fritz, 19, 163
Lanham, Richard, 176
Latinate vocabulary, 27, 89, 167–71
Lawrence, D. H.,
  Attitude toward films, 6
  The Bible and, 83, 105, 197
  Feminism and, 5, 284
  Industrialism and, 6, 13, 76, 117–8, 128, 152, 163, 165, 197, 208–11, 214, 216, 219, 221–2, 228, 231–2, 241
  Midlands dialect, use of, 89, 93, 176
  Metaphysics and, 5, 159, 163, 167, 207, 219, 225–6, 241, 277
  Nature and, 79, 110–12, 114–17, 162–3, 196–8, 206–7, 219, 224–5, 229–31
  Sexuality and, 5–6, 43, 51, 75–7, 110–13, 115, 122–4, 151–3, 161, 169–70, 175, 178, 188–9, 191–2, 201, 207–10, 212–14, 220, 226, 228, 230, 233, 239–40
  Aaron's Rod, 8
  "Boy in the Bush, The" 5, 8
  "Captain's Doll, The" 5
  Fox, The, 5, 7
  "Horse-Dealer's Daughter, The," 34

Kangaroo, 5
Lady Chatterly's Lover, 4–7, 158
Lost Girl, The, 6, 8
Plumed Serpent, The, 8
"Prussian Officer, The," 39, 42
Rainbow, The, 5, 8, 75, 82, 151, 189, 207
"Rocking Horse Winner, The," 5, 12–14, 18, 20–2, 26–36, 38–42, 47–57, 83–4, 88, 91, 95, 98–100, 102, 105, 162, 166, 170, 176–9, 181, 188–9, 196
Samson and Delilah, 5
Sons and Lovers, 7–8, 11, 47, 75–127, 158, 162–3, 166–8, 170, 176–81, 188–91, 195–6, 206–7, 214, 229, 231
St. Mawr, 39
Trespasser, The, 5, 82
"Virgin and the Gypsy, The" 5, 7, 9
White Peacock, The, 8, 82
Women in Love, 6–7, 11, 12, 30, 39, 41, 75, 106, 151–4, 156–63, 166–70, 176–81, 187–90, 195–9, 206–17, 235–6, 280
Lawrence, Frieda, 5–6, 76, 78, 82, 127, 278, 281, 284
Lean, David, 14, 18, 20, 282
Leavis, F. R., 7, 35, 152, 156, 157, 209, 243
Lejeune, C. A., 84
Light and darkness, symbolism of, 24, 37, 89–90, 95, 113–4, 120–1, 123, 165, 197–9, 202, 207–10, 219–21, 229, 231, 234
Lighting, film, 22, 24, 38, 47, 86–8 121, 164–6, 172, 218–21, 236, 277, 286

Linden, Jenny, 155, 219, 244–6, 249–50, 252, 254, 257, 259–60, 264, 267, 270, 273–4
Liszt, Franz, 223
Lodge, David, 38
London Mercury, 151
London Observer, 84, 151
London Times, 84
Loneliness of the Long–Distance Runner, The, 85
Look Back in Anger, 7, 77, 85
Lourdes, 154
Love, theme of, 13, 20–1, 36, 40–1, 45, 49, 51, 56, 73, 76, 79, 91, 94, 99–101, 103, 107, 110–124, 157–61, 166, 171, 175, 182–5, 192–194, 200, 202–4, 209–10, 212–14, 219–22, 227–30, 232, 240, 242
Luck, as theme, 22–3, 30, 32, 35–6, 40, 49–50, 52
Luhan, Mabel Dodge, 7

M

Machinery, images of, 96, 112, 117–8, 180, 197, 203, 206, 208, 214, 216–17, 231
Marat/Sade, 155
Marks, W.S. III, 21, 39
McCabe, Thomas M., 34
McKellan, Ian, 5
McKeown, Marion Smith, 97
Mellen, Joan, 23, 25, 27
Metaphors, 9, 12, 30, 46, 111, 115, 157, 162, 165, 196–206, 225, 275
Metonymy, 11, 200, 225
Metrical patterns, 105–6, 162, 188–9
Middle English, 27
Miles, Christopher, 9
Millett, Fred B., 47

Millett, Kate, 5
Mills, John, 18, 26, 63, 66, 68, 70, 73, 280, 282
Mirren, Helen, 5
Mise–en–scène, 86, 88, 101, 163, 218
Money, as motif/symbol, 13, 16–18, 21–2, 25–7, 28–30, 34–5, 38–42, 45–7, 49, 65, 68–9
Montage, 20, 22, 28–9, 37, 43, 48, 56, 87, 165, 186, 192–4, 200, 226, 228, 277
Moon, symbolism of the, 37, 44–5, 48, 53, 78, 89–90, 113, 123–4, 177, 199, 208–9, 218, 234, 278
Moore, Harry T., 5, 8–9, 156
Mortimer, Penelope, 156, 163
Moynahan, Julian, 76, 153
Mozart, Wolfgang Amadeus, 25
Murnau, F.W., 19
Murry, John Middleton, 7, 151
Musical score
    in *The Rocking–Horse Winner,* 24–5, 280
    in *Sons and Lovers,* 84, 88, 96, 124
    in *Women in Love,* 159, 165–6, 173, 176, 184–7, 192, 194, 218, 223, 226, 237, 240, 278

N

Narrizano, Silvio, 154
Nascimbene, Mario, 84
Nature, images of, 79, 109–10, 112–3, 115–17, 163, 165, 196, 201, 203, 206–9, 219–21, 224–5, 229–31
Neorealism in cinema, 283
New Wave cinema, 85–6, 283
New York Herald Tribune, 84
New York Times,The, 84, 97

Nin, Anaïs, 106
Norse gods, 206, 227
Nottingham, 77, 81, 86, 95, 104, 108, 111, 117–20, 122, 125–6, 133, 143
Nouns, use of, 28–9, 83, 89, 91–2, 98, 162, 166–9, 171, 173, 178, 180
Nudity, 155, 165, 202, 212, 217, 224–5, 230, 240, 285

O

Oedipus complex, 78, 119, 126, 284
Old Testament, the, 83, 197
Oliver Twist, 19, 282
Olivier, Sir Laurence, 24, 43
Onomatopoeia, 35, 83
Ophuls, Max, 19
Osborne, John, 4, 85
Oxymorons, 41, 48, 162, 169, 179, 185

P

Pabst, George Wilhelm, 163
Paradox, 9, 18, 27, 41, 48–50, 57, 99, 102–4, 106, 109, 119, 125, 162, 167, 179, 207, 211–12, 275–6
Paragraph Shape and Rhythm, 12, 18, 27, 29–32, 35–6, 48, 57, 88, 105–9, 187–90
Parallel cutting, 16–7, 20, 32–3, 38, 48–9, 52–4, 101–3, 219, 225, 276–7
Parallelism, 12, 18, 29–30, 34–5, 48, 99, 102–3, 165, 182, 276
Parataxis, 12, 98, 102, 162, 176, 180
Pelissier, Anthony, 11, 14–20, 22–8, 36, 38, 42–7, 53–7, 85, 102, 105–6, 126, 276, 279–83

Peyton Place, 281
Phallic symbols, 95, 121, 124, 213, 216, 230
Picasso, Pablo, 218, 233
Pilly, Charles, 151
Plot changes, 15–8, 78–82, 107, 157–61
Poe, Edgar Allan, 55, 236
Preminger, Otto, 19
Pritchard, R.E., 152, 210
Prose style, 3–4, 9–10, 12, 18, 20, 27, 30, 47–8, 82–84, 88–92, 97–106, 124, 161–3, 166–70, 176–81, 187–90, 195–9, 235–6, 275– 7, 281–2, 285
Puccini, Giaccamo, 25

R

Ragussis, Michael, 167
Rainbow, The, 5, 8, 75, 82, 151, 189, 207
Read, Herbert, 30
Realism
  in British film, 85–6, 283
  in "The Rocking-Horse Winner," 26–7, 38
  in *Sons and Lovers,* 82, 86, 93, 127, 195, 206
  in *Women in Love,* 156, 175, 218–19, 235
Reed, Oliver, 155, 193, 202, 219, 241, 253–6, 258, 260–8, 271, 273
Repetition, 8, 18, 27, 33–6, 39, 57, 83, 91, 95, 99, 102, 105–6, 108–9, 154, 160–2, 165, 169, 174, 179–80, 189–91, 193–5, 205–6, 217, 276–7
Rhythm, 4, 18, 24, 27, 29–34, 36, 83, 85, 88, 91, 94, 96, 100, 104–9, 113, 116, 118, 161–2, 165–6, 179, 181–2, 186–95, 227, 276–7
Richard III, 282
Rocking Horse Winner, The, the film, 4, 11, 14–20, 22–7, 29, 32– 3, 36–9, 42–9, 53–73, 76, 85, 88, 92, 102–3, 105, 170, 181, 191, 275–6, 278–84
"Rocking–Horse Winner, The," the story, 5, 12–14, 18, 20–2, 26–36, 38–42, 47–57, 83–4, 88, 91, 95, 98–100, 102, 105, 162, 166, 170, 176–9, 181, 188–91, 196
Room at the Top, 7, 77, 85, 283
Rossini, Giaochinno, 25
Russell, John, 89
Russell, Ken, 126, 154–61, 163–6, 174–5, 181–7, 191, 193–4, 200, 205–6, 218–35, 276, 278–81, 283, 285

S

Sagar, Keith, 154, 161
Saturday Night and Sunday Morning, 77, 85, 283
Schickel, Richard, 156
Schneider, Daniel J., 34, 48, 109
Schorer, Mark, 38, 75–6, 152–4, 210–1
Sears, Heather, 77, 86, 129, 133, 136–7, 139, 150
Sentence length and style, 9, 29–32, 97–8,
Sexuality, 43, 51, 75, 77, 111, 115, 122–4, 151–3, 161, 169–70, 175, 178, 188–9, 191–2, 198, 201–2, 207–10, 212–14, 220, 226, 228, 230, 233, 239–40
Shaffer, Peter, *Equus,* 43
Shanks, E., 151
Sheybal, Vladek, 203

Index

Shock editing, 165, 186, 191
Shots, types of, 11, 16, 19–20, 22–4, 28, 32–3, 36–8, 42–3, 46, 48, 56, 86–8, 92–7, 101–5, 107–8, 117–8, 121–2, 164–6, 170–5, 182, 184, 186–7, 191–5, 200–1, 204–6, 220, 222–5, 228–9, 236, 241, 277–8
Sillitoe, Alan, 85
Silverstein, Norman, 206
Simon, John, 156, 236
Sinyrard, Neil, 68, 84, 156, 164
Sirkin, Elliot, 156, 164
Skinner, Mollie, 8
Slang, 89, 170, 176
Smith, Julian, 18–9, 282
Snodgrass, W.D., 39–40, 43
Snow and Ice, symbolism of, 94, 107, 116, 153, 158, 163, 165, 172–3, 195, 197, 206, 208, 210–12, 219–21, 226, 230–1, 240–1
Sons and Lovers, the film, 4, 7, 11, 47, 76–88, 92–97, 101–5, 107–9, 116–50, 158, 164, 170, 181, 187, 191, 231, 275–6, 279–81, 283–4
Sons and Lovers, the novel, 7–8, 11, 47, 75–127, 158, 162–3, 166–8, 170, 176–81, 188–91, 195–6, 206–7, 214, 229, 231
Spilka, Mark, 76
Stairs, as symbol, 36–7, 44, 53, 173–4
Stewart, Garrett, 167, 177
Stockwell, Dean, 77, 127, 129–36, 138–9, 142–50, 285
Stychomythic dialogue, 26, 188
Storey, David, 85
Symbolism, 8–9, 13, 18, 20–1, 27, 35, 38–47, 57, 78, 83, 86, 88, 95, 109–24, 153–4, 156, 158, 163, 165, 171, 185, 204, 206–35, 277–8, 281
Syntax, 4, 9, 12, 27, 29–30, 88, 97–8, 100–1, 105–6, 162, 165, 176–87, 195, 277

T

Tarratt, Margaret, 84, 156
Tate, Allen, 39
Tchaikovsky, 202, 218, 224, 272
Thackeray, William Makepeace, 1
This Sporting Life, 85
Tolstoi, Leo, 1
Tone, 4, 9, 47, 52–3, 56–7, 84, 88, 124–5, 163, 166, 235–43, 279–80

U

Understatement, 55, 164
Ure, Mary, 77, 86, 141–8, 278

V

Valentino, Rudolf, 6
Van Ghent, Dorothy, 75–6, 109, 113
Verdi, Guiseppe, 25
Verbs, use of, 27–8, 83, 89–91, 98–9, 162, 166–7, 169, 177
Vivas, Eliseo, 157, 207
Vorticism, 161

W

Wagner, Richard, 25, 38, 83
Wald, Jerry, 7, 76–88, 126–7, 158, 164, 276, 278, 281, 284
Water imagery, 96, 111, 117–8, 162, 165, 172, 217–18, 220, 230
Waugh, Evelyn, 1

Weightman, John, 160, 241
Weiss, Daniel, 115
Weiss, Peter, 155
Welles, Orson, 19–20, 163, 283
West, Rebecca, 151
Whitman, Walt, 83
Widmer, Kingsley, 39
Wilde, Oscar, 55
Williams, Billy, 164
Wilmer, Catherine, 257, 263–4
Wilson, Angus, 157, 191
Women in Love, the film, 4, 11, 154–61, 163–6, 170–6, 181–7, 191–5, 200–6, 218–78, 280–1, 283, 285
Women in Love, the novel, 6–7, 11–12, 30, 39, 41, 75, 106, 151–4, 156–63, 166–70, 176–81, 187–90, 195–9, 206–17, 235–6, 280
Woolf, Virginia, 97–8
World War I, 151, 159, 176, 187, 196, 224, 231, 233, 237, 238, 240, 242, 278
World War II, 14, 19, 43, 282–4
Wrestling match in *Women in Love,* 155, 171–5, 180, 183, 185–6, 218, 220–1, 277

Z

Zambrano, Ana Laura, 182
Zermatt, 155, 230

Literature and the Visual Arts
New Foundations

Ernest B. Gilman
General Editor

Offering works of scholarship and criticism on the interrelationship of literature and the visual arts, this series reflects the rich diversity of subjects and approaches in this developing field. Our authors contribute to an expert's understanding of the topic. At the same time, they speak to readers, lay and professional, with a more general interest in the area. Ideally—and this is the thrust of the phrase "New Foundations" in our series title—works published under the imprint focus on the ways their particular concern leads us to rethink the basic questions of comparative study between the arts, challenging the reader volume by volume continually to remap the grounds, historical and theoretical, on which such inquiry can take place at all.

For additional information about this series or for the submission of manuscripts, please contact:

Acquisitions Department
Peter Lang Publishing
275 Seventh Avenue, 28th floor
New York, New York 10001

OHIO UNIVERSITY LIBRARY

Please return this book as soon as you have finished with it. In order to avoid a fine it must be returned by the latest date stamped below. All books are subject to recall after two weeks or immediately if needed for reserve.

AUG 3 0 2007

CF